Public Relations

Public Relations
A Practical Approach

Ellen Gunning

Gill & Macmillan

Gill & Macmillan Ltd
Hume Avenue
Park West
Dublin 12
with associated companies throughout the world
www.gillmacmillan.ie

© Ellen Gunning 2003
0 7171 3457 1

Index compiled by Kate Duffy
Print origination in Ireland by Paradigm DTP

The paper used in this book is made from the wood pulp of managed forests. For every tree felled, at least one tree is planted, thereby renewing natural resources.

A catalogue record is available for this book from the British Library.

This book is dedicated to
Tony Gunning, Gerard Whelan and Michael Whelan.

Contents

SECTION 7: Examinations

APPENDICES

Preface

This book is a practical guide for public relations students and practitioners. Its contents have been developed over years of practising public relations and constantly striving to find better, more cost-effective, quantifiable, creative and professional ways of doing everything that I have done.

Of all of the subjects you could possibly study, public relations cannot be studied in isolation. To practise PR you need an understanding of the business, political, cultural, social and moral climates within which you practise. PR is about providing a professional communications service, and doing so at a profit. It is about applying creative strategies in order to achieve coverage, or providing excellent advice on how not to become the news. It is about managing your time, your clients and your skills so that the service you provide is efficient and cost-effective, and not injurious to your health!

Although each of the chapters in this book is written as a stand-alone chapter, you will gain much more from the book if you cross reference. For example, take one issue alone — video presentation of the results of the annual report. This will involve the financial chapter (dealing with the results), internal communications (for staff), interview skills techniques (for the chief executive), TV and video skills (to select the video company, determine content, etc.), budgeting (to control costs), event management (so that the function runs smoothly), newsletters (because you will most likely do a follow-up piece), print production (of the annual report), consciousness of corporate image (which must be carried throughout the print, the video and the function), and, of course, they all pull together as strands under the general heading of public relations — understanding what it is, what it can do, and the tools used to achieve those ends.

I have been — and remain — an enthusiastic student of public relations, an enthusiastic practitioner and, I hope, an enthusiastic teacher. The world of public relations is utterly fascinating — you never stop learning. I hope that some of my enthusiasm for my subject communicates itself to the reader. Public relations practice has never been dull; I hope that you will not find studying public relations to be dull either!

Acknowledgments

Let me begin by thanking all of my fellow lecturers in the Academy whose dedication I greatly appreciate, whose company I enjoy, and from whom I always learn. I would also like to thank my students for being such lively and thoughtful contributors in class, and my clients for the wealth of public relations experience they have exposed me to, over the years. I must also thank all of my PR colleagues who shared their notes, gave interviews, cross-checked information and provided visuals.

I must pay particular and special tribute to three lecturers, colleagues and friends. Sincere thanks to John Brophy, NUJ, for his encouragement to approach Gill & Macmillan with the idea for this book.

I cannot begin to thank Ita Glavin MIAPR for the sheer volume of research that she conducted, and her insightful comments. This book could not possibly have been completed on time without her invaluable assistance.

I must also thank Simone Rapple, NUJ, for all the sub-editing and proofing skills she brought to bear on the text. Her ability to tighten and focus sentences, cut superfluous material and suggest alternative phrases was utterly invaluable.

My thanks also to Seán O'Conor and Eamon Brady who sparked the idea to include a chapter on public consultation. I would also like to thank Helen Barry of the Public Relations Institute of Ireland for always saying 'can do' to every request that I made. I must thank Jeanette Curry, Lisa Keogh and Sandra Lindsay in the Academy's office, for shouldering a lot of work in the weeks leading up to the submission of this text. My special thanks to Ailbhe O'Reilly, my editor, for saying 'yes'. Finally, thanks to all my family and friends for their patience and forbearance.

This book is dedicated to the three men in my life — Tony Gunning, Gerard Whelan and Michael Whelan. My husband, Tony Gunning, my greatest supporter, who never fails to believe in me. My brother, Gerard Whelan, for his unfailing encouragement and support. And my father, Michael Whelan, who stimulated my involvement in community activities, which in turn led to a wonderful career in public relations.

The publishers are grateful to the following for permission to reproduce material used in the book:

Department of Public Enterprise, Tetra Pak Ireland Ltd, Railway Procurement Agency, *Irish Independent*, *The Star*, *The Irish Times*, *Evening Herald*, Dublin Docklands Development Authority.

Section 1
PR Foundations

CHAPTER I

An Appreciation of Public Relations

HISTORY OF PR

There are some who say that Public Relations has always existed. They will point to cave drawings as an attempt to educate and inform future generations. The Bible, the Koran and the Book of Kells are cited as early examples of written communication. The Vikings, because they painted the sails of their ships, are credited with the invention of the corporate logo.

As a profession, however, Public Relations is quite new. The person generally credited with founding modern-day public relations is Ivy Ledbetter Lee (1877–1934). Lee was retained as a press officer by the coal industry in the United States of America in 1906, at a time when the industry was attracting a huge amount of bad publicity. He was expected to be the 'mouthpiece' of the industry. A front man was needed and he was chosen.

However, as soon as he got the job, he issued a declaration of principles. The declaration really said that:

- He would deal only with the most senior level of management in the company;
- He must be told all of the facts (not just the version of the facts that the company wanted to issue);
- He alone would have the power to decide which facts, if any, were to be issued to the public;

and, most importantly, he declared that:

- The public could not be ignored, or fooled, or put off by lies.

This statement of principles was revolutionary at the time. No one before had ever insisted that they would deal only with top management — after all, if you were only the mouthpiece of the company, it did not matter who gave you your instructions. It was also extraordinary that he insisted on being told all of the facts. Up to that time, there had been a belief that the press officer was there to tell a story to the public — not necessarily a true story.

By insisting on the facts, he was making sure that he never found himself in a position of having told lies to the public — a huge step. He was the first person to put respect for the public on the agenda. He insisted that he was not there to fool the public, to cover up, or to tell lies that sounded plausible. He was firmly of the opinion that the

3

public had a right to be told the truth. He also believed that the public could not be ignored. No company could put its head down, and pretend that a disaster had not happened. The public had a right to be told what was going on — the bad news as well as the good.

Ledbetter Lee was the first person actually to bring journalists to the sight of a crash — a revolutionary move in those days. He believed that, instead of telling journalists a story, he should bring them, show them, tell them, let them take photographs and write the facts as they saw them. In the early days of his career, he was well regarded for his approach (in later years, he was known as Poison Ivy — but that's another story). After working with the coal industry, Ledbetter Lee went on to work for the railroad industry, and became an adviser to John D. Rockefeller Jnr.

Lee's entry into public relations was followed by that of another of the key influencers in the industry, Edward Bernays (born 1891). Bernays was a PR practitioner, well known for his use of propaganda and persuasion. He also taught the first course ever in public relations at New York University (1923), and wrote *Crystallizing Public Opinion*, the first book on public relations.

The practice of appointing press officers, and later public relations officers, spread. In Britain, after the Second World War, the government appointed a network of information officers — communications experts who would explain new concepts like pensions.

The first Public Relations (PR) post in a public company in Ireland was held by Ned Lawlor. He was appointed Public Relations Officer of the ESB (Electricity Supply Board) in the year of its foundation — 1927. He later went on to become the first president of the professional body, the Public Relations Institute of Ireland. The second PR person to be appointed to a similar position in Europe was Sir Stephen Tallents, who became public relations officer to the Empire Marketing Board in the United Kingdom (UK).[1]

The practice of national governments appointing PR people has continued to this day. Kuwait employed a PR firm to help it communicate with the world when Iraq invaded that country on 2 August 1990. More recently, every member state of the European Union (EU) employed communications experts to explain the Euro prior to its introduction in January 2002.

PUBLIC RELATIONS CONFUSED

Before we look at definitions of public relations, we should first examine what it is not. Public relations is most often confused in the minds of the public with either propaganda or publicity.

Propaganda

Propaganda is a deliberate effort to gain support for an opinion, creed or belief. Propaganda denies, or fails to recognise, the existence of, or merits in, alternative opinions. Propaganda makes an emotional appeal to the heart: 'Believe because I believe'. It is, by its very nature, biased. Propagandists are prejudiced in favour of their topic, and therefore their concentration is on winning your support — not necessarily on being totally truthful with you.

We are all at the receiving end of propaganda during general elections. Think about it. Political party members go out knocking on doors, in the middle of winter, on cold, wet nights, and ask for your vote for their particular party or candidate. If you respond that you have never supported that party, for whatever reason, they will try desperately to convince you that you are wrong. They will not argue that the party of your choice has valuable policies as well, or that the candidate you have chosen to support is, indeed, a very worthy candidate. Rather, they will try to convince you of the error of your ways. This, in its simplest form, is propaganda.

Government press officers are often accused of acting as propagandists because they give only positive, pro-government answers to all questions. The Irish government promoted only a Yes vote in referenda until the McKenna judgement of 1995 (Patricia McKenna MEP), which found the use of taxpayers' money for propaganda purposes in referendum campaigns to be unconstitutional.

The greatest despot will try to propagandise the world into believing that he is a caring and sincere leader. Hitler and Goebbels are well-known examples of highly skilled propagandists.

Public relations, by contrast, concentrates on truth. Where propaganda appeals to the heart, public relations is information — truth — which can be assessed by the mind. With any public relations activity, you are not trying to win people over to your cause blindly. You are trying to give them truthful information, which they may assess, and about which they may develop their own opinions. You are also trying to listen to what they have to tell you — as will be discussed later.

Publicity

Publicity is the other area most confused with public relations. What is publicity? Publicity is drawing attention to something by highlighting the issue, event or occasion in the media. You see it in newspapers and magazines and on television; you hear it on radio; you notice it in bus shelters and on poster sites.

Publicity can be secured by buying advertising. It can also be secured by public relations techniques — by issuing a press release, pitching an idea for a feature article, calling a press conference, or organising a photo-call. Publicists, as a result, are often also referred to as press agents.

There are PR people who specialise as publicists. Max Clifford in the UK is probably one of the best known, and he is extraordinarily good. In Ireland, Gerry Lundberg would undoubtedly be the best-known publicist. He has worked with all of the major theatre and film productions in Ireland, including *Riverdance*, *My Left Foot*, *The Field*, *In the Name of the Father*, *Some Mother's Son*, *Dancing at Lughnasa* and

Widow's Peak.[2] Arts events in particular — film, theatre, poetry, visual arts — would not survive without the valuable work that publicists do. And it is hard to imagine an actor, actress, or performer of note who does not have their own publicist. Louis Walsh, manager of Boyzone, Westlife, Samantha Mumba and Six (among others), is also recognised as a great publicist, and is admiringly referred to by media as 'the spin king'.[3]

The difference between a publicist and a public relations consultant is best explained using a story about Ben Sonnenberg, an early press agent in New York City. Ben was hired by an antique-store owner to get more customers for his store. In the back of the store, Ben found an oil painting of an almost nude lady. He put this painting in an ornate frame and placed it in the front window. This was shocking stuff at the turn of the century! Next, Ben paid a little boy and a little girl 25 cents each to stand and stare at the painting. Then, Ben raced across the street and grabbed a news reporter to take a photo of the children looking at the naughty painting. The result was headlines in the paper. Crowds soon swamped the store. The store owner sold hundreds of printed copies of the painting but not one antique! The moral of the story? Publicity sold copies of the painting, but public relations would have created an awareness of the antiques.[4]

Publicity can be secured by public relations means, but it is not the sole object of any public relations activity. It may be an end result (which is achieved from giving information), or it may be a selected tool used to reach a particular audience, but it is never the primary aim of any public relations campaign.

WHAT IS PUBLIC RELATIONS?

Colleagues tell me that there are in excess of 2,000 definitions of public relations. Here are a few of my favourites:

> Public relations practice is the art and social science of analysing trends, predicting their consequences, counselling organisation leaders, and implementing planned programmes of action which will serve both the organisation's and the public interest.
>
> International Conference of PR Organisations — Mexico City, 1978

More and more, the role of the consultant, in particular, has become one of adviser, analyst and counsellor. In the future, we might see a division in the roles of PR people — some will be employed for their skills (writing the releases, organising the venues for conferences, etc.), while others will be retained for their breadth of vision (giving strategic advice and counsel).

> Public Relations is a combination of philosophy, sociology, economics, language, psychology, journalism, communication and other knowledge into a system of human understanding.
>
> Herbert M. Baus

This definition is one that every student of public relations should learn and use as a put-down for pub bores! All of the elements of the definition are true, and corporations, organisations and individuals are indeed seeking human understanding. Public relations, however, encompasses more, and the problem with this definition is that, having read it, you are no closer to developing an understanding of what public relations actually is.

> Public Relations is the attempt by information, persuasion and adjustment to engineer public support for an activity, cause, movement or institution.
>
> Edward L. Bernays

This definition, in my opinion, comes closer to propaganda than to public relations. A propagandist would seek to 'persuade' (rather than educate). A propagandist would seek to 'engineer' support (rather than earn it).

> Professional public relations evaluates public attitudes, identifies the policies and procedures of the organisation, and executes a programme of action to earn public understanding and acceptance. Professional public relations is strategic and goal driven — it works to predefined objectives. It gets results.
>
> Public Relations Institute of Ireland

This is a good definition, but it lacks the word 'influence'. PR certainly identifies policies and procedures within an organisation, but it also seeks to influence those areas for the good of the organisation, its publics, and society in general. This definition focuses on public understanding and acceptance — two of the cornerstones of PR. And it also, as you would expect of a definition drawn up by practitioners, manages to incorporate an ad for their own services — 'it gets results', and it undoubtedly does.

> Public Relations is the conscious organisation of communication. PR is a management function. The task of PR is: to achieve mutual understanding and to establish beneficial relationships, between the organisation and its publics and environment, through two-way communication.
>
> CERP Terminology Working Group, Berlin Conference, 1999

This definition highlights the conscious decision by the organisation to engage in a process of communications, with the ultimate aim of building strong, lasting relationships. It also tries to outline the tasks of PR. Note the inclusion of the 'environment' — something which would not have been present a decade earlier.

> Public Relations is the strategic management discipline that identifies, establishes and maintains relationships with the publics whose behavior can help or impede an organization's efforts to achieve its goals.
>
> Moshe Dayan, Dayan Public Relations, Israel [5]

This definition focuses on the close relationship and interdependency between an organisation and those publics critical to its success.

PR is strategically planned (systematic, continuous and consistent) and based on the interactive communication effort of an organization or a professional (individual), to establish and maintain relations of mutual understanding (good will) and confidence with their (respective) publics, aiming at a sound (healthy) image, which will help them to achieve their goals.

Thalis P. Coutoupis, Greece [6]

Thalis suggests that one definition is not sufficient. There must be two: one (above) an academic definition for students of the profession, and another, shorter, definition for our clients.

My favourite definition, despite its age, and the one that is most often quoted by PR professionals, remains the following:

Public Relations is the planned and sustained effort to establish and maintain goodwill and mutual understanding between an organisation and its publics.

The British Institute of Public Relations, 1969 (revised)

A select committee of the House of Commons accepted the original definition in 1969 when it was considering the declaration of members' interests.

Let us look at the definition in some detail. Public relations is planned and sustained. It is not something that any company, organisation, charity, voluntary group or individual does on a whim. You do not decide that you will have public relations this year, or this month, but you will not have any public relations next month or next year. It is a deliberate decision, which requires planning and sustained effort over a fixed period of time, working to a pre-planned programme to achieve specific objectives.

It is an effort to establish and maintain mutual understanding. Again, the emphasis is on the long term. You are not only trying to establish a relationship with your publics, you are also seeking to maintain the relationship once it has been established.

And what exactly are you trying to establish and maintain? Mutual understanding. No hint of propaganda. You want to be understood. You want your company and its objectives, policies, and plans for the future to be understood by the various publics. But the understanding is mutual. You are also seeking to understand those publics, to listen to what they have to tell you, to react to it, to improve because of it, to communicate the responsive change to them. And, like every relationship, the communication and the understanding continue to grow, develop and change over time.

Finally, you are seeking to do all of this with 'an organisation and its publics'. 'Publics' is a word peculiar to public relations. It does not mean the general public — the general public is made up of many different types of people, all of whom need to be reached in a different way. Every company has several publics or audiences. There are numerous publics that any company would deal with — employees, shareholders, retailers, customers, to name but a few. All have different needs, so all must be treated differently.

There are also short definitions of PR which, while not defining the skill, serve to highlight some of the functions of PR.

PR is the craft which projects the personality of an organisation.

Organisations need an appealing corporate personality. The personality associated with Microsoft, for example, is young, technically literate, workaholic-types who dress casually. The personality of the Body Shop is of a caring organisation, almost a family, which wants to help the weaker members of society to find their feet; which is kind to the environment; and which seeks to develop a new business style for a new millennium.

Public Relations is about companies making friends and influencing people.

To paraphrase Dale Carnegie[7] — companies, like individuals, need friends. They need someone to defend them in times of crisis. They need key influencers to understand what they are about. They need access to government to explain the impact of proposed legislation on their industry. They need to be respected among their peers as good, sound, ethical organisations.

PR is organised two-way communication.

As individuals, we speak with people all the time. We listen to what they have to say, we respond, we react, we communicate again to make our point of view more clearly understood. Organisations do exactly the same with their publics. They use PR tools to develop a two-way communication flow with their publics — speaking to them, listening to their response and reacting.

PR is a top management responsibility.

Ledbetter Lee insisted that he had access to top management, but nowadays the public relations professional sits on the board of the company, influencing its decisions, counselling on an ongoing basis, being both proactive and reactive. PR is an essential part of business life — it is not an optional extra. Every company needs public relations.

The vital ingredient in good PR is credibility.

Never were truer words written. What you say must be believed. Credibility needs to be earned and, once lost, is hard to regain. We will look at credibility in more detail when we study ethics in the industry.

PR has 3 roles: monitor, communicator, conscience.

Harold Burson [8]

Harold Burson's words are a description of what PR does rather than what it is, but this is a good definition nonetheless. The role of PR includes monitoring and evaluating

trends and societal changes, communicating between the organisation and its publics, and, crucially, acting as the conscience of the business.

PR is 'Managing Your Business Reputation' [9]

This definition/slogan is used on all stationery and emails issued by the Comm-Direct Consultancy in the UK.

PR = IGM: Inform, Guide and Motivate.

Gavin Bennett [10]

Gavin Bennett would prefer that we lose the term PR altogether and entirely replace it with the initials IGM. Inform people by giving them the facts, guide them by offering optional courses and consequences, and motivate them by giving them good reasons to choose the right options. By way of expansion on the above definition, he says that 'Our integrity rests in getting the facts right. Our professionalism rests in assessing/expressing the all-sides options. Our ethics rest in espousing choices of moral merit'.

PR is the building and management of the image.

This definition, from Thalis P. Coutoupis, is one he recommends should be used for the market — our clients and media — as a simple definition of PR. His use of the word 'image' reflects his belief that we are image builders, not image makers. However, I have a difficulty with the word image being used in any definition as I think it leads to confusion rather than clarity.

PR: information ➞ decision ➞ action[11]

More suited to a description of the supportive role of Product PR, this definition nonetheless highlights a sequence of responses from the targeted public — namely: awareness, interest, evaluation, trial, and acceptance. It also reinforces the idea that image alone will not sell a product — trial and acceptance, and, most importantly, delivery of what you promised, are crucial ingredients.

PR is like car maintenance.

Public Relations costs time and money when you don't seem to need it, but saves the expense and embarrassment of major breakdowns!

PR has three ingredients: truth, concern for the public interest and dialogue.

Tim Traverse-Healy [12]

Tim Traverse-Healy's description is hard to fault.

- *Truth.* You must be truthful in every piece of information that you convey to the public. You are not obliged to divulge all of the information in your possession, and will not always tell all of the truth (few companies — or, for that matter, individuals — ever do) but you must never deliberately mislead or lie.
- *Concern for the public interest.* You must respect Ledbetter Lee's dictum that the public has a right to know — and everything that you do must at all times be in the public interest. Behaving in the public interest is also, by extension, behaving in the company's interest.

    Do not confuse public interest with items of interest to the public (an error that journalists regularly make). A decade ago (1994), Imelda Riney, her 3-year-old son, Liam, and Fr Joseph Walsh were killed by shotgun by an (at that time) unknown assailant at Cregg Wood near Lough Derg.[13] The story broke in the media, and was followed closely on radio — a medium that is ideally suited to fast-breaking stories. As the story unfolded, it emerged that the person who had committed these heinous crimes had actually filed the bullets before shooting them, thus making forensic identification virtually impossible. This, in my opinion, is a classic example of confusion about the public interest. It was not *in the public interest* that this information should be broadcast — it gave valuable insider knowledge to the killer. It was certainly *of interest to the public*, who wanted to know every detail of the crime. But the public would have survived without this extra piece of information and would not have been misled or lied to or lulled into a false sense of security by its omission. The simple fact that the crimes had been committed, and that news of them had been publicly broadcast, was sufficient to satisfy the public-interest requirement. The additional information was of interest to the public but should not, in my opinion, have been broadcast or published.

- *Dialogue*. In public relations, there must always be dialogue — a two-way flow of information, feedback, ideas, suggestions, reactions, from which the company and the public benefit.

Finally, as you may now be realising, PR is not something that can be done by instinct — it is too complex a field. PR requires thought, planning, organisation and communication skills to implement and evaluate a successful plan.

An old Chinese proverb says: 'Tell me and I forget. Show me and I remember. Involve me and I understand'. The ultimate aim of public relations is the creation of understanding.

MISCONCEPTIONS SURROUNDING PR PRACTITIONERS

The chapter thus far has attempted to clarify what public relations is all about. We will now deal with the other great misconception — that people actually understand the kind of work we do. They do not. How many times have you heard someone say that their son or daughter is 'good with people' and should, therefore, go into public relations? Being good with people is an essential element of working for any company or industry, in any field. It is very difficult to work with people if you don't make an effort. If you make an effort, you become good with people. Why this should be especially important in public relations is utterly beyond me!

There is also a belief that public relations people are generally young, female, blonde, charming, good-looking and often quite vacuous, and that they spend their days at press receptions, sipping champagne, talking to people, and, naturally, looking beautiful. Who on earth is going to employ you, and pay you money, to look beautiful while sipping champagne? No one that I know of in public relations.

There are many good-looking people in public relations. There are also many very ordinary-looking people, and some downright ugly-looking people. There are men and women, old and young, charming and narky, communicative and non-communicative (it's true), drinkers and pioneers. The same is true of any industry.

The misconceptions have probably developed for four reasons:

(a) No one really knows what we do, so people think they are working in PR, even when they are not. People working in customer care, product sampling, product demonstration, or customer hospitality will all tell you that they are 'in PR'. It is an industry which people want to be in, so they assign themselves the title.

(b) When PR people are photographed at client functions, it is usually the young, good-looking female ones who are photographed (but this is true of most media functions if the photographer is shooting for society pages or evening newspapers).

(c) Utterances by some of the people in the PR industry do not help! Lynn Franks' Californian PR company starts the working day 'by meeting around the kitchen table, lighting a candle, and holding hands for a blessing for the day, and sharing of what's going on for us individually'.[14] Please!

(d) The final reason for the misconception of our role is the way in which the press and media sometimes report PR people. We are either trivialised or stereotyped as baddies.

The trivialisation of PR: In an interview with Mary Finan, managing director of Wilson Hartnell Public Relations (WHPR) and one of the most highly respected practitioners in Ireland, the media subheading read: 'Her childhood was drenched with sweetness; at university she socialised, debated and acted, and still got an honours degree, and she has a seemingly idyllic career as the top public relations executive in Ireland'.[15]

The stereotypical 'baddie' PR: 'He is one of those smarmy PR types who makes the skin of some journalists crawl. He likes to pretend he is your friend. He wants you to know he is there to help.'[16]

What matters in public relations is not how a person looks, but how well they can do their job. And on the champagne scene, all of the best PR people I know have strict rules about not drinking when they are working. If you are dealing with clients and journalists, the last thing they want to do is talk to you about a company when you are nicely merry. PR practitioners may well have a drink when the function is over, but they have too much work to do during any function to be knocking back the champagne.

THE PROFESSIONAL PR PRACTITIONER

If all of these commonly held misconceptions add up to a definition of what a PR person is not, let us turn to look at what a PR person actually is. A good public relations practitioner needs several qualities. At its broadest level, PR people need the following:

- *An understanding of communication processes*. They need to understand how messages are sent and received. They must be able to evaluate the response to a message, and to change and adapt their strategies so that messages are more clearly received and understood.
- *An understanding of the way the media works*. The media is often used as a means of conveying messages to the public. PR people need to understand the deadlines that different media work to, the formats in which information is most acceptable, the needs of print and broadcast journalists. They must understand the influence of the internet, the power of newsletters and magazines, and the value of oramedia (storytelling).
- *A keen understanding of the world of business*. Clients are very often drawn from the world of business. PR people need to understand the demands of business, the profit-making drive, the international repercussions of decisions, the value of trade unions, the implications of industrial relations disasters, the impact of decisions on share prices, and the power of shareholders.

On a personal level, there are certain qualities which undoubtedly help a PR practitioner:

- *A broad interest in the world of media*. Good PR practitioners are readers; they have the habit of reading, and are constantly developing their vocabulary. PR people ideally have a love of language, and take pride in how they would explain a concept.
  - *An interest in what is happening in the media world*. PR people have a knowledge about which journalists write on certain issues. They have enquiring minds, constantly questioning the angles and perspectives that people take, and a curiosity about how a story was covered. They also have a broad interest in the issues of the day — be they national or foreign.
  - *An interest in television*. The PR practitioner wants to know about the latest trends on TV (in particular, the growth of 'reality' television with programmes like *Big Brother* (Channel 4, 2001) and 'Popstars' (RTÉ 1, January 2002). Good PR people know the different TV personalities (and can, therefore, select the most appropriate person to act as a product endorser, or chair a meeting or introduce a video). They constantly look, enquiringly, at the way in which visuals on television portray a message, and wonder whose message they are receiving.
  - *An interest in radio*. Good PR practitioners find it impossible to sit in a car and not listen to talk radio. They constantly study the interviewer, and the style of questioning. They wonder why this particular person is being interviewed at this time. They study how well the interview was conducted, and analyse whether or not the interviewee got their message across. They listen to things like the tone of voice used, the style of questions, and anger/remorse in someone's voice.
  - *Curiosity and enthusiasm about the internet*. What is on the net? How is it

presented? What messages are being transmitted? Who is using the net? Where are they coming from? Are there cultural differences?

❏ *An appreciation of films, theatre, music and the visual arts.*

In essence, the good PR practitioner has an interest in all forms of media.

- *An interest in current affairs.* A good practitioner is someone who can debate the issues of the day. PR people need to know who are the key players — the Taoiseach, ministers, junior ministers, opposition spokespersons. They should be able to identify the policy differences between political parties. A good practitioner will study the influence of groups like An Taisce, the Trade Union Movement and women's groups. PR people will have an interest in changes introduced in the budget and will try to analyse the economic and social impact of those changes. They will study demographic changes, societal issues, trends in employment, and will know what is happening in the wider world. A good PR person follows the progress of bills through the Oireachtas; reads all of the pro- and anti-referendum (any referendum) literature; and studies racism, the collapse of rural areas, and the spending power of young people.

- *Excellent time management skills.* Public relations involves a lot of organisation — organising your own time, so that you can manage a number of clients in the same day, and organising functions like press receptions, press conferences, photo-calls, client meetings, and sponsorships. Without an ability to manage your time well, you will find that you are constantly busy, but achieving little.

- *Thoroughness.* A good PR person will be someone with the dedication to concentrate on the minor and major details of any public relations task, and see them through to fruition. There is no point in organising a function, and getting all of the big details right, only to fail because you did not concentrate on the minor details like organised car parking.

- *An ability to think strategically.* In addition to the ability to concentrate on the small things, a good PR person also needs to be a strategic thinker — to be capable of seeing the big picture. You need to know how your proposals will impact on the business you are advising, to see the developing trends and know how you might incorporate them into your proposals.

- *An ability to deal with people.* This quality is needed in every type of business. You will deal with many people every day — people you work with in the PR office, bank managers, journalists, clients, photographers, etc. You don't need to like them, but you must be able to deal honestly and effectively with them.

- *Honesty.* To work in public relations, you must be honest and trustworthy. You are dealing with sensitive, highly confidential information. You must be trusted both by clients and by the media. You will only be trusted and respected if you are honest.

- *Imagination and creativity.* There are many clients who will approach you with a brilliant idea which you are asked to implement — that is the easy end. There are also many clients who will approach you about their companies, which are perfectly ethical, financially sound, good companies — but they lack excitement. You are the person who needs the creativity and imagination to design something — of interest to the company and the general public — that will attract media attention.

Finally, all of these qualities are enhanced and developed by discussion with other practitioners. Opportunities for discussion usually arise through professional bodies. In Ireland, there are two organisations that represent professional public relations practitioners — the Public Relations Institute of Ireland, which represents all practitioners (and students) in the industry, and the Public Relations Consultants' Association (under the umbrella of the PRII), which represents consultancies. These bodies provide valuable professional and representative advice and offer opportunities to share information and interests with people of like mind.

THE POWER OF BRANDS

The power of brands is particularly obvious when you look at consumer purchases. People buy brand names they know and trust. A brand is bought for three main reasons — functional benefits (because it will do the job), psychic value (because it says something about the kind of person you are), and investment value.[17]

Functional Benefits

Any car with a reasonable engine and four wheels will take you from point A to point B, but no one goes into a garage looking for 'a car'. We look for the car to fulfil a specific function — it must be a four-door to accommodate the children, or it must be easy on petrol because I do a lot of mileage, or it must have big boot space to accommodate my musical instruments. Similarly, a shampoo must actually leave your hair feeling clean — the functional benefit must be present.

Psychic Value

The psychic value is created by the public relations and advertising people. Once we have established the need for a car, and the functions it must have, we then look to the psychic value of the product. We look for a car that says something about us and reflects our personality. We select the car (and often the colour) which best suits our 'type' of person — flashy and sporty (*I want to be noticed*), conservative (*I'm a solid, reliable type*), executive (*I've made it*), 4-wheel drive (*I am a hunting, shooting, fishing guy*).

Look at the ways in which shampoos and perfumes/aftershave lotions are promoted. Any shampoo will wash your hair, but L'Oréal believes you should spend more 'because you're worth it'. Every bottle of perfume or aftershave is a bottle of smelly water, but you either buy cheap and cheerful, or you invest in seductive, expensive or sporty reflections (to your senses) of the kind of person you are. Psychic value is what PR people are really good at. We will build the lifestyle type to suit the product — the salespeople will then go and sell it to you.

Investment Value

And finally, it must be a good investment — the car must actually hold its value; it must have trade-in value in a few years. The investment value of shampoos and lotions is that the investor believes in the product and therefore believes that a higher price is warranted because they are investing in themselves.

ATTITUDES AND OPINIONS

> Creating awareness is one thing, changing attitudes is another. Changing behaviour is the most difficult of all.
>
> Martin Higgins, interim chief executive of the Food Safety Promotions Board[18]

Do not be fooled into thinking that PR people always begin with a blank canvas — they do not. Very often, the job of the PR person is to change attitudes and opinions. This is a very challenging area of PR.

Virtually every decision in life is based on attitudes and opinions. Attitudes and opinions are formed by information, or lack of it. The more you know about a company, the clearer the mental image you develop of it. If the mental image is a good one, you are more inclined to buy the company's products, or give it the benefit of the doubt in times of crisis.

Banks have been promoting pensions to young people for years. They are trying to change attitudes. People think of pensions as something they will need in their old age. Banks are trying to change attitudes and encourage people to take a pension when they are young, so that they will be protected and comfortable in their older years. So far, the response has been disappointing.

Governments invest huge amounts of money in campaigns to try to change attitudes and habits. It is difficult to change attitudes to immigrants, foreign workers, members of the Travelling Community or women, and equally difficult to change habits of voting, saving, disposing of rubbish, etc.

In his 2001 budget, Minister for Finance Charlie McCreevy introduced a new savings scheme called Special Savings Incentive Account (SSIA). The scheme gave a guaranteed extra €1 for every €4 lodged by regular savers. The economic reasoning behind the scheme was clear. The government felt that people were disposing of their income too lightly. As a nation we were impulse buying because there was more cash in the economy (the Celtic Tiger) and because the return on savings, through traditional outlets, was so low that it was almost negligible. Despite the government initiative, the availability of the scheme through banks, building societies and credit unions, the guaranteed return far in excess of anything else available on the market, and a substantial advertising campaign, the initiative failed to capture the public imagination in the initial stages. The uptake on the scheme was much less than the government had anticipated. By January 2002, nine months into the scheme, only about 400,000 people, or 16 per cent of the eligible population, had signed up for the incentive[19] and they were mostly 25-to 49-year-olds from the affluent ABC1 group.[20] Attitudes to saving and habits of spending proved harder to change than the government had anticipated. In the final month, April 2002, perhaps because of the perceived economic downturn, the scheme attracted a rush of applicants.

We grow up with some of our attitudes; we develop others as we go through life. Once those attitudes are ingrained, they are very difficult to change.

CONVERTING NEGATIVE OPINIONS TO POSITIVE ATTITUDES

If you are seeking to convert negative to positive, you should be conscious of what you can realistically achieve.

Jefkins[21] believed that there were four main attitudes:

NEGATIVE	POSITIVE
Hostility	Sympathy
Prejudice	Acceptance
Apathy	Interest
Ignorance	Knowledge

Hostility

If someone is hostile towards your company, it may be because of something that happened many years ago. The PR job is to try to inform that person of why it happened, how it happened, how the company dealt with the situation and how it has implemented changes which would prevent the same thing from ever happening again. What you are trying to achieve is sympathy. You do not expect that someone who is hostile to your company will suddenly become its biggest supporter, but you can expect them to become less hostile and slightly more sympathetic towards you if they fully understand the background and developments within the company.

Since the 1950s, the National Blood Transfusion Board had enjoyed a positive public profile. Donors at Pelican House (or mobile clinics) were plentiful, and the silver and gold pelican pins were worn by donors with pride.[22] All that changed and the board became the object of hostility when the hepatitis C scandal broke in 1994. The eventual outcome was a public tribunal, called to investigate how an organ of the state was responsible for infecting its citizens.

The Blood Transfusion Board tried to change the hostility to sympathy by explaining that improved donor-screening processes had been introduced to ensure that this situation could never happen again. It changed its name to the Irish Blood Transfusion Service (IBTS) and moved from Pelican House to state-of-the-art headquarters at St James's Hospital. The Minister for Health appointed a new chairman, Michael McLoone, and the board probably believed that it had at least begun the process of change.[23]

The national television station, RTÉ, broadcast a docu-drama mini-series in January 2002 called 'No Tears'.[24] The impact of the programme was enormous. It reminded the general public of how angry and hostile they had felt towards the blood bank. The reaction was so strong that the blood bank publicly appealed to people, through media interviews and advertisements, to give blood. They feared that the broadcast of the programme would result in a decline in donations of blood. Elective surgery in the country's hospitals was cancelled. The hostility, which had begun to change to sympathy, had returned to the population.

Prejudice

Prejudice is difficult to overcome because very few people understand why they are prejudiced against a person or a company or a brand. If, by giving people the information they need, you can convert their prejudice to acceptance, you have gone a long way down the road. The consumer who is prejudiced against your brand may never buy it, but, through exposure to public relations techniques, may come to accept that it is a good and reputable brand.

One of the best examples of a conversion from prejudice to acceptance was the Dublin Gas Company. Two people died in an explosion at an apartment complex called Raglan House in Ballsbridge, Dublin, on 1 January 1987. It was several hours before the Dublin Gas Company issued its first public statement. The company was in receivership and the three-person PR department had been made redundant. External PR consultants had to be retained.

People in Dublin were hostile towards a company that did not seem to care. That hostility turned to prejudice when people, in vox-pop interviews, stated that they would not, under any circumstances, have gas in their homes. There was a prejudice against the product and the company that produced it, with many believing that it was unsafe.

To the company's credit, Bord Gáis, which had replaced Dublin Gas as the supplier, not only changed its internal systems, but also communicated the change so effectively that it is hard to imagine a home in Dublin that would now be prejudiced against the gas company. In fact, in 1990, by an extensive PR and advertising campaign (remember the gas company bears and the 50-50 cashback?) Bord Gáis succeeded in promoting gas as a lifestyle choice, which was environmentally friendly. The company not only regained the confidence of consumers, but increased the sales of natural gas appliances by 50 per cent that year. Who would want to deal with dirty grates and buckets of fuel if they could, instead, flick a switch and have the effect of a 'real' fire? It was a brilliant come-back by the company, which had treated seriously the concerns of its customers.[25]

Apathy

Apathy, essentially, is when people just don't care. They have no interest whatsoever in your company. You need to convert that apathy to interest. This is one of the most difficult of all PR tasks. If someone simply doesn't care what happens to the environment, for example, or doesn't care who represents them at national or European level, how do you convert that total apathy to at least a mild level of interest?

Ignorance

Finally, you have to deal with ignorance — people simply may not know anything about your company and, because they know nothing, they cannot form any opinion about you, and are very reluctant to buy anything from you. By converting ignorance to knowledge, you are placing the person in a better position actually to make a decision. This is probably the easiest of the four attitudes to deal with, and the one on which companies spend large budgets. People are reluctant to buy from a company, or to invest in a brand, that they never heard of. Companies are aware of that and consequently spend a large portion of their marketing budgets on research. As Bernadette Coyne, chief executive of Research Solutions has said: 'Research is information and information is power…if you don't know what people think of your brand or they think of the competitor's brand, you are disadvantaged'.[26] As a result, not only marketing budgets but huge levels of PR resources are invested in telling the consumer, the investor and the influencer, about the company, its policies, its location, and its products.

DEALING WITH IMAGES

You will encounter many different images in your dealings with companies, organisations or charities. There are three, in particular, of which you should be conscious:

- Mirror Image
- Wish Image
- Multiple Image

The *Mirror Image* is what companies or individuals believe to be true of themselves. The mirror image may, or may not, be true. It is not that companies are deliberately trying to mislead you, rather that they are deluding themselves. By research, you can establish if you are dealing with a true or a mirror image. We are all guilty of self-delusion in some way. How often have you seen a man or woman walking down the street, dressed in something 'hideous', which they believed was 'beautiful'? Too often! Yet they looked in the mirror that morning and believed that they looked absolutely wonderful. Companies are guilty of making exactly the same mistakes.

A *Wish Image* is what a company would like to be true of itself. It wishes that it could be the biggest in the field, or provide the very best quality service. The wish needs to be identified as such, and moved from being a wish to a goal that the company can attain and is taking steps towards achieving. Your job, as a communications expert, is to harness that goal and ensure that all of your communication strategies work to help the company achieve it.

A *Multiple Image* essentially refers to the fact that different publics have different images of the same company. People develop an image of a company based on their dealings with it: employees will have an image of the company based on their work experience; a retailer will have an image of a company based on the frequency of delivery and the billing method, etc. Each of the publics will have a different image of the company. It is your job, as a PR person, to research and identify those images and use them in your communication with each of the groups.

Corporate Image is an expression much used today. We will look at corporate image and corporate identity in much greater detail later in this book.

Finally, remember that what you are always trying to achieve, as a PR practitioner, is an accurate image of the company — an image that is a reasonable and accurate impression of an organisation and its products or services; an image that is based, most importantly, on the truth.

Key Dates in the History of Public Relations

1877	Ivy Ledbetter Lee (father of PR) born.
1891	Edward Bernays (PR's first educator) born.
1923	First university course on PR, New York University.
1927	Ned Lawler first PR for government body in Europe.
1953	Public Relations Institute of Ireland (PRII) formed.
1955	International Public Relations Association (IPRA) formed.
1959	European Confederation of Public Relations practitioners (CERP) formed by five countries: Belgium, France, Germany, Italy and the Netherlands.
1964	IPRA granted formal recognition by the United Nations.
1965	Code of Athens (ethical code) adopted by CERP in London.
1978	Code of Lisbon (ethical code) adopted by CERP in Lisbon.
1989	Public Relations Consultants Association (PRCA) formed in Ireland.
1997	National syllabus of PR education introduced in Ireland by PRII.
2000	Northern Ireland Government Affairs Group formed.

REFERENCES

1. Michael Colley, *The Communicators : The History of the Public Relations Institute of Ireland* 1953-1993, Public Relations Institute of Ireland, 1993.
2. Mary O'Sullivan 'If the Room Has a View, The Man Has the Vision', *Sunday Independent,* 2 April 2000.
3. Jennifer O'Connell, 'Louis the Spin King', *Sunday Business Post,* 20 January 2002, Agenda section.
4. Jack Felton, Institute for PR, University of Florida, quoted in *IPRA Digest,* no. 68, 16 January 2001.
5. Moshe Dayan, Dayan Public Relations, Israel. Definition downloaded from the internet in September 1995, quoted in *IPRA Digest,* no. 16, 14 August 2000.
6. Thalis P. Coutoupis, Greece, quoted in *IPRA Digest,* no. 17, 17 August 2000.
7. Dale Carnegie, *How to Win Friends and Influence People,* Hutchinson, 1994.
8. Harold Burson, quoted by Alasdair Sutherland, in *IPRA Digest,* no. 62, 12 January

2001. (Alasdair Sutherland is Executive Vice President, Manning, Selvage & Lee, and was IPRA President, 2001.)

9. Alison Tipping, CommDirect, UK, quoted in *IPRA Digest*, no. 18, 18 August 2000.

10. Gavin Bennett, Kenya, *IPRA Digest*, no. 157, 17 October 2001.

11. Professor W. R. Spence, presentation at Irish Academy of Public Relations course entitled 'Public Relations Skills for Practitioners', at Skull Kommunikációs Iskola, Budapest, 1997.

12. Tim Traverse-Healy, *Actions Speak Louder than Words*, video, PRTV, UK, 1991.

13. 'Witness Denies Garda Pulled Killer from Car, *The Irish Times*, 6 April 2001, p. 1.

14. Patricia Deevy, 'Franks, My Dear, I Don't Give a Damn', *Sunday Independent*, 2 April 2000.

15. Patricia Deevy, 'It's a Wonderful Life', *Sunday Independent*, 20 February 2000.

16. Jody Corcoran, 'Forget about the Dead Man, Let's Talk about Frank', *Sunday Independent*, 16 April 2000.

17. Jon White, *Actions Speak Louder than Words*, video, PRTV, UK, 1991.

18. Ella Shanahan, 'Food safety is no laughing matter for entertainer', *The Irish Times*, 18 January 2002, Working Life feature.

19. Samantha McCaughren, 'Take the money Charlie's giving away for free', *Irish Independent*, 26 January 2002, Your Money section.

20. Clare O'Dea, 'SSIAs are now held by 25% of adults', *The Irish Times*, 25 January 2002, Business This Week supplement.

21. Frank Jefkins, *Public Relations Techniques*, London: Butterworth Heinemann, 1994 (second edition).

22. 'Giving Blood', Opinion/The Irish Times on the Web/ireland.com, 24 April 1998.

23. Paul Anderson, 'Minister names new blood service chairman', Breaking News/The Irish Times on the Web/ireland.com, 6 September 2001.

24. RTÉ Drama — 'No Tears'. Four-part drama series — one-hour-long episodes. Dramatised account of the true story of Ireland's hepatitis C scandal. Started on Monday, 14 January 2002 at 9.30 p.m. Also broadcast on Monday, 21 January; Monday, 28 January; and Monday, 3 February. Producers: Jackie Larkin and Lesley McKimm. Series written by: Brian Phelan. Directed by: Stephen Burke. An independent commission for RTÉ. 'No Tears' was produced by Little Bird in association with Comet Films and is supported by the Irish Film Board. RTE Online http://www.rte.ie/tv/notears/index.html

25. www.naturalgas.ie

26. Elaine Larkin, 'Firms realise information is power', *The Irish Times*, 5 February 2001, finance section, www.ireland.com/the Irish Times — FINANCE

CHAPTER 2

Ethics

The only way to compel man to speak good of you, is to do good.

Voltaire

Truth and ethical behaviour will be a recurring theme, so it is important, in the early stages of this book, to outline the Codes of Ethics by which PR professionals are bound.

ETHICS AND BRANDS

Brands have already been referred to briefly. Consumers buy brand names they know and trust. Major corporations with wide product ranges, devote huge resources (people, money, PR, advertising) to promoting brands. We may know little about the company itself, but we know and understand something about the brands it produces.

You need only look at teenage spending patterns (or yuppie spending patterns) to see the power of the brand. Teenagers will 'allow' their parents to buy only certain brands of trainers and leisure suits; 'other' brands are dismissed as 'uncool'. People wear brands prominently on their persons — look at the Tommy Hilfiger range of clothing — to broadcast their brand consciousness.

Consumer focus on ethics also affects brands. The sportswear giant, Nike, one of the world's biggest brand names, was seriously undermined in the 1990s by several exposés of its manufacturing processes. In 1998, Nike's CEO, Phil Knight, admitted that the shoes 'have become synonymous with slave wages, forced overtime and arbitrary abuse'. At the time, workers in one Indonesian factory producing $100 trainers were being paid 80 cents an hour, while Michael Jordan was paid $20 million a year to promote the brand. By the 2002/2003 season, however, Nike had bounced back and joined forces with the Manchester United Football team. Nike is by no means alone, and Naomi Klein's book, *No Logo*, makes compulsive reading for ethical consumers, corporate heads of business and PR practitioners.[1]

INVESTORS AND CONSUMERS

Among the key publics of any company are: employees, consumers, investors, suppliers, the media, pressure groups, the competition, the community, legislators and the trade. All of these publics are conscious of and concerned about ethics. They expect companies to behave ethically — to tell the truth when disaster occurs, to explain investment policies, to treat their staff well, to deal with customer complaints. There is such a wide choice of companies in which to invest, and products to buy, that we, the consumers and investors, see no reason why we should put our money into a company that does not behave ethically. There are numerous examples of companies that saw profits and share prices decline sharply after unethical behaviour had been revealed. Customers will not buy from companies that test their products on animals, or use child labour in the production of their goods, or adopt policies in developing countries which they would not adopt in the first world. It is in a company's interest to behave ethically, and the company, its customers and investors, and the media have a right to expect that the company's PR people will do the same.

ETHICAL PR

PR practitioners, in my experience, are a very ethical group of people. They take their responsibilities seriously and are truthful in their dealings with media, clients, consumers, investors and the public. Mary Finan perhaps summed it up best when she said: 'You're here for the long haul. The most valuable asset…is our integrity. No client, no matter how much they would spend, would be worth me telling a lie for'.[2]

However, the year 2000 also saw Frank Dunlop, a leading Irish PR consultant, give evidence before the Flood Tribunal. It was the first time that a PR consultant had appeared in this role, and the first time that a consultant had given evidence of making payments to influence decisions. Frank Dunlop tendered his resignation from the Public Relations Institute of Ireland (PRII) shortly after giving evidence. The media, once his friend, rounded on this 'spin doctor' ruthlessly.

> The thing about Dunlop was that he spun beautifully. He never refused a request for a chat even though he rarely spoke on the record. He spoke at such length and with such volubility that you were inclined to believe that he was telling the truth. How could a guilty man speak with such apparent openness and with such detail I wondered, forgetting, of course, that the best lies are those that are dressed up with lots of little frilly — and usually inconsequential — bits.[3]

CODES OF ETHICS

Every profession has ethical standards which its members must observe. Public relations is no different. There are two codes by which public relations practitioners are bound — the Code of Athens and the Code of Lisbon (see Appendices).

The codes bestow obligations and place restrictions on PR practitioners in their own interests, in the interests of media and in the interests of their clients. The codes do not specifically mention every national law by which you must abide. It is stated, and understood, however, that all of your actions will be legal. That being said, the obligations and restrictions can be divided into fifteen areas as follows:

- Lifetime confidentiality
- Insider trading
- Integrity

- Ignorance
- Staff
- The profession
- Public interest
- Elected public representatives
- Influencing government, legislators and media
- Declaring financial or other interests
- Accepting third-party commissions
- Varying fee structure
- Representing conflicting interests
- Guaranteeing results
- Competing for business.

We will look at each, in turn.

Lifetime Confidentiality

A PR practitioner is expected to deal honestly and fairly with employers and clients (past and present). Whether you work in-house for a particular company, or handle several clients on a consultancy basis, you are privy to highly confidential information. The Codes oblige you to respect that confidentiality for life. The fact that you have ceased to work for a particular company does not allow you to start talking about commercially sensitive information you became aware of while you were employed by that company. Just as a priest would never discuss information he was given in a confessional, or a lawyer would never discuss confidential client information, so too you must never reveal information, except in a court of law.

Insider Trading

The Codes also make it abundantly clear that any information you have gained may not be used for your own financial advantage. If you know that a company you are working with is about to introduce a new product, and that this might increase the company's share price on the stock exchange, you may not buy shares for yourself in advance of any public announcement. If you did, you would be improperly benefiting from confidential information to which you were privy. Similarly, no member of your staff may purchase or sell such shares.

Integrity

The word 'honesty' appears many times throughout the Codes. Honesty is terribly important in public relations. After all, you are not only the public face of an organisation, you are also its conscience. You are aware of everything that is happening in the company, and you are advising on issues on a daily basis. It is vital that your clients, the media, and your colleagues respect you as an honest person.

Ignorance

Ignorance is no excuse for poor conduct. As a professional practitioner, you are obliged to respect the Codes of ethics which are binding on you as a professional. You are also duty bound to be aware of the contents of the Codes, and any changes that are made to them. It is simply not good enough to say that you were unaware of a new clause that had been recently inserted. You have a duty to be aware of, and behave in accordance with, your codes of conduct.

You also have a duty to be thorough in establishing all of the facts in any situation. You are further obliged to check, to your own satisfaction, that the facts you issue to the general public are correct. The media, and through them, the public, must trust the information you are issuing. You can issue that information with confidence only if you are fully informed yourself.

Staff

Not only have you a duty to abide by the Codes yourself, you also have a duty to ensure that other members of your profession do likewise. Particularly important to note is the fact that you cannot allow any member of your staff to breach the Codes. It is not necessary for all members of staff to be members of the profession, but all are bound by the PR codes of conduct. As a member, it is your duty to ensure that staff-members abide by the codes of conduct, whether they are PRII members or not.

This is an important element, because it highlights honesty yet again. It prevents an otherwise unscrupulous practitioner from deciding to bend the rules. As a PRII member, you cannot defend your conduct by saying that you did not break the rules, but unfortunately some members of your staff did. That's not good enough. You are responsible for your staff and, if you are an honest practitioner, you will not condone any breach of the Codes either by a junior member of staff, or by a fellow practitioner.

The Profession

The codes of professional conduct impose an obligation on you not to damage the reputation of either your national institute or your profession. As a practitioner, you must be conscious of the respect in which your profession is held. You may not do anything to jeopardise that respect. If public relations is to maintain (some would say 'earn') its good reputation, all PR practitioners must behave ethically and honestly.

As a PR practitioner you are obliged, not only to respect the rules of your own profession, but also the rules and codes by which other professionals are bound. Just as you are forbidden to encourage a member of your own staff to breach the PR codes, so too are you forbidden to encourage a member of any other profession to break their codes of professional practice.

Public Interest

It is enshrined in the Codes that all activities must be conducted with proper regard to the public interest. If something is in the interest of the public, it is also in the interest of your company. The focus of public relations practitioners is always to ensure that what they do is in the best interest of the public. If your primary focus is always on your client, it is possible that you might lose sight of what is in the best interest of the public. A natural desire to protect or shield the client might, somehow, take over. If, on the other hand, as these Codes demand, your focus is always on the public interest, there is no danger that you will, however inadvertently, do something that could be regarded as an improper activity.

Nothing that the public is entitled to know is secret. You have a duty to ensure that the interests of any company you deal with are fully declared (e.g. is the company being open about the subsidiary in Asia — an associated sister-company with a different name?) You are encouraged to ensure that the companies you deal with behave ethically. It makes sense. How can you deal honestly with the public, on behalf of a company that does not deal honestly with you? It is impossible.

Elected Public Representatives

A small but growing number of Irish politicians also work as consultants. This issue is dealt with in greater detail in the chapter on Political PR. However, this trend has ethical implications for PR practitioners. If your consultancy retains a publicly elected representative to lobby on your behalf, or on behalf of others, this appointment should be made public. Public representatives, at local, national, and European level, make regular contributions to debates representing the interests of their constituents. That may often involve them in lobbying to have changes made to certain laws, or planning permissions, or EU directives. The behaviour of the representative is perfectly ethical.

If, however, that same public representative is a director of your company, or has been retained by your consultancy to lobby colleagues, his or her 'interest' in the issue should be declared.

It is perfectly ethical to retain an elected representative to lobby on your behalf, or to have an elected representative join the board of a client company. If the public is unaware of these facts, however, they might feel that perfectly good amendments to legislation or planning permissions occurred only because the representative had a financial interest in the outcome. You risk damaging the reputations of the elected representative, your client and yourself.

My own personal opinion on this subject is that a public representative should never be retained as a lobbyist. I have no problem with former public representatives, but sitting Councillors or TDs or MEPs are a different matter. The public perception will be that you are retaining someone 'inside the circle' to 'have a word in a few ears'. It does the profession of public relations no good at all to be involved in this form of lobbying, and I believe that it will ultimately damage the public belief in politicians and PR people alike.

Influencing Government, Legislators and Media

As a practitioner, you may well be asked to influence any of these bodies, as part of a legitimate public relations campaign. For example, you may be retained to lobby government ministers and spokespersons, to ensure that a law which is adversely affecting your company, and could possibly cause redundancies, is changed. That is a perfectly legitimate public relations objective. You may not, however, improperly seek to influence the outcome (e.g. you could not offer a TD a financial inducement for changing the legislation, or a holiday in Barbados, or free printing at the next election). It is hard to imagine any offer of this nature which would be consistent with the public interest! How could such a change be in the best interests of the population, if you needed to bribe people? It would also not be in the interest of your profession. If you are a professional practitioner, and there is a good reason to change a law, you should be using your communications skills to effect the change.

There are PR practitioners who specialise in lobbying and are expert in the art of communicating the need for legislative change.

Declaring Financial or Other Interests

You also have a duty to inform your client company of any relevant financial connections that you have. If, for example, your public relations consultancy also owns a photographic agency, and you propose to use that agency for a photo-shoot for your client's corporate brochure, you must inform the client of the connection. Otherwise, you are not dealing fairly with the company which has retained you. Your clients may not have any objection at all, but they are entitled to be told. Similarly, other connections not directly financial — your spouse owns the printing company that you are recommending, or your sister is the managing director of the video company you propose to retain — must also be declared to the client.

If one of your employees has shares in a client company, the client company must be made aware of it. It protects your employee from a charge of 'insider trading' and again it ensures that you cannot instruct a junior member of staff to behave unethically. Remember that you should be declaring *all* of your financial interests to your clients, and that includes any stocks or shares in their company held by you, or any member of your staff.

Accepting Third-Party Commissions

If, for example, you receive a commission from a company for putting business its way, you must declare that commission to your employer or client. In public relations you are constantly dealing with a number of suppliers — you will regularly retain photographers, book video-shoots, buy print, work with graphic designers, etc. There is nothing wrong with a print company telling you that, because it values your business, it will pay you a 10 per cent commission on each piece of business that you give it. It is wrong, however, not to let your client know that you receive such a commission. Similarly, in the case of a hotel offering you a free weekend to thank you for the level of business you have put its way, the free weekend should be declared to the client and offered to them instead. After all, you recommended the hotel because of its location, décor, pricing, etc. and not because you would get a free weekend!

Varying Fee Structure

The Codes of ethics establish the practitioner's right to charge a fee — not necessarily a flat-hour rate — that reflects the level of skill acquired over the years. For example, a client may call you in to advise on a crisis situation. Because you have dealt with many crises throughout your career, it may take you four hours to advise the client. However, if you were to charge four hours at, say, €100, the total fee would not accurately reflect the level of skill and experience you needed to enable you to advise the company in such a short space of time. You are perfectly entitled to strike a higher fee which takes into account factors other than the number of hours worked.

Representing Conflicting Interests

You may not represent conflicting interests. How could you? If two companies are in conflict with each other, how can you expect both of them to give you sensitive or confidential information? Of equal importance, how could you, as a professional, handle these conflicting interests honestly? It would be very difficult if not impossible. You may, however, represent competing interests — two chain stores handling fashion items, for example — provided that both are made aware of the fact that you are handling their competitor, and that both agree.

Neither do the Codes of ethics prevent you from performing the same function for competing companies. If, for example, you are a public relations consultant working in a specialised area like finance, or information technology, or agriculture, there is every chance that all of your clients compete with each other. Each will be aware of your client list. All will accept that you will, to the best of your ability, operate a system of 'Chinese walls'[4] within your consultancy. And all will be willing to work with you because your expertise cannot be found, or found to the same degree, in other non-specialist consultancies.

Guaranteeing Results

Practitioners may not guarantee results that are beyond their powers to achieve. For example, you could not guarantee that a client would achieve feature coverage on page 3 of a national newspaper, next Tuesday, if they were to give you the contract. How could you make such a guarantee? You do not own the newspaper, or the journalist, and you are not buying an advertisement. You are offering a guarantee to the client over which you do not have total control. You *could* guarantee the professionalism of your service and the effort that you would put into having a story covered. You could show the level of coverage achieved from previous campaigns. All of that is perfectly legitimate. You could not, however, guarantee newspaper coverage.

Competing for Business

You must also be ethical in your conduct towards your colleagues. You must treat them with the same high standards of truth and honesty that you apply to clients. You are specifically forbidden to make unfair comparisons or to claim credit for ideas that are not your own. This applies particularly in a situation where, as in all professions, you are competing for business against a fellow professional. You may fairly win the public relations contract — that is acceptable business practice. But you may not imply something about another consultancy, or steal some of the proposals that it put forward and pretend that they are your own. The word 'honesty' is surfacing again. You must at all times deal honestly with your colleagues.

REFERENCES

1. Bernice Harrison, 'The price of a label', *The Irish Times*, 5 February 2000.
2. Patricia Deevy, 'It's a wonderful life', *Sunday Independent*, 20 February 2000.
3. Emily O'Reilly, 'The spinning of an elegant web of deceit', *Sunday Business Post*, 23 April 2000.
4. Chinese walls: if a consultancy is handling two competing clients, it is understood that two different teams of account handlers will be responsible for each client, and neither team will divulge information to the other. Although both teams work for the same consultancy, in the same building, a system of 'Chinese walls' means that confidential information about the client remains within the 'walls' of the team responsible.

CHAPTER 3

Objectives, Publics and Techniques

At the beginning of any public relations programme, you need to set objectives. If you do not know what you are trying to do, how can you design a programme that will achieve anything?

Objectives are usually set for a twelve-month period. They are set at the beginning of the year, and they clearly identify what you want to achieve by the end of that year.

After you have set your objectives, you define the publics you intend to reach. You then structure a programme to reach those publics and achieve your objectives. Finally, you also build in a method of evaluation which would allow you an opportunity to assess whether or not your proposals had the desired effect of reaching target audiences and achieving the objectives.

OBJECTIVES SHOULD BE SMART

Objectives should be SMART[1] i.e.

S	Specific
M	Measurable
A	Achievable
R	Realistic
T	Time-sensitive

Specific

Whether you have just joined the company as a PR executive or have just been retained by the company as a consultant, you must begin by establishing what the company's goals are. You must know what the company wants to achieve over the coming year (and in most cases companies will be able to give you a clear set of goals for a five-year period) and gear your public relations objectives towards the achievement of those goals. Your objectives should also take into account those issues which may become problems in the long-term. Objectives should not be confused with aims. An aim is general, an objective specific.

Measurable

There is absolutely no point in writing an objective for a company which states that the company should 'increase public awareness' of what it does. This is the 'wannabe' syndrome ('I wannabe famous') and is totally unprofessional. Increase the awareness of what? Is it everything that the company does? Or a specific brand? Or a new sponsorship?

'Increase public awareness' by whom? Employees, teenagers, investors? You must always divide the general public into specific groups first, and then target them.

'Increase public awareness' from what level? In order to increase awareness, you must know what the level of awareness currently is. Have studies been done to establish how well known the company is? If so, what did they reveal? If only 5 per cent of office workers (assuming that they are your audience) could identify what your company does, what do you want to increase the level to?

Making objectives measurable means that instead of having an objective 'to increase awareness of the company', you would instead have an objective:

> To increase the awareness of the company, as a major employer, among office workers. The awareness should rise from 5 per cent to 7 per cent over a twelve-month period.

Achievable

An objective should be achievable — that is, what you are aiming for should be possible. Is it possible to attract the number of subscribers you are looking for? Can the required level of understanding be achieved in a short time-frame? Is it possible to change attitudes of buyers within a six-month period? There is no point in designing plans for objectives that are flawed. If the objective is unrealistic in the first instance, all of the work you put into achieving it will be wasted.

Realistic

Your objectives should also be realistic in terms of the budget available to you. If your company or client has allocated a budget for public relations, you must work within that budget. There is no point in identifying objectives which would cost more to achieve than you have to spend.

Time-Sensitive

Objectives can be immediate (short term), in the near future (medium term) or distant (long term).

Make sure that the objectives can be achieved within the time allotted to you. You may have a number of objectives, all of them worthy, which would take two years to achieve. If you have only a one-year contract, or have been asked to prepare proposals for a six-month period only, it is far better to detail the objectives that can be realised within the time available. You should also note (for future reference) those other objectives which could be added in the following years.

SMART

It might be your aim, for example, to work in the public relations industry. Your objective, however, might be, in the first instance, to achieve a professionally recognised qualification. So, you would need to establish which courses are available, at what venues, cost and times (**S**). Your timescale might be three months (**T**), during which time you might study newspaper advertisements, surf the net and have discussions with colleagues (**M**). Over the following three months, you might enrol on your chosen course of study and arrange finance through your company or by student loan (**A**). The evaluation of the success of your objective would be reflected in your examination results (**R**). The aim of working in the industry will never be realised if you do not reposition it as an objective.

Any company or organisation will have a number of objectives it wishes to achieve. These might include: improving community relations, changing the image of the company; improving the quality or number of job applicants; educating new markets about the company or its products; preparing the stock market and investors for a new share issue; educating users, influencers and consumers about a new product; making legislators aware of the company; or highlighting the company's research and development activities.

Again, bear in mind that all of the skills interlink. If you are trying to improve the number and quality of job applicants, you need to look at the reasons why you are not attracting the calibre you need. Is there an economic recession (people just want a job)? Is the salary scale too low? Does the company have a good reputation (if you have a choice, as an employee, you will exercise it)? Is the company's location difficult to reach (should you introduce company buses)? Does the company have any gym facilities/sport societies/amateur drama groups, which would help to attract potential employees? Has the company a history of poor industrial relations? Where does it advertise?

A broad objective will help you to define the questions that you need to answer, in order to identify the publics and target them with appropriate techniques.

DEFINING 'PUBLICS'

Until a few years ago, the word 'audiences' was used to describe the people a company was trying to reach. 'Audience' is not a good word — an audience is passive, waiting to be informed or amused, and not expecting to have to contribute anything to the proceedings. You are a member of an audience when you go to the theatre or cinema — you do not expect to have to do anything, do you?

Instead of 'audiences', practitioners now use the word 'publics'. Publics is a term peculiar to public relations. Every company has numerous publics with whom it must communicate. The use of the word 'publics' is a clear reminder that we are not dealing with the general public. The general public includes everyone. How do you reach everyone? By dividing the general public into sub-groups — publics — and targeting each of them in turn. Identifying publics is fundamental to any public relations programme. If you do not know, precisely, who you are trying to reach, how can you possibly design a communications programme to reach them?

Publics may be a diversity of minority groups, in which case you will need to use specialised and highly targeted forms of communication. You may need to create private media for them, like slides, films, video tapes, house journals, educational literature, private exhibitions or seminars. Remember too that public relations includes the spoken word, face-to-face meetings and lunches.

More mainstream publics can be reached through a mixture of specially created and mass media. The majority of individuals can be categorised in several different ways; for example, one man may be all of the following:

- City office worker
- Suburban dweller
- Husband
- Parent
- Motorist
- Golfer
- Gardener
- Amateur photographer.

He probably reads a daily newspaper, listens to the car radio, watches TV and surfs the internet. He can be reached by mass media. But which person are you trying to reach? Do you want to reach only the 'amateur photographer'? If you do, then mass media may not be the route to choose — there are probably better ways of communicating with him, which are more direct.

So, you begin by looking at every public a company has to deal with. When you have listed all of the publics, you should prioritise them. You should then analyse how well you currently communicate with each group.

You may not have sufficient funds in your budget to enable you to communicate with all publics to the extent that you would wish. However, they all need some level of communication. It is very easy to overlook a small public when things are going well and realise, too late, in times of crisis, that, if you had paid a little more attention to them over the last few years, your crisis might not be so acute.

SOCHIA

Each business ranks its publics in order of importance. This determines the frequency with which they need to contact them. Over the years I have developed a weighting system, as follows:

33

The SOCHIA Weighting System for Publics

S	Support is desirable
O	Other (less important)
C	Crucial to our success
H	Helpful in achieving our goals
I	Important on an on-going basis
A	Activist (usually special interest).

We all, as individuals, prioritise our friendships, and communicate at different levels with different friends, but we do not usually think of it that way. Think of your own circle of friends. There is the person that you simply 'must' speak with each day. There are people that you meet for lunch once a week/month. There are the friends that you always meet in the pub on a Sunday. There are the ones that you e-mail (and they divide into the people on your group list for jokes, or the people you communicate with by mail). And there are people to whom you send annual Christmas cards — usually with a note saying, 'We must meet'. Without realising it, you have categorised your friends in order of priority — the most important being the daily phone call, the least important being the annual card. However, all are friends, and all are important to you. It is just that you have allocated your resources (in this case your time) to the highest-priority friend.

Companies list their publics in exactly the same way. They prioritise them and then select the tools which are most appropriate to communicate with them. Some publics need regular communication, some less regular. Some need face-to-face interaction, others might receive a newsletter.

The basic publics for any company are:

- Community
- Potential Employees
- Employees
- Suppliers of Goods and Services
- The Money Market
- Distributors
- Consumers and Users
- Legislators and Opinion Leaders
- The Media
- Pressure Groups
- The Competition
- The Trade.

This is a framework or target approach. It gives us a framework of categories of publics which we might target. Let us look at each in some detail, and look at the techniques that might be employed to reach them.

Community

Every company must be conscious of the community in which it is based. The community contains current and potential employees, their families and neighbours, other businesses, residents' associations, retailers, schools, and possibly customers.

Even if the company exports everything it produces, it should still maintain good relations with the community.

There are many ways in which a company can communicate with the local community:

- Provide 'open days' which would allow members of the local community to visit the office or factory and see for themselves the work the company is doing;
- Keep in touch by submitting news to the local newspaper or free-sheet;
- Allow the use of the company boardroom as a meeting place for local committees;
- Host an annual dinner for senior citizens in the company canteen;
- Allow members of the residents' association to use the company sports facilities;
- Sponsor local events, such as music festivals, summer projects, local theatre groups;
- Offer financial support to enable (for example) a local art gallery to be built.

The company could also become involved through flower shows, sports events, schools, libraries, parks, hospitals, art galleries, and community events (e.g. senior citizens' weeks).

The opportunities for companies to become involved in their communities are plentiful and can be tailored to suit the company's budget. The object of the exercise is that the company should be seen as part of the community — not just a factory/office providing employment.

Potential Employees

Every company wants to attract the brightest and best employees. Companies also want people who *want* to work for them. It is nice to be seen as a good employer, with a good track record, for whom school-leavers or college graduates want to work.

There are many ways in which companies can attract potential employees. They can provide information to career guidance teachers, advisers and appointment officers of local schools and colleges. They can exhibit and show a video at careers exhibitions and recruitment fairs. They can sponsor school projects. They can arrange for senior pupils to have an opportunity to visit the plant and learn about the industry. They can offer awards and placements to university graduates.

Employees

Existing employees should not be forgotten. They are, undoubtedly, the company's greatest asset.

There are many ways in which you can communicate with existing employees. If the company is very large, it would be nice to give each new member of staff a one- or two-day induction programme. Show how the company works, what the management structures are; explain the nature of the job, the importance of observing safety regulations, how the other branches of the company work and what their function is.

Companies can also provide training for their employees in new technology — or provide training for managers who will explain to workers the impact of the technology.

Companies can produce staff newsletters which give an opportunity to both staff and management to put their points of view (we will return to newsletters in a later chapter).

Staff reward schemes or staff ideas schemes are also popular. It is nice to be recognised for what you have done, and a reward scheme does just that. The reward might be for making a supreme effort to help a difficult customer — it should not be linked to sales reward schemes which have a different purpose entirely. Superquinn has an 'employee of the month' scheme and the employee is nominated by the customers. It is a nice recognition and the cost to the company is small in terms of budget, but the benefit is huge in terms of morale.

Similarly, ideas schemes encourage employees to put forward ideas for change, improvement or development within the company. The Revenue Commissioners operate this type of scheme, called an Input Awards Scheme. It was started in the early 1990s, and entries are invited from staff up to managerial level. The scheme, which gives monetary awards, seeks ideas from staff about how processes or systems could be improved. To win an award, the idea does not have to be implemented — it just has to be a good one.[2]

Disillusionment or lack of knowledge can create major problems for any company. Employees who are not informed of the company's financial policy or performance until they read about it in the newspapers are unlikely to thank you for keeping them 'outside the loop'.

Suppliers of Goods and Services

The people who supply your company are also an important public who should not be overlooked.

Goods suppliers include the people you buy from — raw materials, components, print and packaging, fuel, transport, canteen supplies.

The suppliers of services are equally important and are wide-ranging. They would include the company's solicitors, accountants, bankers, PR consultants. The suppliers of public services (health, refuse, water, police and fire brigade), as well as those supplying the educational needs of your industry (schools, colleges and training bodies) should not be forgotten. And you might also include trade associations, research and advisory bodies.

The Money Market

The money market is vital for any company. It would include shareholders, advisors, bankers, investment analysts, stockbrokers and institutional buyers. Shareholders, after all, have invested their money in your company. You should be communicating with them regularly. They should know how well your new product is doing against stiff competition. They should know who your key employees are and what their jobs involve. They should know that you are involved with the local community.

At the end of the day, shareholders should feel that they are 'close' to the company in which they have invested. Shareholders who know your company may decide to stick with you through thick and thin (when your quoted share price is falling) because they believe in you. On the other hand, if there is a hostile take-over bid for your company, and shareholders have only a brief outline of what you do, they may not feel any compulsion to stick with you and may simply decide instead to realise the value of their shareholding and sell to the highest bidder.

Companies neglect the money market at their peril. My consultancy was approached by a small company some years ago looking for a 'big splash' in the national media. When we discussed their needs in greater detail, it transpired that the bank manager had threatened to pull the plug on the company and the owner/manager wanted to impress him with publicity. It took a long time to explain to him that what he should have done, some months previously, was approach the bank manager and explain the difficulties he was encountering. It might not have prevented the closure, but it might have given him the benefit of professional advice and guidance at an early stage.

You need to communicate with the money market in order to build up loyalty and understanding of your company.

Distributors

Depending on the actual company you are dealing with, distributors could include wholesalers, cash and carry outlets, van drivers, mail-order companies, shops, super-markets, co-ops, exporters and importers.

Distribution outlets wield a powerful influence over the consumer which should not be underestimated. When I bought a new television two years ago, I selected three that seemed to meet my requirements. I then eliminated one, because I had never heard of the make. I called the shop assistant and asked him to advise which of the two remaining well-known brands I should buy. He said that both were good. So I asked him which brand sold in greater volume. I bought that one.

Another example involves my company, Elton Communications, which did research for a company that produced an electrical item sold to the home market. We wanted to do some unscientific research to see for ourselves how well the product sold and what people thought of it. We visited a number of outlets selling it, and asked the shop assistants whether it was any good. Every single shop assistant told us that it was good, but that it was seriously overpriced, and they would recommend another manufacturer's model — cheaper in price, but which performed exactly the same function. When we gave this feedback to the company, the reaction was horror. It had never crossed anyone's mind to go into one of the shops selling their goods and ask for honest feedback.

Finally, on the other side of the coin, there is nothing more annoying than dealing with someone who knows nothing about the product. It is your job, as the manufacturer, to make sure that people are informed. The customer will not buy if the assistant 'never heard of them', doesn't know anything about the company, has no idea where the company is based, or what other products it makes.

Consumers and Users

Never forget the end customer — the person to whom your product is sold. You should also include in this category people who can recommend your product to consumers. For example, if you are a carpet manufacturer, interior designers would be an important public for you. They, after all, can use your product in showhouses or recommend it to their private clients.

Marketing departments now invest heavily in customer research. They try to establish who is buying their product (what age, sex and background profile); whether they bought it for themselves or received it as a present; whether the customer has bought any other product the company makes; if the customer can suggest other products the company should make.

Consumers also have a power of boycott which should not be forgotten. A happy customer will tell three people of an experience; a dissatisfied customer will tell eleven! An angry consumer can do a company a lot of damage, even if the company is not directly related. When the French government decided to conduct nuclear tests in the Mururoa Atoll, consumers throughout the world were furious. The most prominent exports from France were wine and apples, so consumers boycotted these products in huge numbers. The boycott was so effective that both of these industries ended up lobbying their own government. And don't forget the power of the internet in this scenario: there are at least 10,000 matching pages on the internet on 'Consumer' and 'Boycott'.[3]

Opinion Leaders

Opinion leaders are people whose attitudes and opinions influence others because they speak from a position of authority. That position of authority is bestowed upon them by the people who listen to them; it is not necessarily related to the position they hold in society.

There are four types of opinion leader:

- Opinion leaders by position
- Opinion leaders by education and experience

- Opinion leaders by popular acclaim
- Opinion leaders by organisation.

Opinion leaders by position

These are people who hold a position of authority within the community. These opinion leaders would include local councillors and town commissioners, elected members of the national and European parliaments, the parish priest/vicar/rabbi, the local bank manager, and the Garda sergeant — to name but a few.

Opinion leaders by education and experience

These opinion leaders are people who give guidance and express opinions in specific areas. They are to be found in all walks of life. David Bellamy influences opinion when he speaks on conservation issues. Donegal woman Bridget McCole influenced the entire nation by her courage and determination (Positive Action). And who would dispute the incredible influence of Adi Roche (Chernobyl Children), Bono (on third-world debt) or T. K. Whittaker (economics)?

Opinion leaders by popular acclaim

These opinion leaders have been given positions of authority within their communities by popular acclaim (usually by election). The chairperson or secretary of the local residents' association, senior citizens' club or local action group would come under this category, as would those without a formal position whom the community respects. A senior citizen living in the community could be held in great respect because of the historical knowledge of the area he possesses. An unemployed person who has spent a lifetime working for the good of the area, without ever serving on a committee, might be well respected and listened to. If people are afforded the respect of the populace, then they are, by definition, opinion leaders.

Opinion leaders by organisation

These opinion leaders are 'bodies', not individuals. They include groups such as An Taisce, Greenpeace, Council for the Status of Women and Chambers of Commerce.

The Media

The media are another important public both in themselves and in their influence with their readers. As with financial publics, you should, as a matter of courtesy, keep journalists informed of developments — not only when you are seeking publicity through press releases, but you should keep them up to date on ongoing developments which might interest them. Keep them informed, even when there is no story in which their readers will be interested. They like to know what is going on.

Local media — print and radio — will obviously have an enormous impact on the local community. National print, radio and television will influence a wider audience of consumers and investors. Specialised media like newsletters and magazines will influence other professionals, specifiers, industry leaders.

For a long number of years, the public relations industry has been debating whether media should be categorised as a public, or a channel to the public. I believe that they are both. They undoubtedly are a channel or a conduit which practitioners use to reach members of the public. However, they are also a public in themselves. The growth of specialist writers and media commentators puts an onus on organisations to treat media as a public. These are experts in their field with an interest in your organisation. They are undoubtedly a public and might also be classified as a fifth type of opinion leader.

Pressure Groups

Pressure groups have changed over the years. There are now two categories of pressure groups — established and self-selecting.

Established

A decade ago, any organisation could write a list of pressure groups which might act/react with them — groups like Greenpeace, An Taisce, or the local residents' association. These are established pressure groups. They are formed of people with a common interest. They provide an identifiable public for a company or organisation to communicate with.

Their 'common interest' is generally something that benefits the entire community, and their media skills are excellent. For example, the Shell Oil Company decided to sink an old drill platform, the Brent Spar, in the North Atlantic in 1995. Greenpeace believed that this action would cause enormous damage to the environment. Its campaign, and the worldwide media attention it attracted, eventually led to a reversal of the decision by Shell.[4]

Self-Selecting

The second type of pressure group is self-selecting. These groups cannot be determined in advance. People come together to form pressure groups issue by issue. In effect, people select themselves to become members of a pressure group in reaction to a company or council or government initiative.

A group may spring up to defend the environment against a new high-rise apartment complex, and it might comprise local residents, members of An Taisce, environmentalists from outside the area, people who have previous experience of dealing with the builder, public representatives, parents and senior citizens' groups. When the issue has been resolved to the satisfaction of its various component members, this self-selecting public disappears as quickly as it originally appeared.

The Competition

Companies also need to communicate with their competitors — other companies who operate within the same industry. It is a necessary business link, usually kept through professional organisations or meetings with each other at chamber of commerce functions. It is nice (and profitable) for your competitors to speak well of you. In every industry, there are 'cowboys' — people who let down the profession. Your business wants to be neither a cowboy nor an unknown. The ideal is that you would be well thought of as a fair (and possibly tough) competitor. Different tools may be used for each public — so, let us look at some of the tools and techniques of the public relations practitioner.

PR TECHNIQUES

In addition to all of the techniques outlined in the preceeding pages, public relations professionals offer a range of skills and services which draw further on the pool of techniques available to them. The services include:

- Annual reports
- Communications audits
- Competitions and award schemes
- Conference co-ordination
- Corporate advertising
- Corporate brochures
- Corporate entertainment
- Crisis management
- Direct mail
- Event management
- Exhibitions
- Media training
- Management of design
- Market research co-ordination
- Media monitoring
- Newsletters
- Open days
- Photography and photo calls
- Plant openings
- Platform/public-speaking training
- Press relations
- Product launches
- Public/Government affairs
- Script writing
- Sponsorship management
- Staff publications

- Video and audio-visual presentations
- Website design, management and monitoring.

The best form of communications, always, is face-to face. Second best, probably, is personal contact by telephone, followed by contact in writing (letter, fax, e-mail). Every company would wish to meet all of its key publics face-to-face, but it is not physically or financially viable. A range of PR Techniques is deployed to achieve the communications goal instead. Among the techniques used are:

- Media Relations — coverage in national and regional media by press release, feature article, interview, photograph, interviews, guest appearances
- Internet — world-wide web and e-mail
- Print — newsletters, posters, brochures, information packs
- Functions — receptions, dinners
- Public meetings
- Exhibitions — own, joint-venture, or by participating in established exhibitions
- Seminars, Workshops, Conferences — guest speakers, hands-on experience, position papers, platforms
- Sponsorship — large or small, enhancing the reputation of both the sponsor and the sponsored.

IMPORTANCE OF MONITORING LIFESTYLE AND SOCIETAL CHANGES

It is important that you do not make the mistake of simply sub-grouping the publics, without making some effort to identify their lifestyles and interests. The lifestyles of the people with whom you are trying to communicate will determine the techniques and tools you use to reach them.

For example, the typical Irish business leader under 45 years of age most likely drives a BMW, is family-oriented, has a working partner, is into mobile technology, uses the internet, desktops and laptops, and is not overly concerned about the media.

The over-45-year-old business leader, by comparison, drives a Mercedes, likes to play golf, is loyal to his company, has a non-working partner, uses mobile and desktop technology, and is concerned about what the media thinks about his business.[5] The current trend among the over-40s in the United States is that they like to refer to their 'middle youth' (and not their middle age).[6]

Clearly it is necessary to use very different approaches, techniques and tools to reach each business leader effectively. Selecting the technique and knowing how best to use it to maximum effect requires an ability to think creatively.

THINKING CREATIVELY

Once you have set your broad objective, you can begin to identify the publics who need to be reached. You then look at the techniques for reaching those publics, and establish how creatively they can be applied. This is what separates the successful from the unsuccessful consultant — the power to think 'outside the box'. Consultants should be regularly challenging their minds creatively by reference to texts — they keep your mind fresh.

Joseph Rossman (1930s) identified the following stages of creativity:

- Observation of need or difficulty
- Analysis of need
- Survey of all available information
- Formulation of all objective solutions
- Critical analysis of these solutions for their advantages and disadvantages
- Birth of a new idea — the invention
- Experimentation to test out the most promising solution
- Selection and perfection of the final embodiment by some or all of the previous steps.[7]

Alex Osborn (1950s) divided the process into seven sections:

- Orientation — pointing out the problem
- Preparation — gathering pertinent data
- Analysis — breaking down the relevant material
- Ideation — piling up alternatives by way of ideas
- Incubation — letting up to invite illumination
- Synthesis — putting the pieces together
- Evaluation — judging the resulting ideas.[8]

Professor Morris Stein established a three-stage model:

- Hypothesis formation
- Hypothesis testing
- Communication of results.[9]

And Andy Green devised a mnemonic — the five 'Is': information, incubation, illumination, integration, illustration.[10]

Theories abound and there are numerous well-written and thought-provoking books on the subject with which you should familiarise yourself. For the purposes of this chapter, however, we will look at two types of thinking — vertical thinking and creative thinking.

Vertical Thinking/Logic

Vertical thinking is high-probability thinking. Without it, life would be impossible. There are numerous ways in which vertical thinking is used in PR practice. Among them are:

- Research
- Identification of problems

- Definition of publics
- Evaluation methods.

Lateral Thinking/Creative

New ideas depend on lateral thinking which is sometimes highly creative, and sometimes just a new way of looking at things. It is often referred to as 'thinking outside the box'. The ability to think laterally is not related to intelligence, but to developing a habit.

Edward de Bono,[11] the acknowledged 'father' of the science, gives numerous examples of the ability to 'think outside the box'. We will discuss just two of these.

- Edward Jenner found a cure for smallpox when he shifted his attention from asking why people got smallpox to figuring out why dairymaids did not (harmless cowpox gave protection against deadly smallpox).
- Sherlock Holmes solved one of his cases when his sidekick, Dr Watson, claimed that a dog was an unimportant part of the case because it did nothing. Holmes took the opposite view. The dog's inactivity, when it would reasonably have been expected to do something, was highly significant.

Creative thinking should not be confused with an ability to toss ideas around. Certainly you need to generate ideas. But, as a professional, you also need to hone those ideas, think about them carefully, and plan them fully before you recommend them to a client.

Creative or lateral thinking is most often used in PR practice for:

- Solving client dilemmas
- Designing innovative proposals
- Finding new ways to reach publics.

The most widely publicised photo-calls began with someone thinking vertically that a media exposure opportunity was needed, and then applying lateral thinking to create something 'different' which would appeal to the media and the public. Vertical thinking will help you to analyse the problem and design the broad brush strokes of the solution. Lateral thinking will enable you to apply the technique with humour, panache, flair and, ultimately, success.

THINK-TANKS

Many consultancies use creative think-tanks to apply innovative solutions to client problems. The larger photographic agencies also hold daily meetings to look at approaches to their clients' needs and try to design a photo that will attract media attention.

The skill in successfully managing a think-tank is to allow everyone to contribute an idea, and to move instantly to the next idea. Instead of stopping to analyse the first idea, you proceed to the second and the third — and it is only when all ideas have been exhausted that you go back to revisit each and see if any had potential, or could be married with other ideas to solve your need creatively.

It does not matter how the problem is defined, as long as it is defined thoroughly, and each element is given equal consideration. The object of the exercise is to keep shifting the focus of your attention, thereby enabling you to see the problem from a different perspective and find a solution from 'outside the box'.

Consultancies also use this technique when looking for new business.

REFERENCES

1. Helen O'Sullivan, a distance-learning student of the Irish Academy of Public Relations.
2. Paul McDonald, Press Office, Revenue Commissioners, Dublin.
3. Presentation at CERP Conference, Copenhagen, October 1996.
4. http://www.ex4all.nl/~evel/brenteg.htm, March 2002.
5. Ella Shanahan, 'Mercs, perks and clubs define the modern Irish manager', *The Irish Times*, 26 May 2000.
6. Carolyn Fazio, former president IPRA, 10 January 2001.
7. Andy Green, *Creativity in Public Relations*, Institute of Public Relations (UK)/Kogan Page, (1999).
8. Ibid.
9. Ibid.
10. Ibid.
11. Edward de Bono, *The Use of Lateral Thinking*, Pelican Books, 1972.

Section 2
PR & Media

CHAPTER 4

PR and the Media

Public Relations people depend on the media to reach a broad audience for them. They also use the media to publicise events, build personality profiles, and put issues 'on the agenda' for debate. Before we begin to look at how PR people link with media, however, we should look at the media itself.

MULTI-MEDIA SOCIETY

We live in a multi-media society in which it is becoming increasingly difficult to catch and hold people's attention.

Television

No longer are people confined to a national television station. Cross-border television (UTV, Channel 4, BBC) was closely followed by satellite and pay-TV in which the viewer selected additional channels of specialist interest (children's channel, CNN, Disney channel, National Geographic, sports channels), and will soon increase again with the introduction of digital television.

There is also the growth (admittedly slow) of local television channels like Cablelink in Dublin and Channel 9 in Derry/Donegal. The choice of television channels available to people has made it more difficult to reach them, or, for that matter, to monitor their viewing habits. In the 1960s/1970s it seemed that most families in the country watched *The Late Late Show* on RTE 1 on Saturday nights. They were a captive audience. Could the same be said of any programme these days?

Viewing habits have also changed. The introduction and widespread use of video recorders means that the viewer no longer needs to be in front of a television set in order to see a programme. Viewers don't even have to be present to start the taping. This means that they can watch the programme at a time of their choosing, which might be later that night, or the following Sunday afternoon. It removes some of the 'currency' of the debate from the issues (which may have been covered extensively in the newspapers in the intervening days). It also gives viewers the power to 'skip' sections of the programme — perhaps your client's interview — which they deem to be boring. You cannot do this if you are watching a live broadcast. The viewer also has the 'power' to skip those sponsorship messages or ads so carefully placed between sections of the programme.

Again, going back to the 1960s and 1970s, people were lucky if they had one television in their home. The entire family, therefore, watched the same programme at the same time. Nowadays there is a television in each room, and four people sharing the same house might be watching four different programmes on four different channels at the same time on the same evening.

Newspapers

Thirty years ago, the nation had a choice of three national newspapers, and readers were defined by their choice. Readers of the *Irish Press* were of Fianna Fáil stock, the *Irish Independent* attracted Fine Gael supporters, and *The Irish Times* was read by the upper middle classes and people of Protestant origin.

The *Irish Independent* and *The Irish Times* still publish daily. The *Irish Press*, unfortunately, is no longer with us, although the title may re-appear in the future. The *Cork Examiner*, which was a Cork/Munster paper back then, has now become a national title (the *Irish Examiner*). All three now compete with English broadsheets, and a wide range of Irish (or English with Irish-section) tabloid newspapers. The evening newspaper market declined with the loss of the *Evening Press*, but the expansion of the *Evening Echo* beyond its Cork base into Limerick may be early signs of a revival.

The Sunday newspaper range is very substantial, with large numbers of British papers (again mostly with an Irish section/flavour added) capturing a sizeable share of the Sunday market. This was helped, of course, by the size of the print runs in Britain, and their ability to do split print runs (the Irish newspaper market is too small for split runs). Sales were also boosted by the 'value for money' or 'loss-leader market penetration tactics' (depending on your perspective), represented by the cover prices of the papers themselves.

Any analysis of newspapers, no matter how brief, would be incomplete without reference to the issues of media ownership, control of media outlets, and cross-media ownership. In Northern Ireland, for example, Tony O'Reilly controls 99.7 per cent of the Sunday newspaper market through the *Sunday World* (55.8 per cent), the *Independent on Sunday* (1.7 per cent), and *Sunday Life* (42.2 per cent).[1]

Local or regional newspapers still attract a wide readership. The growth of local newspapers, particularly in cities (especially Dublin) has been huge. People like to read about things that are happening in their own areas. Similarly, papers produced for a wider local area (like the *Kerryman* or the *Connacht Tribune*) are well read for the local 'angle' on a story, and for the fact that they provide coverage of events which would not be covered in national media.

Newspapers no longer need to be read in print. They can now be read online. However, free access to newspapers on the web will probably not be available in the future. Currently, very few papers make money from their online services. The *Financial Times* is losing money. The *Wall Street Journal* has 625,000 online users. It

ABC Circulation Figures, January–June 2001	
Title	**ABC Circulation Figures**
Mornings	
Irish Independent	168,300
The Irish Times	119,252
The Examiner	63,619
Star	97,315
Evenings	
Evening Herald	104,300
Evening Echo	28,222
Sundays	
Sunday Independent	310,600
Sunday Tribune	90,190
Sunday World	301,748
Sunday Business Post	55,350
Ireland on Sunday	46,658
Irish Farmer's Journal	73,401
Magazines	
RTÉ Guide	145,921
Image	22,207
Hot Press	16,052
Phoenix	21,288

Source: *Irish Media Contacts Directory*, Media Information Services, November 2001.

Note: Estimated readers per copy
Evening Herald (4.5), *Evening Echo* (4.3), *Irish Independent* (4.0), *The Examiner* (3.9), *Sunday World* (3.8), *Sunday Independent* (3.6), *Sunday Tribune* (3.2), *The Irish Times* (3.0), *Star* (2.9) and *Sunday Business Post* (2.0).

broke even in 1999 but has lost money ever since.[2] In Ireland, the well-read version of *The Irish Times* online underwent searching analysis when the paper revealed in 2001/2002 that it was in severe financial difficulty.

Another issue for online editions is the format that they will adopt in the future. Currently online versions of newspapers are merely a cyber-copy of the printed version. Will interactive elements be added in the future?

Then, there is the great debate about the future of the newspaper industry itself, now that most people have access to the internet. Jon Katz[3] believes that newspapers are 'almost stupefyingly oblivious to the fact that they aren't in the breaking news business anymore. Most newspapers reported the news on page one the next morning as if none of their readers had heard it before, despite the fact that almost all of them had'. Perhaps the newspapers of the future will need to compete with the 'breaking news' media?

Finally, the profile of journalists entering the profession has changed, and this is causing concern in the US and throughout Europe. The American Society of Newspaper Editors constantly conducts surveys to establish the gap between the people who write the news and the people who read it. According to James Fallows,[4] until 1965, journalists came from the upper end of the working classes. Now, they have university degrees and live in what he calls 'money and brains' neighbourhoods (two-earner couples, expensive condos or townhouses, few children, their own jacuzzi and a liking for jazz and sailing). These same journalists avoid 'shotguns and pickup' neighbourhoods (low real-estate prices, families who eat Wheaties, drink whiskey and go car racing or bowling). This, he believes, leads to the media having more empathy with the 'haves' than the 'have nots', and, as a consequence, they no longer reflect the interests of their readers.

Magazines

The number of magazine titles (home-produced and foreign) has also grown in recent years. Choose any category of magazine (current affairs, women's or men's interest, photography, gardening) and just look at the range of titles available. If you look only at Irish-produced magazines, you will find at least thirty which deal with business/current affairs, about thirty-two covering sports and leisure, a minimum of eleven magazines of women's interest, and about fifteen which deal with religious issues.

Categories of Irish-Produced Magazines	
Category of Magazine	**Number in Circulation**
Accountancy/Banking/Insurance	7
Advertising/Marketing	5
Agriculture	14
Arts/Music Entertainment	18
Building/Construction	18
Business	22
Communications/Films	4
Company Staff Newsletters	6
Computers/Internet	8
Economics/Social Sciences	2
Education/Science	15
Electrical/Electronics	3
Employment	6

Engineering	3
Environment	4
Fashion/Lifestyle	18
Fishing/Marine	3
Food/Drink/Catering	14
General Interest/Current affairs	8
Grocery/Drinks trade	10
Hardware	1
Health	6
Hobbies/Interests	3
Industry	7
Interiors/Property	18
Irish abroad	5
Irish Language publications	3
Legal	20
Management	4
Medical	20
Motoring/Motor trade	18
Political	2
Printing	1
Public Affairs	2
Public Service	2
Publishing	2
Religious	15
Security	5
Social Issues	10
Sport	29
Tourism/Travel	16
Training and Development	1
Transport	4
Trades Unions	2
Veterinary	2
Voluntary Organisations	3
Weddings	4
Women's Interest	9
Young People	2

Source: *Irish Media Contacts Directory*, Media Information Services, November 2001.

To this range of Irish-produced magazines must be added imported titles which sell so well. Magazines of British and American origin are widely available on Irish shelves, as are cross-border magazines like *Hello*, which is produced in several languages for different markets. Most use the services of Irish journalists and photographers, and some, like *Hello*, have Irish offices. So, what do Irish people read? *VIP* and *Image* magazine are the bestselling monthly Irish titles. The top UK sellers in Ireland are *Cosmopolitan* and *Marie Claire* (for women); *FHM*, *Loaded* and *Maxim* (for men). The bestselling weekly titles are *Bella*, *Talk*, *That's Life*, *Now*, *Hello*, *Woman*, *Woman's Own* and *Woman's Way*. In its category, the *RTÉ Guide* is also a best-seller.[5]

Finally, it should be remembered that, in addition to over-the-counter sales, there are also closed-circulation magazines (distributed to members of particular organisations or industries), subscription magazines by post, and free and subscriber e-zines on the web.

Radio

The radio landscape has also changed. The number of national stations has increased from the original Radio Éireann to include, in addition to RTÉ Radio 1, 2FM and Today FM, which are capturing the younger listener. Moreover, the local stations command very sizeable listenership figures within their broadcast areas: Dublin FM104 (29 per cent), 98FM (27 per cent), Cork 96FM (62 per cent).[6]

Local radio and easy-listening stations will continue to grow in the future as the Broadcasting Commission of Ireland (formerly the IRTC — Independent Radio and Television Commission) awards more licences. In May 2000, Dublin got a new music station, Lite FM. In 2002, Newstalk106 was launched in Dublin, and Red FM began broadcasting in Cork.

Internet

People use the internet to search for information, read magazines online, and debate issues in chat-rooms. They also receive information by e-mail. Current estimates suggest that by 2004 more than 200 billion e-mails will be sent annually in the US.[7]

Targeted Information

Each newspaper, magazine, television station and radio station — in fact, each section or programme within those categories — has almost a photo-fit picture of the reader/viewer/listener. The range of media listed above simply would not survive if they all covered the same information, in the same way.

The differences in media, their approach to a story, their style of writing and the columnists they employ, play a huge role in determining which media the reader/viewer/listener will select.

As a PR person, you need to understand all of the media, their audiences, their journalists and their 'ethos', in order to be able to target information to their readers. For your message to achieve coverage, it must be relevant to the media to which you have issued it.

WORKING WITH THE MEDIA

Press, radio and television provide the PR practitioner with an essential channel of communication between clients and public (i.e. sender and receiver). You should try to develop an amicable working relationship with media colleagues. This is not always possible, particularly if you are working with a consultancy firm, where the breadth of clients you handle is matched by a breadth of media covering those issues. However, it is not necessary to know a journalist in order to submit a press release. Every journalist is looking for a good story — whether they know the sender or not is of little consequence.

Either way, your relationship with the media should be consistent: honest, factual and accurate. You should always check the content of media releases before issuing — for sense, accuracy, grammar and spelling — and you should always be clearly identified as the source of the information.

Having good relations with the media also means respecting them as journalists. Their job is to find good newsworthy stories of interest to their readers. It is not their job to provide you with free publicity. Nor are they obliged to provide you with 'good' publicity (they will cover the bad news as well). Journalists, for their part, should respect you as a professional, and appreciate the service you provide. Respect on both sides is a great foundation for a lasting working relationship.

What Type of Media?

To work with the media you need to develop an understanding of how they work, the time constraints they are under, the kind of stories that appeal to individual journalists, their lead-in times, their readers, their deadlines, and — most of all — their need for news.

When people think of the media, they are inclined to think of one element only (i.e. they think of press or radio or television). A good media campaign involves as many combinations of media as possible.

If you have a press release to issue, or a story you want told, you should look at all of the opportunities, including:

- Press
  - Daily national morning newspapers (broadsheet and tabloid, Irish, UK, and mixed) — *The Irish Times, Irish Independent, Irish Examiner, Star, Daily Mirror, Irish Sun*
  - Daily evening newspapers (Dublin, Cork and Limerick) — *Evening Herald, Evening Echo*
  - Sunday newspapers (broadsheet and tabloid, Irish, UK, and mixed) — e.g.

Sunday Independent, Sunday Business Post, The Sunday Times, Sunday World, Ireland on Sunday, Sunday Tribune

- ❏ Weekly provincial/regional newspapers (broadsheet, at least one per county) — e.g. *Kerryman, Donegal Democrat, Connacht Tribune, Anglo-Celt*
- ❏ Freesheets and local newspapers (mostly tabloid, distributed by community or city area) — e.g. *Carraigdhoun Weekly, Northside People, Liffey Champion*
- ❏ Trade Magazines (monthly, subscription and counter sales, specialist interest) — e.g. *Inside Business, Shelflife*
- ❏ Consumer magazines (weekly, fortnightly or monthly, general interest) — e.g. *Image, VIP, RTÉ Guide, Woman's Way*
- ❏ Specialist magazines (monthly, specialist interest, sold over the counter or by subscription) — e.g. *Phoenix, Magill, House & Home, metro éireann*
- ❏ In-house magazines (monthly, distributed to staff or members) — e.g. *Gasette* (Bord Gáis), *Public Sector Times, Revenue Review, Electric Mail* (ESB)
- Television
  - ❏ National television — RTÉ 1, Network 2, TG4, TV3
  - ❏ Cross-border television — e.g. UTV, BBC, Channel 4
  - ❏ Subscription services — e.g. Sky Sports, CNN, National Geographic
  - ❏ Local/community television — Cork, Navan, Dublin, Derry/Donegal
- Radio
  - ❏ National radio — RTÉ Radio 1, 2FM, Today FM
  - ❏ City radio — e.g. 98FM (Dublin), 96FM (Cork)
  - ❏ Regional radio — e.g. 95FM (Limerick), Galway Bay FM, LM/FM (Louth/Meath)

The range of media available to you is enormous. There is ample scope to have any press release or story covered, provided that you know how many possibilities for coverage exist, and you choose the most suitable.

DEADLINES

When issuing a press release or organising a function, you should be conscious of the deadlines of the media to which you are issuing. There is nothing more frustrating than sending a well-written and relevant press release to a journalist too late for coverage — or, for that matter, arranging a function at the wrong time, so that you miss your main media target. There are some deadlines of which you should be particularly conscious.

Press

Morning newspapers are collected for distribution at about 4.30 a.m. daily. So, if you hold a function on a Tuesday morning, it is in ample time to be covered in Wednesday's daily newspaper. Remember, however, that a function early on Tuesday morning may also be covered in the late edition of Tuesday's evening papers. This may or may not be to your advantage. If your main audience is the evening newspapers, radio and TV coverage — that's fine. If, however, your main audience reads the daily newspapers, there is always a danger that your story, having been well aired on radio, TV and in print on Tuesday evening, will be regarded as 'old news' by Wednesday morning and may not be covered.

Every newspaper contains **special supplements** and you should be aware of the days for each supplement (education, arts, business, property) and the deadlines for receipt of press information.

The early edition of the **evening newspapers** is on the streets at 10.30 a.m. You can buy this evening's paper and read it over your coffee break mid-morning.

Be conscious that each **consumer magazine** works to a different deadline. For example, if you were to suggest feature coverage to most women's magazines, you should know that they work with a six-week lead-in time. There would be no point in approaching them at the end of November with an idea for their Christmas issue. Even if it was a brilliant idea, they could not cover it because your approach would be too late.

It is important to know on what day of each week **weekly business magazines** are available for sale, and on what day of each week they go to print. A consumer magazine that is on the newsagent's shelves on Thursday morning of each week will most likely go to press on Tuesday evening/early Wednesday morning. If you are holding a 'business' press conference and you arrange it for a Wednesday morning, you are too late to have your conference coverage included in that week's edition of the business magazine. By the following week, the conference may have received so much exposure in the daily and Sunday newspapers that it would be 'old news' to the readers.

Trade magazines should be treated in a very different way from consumer magazines. If you have a story about a product launch, the type of press release and the timing of your release will differ greatly between the trade and consumer magazines.

With a trade magazine, you are giving the readers information about a product that you would like them to stock and sell to the end-user. Therefore, you need to approach trade press with information for publication before the coverage appears in the consumer media.

Trade magazines will charge you for the use of product photographs (in theory, a reproduction fee) as will some of the consumer press, depending on the section you target.

There are many categories of magazine, among which are: Agriculture, Business/Current Affairs/Finance, Company/In-House magazines, Construction, Education, Food/Drink/Tobacco, Language publications, Marketing/Advertising, Medical/Veterinary, Music/Theatre, Public Service, Religious, Security/Defence/Law, Sport/Leisure, Technology/Computer, Tourism/Travel and Women's magazines.

Don't assume that every magazine in a particular category should receive the same release. They should not. *Cosmopolitan* magazine will treat a story in a very different way from *Woman's Way*, although they are both 'women's' magazines. The *Magill* treatment will differ from that of *Phoenix*, although both are political/current affairs magazines. In each category, each magazine will apply a different treatment to a story, so you need to write a different press release for each.

Radio

If you are writing a press release for radio, remember to adjust your style of writing to suit the broadcast media generally and the programme listenership you are targeting specifically. Radio is an aural media, so it is the spoken word that makes the impact. Remember to write the way people would speak. If your target is a news or current affairs programme, your press release should be concise hard news of interest. If you are issuing to a morning chat show which is personality-driven and takes phone-ins live on air, your release should be snappy, upbeat, likely to generate debate, and you should always offer a telephone interview. It is a 'listeners' medium after all.

Television

Television news seldom uses news releases. More often, you will contact the researchers in advance of a function and seek to interest them in sending a crew to record the event visually. Television needs moving pictures. The only time you see still photography or hear the equivalent of a press release being read is if someone dies, or if the reporter cannot be contacted by video link-up. Remember too that you have the option of issuing a Video News Release to television stations.

MERITS AND DEMERITS OF VARIOUS MEDIA

When choosing the media to which you will issue a release or suggest a feature article or interview, you should be aware of the merits and demerits of the medium you have chosen.

Merits

- Newspapers can cover information in much greater depth than a radio news programme.
- Newspapers and magazines can be read anywhere (on bus or train) and can even be read online.
- Magazines have a very long shelf life. Have you ever seen a current magazine in a dentist's surgery or a doctor's waiting room? Magazines are inclined to be kept for months.
- Press-cutting libraries store information from the print media. They file printed matter by company and category, extending the shelf-life of any article. These abstracts from print media may also be stored on CD-ROM and Microfiche.

- Feature articles are often cut out and kept. People with a particular interest — for example, a hobby (gardening, photography, baking), or business (managing stress, negotiating with staff, monitoring finances) — are inclined to keep articles for reference.
- Television combines the powerful impact of movement and words. Although exposure on the TV news may be very short, the impact of the visual accompanying a story means that you will probably remember the story for longer.
- Radio can encapsulate a news story in a few short words.
- You do not need to 'make time' for radio. Radio does not intrude on your life, you can be doing other things while you listen.
- Provincial and Sunday newspapers have a shelf life of at least a week. They are seldom discarded before the next edition is bought.

Demerits

- Daily newspapers are inclined to have a very short life. Tabloid newspapers might be bought and read on the train going to work, and discarded by 9 a.m!
- Broadsheet papers are inclined to have a longer, same-day life. They are often brought home in the evening for another member of the household to read.
- Evening newspapers are usually bought on the way home but, again, they are never read the next day.
- Even if your story is covered in a newspaper or magazine, it will not be read by everyone who buys the publication. Very few people read a paper from cover to cover. We all 'skip' sections which do not appeal to us.
- Newspapers and magazines occasionally get their facts wrong. Even if the paper publishes a correction the next day, it may not be seen by all of the people who read the original piece. This is particularly true of magazines.
- If there is a breakdown in transmission, your TV appearance or coverage may not be seen. The audience has been lost to you forever.
- The journalist covering your story (print, radio or TV) may do further background research beyond the release. Their report of your story may not be as favourable as you would have wished.
- You need to 'make time' for TV (plug it in and sit in front of it) and for newspapers and magazines (have a coffee and read).

CATEGORIES OF READERS AND VIEWERS

You have often heard the term 'ABC Readership'. What it means is that readers are divided into categories based on job and income. Frank Jefkins[8] described the social grades in Britain thus:

	Class	Description	Percentage of total
A	Upper middle class	The head of the household is a successful business or professional person, a civil servant, or has considerable private means	About 3%
B	Middle class	Senior people, not quite at the top	About 13%
C1	Lower middle class	Tradesmen, non-manual workers, 'white-collar' workers	About 22%
C2	Skilled working class	Usually apprenticed workers, 'blue-collar' workers	About 32%
D	Semi-skilled and unskilled working class		About 20%
E	Those at lowest level of subsistence	Pensioners, casual workers, those dependent on social security	About 9%

In some countries, 'class' may not be the most important factor when categorising readers. They may be categorised by education, race, language spoken, disposable income or, as we have seen was the case in the Ireland of old, by political allegiance.

OPPORTUNITIES TO SEE (OTSs)

Audited circulation/viewers/listeners figures are available every six months. With the print media, estimates are also made of how many people read each newspaper. One copy of a paper may be read by 4 people.

- The number of copies of a newspaper sold = **circulation figure**
- The number of estimated readers per copy = **readership figures**
- The circulation figure multiplied by the readership figure gives you the **OTS** (i.e. total number of people who had an Opportunity To See the article).

MEDIA INTERVIEWS

One of the things you will be required to do, as a PR professional, is suggest interviews to journalists, provide them with people to interview, and prepare your clients to meet those journalists. These occasions will arise from suggested feature pieces, press briefings given by your client, and press conferences which your client must host.

There are two key areas, from a PR perspective, when it comes to media interviews: knowing the needs of different media, and preparing your client for each.

Needs of Different Media

There are some simple but very real differences between media. You should be aware of these differences, and you should prepare your client for them.

Print

It has already been mentioned that one of the great advantages of print media (newspaper or magazine) is the ability of that medium to cover a story in some depth. This, in turn, means that interviews with print journalists tend to be longer than with other media. Their need for information is greater, they have more space to fill, and they therefore require more time from your client.

Most reporters will still use a notebook, even if they use it only as a reference for key words. Most will also use a hand-held tape recorder. There is nothing at all wrong with this — it saves a lot of writing, and gives the journalist access to totally accurate quotes from the client. However, your client should be aware of the tape recorder at all times. It is very easy to forget that comments are being recorded, particularly if the impression is created by the journalist that your comments are 'off the record'. This is not to say that they would report an off-the-record comment, but your client may not be able to distinguish.

For example, at what appears to be the 'end' of an interview, the journalist formally thanks the client for the interview. The client relaxes, but the tape is still running. The journalist then leans over (as if just chatting) and asks another question. The client presumes that what is said now is off the record. In fact, the tape is still recording. It is your job to brief the client in advance – thoroughly.

Finally, your client should also be aware that some telephone conversations are recorded. This is happening more frequently. The journalist should tell the client that the call is being recorded but, because the client cannot physically see the machine, it is easy to forget about it.

Radio

It seems almost pointless to say it, but how you look is utterly irrelevant on radio. Unlike a photograph to accompany a feature piece, or television footage of your interview, a radio interview can be conducted in your 'sloppies' and no one will know, nor will it affect the impact of what you are saying.

How you sound on radio is crucial. The tone, pitch and speed of your voice all give indicators to the listener, who draws inferences from them. The Irish, in particular, are known for speaking fast. It is a fact that people speak even faster when they are under stress or pressure. Since being interviewed on radio is not a 'natural' thing for your client, the temptation is to speak faster when being interviewed. However, on radio, if you speak too quickly, your words run into each other and your message is lost. You must train your client to slow down when speaking.

The opposite is also true. If your client speaks too slowly, people lose interest. Long gaps in your client's response only encourage people to switch stations. Journalists are also aware of this and will try to speed the reply. If the client has not been trained, an opportunity has been lost to get the message across and influence listeners.

Someone speaking with an air of authority is fine, if they are in a position of authority. But sometimes the 'authority' sounds like 'superiority', which switches people off. By rehearsing interview techniques in advance, you will have an opportunity to iron out these difficulties before they are aired to the nation.

Your client should also be comfortable with the amount of information to be imparted in the space of a short radio interview. Huge amounts of detail simply cannot be absorbed by radio listeners. On television, you can show a graph which simplifies large quantities of information; on radio you cannot. In the 1997 general election, Fianna Fáil told people over and over again that they would 'cut taxes'. It was simple, short, effective and easily understood. Fine Gael, on the other hand, tried to explain how they would widen the tax bands, lower the ceilings for entry into tax brackets, change the allowances, etc., and utterly confused people. The end result of their proposals would have been the same — a reduction in taxes — but the complicated nature of the message meant that it was lost on most people.

The requirements of and preparation for radio interviews vary with the programme that your client is on, and the reason for the interview. If the programme is a news programme, the interview will be quite short and will deal only with the salient or crucial points. If the interview is on a chat show, it will be longer in duration with more time to flesh out different points, and more time for your client to win or lose listeners. Chat shows are inclined to have a phone-in element which is completely unpredictable. Neither the interviewer nor the interviewee knows in advance who is likely to phone in, or what points they are likely to raise, or — worse — what tangent they are likely to go off on. It all makes for good radio, but it can be a harrowing experience for the client.

Finally, each of the points above refers to being interviewed in studio. A lot of interviews are done by telephone. This enables the client to conduct the interview from a location that suits them (the office or home), on an apparatus with which they are completely familiar (the telephone). However, there are dangers in telephone interviews. Because the telephone is such a familiar instrument, it is easy for people to forget that they are speaking not only to the interviewer, but also to every listener in the country. Because telephones are used in one-to-one conversations, it can be difficult to keep this crucial point in mind.

Telephone interviews also deprive the interviewee of visual contact, which is extremely important. If you are sitting opposite the interviewer, you know immediately if they are becoming confused or angry or bored with your response. This is much harder to gauge at the end of a telephone line. You can miss vital visual signals. One classic example occurred during the presidential campaign for the late Brian Lenihan when Pádraig Flynn gave an interview on *Saturday View* on RTÉ Radio 1.

The programme participants included Michael McDowell in studio in Dublin, and Pádraig Flynn by link from Mayo. The studio discussion had been running for some time and Pádraig Flynn obviously felt that he wasn't being given a fair share of air time. When he was given the opportunity to contribute, he did so. He was on the programme in support of Brian Lenihan's candidacy, and proceeded to talk about Mary Robinson (later President of Ireland), who was Brian's opponent.

As the show was coming to a close, Pádraig Flynn went off on a tangent, saying that Mary Robinson had apparently re-invented herself for the campaign. Flynn's infamous comment, '…none of those who knew Mary Robinson very well in previous incarnations…' was the launching pad.[9] The substance of his point was that he could not accept the sincerity of the way in which she was wearing a new type of clothing, had changed her hairstyle and was now projecting a 'new' image as a caring family person and mother.[10]

According to Liz McManus TD, Flynn 'made the most extraordinary attack on Mary Robinson, saying that she had suddenly discovered her role as a good mother of her children. And it lost Fianna Fáil the election.'[11]

Pádraig Flynn's disadvantage was that he had no visual contact, so he could not see how furious the panelists in studio were getting. Michael McDowell interrupted him and demanded that he apologise and retract some of the remarks about Mary Robinson. The interview has since passed into history and folklore as one of the factors which contributed to Mary Robinson's election. Had Pádraig Flynn been in studio in Dublin, he would have seen the reaction of the other panelists and would have had time to correct what he had said, before it became an issue of controversy.

Television

Television is a highly visual medium and, since 60 per cent of what you learn comes through your eyes, it is also a powerful medium. It is a medium with which the viewer is very familiar. Viewers are used to confident, competent performers, and expect no less from a business person making their first appearance on television. Your client needs to be comfortable with the medium.

It is immensely important that your client looks well on television. Physical appearance, eye contact and hand movements are important. Your client should be advised about what to wear. Wearing pale colours on television will make the interviewee look washed out. Tight check patterns will 'flutter' on screen. Wearing the same colour as the seating will make your client look like some sort of puppet with head, hands and legs only. Make-up (for men and women) should be professionally applied to suit the needs of television.

Adopting the correct posture on television is also important. Too relaxed and your client will look sloppy or disinterested; too far forward in the chair and the interviewee will look too anxious.

Hands should be kept as still as possible. Remember the habit that Mary Robinson had with her hands? Many who watched her being interviewed were aggravated by the constant gestures of both hands (thumb and middle finger joined together at the tips, hands moving up and down, gesticulating as she spoke). This is not a minor thing. Any hand movement distracts the viewer from the message, and instead encourages them to focus on the source of their annoyance.

Eye contact is also important. Viewers have placed their trust not in the interviewee, but in the interviewer. If Bryan Dobson is interviewing on the *Six-One News*, the viewer looks to him for a reaction. It is vital, therefore, that the interviewee makes eye contact with the interviewer and keeps it. Failure to do so will make your client look 'shifty'.

It should be stressed that looking good on television has absolutely nothing to do with being 'good looking'. Beauty, after all, is in the eye of the beholder. Looking good on television simply means being prepared: wearing the right clothes, being relaxed, having no distracting hunches or twitches or hand movements (you can be trained out of all of these), paying attention to the questions asked, and answering them as calmly and fully as possible.

PREPARATION FOR INTERVIEWS

1. Establishing Facts

As a professional, it is your job to establish all of the facts of the interview in advance, and to brief your clients fully before they meet the journalist. The following are among the items to establish.

- *What is the name of the journalist?* This is always worth double checking on the day in case someone has called in sick, or been delayed.
- *Who are they writing for/ recording for/ filming for?* Your client should know which newspaper, radio or television station they are conducting the interview with.
- *How long do they want for the interview?* The journalist should be able to tell you exactly how much time is needed, and you, in turn, should be able to establish if the time required is fair. Particularly in a crisis situation, where your client has many media demands, you may need to shorten the length of time available. There is also an inherent danger in allowing too much time for an interview — the more time the client has, the more likely it is that a mistake will be made.
- *Where does the journalist want to do the interview?* If it is radio, you will want to be sure that the location has a quiet background — otherwise the noise of people drinking tea, or of machinery or cars in the background, will detract from

the interview. If it is television, you may need to prepare the interview area (in the chief executive's office, for example, you might remove files from the desk before the journalist arrives).

- *What is the journalist trying to establish by the interview? (Angle?)* If you were not instrumental in setting up the interview, or if the interview came out of the blue, it is always nice to know why your client is of interest at this particular time. Publicity is often the name of the game, and few clients like to turn down interview opportunities. They will not thank you, however, if the journalist has an 'angle' which was not anticipated, and they were ill-prepared for the questions asked.

- *What is the deadline?* This is particularly important in a crisis situation. The radio news bulletins are broadcast on the hour; television news is broadcast at least three times a day; and newspapers are published the following day. The deadline may well determine the order in which interviews are given.

- *How many people will be present?* This is really just to put the client at ease. It can throw even experienced interviewees if they expect one journalist and, instead, are confronted with an interviewer, a soundman and a cameraperson. Similarly, if you, as the PR person, intend to be present at the interview, you should inform the journalist as a courtesy. Most journalists will not thank you for being present, but many clients feel more comfortable knowing that there is someone present who is watching out for them.

- *Will the pre-recorded interview be edited?* For radio or television interviews which are pre-recorded, the rule of journalists is that they normally record more than they need and then edit it down. From your client's point of view, and from your own, you have no control over the edited version (this is entirely at the discretion of the journalist). You should therefore aim to give an interview which lasts close to (and not much more than) the amount of 'finished' product required.

- *What is the journalist's style of questioning?* You probably know this already, but you must advise your client and discuss it with the interviewee. Different people have different styles. Some interviewers ask short questions and allow interviewees to take their time answering. Others ask short questions but interrupt after a couple of minutes. Others again ask long detailed questions, leaving the interviewee with short answers. Establish the style in advance.

- *Has the crew/team had an opportunity to visit the scene?* This is particularly important in a crisis situation. Has the journalist or photographer or cameraperson had an opportunity to visit the plant, or see the plane sitting off the runway, or get access to the river which burst its banks? Your client will not have time to go with them, and probably will have no desire to do so either, but you should ensure that they have all of the footage they need to accompany the interview clip.

2. Determine

- *What does your client want to say?* Why is your client giving the interview? No one should give an interview simply because a journalist requested it. If your client is going to be available to media, there must be something in particular to share with the viewers, readers or listeners.
- *How many points can be reasonably covered in a short space of time?* The general rule is that your client will not be able to cover any more than three points in any one interview. More than that, and the message is lost. Establish the three points clearly in advance of the interview. If it is for newspaper or radio, the client can bring to the interview a piece of paper with three points written on it. If it is for television, this is not advisable. Interviewees who keep referring to pieces of paper can give the impression of being unsure of their subject. A card with three points on it is particularly necessary if your client is doing back-to-back interviews. We had clients in the US some years ago who between them (there were two) handled twenty radio interviews in the space of approximately thirty minutes. Under these circumstances it is virtually impossible after the third or fourth interview to remember what you have said, and to whom. A new card for each interview allows you to tick off the points as you make them, and serves as a reminder, before the close of the interview, that the final point has not been made.
- *What is the key message you want to leave with the general public?* Of the three points your client is making, which is the most important? This establishes which one should be highlighted or repeated in the event of the interview running over time.

3. Think Like a Journalist

The only way that you can adequately prepare your client for an interview is if, in advance of the interview, you think like a journalist.

- *What other questions are likely to be asked?* Since you have established the journalist's style, the purpose of the interview, and the length of time allocated, you should be able to anticipate the questions that are likely to be covered.
- *What other tangent could the interviewer take?* This is even more important. People find it easy to answer the easy questions. Your real skill, as a PR professional, is in preparing clients for questions they do not want to be asked. Has the company had any bad industrial relations in the past year? Is there a problem in the industry, or related to your company, which might be raised? How did the company deal with the financial scandal it found itself involved in a few years ago? Is there any truth in the rumour that one of the directors is under investigation for sexual harassment? Your skill as a PR person is to toss out the difficult questions to your client, in advance of the interview, so that there are no surprises on the day.

4. Location

Visit the location in advance of the interview. This section is particularly geared to television interviews. If the interview is to be held in an office, what is to be seen behind the desk? Can the names of files be read? Does the wall planner contain any sensitive information? Are there papers on the desk which shouldn't be there? Is the office simply too busy — should you re-locate to the boardroom or another office? Is there any possibility that something on the desk, the shelves or the wall, might distract or detract from what your client is saying?

REFERENCES

1. Simon Carswell, 'Unionists cry monopoly over Tel takeover', *Sunday Business Post*, 19 March 2000.
2. *Sunday Programme*, RTÉ Radio 1, 10 March 2002.
3. Jon Katz, 'Has print had its day?', *The Irish Times*, 13 March 2000.
4. Joe Carroll, 'Readers at risk in journalists' upmarket drive', *The Irish Times*, 22 April 2000.
5. Stephen Comyn, 'It's magazine time', *Shelflife*, September 2000.
6. Independent Radio and Television Commission (IRTC), 22 February 2000.
7. Carol Power, 'E-mail marketing software to grow 40% annually', *The Irish Times*, 17 March 2000.
8. Frank Jefkins, *Public Relations Techniques*, London: Butterworth Heinemann, 1994 (second edition).
9. Ciarán Swan, 'Red Roses for the President', *CIRCA Art Magazine* (Back Issues CIRCA 89), www.recirca.com/features/index.shtmL.
10. 'The Flynn Saga Continues' http://www.mayogazette.com/mayo/issue20A.html.
11. 'Interview with Liz McManus' www.tallgirlshorts.net/thewayofwomen.

CHAPTER 5

Writing News Releases

WHAT IS A NEWS RELEASE?

Let us begin by asking the vital question: what is a news release? A news release is a method of issuing news to journalists. Its purpose is to impart news to journalists in a style in which they would have written it. It is information of a newsworthy nature. It is news that would interest the readers/listeners/viewers of the medium. Simple.

The term 'news release' has replaced the more old-fashioned 'press release'. Press means the printed media only. The more appropriate title for releases is 'news release' as the information is issued to print, radio and television media.

A news release is only one method of issuing news — there are several ways in which it could be done. You could call a press conference instead, or you could make a telephone call to arrange an interview. A news release is just one way of issuing news, but it is the most basic and one of the most effective methods, used daily, by practitioners.

WHAT IS NEWS?

The emphasis in a news release is on news. What is news? News, according to William Randolph Hearst, is 'something somebody doesn't want printed; all else is advertising'.[1] News is something of interest that you have not heard before. The key element is that it is information 'of interest'. This is not some sort of free advertisement — if you need to advertise something, you should buy space. Nor is it a way of getting a free mention in the newspapers — if you have nothing newsworthy to say, no one is going to publish it anyway. News is something of interest to a journalist, whose basic requirement is to write stories of interest to readers. Therefore a news release issued to a national newspaper should contain information that you believe is of interest to readers nationwide.

News is generally also new. It is fresh information about something that has happened either on the day or the previous day. However, news does not always refer to something that happened recently. The 'discovery' of a Caravaggio is not news because he painted the scene recently; rather it is news because this 'old' painting has now been attributed to Caravaggio. *The Hitler Diaries* were news because the diaries had recently been discovered to exist, not because (as it later transpired) they had been recently written. (*The Hitler Diaries* were a hoax).

WHAT IS THE DIFFERENCE BETWEEN HARD NEWS AND SOFT NEWS?

Hard news has an urgent, vital quality. A hard news story is very important and the media will want to cover it. Hard news is usually not issued by press release. If your company has had a disastrous year financially and as a consequence made 200 people redundant, you have a hard news story.

Hard news stories are those which 'must' be covered by all media — the government calling an election, for example. If you picked up your newspaper and did not find any reference to the election, you would be horrified — and would probably change the newspaper you buy daily. Hard news is common to all media. One of the most recent examples of international hard news was the twin towers incident on 11 September 2001 in which thousands of people lost their lives. It was a story of such magnitude that it 'demanded' to be covered by all media.

Soft news, on the other hand, is of interest but does not have the same urgency. If a charity is launching a new fundraising drive, or your managing director has been appointed to a prestigious committee, or your company has launched a new spreadable butter, what you are dealing with is soft news (pardon the pun!) This is news which does not 'demand' to be covered. In fact, you might not even notice that the fundraising drive was not covered by your newspaper. It would not be an issue of 'crucial' interest. A lot of soft news is issued by news release and photo-call.

Be careful not to confuse soft news with advertising. If your company is launching a new product and you write a press release giving information about the retail outlets in which it is available, and the cost of the product, your release amounts to advertising copy. There is no news value. If, on the other hand, your release covers the research that was done, the number of new jobs created or the value of the new product to users, you have a news story. The news story will generate interest in your company and its products. Advertising will take care of the sales.

UNDERSTANDING THE MEDIA

In order to write a good release, you need to study the media. You must be aware of what a journalist is looking for. If you can write the news in a style that is consistent with the newspaper (or magazine, radio programme, etc), and which satisfies the journalist's basic requirement for news, you are well on the road to having your release covered the next day.

If you understand the mind of the journalist, you must also understand the way the journalist reads and edits. The average journalist receives hundreds of news releases every day. Journalists' desks are covered in them. Your job is to make sure that, at the very least, your release is read. With so many releases, the journalist will look quickly at yours and decide, in a matter of seconds, whether or not to read further. Your subject matter, title and opening paragraph, therefore, are vital. When the journalist has read the opening paragraph, the release will either be consigned to the bin, or read in greater detail.

SELECTING THE RELEVANT JOURNALIST

It is important that your release is issued to the right journalist — either the specialist who writes in that particular area, or a journalist who has an interest in the subject of the release. There is no point in sending a sports release to a business journalist.

You should know the journalists writing in each area and target your release to the journalists who are most likely to cover the story.

You should also keep your contacts file up to date. Directories are published annually which list newspaper deadlines, editors and correspondents. However, people move position within media, they move to other media, they retire and they die. Your contacts file should be continually updated.

NEWSPAPER PRACTICE

You must also be aware of how a newspaper edits a story. If you are writing a news release, the most important information should be contained in the first paragraph. As you go down through the release, the lower down the page you get, the less important the information is. Newspapers edit/cut from the bottom up. If your news release has been properly structured, the loss of the last two paragraphs will not affect the reader's understanding of the story. The reader will still have read the most important pieces of information.

WORDS

The words that you use in a news release are also vital. Never use big words when you can use little ones. It is a simple rule, but one that many people overlook. The people reading the newspaper are busy, have limited time at their disposal and their attention will not be held by a story which uses words that they do not understand. This is not to insult the average reader — rather it marries their tight time schedules with your requirement to communicate. If you use long words, you are more likely to create confusion. Remember, the purpose of the release is to tell the reader some news, not to impress people with your brilliance!

Newspapers print stories in columns. The columns are quite narrow. If the words or the sentences you use are too long, they will become broken. A paragraph in which several words are divided over two lines will lose its flow, and the reader will move on to another story. You should also keep your words short because (general) news should be capable of being read and understood by a 7-year-old. If you are writing for the national media, you must use short words.

The general rule is that you should use no more than 25–27 words per sentence, and your first paragraph should not exceed 50 words.

I have often dreamt that the 'long word' version of this well-known song was written first. Then someone with a good journalistic eye amended it and wrote the short version. See what you think!

Long Word Version

Kindly indicate the way to my abode
I'm fatigued and I wish to retire
I had a little drink about sixty minutes ago
And it's gone to the top of my anatomy
No matter where I perambulate
On land or sea or atmospheric pressure
You will always hear me chanting this refrain
Kindly indicate the way to my abode

Short Word Version[2]

Show me the way to go home
I'm tired and I want to go to bed
I had a little drink about an hour ago
And it's gone right to my head
No matter where I roam
On land or sea or foam
You will always hear me singing this song
Show me the way to go home.

USE OF LANGUAGE

The language that you use in a news release is vital. Watch the construction of your sentences. Never use words that are likely to imply something e.g. 'the Managing Director *admitted* that profits were down this year'. Did he admit it under pressure? Did a clever journalist force the admission from him? Or did he state that the profits were down?

Never personalise a release e.g. *'We are pleased to announce'* or *'The benefit to you, the customer, is'*. Journalists do not directly address their readers, and neither should you.

Do not use the company name over and over again in the release. Aim to name the company not more than twice in four paragraphs.

At all costs avoid flattering your client. The client might be delighted — the media will be completely unimpressed. Remove flattery such as: the *highly reputable* marketing manager, *the world-leader* in the electrical trade, the *well-known* estate agency.

Be brief. Never use two or three words where one would do. Here are a few examples: 'The investment is believed to be *in excess* of £2 million...' could be shortened to 'The investment is believed to be *more than* £2million....' 'The *position, at the present time*, is that refunds will not be issued' could become 'The *current position* is that refunds will not be issued'.

Ruthlessly cut unnecessary adjectives, adverbs or padding. For example: *past* memories (is there such a thing as future memories?), *true* facts (if they are facts, we do not need to be told that they are true), *invited* guest (the only interesting thing about guests is when they are uninvited gate-crashers). These words add nothing to our understanding of the story, take up precious print space, and force the journalist to spend time editing your text.

Avoid the use of foreign expressions — they create barriers to communication. 'The directors were given *carte blanche* to investigate the misdemeanour' would be clearer if you used only English: 'The directors were given full powers to investigate the misdemeanour'.

Avoid industry jargon, unless you are writing for specialised media. Bear in mind that you will sometimes need to remove the jargon entirely and explain the development or product in simple English. For example:

- 'The use of CFL bulbs has been shown to reduce energy bills effectively' — jargon.
- 'The use of Compact Fluorescent Light bulbs (CFLs) has been shown to reduce energy bills effectively' — jargon explained, but still not clear.
- 'The use of special long-life bulbs, called CFLs, has been shown to reduce energy bills effectively' — much clearer.

Avoid sexist or racist language where possible. While too much use of his/her can actually confuse, you should be able to find alternatives. A *'businessman'* could be referred to as a 'business person', 'chief executive', or 'business leader'. An *'air hostess'* could be a 'flight attendant' or 'cabin crew'.

Avoid the abuse of the English language which is so common in speech nowadays. Check that you are using words in the right context. Words like 'bemused' are commonly abused in the spoken language. For example: 'The act was outrageously funny. I was totally *bemused* by it' —bemused means muddled or stupefied; surely 'I was totally *amused* by it' was what was intended?

Use simple punctuation. Brackets, dashes and dots strain the eye and disrupt the sentence flow. Use commas and semi-colons only where the meaning is in doubt without them. If a sentence needs a lot of commas or semi-colons, split it into separate sentences. Do not use exclamation marks.

Use active rather than passive verbs. 'The *truth was told* by the boy' becomes 'The boy told the truth' or 'The meeting of the *class will be held*...' becomes 'The class will meet....'

Finally, verb tense should almost always be past. Most news releases are issued on the day on which something happens. Therefore, by the time coverage is achieved (even if it is one hour later, on radio) the story has to be told in the past tense. There are exceptions of course, but as a general rule, it is the past tense that is used. Remember too, irrespective of what tense you choose, to check that the same tense is used throughout the release.

NEWSPAPER STYLE

Your news release should be written in the newspaper's style, not in the style of a letter. If you were writing a letter to the Lord Mayor of Dublin, for example, you would address your letter to: the Right Honourable, the Lord Mayor of Dublin, Councillor Tom Kenny TD. However, if you were referring to the same man in a news release you would be more likely to refer to him as: Dublin's Lord Mayor, Cllr Tom Kenny.

The same goes for the use of full stops and capital letters. The letters T.D./M.P. stand for Teachta Dála/Member of Parliament, but most newspapers omit the full stops and use simply TD/MP. Full stops take up space! Most managing directors like to refer to themselves using capital letters for their title e.g. Mary Maguire, Managing Director of Maggiemay Ltd. This looks well if used in a letter, but newspapers do not generally use capital letters for titles. If the same wording appeared in a news release it should read 'Mary Maguire, managing director of Maggiemay Ltd'.

READERS

Always remember the readers you are writing for. If you are issuing a release to foreign media, be sure that the words you use are understandable to a foreign reader. For example, the prime minister in Ireland is called 'An Taoiseach'. Few outside Ireland would understand a release about a Taoiseach in Ireland — you would have to call him Prime Minister. Also try to make connections for the readers if possible. If someone previously had an international reputation in the sports world, and you were writing for sports media, it might be more appropriate to describe him as 'Joey Bloggs, former rugby international'.

If you used either of these descriptions for a national audience, they would think that you had lost control of your senses. The personality would be so well known that any description would be completely unnecessary. Write with your readers in mind.

With national, regional or local media, readers are equally important. Journalists understand their readers and what it is they want. It is the job of journalists to write for 'their' readers. So, when issuing releases, you must bear the readers in mind. Just as different papers have different styles, so too their readers differ one from another. The person who reads the *Star* is unlikely to read *The Irish Times*. The reader of *The Sunday Times* is unlikely to read the *Sunday World*. Make your release relevant to the newspaper's readers.

IDENTIFY THE 'ANGLE'

Finding the angle in a story is one of the greatest skills of a professional PR person. The story must be written with a particular angle in mind. The angle must grab the attention of the journalist and the reader. This means that you may, in fact, use several different angles when issuing the same story.

The first challenge of the PR person is to find the angle within the story. The company brief may have identified the story as the opening of new premises. The PR angles, however, might also include job creation, use of new technology, and regional investment arising from the opening of the new premises. The story has a better chance of coverage if it has interesting angles to it.

The job-creation aspect might be the angle used in a news release to the *Irish Independent*. The use of new technology might have a better chance of being covered in the *Sunday Business Post*. Investment in the region might be of interest to *The Irish Times*, and the opening of the new premises would definitely attract the interest of the local media.

There are angles within the story which need to be developed to get the best chance of media interest, and different angles will interest different media and therefore give you the widest possible spread of coverage.

NEWS RELEASE FORMAT

News releases are written in a very definite style. When journalists write a story, they always seek to answer six questions. A news release should do exactly the same thing. In every release that you write you should answer the 5 Ws + H:

- Who?
- Where?
- What?
- When?
- Why?
- How?

These are the most important elements of any news. When constructing your release, you should aim to answer these six questions in the first two paragraphs. A news release should not read like a detective story. You do not first create the atmosphere, sketch the scene, and introduce characters and plot before getting to the nub of the story. A release tells you instantly, upfront, in the first two paragraphs, what the story is about. It gets straight to the point.

The way in which you combine the six elements will differ with each medium you release to. The 'What' generally makes it into the first paragraph — it is important to know what you are reading about — as does the 'When' — you need to know if the news is recent.

If the 'Who' is someone like Bono of U2, then 'Who' must be dealt with in the opening line. On the other hand, if it is the local managing director, unknown outside the company, you might leave the 'Who' until later in the release.

If the 'Where' is Wexford, this information would be vital to media in the county, but less important in the national media.

'Why' can be at the heart of the release: why the new product was introduced, why the business needs massive expansion, why the director has resigned, why so many employees have been made redundant. In a crisis situation, it can be the hardest to deal with: why did the plane crash? Why was the victim murdered? Why did the explosion happen? Why was no one monitoring the situation?

The 'How' is a similar situation. Again, it might be at the heart of the release: how the company won the contract against stiff competition, how this young singer was given her break, how so much money was raised for charity. Or the 'How' can be, again in a crisis situation, closely linked with the why, and therefore difficult to answer: how did no one foresee that this might happen? How were so many people poisoned? How did so much money go missing, etc?

INVERTED PYRAMID

News releases are also written using an 'inverted pyramid' style (i.e. an upside-down pyramid). The most critical information is contained in the first two paragraphs of the story; the less critical information follows. Releases are written in this way because media people edit from the bottom to the top. Space is at a premium and a well-written two paragraph piece can tell a story adequately. This is why the first two paragraphs contain the 5 Ws and H. They must tell the story, in full, for the reader. The next two paragraphs put flesh on the bones.

For example, the first two paragraphs of a news release might deal with Maggiemay Ltd. (*who*) which opened a new factory (*what*) in Ennis, Co. Clare (*where*) today (2.2.2004) (*when*) to produce Aran jumpers for sale on the American market (*why*). Ennis was chosen because of its proximity to Shannon Airport (*how*).

The following two paragraphs would give the less important information such as: how many people Maggiemay Ltd employs, how long the company has been in business, what other products are in its range, which other markets it sells into, etc.

If readers see only the first two paragraphs, they have the essence of the story. If four paragraphs make it into the paper, they have a fuller picture. But the picture was not incomplete if only the first two paragraphs were covered.

HOW TO TITLE A NEWS RELEASE

The title of a news release should state quite simply what the release is about. The purpose of the title is to tell journalists what they can expect to read about. The title covers the subject matter of the release.

Never confuse the title with headline writing. Writing a headline for the story is someone else's job. Your job is to impart the information. The following are some possible headlines and news release titles:

- Your company has introduced a new brand of hair restorer for men. This new product will restore hair to an otherwise bald patch over a one-month period. The title of your media release may read: *'New product restores hair growth'*. All you are trying to do is let journalists know what they will be reading about. The headline writers in the newspapers, however, may run with: *'Gone today, hair tomorrow!'*

- You work for a member of the European Parliament. He has discovered that a little-known, illegal, hallucinogenic drug is available in the EU because of a poorly worded section in a piece of legislation. He wants to change the legislation. The title of your media release might read: *'MEP seeks change in legislation on illegal drugs'*. The headline in the newspapers might well read: *'EU makes halluc- inating drugs available in Ireland'*.

PRESENTATION OF NEWS RELEASES

A news release should always be issued on headed notepaper (either that of the con- sultancy or that of the client firm). The source of the release should be immediately identifiable.

The top left-hand corner of the release should contain the words 'Press Release' or 'News Release'. This identifies the information as news, written in a journalistic style, issued free of charge and without obligation to the journalist. It also avoids confusion with advertising copy, a letter to the editor, etc.

The top right-hand corner should always contain the date on which the release was issued and the time (if relevant). It is important for the journalist to know when it was issued. A clearly dated release is also of benefit to a journalist who has been away from the office for a few days. The inclusion of the date of the release clearly indicates that it was issued some days ago. This may mean that the journalist bins it, or it may mean that you receive a phone-call to see if the story was covered by someone else at the paper, or to look for developments on the story, or a fresh angle.

The news release should be clearly titled. The title should reflect the subject that the journalist can expect to read about in the first paragraph.

Any reference to the timing of an event, usually contained in the first paragraph of the release, should also be dated. If you make reference in the release to 'today' or 'yesterday' you should always put the date in brackets afterwards. This helps the journalist to know if you have written the release properly. For example, if you were issuing a release on 3 February 2004 to be covered in the national media the following day, your news release should be dated 3 February 2004, but the opening sentence would refer to 'yesterday (3.2.2004)' because it will have happened yesterday by the time the readers see the story. If you are issuing a release to the US, it would read as 2.3.2004 (in America, dates are listed by month, day and year).

You should always leave a wide margin down either side of the page and double space (or 1.5 line space) your sentences. These two rules are a hang-over from olden days when releases were mostly issued on paper, and journalists needed to make comments in the margins, or write alternative words in the gaps between sentences, before the story was sent for setting.

The best news releases seldom extend beyond two pages at most. Many news releases are a single page. If the information you are trying to impart as news cannot be reduced to fewer than three or four pages, you should find another way of issuing that particular news story. Long news releases are time-consuming to read, and usually contain information that is unnecessary. Keep your releases to one page if at all possible, and a maximum of two. Remember that your release can be accompanied by additional information. These sheets of additional information may contain a lot of the background information on the formation of the company, idea behind the initiative, etc., which you deemed necessary for the journalist to know, but not relevant for inclusion in the release.

Finally, a news release always concludes with the name and contact phone numbers of the person who issued it, e.g.

Further details: Oonagh Monaghan
Professional PR Ltd
Tel: 123 4567 (work)
086-1234567 (mobile)

Journalists do not work a 9 to 5 day; neither do PR people. Journalists may well need information about your release during *their* working hours (8 p.m. is not unusual). You need to give them a home or mobile number so that they can contact you at *their* convenience. After all, *you* want the coverage.

It is also inadvisable to clog the end of the release with a multiplicity of contact numbers (home, work, mobile, e-mail, fax, etc). The journalist requires, ideally, one phone number at which you can be contacted for further information. Journalists will not e-mail or fax you an enquiry because it is too time consuming, and you might not be in the office late in the evening and capable of responding in time to meet their deadlines.

Finally, bear in mind that whether the news release is sent by courier, fax or e-mail, the same rules apply.

USE OF EMBARGOES

Your news release may also be issued in advance, but not for publication/broadcast/coverage before a certain time. This means that you place 'an embargo' on it. In this case, in the top right-hand corner of the release (where the date would appear), the words Embargo: 3.00 p.m.: 2 February 2004 (or similar) would be inserted. This indicates to journalists that they have received the information in advance, but may not use it before the specified time.

Many government ministers send their speeches, or news releases about their speeches, to media in advance, embargoed until they have actually spoken. In a lot of cases, this is completely unnecessary as there is little of newsworthy value in the release. In other words, it could as easily have been issued after the speech was delivered.

An embargo is intended as a form of assistance to media. For example, in Britain, the Queen's Annual Honours List is issued to media, embargoed, a couple of days in advance of her announcement. This enables media to assemble photographs and biographical details of the recipients in advance of any announcement.

Embargoes can be abused by both sides, however. Media often accuse PR people of putting an embargo on a story with the sole purpose of allowing one arm of media to gain a 'scoop'. For example, an embargo until 6.15 p.m. might be seen to favour television news (the hourly radio news bulletin would be over, and print media — even the evening newspapers — could not report till the following day).

Embargoes are also abused by the media. PR people accuse media of observing embargoes almost 'in the breach' and of breaking embargoes on 'slow' news days. Unless the practice of applying embargoes is curtailed, and unless both sides reach agreement about the ways in which embargoes should be applied and respected, the practice will decline in future years.

COVERAGE

Last, but by no means least, remember that when you issue a news release, you are giving information to the media. There is no obligation on them to use this information, nor are they under any obligation to use the information in the way in which it was given to them.

On the next pages you will see a news release issued by the Irish Academy of Public Relations, and the coverage arising from that release, which appeared in the *Evening Herald* newspaper. The journalist who wrote the piece, Lance Contrucci, attended the graduation ceremony and the two of us had a grand chat. I honestly thought that the resulting piece, while inaccurate, was tongue in cheek. However, the PR industry was horrified and the PRII sent a letter to the editor arising from the piece. See what you think.

(a): IAPR Press Release

IRISH ACADEMY OF
Public Relations
Academy House, 1 Newtown Park
Blackrock, Co. Dublin
Telephone: 2780802
Fax: 2780251
E-mail: info@irishacademy.com

Press Release   12/5/99

60 STUDENTS GRADUATE FROM PR COURSE

Sixty students were awarded 'Certificates of Achievement' this evening (12.5.99) in the Shelbourne Hotel. The students had all completed a ten-week 'Introduction to Public Relations' course with the Irish Academy of Public Relations.

Commenting at the graduation, Ellen Gunning, the Academy's director said, 'The aim of this course is to give participants a flavour of the PR industry. To whet their appetite about dealing with the media, organising functions, and designing newsletters'.

Presenting the certificates Mr Aidan O'Hanlon FPRII, the Academy's extern examiner, encouraged students to read as widely as possible, and to continue their studies if they wanted to work in the business.

Many students, particularly the honours graduates, will return to college in October to study for the Academy's Diploma in Public Relations.

The Irish Academy of Public Relations is the largest private provider of public relations courses in Ireland.

Further details: Ellen Gunning
                   Tel: xxx xxxx

(b): Evening Herald article

Dubliner's Diary

Thursday, May 13, 1999

Lance Contrucci

That's what it said in the handout

SIXTY students were awarded certificates of achievement by the Irish Academy of Public Relations last night.

The academy's director, Ellen Gunning, told me the class concentrated on 'Ethics, Press Releases, Organising Functions, Photographers'.

Excuse me, Ellen, while I wipe the tears of laughter from my eyes. It's just that I've worked with people in PR for a long time and I didn't know there were any schools or degrees for the profession.

I figured people just gravitate into PR after a lot of soul searching, ie: 'Gee, what should I do? I like to go to parties and wear a suit — I know, I'll go into PR.'

I know the firms have very stringent hiring requirements. They won't just let anyone work in PR.

You have to know how to **SMILE**. And they like people who are physically strong, the better to shove reporters in front of the dozens of 'experts' at solemn events, such as the launch of an important new nappy.

And those courses. Ethics? It's commonly believed that PR firms have the ethics of rattlesnakes ... but that's being very unfair to snakes.

If anything, the course is probably called 'Ethics: How to give them up'.

Other courses might include 'What Kind of Whiskey to Serve to a Journalist'.

In fairness, I have to say that the work isn't as easy as it looks. The press releases have to be very well written because they often go straight into the paper below the journalist's byline.

And one must be very creative to coax reporters to media events, away from the warm, friendly confines of the pub beside the office.

PR is a very decent business, and those who are interested in pursuing it would do well to check out the Irish Academy of Public Relations.

At least that's what it says in the press release ...

REFERENCES

1. William Randolph Hearst, 'A Collection of Quotes Based on the Name William', Advertising Quotes, www.allthingswilliam.com.txt
2. Irving King, 'Show me the way to go home', www.voicesinmyhand.com

CHAPTER 6

PR Photography

As a public relations practitioner, you will not be expected to take photographs. Many people study photography as a hobby or profession. They learn how to use a camera, study different shutter speeds, apertures and filters. You, on the other hand, are working as a PR person and therefore need to study photography from a different perspective.

Your job requires that you understand what can by achieved by photography. PR people must:

- Understand the best uses of the medium
- Select the best photographers for each job
- Choose the most appropriate shots for each newspaper or magazine
- Create and commission props.

PR people are keenly aware of the need for compatibility between photographers and clients, and of the different requirements of various media, from slides to photos to transparencies.

PR photography is very varied, challenging and professional. PR people are responsible for commissioning photography for annual reports, corporate brochures, crisis files, websites, newsletters, boardrooms, photo calls and press conferences.

Professional PROs also need to understand the NUJ rules regarding photography and the legal issues surrounding copyright. They are responsible for monitoring photographic coverage of the company, building historical picture libraries, replacing old photos on media files, and controlling the image of the company through its photographic representations.

There is a lot more involved than the photographer's job. No matter how good they are, the photographers' work is finished when the image is sent to the consultant. In many cases, the real PR work is only beginning.

CREATING VISUAL IMAGES.

'A picture is worth a thousand words' is oft quoted, and very true. People remember visual images quicker than they remember a story they have read. This is also true of video and television. Often we do not even hear the story. We see a visual of, for example, starving people, and we know that the story is about famine. Similarly, a photograph of someone on the steps of the High Court, with their hands in the air, celebrating their win, seems to tell you the story. But what if the opening paragraph of the story said something like: 'When Michael Bloggs appeared on the steps of the High Court, he adopted an unusual pose for a man who had just been found guilty of...'? How many people would read the story? How many would see the photograph and believe that they 'knew' what the story was about?

Every photograph you commission should enhance the image of your organisation. Most photographs, and certainly all photos for media release, should tell a story. Many shots will require the use of exotic locations, celebrities or created props. In PR you are trying to communicate something visually, verbally and in writing. Your photographs, like your news releases, need to tell a story, convey an impression, enhance the corporate image, and add to the store of information which the public already knows about your organisation.

There are two types of photographic occasions — photo shoots and photo calls.

PHOTO SHOOT

A photo shoot is a closed event. Unlike a photo call, there is no open invitation to media photographers to attend. The only photographer present will be the one whom you have retained for the shoot. Photo shoots are used regularly for corporate brochures and annual reports. You would also use a photo shoot to prepare a catalogue for a fashion show, for example. You are not going to invite the media, although it might well be of interest, because you want to save the coverage for a later time — perhaps when the models are on the catwalk.

PHOTO CALL

For media events, you will be required to issue a photo-call notice. This is an open invitation, sent to photo-editors/photo-journalists/photographers, to attend and photograph an event that you are organising. The photo-call notice has a set format.

Like a media release, the top left-hand corner will contain the words 'Photo-Call Notice' and the top right-hand corner will show the date of issue. A title will also appear which gives some flavour of the event. Beneath this is an indented section, which gives details of the venue, date, time and people attending, followed by no more than 2.5 paragraphs giving slightly more detail.

On the next page you will see a photo call notice and you will see the photo coverage which this photo-call notice achieved. The following day (Saturday) photo-coverage appeared in *The Irish Times, Irish Independent, Star,* and *Evening Herald.*

The purpose of a photo call is to attract media attention and secure coverage. However, there are two key issues you should bear in mind.

Media Obligation

There is no obligation on the media to attend the photo call. Neither are they under any obligation, if they attend, to publish those photos subsequently.

Photo-Call Notice: Baby and Kids Show

PHOTO-CALL   2.5.1995

Baby & Kids Show

WITH:	The Lord Mayor of Dublin, Cllr. John Gormley,
	Babies and children (up to 3 yrs. old),
	Clowns, jugglers, face-painters
AT:	1.45 p.m.
ON:	Friday 5th May 1995
IN:	The RDS, at the Baby & Kids Show
	On the lawn outside the front doors (weather permitting)

The Lord Mayor of Dublin, Cllr John Gormley, will officially open the Baby & Kids Show in the RDS on Friday 5th May 1995 at 1.45 p.m. The show provides entertainment for children each day, including clowns, face-painters, tell-a-joke on the big screen, and discos.

As well as live entertainment, the show includes a seminar programme dealing with issues such as the challenge of the year after childbirth, pregnancy over 35 years, and the 10 things women worry most about during pregnancy.

The Baby & Kids Show continues at the RDS through Saturday and Sunday (6–7 May) from 11.00 each morning.

Further details: Ellen Gunning
Tel: xxx xxxx

Photo Coverage in the Media

Fun in the sun . . .

● Living it up in the sunshine at the Baby and Kids Show in the RDS yesterday were these three little Dublin bundles of joy, from left, Orla McCarthy (nine months), from Phibsboro, John Robinson (six months), also from Phibsboro, and Taylor Watson (13 months), from Crumlin. The show, which inclu... ...hibition of baby products, with seminars for parents and entertainment for children of all ages, continues today... *Picture by Bryan O'Brien*

CHILD'S PLAY!

● LITTLE Lorna Buggle (2) from Leixlip was one of the star attractions at the launch of a unique children's fair yesterday.

● The Baby & Kids Show at the RDS kicks off at 11am today and features hundreds of products for the toddler market, from toys to clothes.
Pic: GER MOONEY

☐ SUNNY SMILES: Orla McCarthy (nine months), Phibsboro, John Robinson (s... (13 months), Crumlin, at the Baby and Kids Show which continues today and to...

n reactions: Orla McCarthy (9 months), from Phibsboro, taking a close look at the chain of office of the Lord Mayor of Dublin, Mr John Gormley, at the officia... opening of the Baby and Kids Show at the RDS yesterday. John Robinson (6 months) seems less impressed. Photograph: Frank Miller

Control

Although you have designed the photo call in a certain way, you have no control over the photographs that appear. For example, the photographs that were published showed happy babies and children. But the photographers might have used, instead, a photo of workmen erecting a sign, or an unflattering shot of the Lord Mayor or the organisers. You make the best pitch possible for the photo call, but you have no control over what is photographed when the photographers arrive.

Diary

You should phone the Picture Desk in advance, and see if your photo call has been listed in the diary. If it is not in the diary, someone has taken the decision that it is not of sufficient interest to send a photographer. They might, however, be interested in receiving a photograph from you. If so, you should establish the name of the person to whom it should be sent. If it is in the diary, there is a fair chance that it will be covered by the newspaper. There is still a chance that it will not.

Whether newspapers indicate that they will attend or not, you should always have your own photographer present. The photographer can 'cover' for any newspaper not present (i.e. take photographs in their style which will be issued to them immediately afterwards). The photographer will also take shots for all of the other outlets you have identified. These might include the staff newsletter, a commemorative photo for the boardroom, and various consumer and trade magazines which would have an interest in the event. It goes without saying that you should always cross-check, after the function, which newspapers were represented. Photos should immediately be sent to newspapers that were not present.

If the photo call was held in conjunction with a press conference or an exhibition, it is possible that the newspaper might send a reporter, but not a photographer. If a reporter has been present, you should still send the photos to the picture desk. However, in this case, you should reference them back to the reporter, e.g. 'See news item by Máire Mulreany, reporter'. The newspaper may still choose not to use the photo, but, again, you are improving its chances of being used.

TYPES OF PHOTOGRAPHY

Specialised Photography for Annual Reports

If you look at the front covers of annual reports over the past ten years, you will see from the quality of photography, paper and binding how this aspect of public relations has changed over the years. Instead of boring old shots of cows in a field (for the agricultural sector) or company headquarters (for just about every other sector) or plain covers with large text, annual reports now look sexy. The quality of photography is excellent and the entire look enhances the corporate identity of the company.

Front-cover photography for an annual report is highly specialised and extremely expensive, especially if you are trying to photograph a process. I remember, as a child, watching glass milk bottles being made. Could you imagine trying to get a shot of hot molten glass going into a mould from which it will emerge as a milk bottle? The photography would take a lot of organisation, time and money.

The organisation could involve clearing a particular section of the factory while the process is being photographed, and might include repainting walls or polishing installations. Then there is the recce by the photographer to establish what the light conditions are, where the electric sockets are located, and the speed at which the molten glass travels. The photographer will set up the lighting required (which can be disruptive for staff), and it might take anything up to four days' photography before you get a shot with which both you and the photographer will be happy.

The end product, however, would be a shot that represents at least part of the product of the company, while arousing curiosity, looking visually stunning and also enhancing the corporate image. Even at 2001 rates (for this imaginary shot, approximately €5,750) it represents great value for money.

This, of course, is not the only type of shot that might be taken. You might require an aerial shot of the location of the new factory, as yet un-built, which will require the use of a helicopter and the willing co-operation of the weather — not easily obtained.

Whatever the shot, it will take time, creativity, expertise and money to create. It will probably involve additional peripheral costs (painting, etc.), some staff disruption (over the days on which the shot is being taken), possible accommodation for the photographer (away from a home base). But in the end, the annual report, which has the longest shelf-life of any corporate print product, will have a front cover worthy of the organisation.

Product Shots

Product shots (excluding the needs of the advertising department) are taken, usually, for crisis files. These shots show each type of product in the company's range. So, if the company produces baby-food products, the PR executive will need to arrange shots of every single brand of baby-food, each individual product (from the carrot juice to the banana pudding), in each of the flavours in which it is produced. The shots will need to be taken in black and white, and colour, in photo and slide format, and on video clip. These are the shots that will be used in the event of an emergency recall of the product. These shots are vital for the worried consumer because they enable people to identify, precisely, which product has been recalled. Taking a newspaper photograph into your kitchen is by far the easiest and most effective way of checking whether or not you have a recalled product in your possession.

No company plans a product recall. That would suggest sloppy practices which might lead to such an event. But every company with product knows that this is a 'likely' crisis which might befall them, through either their own fault or the fault/sabotage of others.

Product shots need to be regularly updated to ensure that the full range is recorded on film, and naturally any change in corporate branding means that the entire range of products must be photographed from scratch.

Production Processes

The ideal time to photograph production processes is when the plant is newly built. The machinery is all sparkling new, walls are freshly painted and the job involved in taking the photos is much easier. Whether or not the plant is newly built, the photographs must be taken.

Location Shots

Location shots are also taken for crisis files. These shots, both exterior and interior, are the responsibility of the PR person. You will need to gather exterior photographs of the plant in its natural surroundings, entrances and exits, vans and trucks. Interior photographs will include every stage of the production process, safety procedures, and storage areas for both raw and finished product.

Essentially you are trying to ensure that, should a crisis arise, you have photographs on hand which show the plant, the processes and the procedures, together with the exact location within the plant, and the exact stage of the process, at which the 'problem' occurred.

Both the product and location shots should be stored, in hard copy and electronically, for immediate distribution to media in the event of a crisis.

Head and Shoulders Shots

These are head and shoulders shots of key company executives. They are necessary for two reasons: inclusion in the crisis file (so that when people are quoted they may also be seen) and for standby purposes for media. These are 'insurance' shots on which you will draw should a journalist ring you looking for a head-and-shoulder of the person quoted in the release you have just issued, or to accompany a feature about your industry, for example. Three or four photographs should always be kept on file, and each should be referenced with the photographer's name and relevant details (roll and picture numbers) for easy retrieval and re-ordering.

Three different types of head-and-shoulder (portrait) shots of each executive should be taken. These should be reviewed annually. The three shots are: winter business, summer business and what I call 'casual chic'. This is simply good forward planning. If the crisis happens in winter, you don't want to issue a photograph of someone in a light suit — they will look silly; similarly if the crisis happens in summer and the person is in winter dress. The casual chic shot is really not a crisis shot, but it is worth having it taken at the same time. It is a shot you keep on standby in the event of an announcement of a sponsorship, for example. If the sponsorship is of sports people, or a regatta, a serious corporate shot might look incongruous. The casual chic shot should be used.

These photos should be taken in studio, away from the office. The participants should be told exactly what they should bring with them for the photo session, and they should be given ample time to prepare. The photos will be used for a twelve-month period, so you need to give people time to dye their hair, or take sunbed treatments, or buy a few new suits. After all, they too are projecting an image — a personal image — and that is just as important to each individual as the corporate image of the company. This is not a fashion shoot — the Press Officer is not trying to generate highly flattering, air-brushed photographs of the individuals. Rather, you are trying to get good photos which can be issued to media.

If your key company executives are spread throughout the country, or the globe, it may be necessary to have these shots taken at the annual general meeting. If this is the case, you should also take a group shot of the board.

These head-and-shoulder shots should be reviewed annually because people change their looks, sometimes quite dramatically, over a period of time. People who had brown hair are suddenly blonde; those with greying temples have 'returned' to their natural colour; people who wore glasses now wear contact lenses; the bearded become clean shaven over time; and the clean shaven grow moustaches. It is possible that the individual has not changed in the twelve-month period, but the photos should be checked annually anyway.

Finally, these photographs may also be used in the annual report.

Corporate Brochures

Corporate brochures are another important tool in the printed armoury of the company. The corporate brochure will require special photos to be taken and, again, a lot of planning will go into the event.

We handled photography for a corporate brochure for a catering company some time back, and a considerable amount of work went into the preparation and execution of the event.

- Staff had to be photographed in uniform. This meant selecting a non-working day on which most staff members were available for the shoot. This had cost implications for the organisation.
- The staff shots were to be taken outdoors, in a location in which the company catered but did not own. Permission had to be granted to access and photograph on site. Staff had to be briefed in advance, and then a very large group of people needed to be arranged into a photo that reflected the corporate image of the company. With so many people, the amount of time moving small people and tall people, asking others to uncross their legs, straightening ties and pins, tidying loose ends of hair (which were hardly visible to the naked eye) required a lot of time, patience and co-operation on the part of the staff.
- The kitchens, the hub of the organisation, also needed to be photographed. These were absolutely impeccable — you could see your own reflection in the stainless steel. Yet the photographer arrived, checked through the viewfinder, and began to identify areas that needed to be re-cleaned. Knowing how utterly spotless the operation was, the owner and I both insisted on looking through the viewfinder and, sure enough, blemishes were evident.
- The brochure also needed photographs of food. This was, after all, a catering company. The chefs had to decide on the menus that they wanted shown in the brochure. The ingredients had to be prepared and the food cooked, in the first instance, and then enhanced for photographing. After that, it took hours to get the right shots.

Intranet Photographs

Many companies use photographs on their intranet sites which would not be used on their websites. For example, if the company is building a new factory, in a location distant from the other locations in which it operates, it is a great idea to keep staff updated on progress by putting shots on the internal intranet system. This allows everyone to see the progress of the building.

These shots would be of little interest to customers/potential customers visiting the corporate website, but they would be of interest to an internal audience. The PR role is to ensure that the photographs are regularly updated and accompanied by reports of the site's progress.

Website

There are many photographic agencies from which photographs can be bought, and in some cases it is possible to buy the 'type' of photograph you need (either for a corporate brochure or for a website). A shot of executives meeting in a boardroom for example, or three people viewing a computer screen, can easily be acquired. Most of these shots come at a cost, but there are agencies from which photographs may also be used free of charge.

However, it is not always possible to buy the shots that you need, and often you need to retain a photographer and 'design' your shot. Putting photographs on your website is fraught with problems. Because the photo is now in 'cyber-space' and can be downloaded and manipulated (by the addition of long noses, or a third eye or something), celebrities, in particular, are very reluctant to grant permission for their image to appear on websites. It is important that, no matter whose photograph you use, you seek their permission first. Photos on the web are, after all, deemed to be 'published'.

Media Shots

Photographs for media release must be interesting. The picture desks have hundreds of shots to choose from each day. If your photo is 'boring', it hasn't a hope of securing coverage.

Branding

The purpose of a media photograph is to tell a story visually. Your picture should convey a message — possibly even incorporate the company name — but it should never be blatant advertising. You should never, for example, photograph people standing in front of a sign with the company name on it, unless the photo is to be used in an advertorial. For PR photography, you could have people photographed showing the logo or company name to the side of the picture instead — again, provided that it's not blatant. And remember, the photo does not have to include the company name or logo at all.

People

Have you noticed that the most interesting photographs usually have people in them? We are all curious about people. We are certainly more curious about people than we are about things. If the photograph is intended to show a new building, the latest type of tractor or a new range of shoes — put people into it. Show a bricklayer building a wall, or a government minister in wellingtons climbing onto the tractor, or a hill-walker wearing your boots. Involve people and action where possible.

The people should be relevant to the picture and the story. There is no point in showing a woman in a bikini getting onto a tractor, although, regrettably, car companies do not seem to be able to break the link between women and cars!

Action

You should also try to incorporate action where possible. Machines are more interesting when they are working; planes are more interesting when they are flying; cars look more appealing when they're being driven past houses or on the open road; buildings look more appealing if there are people walking into them, etc.

Celebrities

Use celebrities in photographs. We are all curious about anyone with 'celebrity' status and will be instantly drawn to the photograph. Once readers have been drawn to the photo, they will read the caption to see what it is all about.

Props

Props can also be used to great effect. For example, we handled a photo call to announce the winners of a school competition about environmental awareness. The winning group of schoolgirls was brought to Dublin to accept the prize. Their submission was a videotape in which they 'put the world on trial' for damaging our environment. The photograph of a group of schoolgirls would have been nice, but might not have achieved the kind of coverage we were looking for. So, we hired wigs and gowns and gavels and dressed them all as judges — great coverage.

Locations

You can also use locations to great effect. Put people standing on a spiral staircase, or looking at their own reflections in a gilt mirror, or viewing Dublin from the top of a building, or looking out through a Georgian window. It can add interest to what would otherwise be a 'dull' shot.

Children

There is an old adage which says that you should 'never work with children or animals'. Certainly they are both uncontrollable 'elements' in a photograph, but they can also generate great shots, and a combination of both is usually too good an opportunity for media to pass up.

With animals you are virtually guaranteed that they will not do what they are bidden to do. We have photographed 'placid' dogs which managed to look like they were strangling themselves on their leads, and ring-tailed lemurs which jumped off branches and landed on people's shoulders, instead of standing on tables to be hand-fed. Photographing animals is very unpredictable — the shots are seldom as you outlined in the brief, but the results can be stunning.

Children can also be difficult to work with, and you must ask the parents' permission if you want to photograph them. Parents too can be very awkward or very helpful — a bit like their offspring? I did a photo call for the first-day opening of a new school, in which I tried to get a little girl to hold a little boy's hand. The little girl was willing; the little boy would not hold hands under any circumstances. Eventually, in sheer exasperation, I asked if there was a parent present. The father emerged from the crowd. I asked him to remove the child because *The Irish Times* and I were tired of asking him to hold the girl's hand. We would use another child instead. I admit that I was very short with the father and really expected that he would tell me that I was treating himself and his child badly. Instead, he had heard the words '*Irish Times*' and nothing else, and proceeded to tell his son, in no uncertain terms, to hold that girl's hand 'immediately'. Ah, the power of parents! He was rewarded, as were we, with a great shot in the paper the next day.

Local Media

National and local media need interesting photographs, but local media, in particular, need local people. Local newspapers are read for local news, so you need to have local interest in your photographs. Select people from the local area, and have them photographed with the 'celebrity'. Remember that you might be handling a conference which has people present from every county in the country. Every one of those groups with the celebrity gets you into another newspaper — Donegal people with the celeb, Kerry people, Carlow people, etc. All have their own local media and all will use photographs of local people, or people with a local connection in their newspapers. It is important to remember that people with a local connection are just as good as local people. John Delaney, originally from Cork (whose parents still live in Irish Street, Macroom), would make a great shot for the local papers. Certainly people mightn't have seen him in years, but that is no disadvantage. His photo will generate curiosity. What is he doing with himself these days, and why was he attending a big medical conference in Dublin? The local 'connection' feeds the newspaper's need to be relevant to its readers, and delivers a wider audience to you.

MONITORING PR PHOTOGRAPHS

The PR person is also responsible for monitoring photographs. You are the person who receives the press cuttings, analyses the impact of the coverage, and estimates how many people had an opportunity to see the shot. You are also the person who cross-evaluates the number of shots issued versus the number of shots covered.

The PR person will also keep an eye on 'stock' photography — those photographs that newspapers keep on file because the person is well known or the team is prominent. The well-known person may well have changed their style since the original photograph was taken. With the exception of people who like to use photographs that are a decade old (making them look younger), most people prefer to see themselves appear in media as they actually are. Likewise with sports coverage — if your company has recently become a team sponsor, you will monitor the photographic coverage to make sure that stock photographs (with the old sponsor's name emblazoned on the jerseys) are not used. You may well need to contact the newspaper offices and replace the 'offending' shots.

THE PICTURE EDITOR

The bottom line for all picture editors is that they are looking for pictures that will enhance a page and appeal to their readers.

Each newspaper has a different style of photography. You should be familiar with each newspaper or magazine to which you are submitting, and therefore capable of identifying its style. As a PR professional, you should know the type of photograph each newspaper will want. A photographer, if you are using one, should also be able to advise you.

Bear in mind, always, that the newspapers' preference will be to use pictures taken by their own photographers. Newspaper photographers will photograph several events during the day, and always take more photos than the paper will use.

If you are submitting a PR photograph, you are competing with every photographer working in that newspaper, and every other PR person submitting on that day, and all of the photographs arriving over the wire services. This is the range from which the picture editor selects every day. It is much more difficult to have a photograph used than a media release. Photographs are expensive to produce. You should be sure that, at a minimum, you are issuing the type of photograph the newspaper would be interested in.

Never make the mistake of choosing your 'best' photograph and sending it to all the newspapers. Even if all of the daily newspapers are covering the same story, each will look for a different photograph. The photo may be only slightly different — but you will seldom see exactly the same shot in two or more newspapers.

Sunday newspapers are seldom interested in events that happened early in the week. These would already have achieved coverage in the daily papers.

Remember too that it is sometimes worth considering offering an exclusive photograph — for example, to a business supplement of one of the daily papers.

Finally, newspaper journalists and photographers are members of trade unions (in Ireland it is the NUJ — National Union of Journalists). If you are submitting photographs to national media, be sure to use an accredited photographer who is a fellow union member. You too, as a PR practitioner, should be a member of the same union.[1]

The union rule applies to national newspapers. You can use a non-union photographer for all kinds of other shots — slide presentations, corporate brochures, company newsletters, etc.

WORKING WITH PHOTOGRAPHERS

Selecting the Photographer

Different photographers handle different styles of photo. There are great portrait photographers, food photographers, fashion photographers, and PR photographers. As with every industry, there are also some bad ones. When selecting a photographer for the first time, ask colleagues to advise you about photographers they have used in the past, and whether or not they would recommend them again. Alternatively, the NUJ is always happy to provide a copy of its list of accredited freelance photographers. Ask to see a portfolio of work before retaining a photographer. There are many who are 'willing' to handle PR work, but you do not want to be their first 'guinea pig'. PR photography, especially media photography, is very different from product shots or wedding photography. Photographers' portfolios will show you whether or not they have done this type of work before, and they will also indicate the level of creativity they bring to their photos.

Matching Personality Types

Match the personality of the photographer to the subject. This is of critical importance. Few people, with the exception of the phenomenally famous, really feel comfortable in front of a camera. It helps enormously if the photographer's style matches the style of the subject, as the following two examples illustrate.

We sent a photographer to the home of a well-known female celebrity to take photos for us, with our client, early one morning. We booked and briefed the photographer who, with the benefit of hindsight, was too young and too stressed. When client and photographer arrived, they found a typically busy early-morning family home — children getting ready for school; organised chaos! My client had the good sense to position himself in the kitchen, where he drank tea and stayed out of harm's way until all had departed the home. The photographer, on the other hand, paced constantly, and continually reminded the celebrity that she was late for the photo shoot. By the time the photos were taken — about fifteen minutes later than planned — our celebrity was aggravated and stressed. A personality clash resulted in 'nice' photographs which could have been 'great'.

On the positive side, we also handled a photo shoot with three businessmen who were announcing a major development in the capital city. The three had flown into Dublin from around the globe, and were on a tight schedule. In the event, we had exactly 45 minutes in which to take the photographs, after the business of the meeting had concluded. The photographer got lost (these things happen) and arrived with five minutes of the allotted time left. I explained that there was little point in going into the room as it contained three men, with high stress levels, who were not used to being kept waiting. A relaxed shot would be almost impossible to achieve. The photographer went through the door and instantly began to advise them to tuck in their tummies, or straighten their ties, or look to the right because it was a better profile. Within seconds, he had them relaxed — a personality match that resulted in good photography.

Briefing the Photographer

There are hundreds of good photographers who can fulfil any brief you give them — but you must give them the brief. No photographer can be expected to guess what you are looking for. So, how do you brief a photographer?

Create the Photo

It is your job to achieve the coverage — that, after all, is the purpose of a photo call. It is, therefore, well worth your while spending time in advance with the photographer creating the shots. You will have only one opportunity to capture the visuals you need.

Book the Photographer Early

If you are organising a press reception, you should book your photographer when you are booking the venue. Give the photographer as much notice of the function as possible. An early booking ensures that you get the person you want on that particular day.

It is important that you give the photographer an opportunity to think about the function long before it happens. A photographer will often come up with great ideas about props that could be used to make the picture more interesting. However, very few people are creative under pressure. You are not doing justice to yourself, your client, or your photographer if you do not give sufficient notice.

Brief the Photographer about the Client and the Function

The photographer should know who your client is (i.e. what company you are working for). You should tell the photographer who the important people in the company are and give a brief description (e.g. 'The finance director must be included in some photographs. He's a small, stocky man with grey hair and a bushy beard'). You should also warn the photographer about other company members or guests attending the function who have a tendency to step into photographs because they believe they are important!

Tell the photographer what the purpose of the function is: e.g. the chief executive is making a presentation to the foreman who is retiring after 50 years' service, or the company is introducing a new range of frozen food. The photographer should know what to expect: the presentation is a small piece of crystal which might be difficult to photograph, or you intend to have six chefs cooking the frozen foods, so there will be plenty of high white hats and steam.

Recce

Visit the location in advance and take note of all of the positive and negative features of the venue. This is known as a 'recce'. 'Recce' is short for reconnaissance or reconnoitre — a preliminary survey of the location.

Location

Brief the photographer about the location, giving as much information as you possibly can. Let the photographer know of any possible problems because of the location (e.g. low ceilings or lack of natural light). Point out the photographic features (e.g. the waterfall feature in the gardens or the old-fashioned love-seat in the reception area). If you have doubts about the location, ask the photographer to visit it in advance and advise you where the best shots could be taken. If possible, accompany the photographer on this recce as you will have a better understanding of the 'logistics' of moving people from one end of the hotel to another for a photograph.

Always take account of the Irish weather. Regardless of the forecast, plan for disaster and hope that it doesn't happen. If you are photographing outdoors, you need a good location bathed in sunlight. If the weather is bad, you might photograph outdoors, but the shot might be of two people battling against the elements as they arrive at the meeting. More often, bad weather, or the threat of it, means that you should have an alternative indoor location on standby. This also needs to be arranged in advance.

Coverage

You need to tell the photographer where you expect the photographs to be used. The photographer should be thinking about possible shots for different media, so provide a full list of media in which you hope to achieve coverage, even if the event is a photo call. It is easier to remove a newspaper from the list (because a staff photographer has been sent) than it is to add one at the last minute.

In addition to the national media shots, you might need local media also. For these shots, you will need to incorporate different groups of people, and the photographer will need to know how many groups, for which media, and at what times the photographs will be taken.

Don't forget the in-house magazine. This will require a different style of photograph altogether. The photographer will need to use staff in the photos. The photos will also be more relaxed in style, showing staff chatting over a cup of tea or relaxing in the gardens during the lunch-break. The list of possible uses of the photographs is, as we have seen, virtually endless.

If the brief extends to a number of different styles of photography, and particularly if there is not a lot of time available to you, you might be wiser to book two photographers — one to look after the national media shots, and possibly the annual report; another to look after local media and in-house publications. The results will almost always justify the additional cost involved, and will add to the smooth running of the event.

Be mindful also that if you require different outcomes, a mix of photos, or slides and transparencies, for example, you might also need two photographers to cater to the different lighting requirements.

Colour or Black and White?

This is less of an issue now than it was some years ago. Until about 1997 all media photography was done in black and white. This was primarily because newspapers used photos in black and white in their publications. However, between 1997 and 1999, the number of colour photographs appearing in newspapers increased and, thanks to better technology, colour photographs can be stripped of colour and used as black and white. By 2000, virtually all photos were being taken in colour. All national print media will now accept colour photographs and reserve the right to use them either in colour or in black and white.

Contact Sheets

Very often, you will ask the photographer to send you contacts or contact sheets. These are 10"x8" (the same size as the photographs you will eventually order) and contain miniature versions of the photographs that have been taken at your function. Many one-hour photographic services (which look after your holiday photographs) produce a contact sheet with your negatives and photographs.

The contact sheets are always marked with a reference number, which will probably include the year (e.g. 1511-2005). Each photograph on the contact will be numbered for ease of ordering.

It should be noted that when selecting from the contacts, you should never do so with the naked eye. Always use a magnifying glass to make sure that everyone's eyes are open!

Lastly, you should always have a set of contacts on file, whether you are in-house or consultancy.

Copyright

Until 2000, copyright (ownership) of photographs belonged to the person commissioning the photography — usually the public relations professional on behalf of the client. With the introduction of the Copyright and Related Rights Act, 1999, copyright of photographic images transferred to the photographer.

Timescale

The photographer will also need to know how quickly you need contact sheets, prints or images sent by ISDN. You need to tell photographers this when you book them because it will impact on the other jobs they are doing that day. If you book a photographer for a function from 11 a.m. to 12.30 p.m., and you need contact sheets by 2 p.m. the same day, the photographer may need to leave the time free to get back to base and develop them for you. This is particularly true of the smaller one-person agencies which operate outside the major urban centres.

In urban areas, in most cases, you will be dealing with photography companies. These will charge an additional fee for a 'fast turnaround' of photographs, but you are really paying their administration costs. The photographer will leave your job and travel to the next assignment. Your film will return to base on a courier's bike!

Arrival

You should ask your photographer to check in with you on arrival at the function. This will allow you to give an update on any changes (e.g. chief executive is sick, managing director is deputising). You also have a chance to brief on which newspapers have sent photographers — your photographer won't want to take the same shots as they do, and they can be taken off the list of media to issue to.

Photographers should be given the time and space to do their job. You should move around with photographers, but don't fuss over them or get in their way. They have been fully briefed — let them respond to that brief.

Protect your Clients

With photography you are projecting the visual image not only of the organisation, but of the individual as well. Protect your clients when they are in front of the lens and don't let them do anything which would look foolish (even for a national newspaper photographer). Try, if you can, to prevent unflattering photos being taken — ensure that clients' ties are straight, their hair is combed, their tummies are tucked in, and their shoulders are back. Check their jackets for signs of dandruff — believe me, they will not mind, they will appreciate it. Remind someone wearing glasses that they should be removed (if they do not like to be photographed wearing them). Act as a minder for people's handbags, briefcases, wine glasses, cigarettes and cigars. Do not allow people to 'hide' things behind their backs. They are never 'hidden' in the finished photo. Wine glasses behind your back distort the shape of your shoulders. Cigarettes give the impression that you have a small fire burning at the back of your jacket. Handbags cut the look of the shoulder of a jacket.

Also watch your clients when they are seated. A woman at a top table, in a short skirt, will appreciate a nod that her legs should be uncrossed. A man sitting in relaxed pose will appreciate it if he catches your eye and you are visibly tucking in your tummy. He'll get the message instantly.

You cannot prevent every unflattering photograph, but you should do your best. These people are, after all, your clients.

Dispatch

The photographer will be sending you either contacts or prints that afternoon. Some will give you a password/code and post your contact sheets on their website. You make your selection from the contacts and, by telephone or e-mail, order the photographs you need.

If time is short, you may prefer to ask the photographer to select pictures and send them directly to the relevant media. You may have to write the caption and e-mail it to the photographer who can forward it with the shots. Later, the photographer can send you a note of the references, and a list of papers to which the pictures were issued.

The growth in use of ISDN lines, particularly in the past few years, has meant that newspapers can now receive images, computer-to-computer, directly from the photographer. Some smaller magazines and local media still use actual photographs — but this practice will probably disappear in the near future.

THE PHOTO CAPTION

Gathering Caption Material

It will be necessary for the photographer, the photographer's assistant, or you to gather caption information as the photos are being taken. You need a list of the order in which photographs were taken, and the people who appeared in them, listed always from left to right.

Be sure that you check the correct spelling of people's names, why they are at the function (e.g. addressed the conference or attending the conference), what part of the country they are from, or which county they are from (it gives you potential additional uses for the photograph afterwards), which company they are representing (if any) and what position they hold within the company.

Try to gather as much information as possible so that the captions you issue are correct.

Captioning

When issuing the pictures you should always caption them.

If you are sending a photograph physically, the caption should be typed on a plain piece of paper and attached to the back of the picture, using two pieces of sellotape, one on either side. Never write on the back of a photograph as the pen mark may show through on the front. Never use a sticker. The idea of applying a piece of paper with sellotape is that it is easily removed. Picture editors do not enter captions in newspapers — this is the job of a sub-editor.

Be careful of paper clips and staples — they can destroy a photograph. If you are sending the picture with a press release, do not attach it with a paper clip. If the release is two pages long and stapled together, put the picture on top of the release (so that the staple can't damage it).

Always issue pictures in a picture envelope — soft top, hard cardboard back. This prevents the courier from bending the envelope inadvertently and tells the receiver that there is a picture enclosed.

A photographer who is sending the photograph by ISDN should have been given the caption in advance (by you) to send with the image.

Writing the Photo Caption

The caption should give a brief description of what happened on the day, and name the people from left to right (L–R), unless the photo involves a celebrity or a large group of people.

Give the picture a title, then list beneath from left to right who is in the picture. Add a brief description of what was happening and always give your name and phone number for further details, as in the following example:

> At the launch of the 2004 edition of Eurofood yesterday (2.2.2004) were (L–R): Mr Pat Brophy, managing director of Katering Inc., national distributors of the directory, Pierre Gourmet, chef at Le Petit Pan Restaurant, and the Minister with special responsibility for Consumer Awareness, Ms Mary Malone TD.
>
> Further details: name
>
>   phone numbers (work and mobile)

A celebrity in the photo would usually be named first. For example, in a shot containing four people (all unknowns) you would caption '(L–R): Mr Joe Murphy, Ms Joanne Keogh, Ms Jeanette Lindsay and Mr Brian Maguire'. If there is a celebrity in the shot, the caption would read: 'Gabrielle with three of her biggest fans, (L–R) Joe Murphy, Joanne Keogh, and Jeanette Lindsay.'

If the photograph is a group shot — a conferring ceremony, a newly elected committee, or a choral group, for example — you would simply caption the photo with the name of the group and not list each of the individuals in the shot.

The caption should always include a date in brackets, and should give your name and phone numbers as a reference point.

Some photographers like to stamp their shots with 'not to be reproduced without permission'. Personally, I find this practice confusing. The PR consultant, on behalf of the client, has bought the shot and issued it to the media. The company wants it to be used, and permission is implicitly given by submitting it free of charge to the media. The note about reproduction may be very relevant for future or additional use of the photograph. I believe, however, that photographers need to find a different form of wording which clarifies that immediate use, in conjunction with a press release or caption, does not require permission.

COST OF PHOTOGRAPHERS

A photographer will usually charge an hourly fee for attending your function. You will be liable for travelling expenses in addition. Photographers will generally charge half the hourly fee plus mileage for their time travelling to and from the function.

Most photographers will charge double the hourly rate if you need the contact sheets in a hurry — which is usual with media functions.

You will be charged separately for each of the contact sheets and every photograph you order. In addition, you may also be charged a fee for each roll of film used.

Finally, the cost of 'paper' photographs (which will be issued by courier) is approximately 60 per cent of the cost of sending the image by ISDN. The technological option is more costly, but it is also much quicker. Costs of ISDN images will decline proportionately in the coming years.

EDUCATE YOUR CLIENT

Clients often believe that their 'celebrity guest' will be the focus of photographs. This is not always the case. The person may have had too much media exposure recently, or may be unknown outside an elite group of people, or may have been extensively covered on the political pages. It is your job to advise the client about the type of photography that you believe will achieve coverage. It is also your responsibility to advise the client of the likely coverage achievable.

BRIEFING MEDIA PHOTOGRAPHERS

At the photo call, you are keeping an eye not only on your own photographer, but also on the media photographers who attend. After all, you have invited them — you want to be sure that they get the pictures they want. It is your job to link with them on arrival and make sure that they get that picture.

You are also watching the people they use in their shots, and the angles at which they are taken. This can be important, for example, if another newspaper photographer arrives late to the photo call. You will often be asked which other newspapers have attended and what shots have been taken. As a professional, you should be able to brief them fully. You should also be able to offer them alternative angles.

REFERENCES

1. Public Relations practitioners are eligible for membership of the Publications and Public Relations branch (known as P&PR) of the NUJ.

CHAPTER 7

Print, Video and Internet

INFORMATION OVERLOAD

The average person probably reads a daily and evening paper, a regional paper once a week, at least one or two Sunday newspapers, magazines which are relevant to their employment, special-interest magazines, and a variety of newsletters. The same person watches a broad range of television stations, listens to local and national radio, and surfs the net (at work and at home).

In addition, that person might work, run a home, mind elderly parents or children, hold dinner parties, go to the cinema, theatre or pub, compete in or watch sporting events, read books for leisure, undertake courses of study, garden, cook or do DIY. The average person writes letters, sends and receives e-mails and text messages, and makes and receives telephone calls.

As a PR person, your message is competing with every other form of information and entertainment available to an individual. To have impact, it must be targeted and relevant — hence the need for specially created PR literature and media. These include: creating various types of printed literature, videos, CD ROMs, slide and overhead presentations, audio tapes, films, and commissioned programmes for broadcast.

All have value, and all have their place in a full public relations programme. For the purposes of this chapter, we will look at them in three separate sections: Created Print Material, The PR Video and Internet.

It is becoming increasingly difficult to catch and hold people's attention. The reason you create media is so that you can target a message directly to the publics, with information they will want to receive. You have total control over the content, the mailing list and the delivery method. Before we look at PR print, we should first distinguish it from direct mail.

Growth of Direct Mail

Huge growth in direct mail and direct marketing/selling over the years has created an industry in itself. There are companies that compile, edit and update mailing lists which can be purchased for use (e.g. Kompass).

There are also companies that sell their mailing lists to others. You have often completed a form and seen a box at the end which asks if you wish to receive other 'related' information (or worse, asks you to tick if you do not wish to receive this information). These lists are sold to companies who are looking for databases made up of people like you — who buy concert tickets, or attend the theatre, or subscribe to charity or purchase books on the net.

Direct Marketing companies use these lists and others to design a letter, brochure or 'gimmick' to send to the target market with a strong, persuasive selling message.

Everyone has received direct marketing/selling messages at some stage. The most obvious and widespread are those which arrive in an envelope with a message saying something like, 'This envelope contains your key to a $1 million fund' or 'You have been specially chosen to receive a prize' or 'Important information. The contents of this envelope could change your life forever'. This is unsolicited direct mail. Your name has appeared on a list somewhere and you will receive these offers forever!

Direct marketing people believe that they have about 30 seconds in which to grab your attention. After that, you bin the letter.

There is a backlash against this form of direct selling. People object to being inundated with what is commonly called 'junk mail', and there are environmental implications — a huge waste of paper is involved. There are moves in certain EU states to allow you to refuse unsolicited mail.

With public relations, direct mail is intended not to sell but to tell. The object of the exercise is to keep a particular target public informed of developments and not, as with direct marketing, to encourage them to buy something.

CREATED PRINT MATERIAL

We will begin by asking the crucial question — why print? PR is about communications. It is about seeking to influence attitudes. It is about using all of the tools at your disposal to reach your key publics. One of the tools available to you is printed material.

So why do PR people create printed items? What is the big attraction of print?

Message Control

One of the biggest advantages of creating your own printed message is that you have total control over the content. You decide what information is contained within the printed item. You control the tone of the message which, in turn, affects the way in which the message is received by your public. You control the look of the message: the use of colour, the selection of photographs, even the type of paper.

Printed PR material gives you message control which cannot be achieved with a press release. A journalist receiving a press release may choose to use it, discard it, or write the story in a different tone or from a different angle from the one you proposed. You do not have control over the final printed message as it appears in a newspaper. With PR literature, you do.

Print Endorses Company Profile

Well-executed printed items undoubtedly endorse your company profile. A printed brochure can tell you much about the company, its mission statement, its staff, its attitudes, its policies and products. The very fact of producing a print item makes a statement about your company, its quality, its professionalism.

There is also a certain status attached to printed items. You would be reluctant to deal with a company that had absolutely nothing about itself in print, wouldn't you? You would see it as somewhat strange. If people are not prepared to commit to paper any information about themselves, why should you commit to them as an employee or a customer?

Finally, print has a permanence about it. The printed item is inclined to have a long shelf-life. It is a permanent record of your company's achievements and policies, and a historical record of changes in the company over the years.

Need for Written Information

There is undoubtedly a need for written information. People believe that what they read is true — after all, companies would not commit a lie to paper. Print gives the company an opportunity to provide a detailed level of information which might not be possible in another medium. The 'story' might achieve media coverage, but not in the same depth. Printing your own literature gives you just that opportunity.

Printed items can also be used as a resource by media. If you are briefing a journalist about developments within your company, it can be very useful indeed to be able to provide printed information about the organisation. This acts as background, briefing material from which the journalist can source additional information.

Finally, despite all of the other media available to people, and all of the other tools available to you as a PR person, it can be extremely difficult — impossible, in fact — to reach everyone face-to-face. Print overcomes that gap and allows you to reach large numbers of people in one fell swoop, with the same information, in the same detail, on the same day. There is a lot to be said for that.

Danger of Overdependence

Print acts as a security valve which gives the PR person control, but it can also act as a barrier to communication. The disadvantage of creating your own material is that you may become too reliant on it. Be conscious that if you become overdependent on print, you may lose touch with the very people you are trying to reach. Print gives you control, but media coverage gives you endorsement.

If you are introducing a new service, a printed brochure might be distributed to customers at a special event. The same print item might also be used as information for media at a press conference and photo call.

Remember always that print is just one of the tools in the armoury of the PR person; it should never be used as a substitute for the others but is a great way of enhancing messages received through other channels.

When to Print

You should consider producing a print item when you are introducing a new concept or product (you can explain its benefits in detail). Print can explain, for example, the end-of-year profit figures or the outcome of a crisis (how it happened and the new measures you have introduced in the meantime). You can obviously print only when you have money in your budget — print is expensive. And you can print only when you have a specific outlet, such as an exhibition, a series of school visits or a mailing list of potential recipients.

Types of PR Print

Some of the broad range of print items for which you will be responsible include:

- Letterheads, compliments slips, business cards
- Annual reports
- Posters and wall charts
- Calendars
- Invitation cards
- Leaflets and booklets
- Instruction cards
- Video print inserts
- Press kits
- Questionnaires
- Diaries/clocks/promotional material
- Information for schools
- Souvenirs/mementos
- Anniversary print (e.g. tenth year in business)
- Induction material
- Information brochures
- Competition literature
- Education packs
- Newsletters.

Print Management

Regardless of the print item you are producing, there are certain factors which are common to all, and a certain procedure which should always be followed.

Put a Team Together

You can begin to put a team together only when you clearly know what it is you want to print. You need to know who the public is, how many copies of the print item will be needed, how it will be distributed, and what key messages it should contain. When you have reached this stage, you can begin to assemble the team for the job.

Selection and Briefing

- *Designer.* You will need to select a designer — someone who has worked with print material before (and ideally has worked with you); someone who has designed for this particular public in the past, be it shareholders or transition year students; someone who can show you a portfolio of their work. You then need to brief the designer about the impression you are trying to create through this item of print. What overall 'feel' are you trying to create? Up-market, fun and adventure, or seriously academic? You do not need to produce a mock-up of what you are looking for. You are not a designer after all, and you have gone to the trouble of retaining someone who has this particular skill. Give the designer the outline of what you are looking for and then leave them to do the job — let their creative juices flow! Finally, check whether or not you will need graphs or cartoons and whether this is your responsibility or the designer's.
- *Printer.* Like designers, there are horses for courses. Some printers are very good at producing single-colour or spot-colour jobs, but not well skilled at producing high-quality, glossy, full-colour print. Check the portfolio of their work and write a very detailed brief. Your brief should include type and weight of paper, use of colour, pantone references (especially for the corporate logo), format in which the print item will be sent to the printer, quantity required, deadline for delivery and type of finishing (e.g. stapled or wire bound). The printer will quote you for everything you include in the brief. A printer is under no obligation to tell you that you have forgotten to include something that will attract an additional charge, so make your brief as thorough as is possible.
- *Copywriter.* Select someone to write the text. It might be the case that you will write it yourself. More often, you have too many other things to look after so you will retain a copywriter. You need to look at a portfolio of their work. They might write brilliantly for shareholders but be incapable of writing for 15-year-old schoolchildren. You need to brief the copywriter about the number of words you require and whether you are paying by word or by finished article. You need to discuss the deadline by which you require the text. You will also need to brief them about the purpose of the printed item, the amount of background information you can make available to them, the opportunities they have to speak with people in the organisation, or the need for an interview with the chief executive. Copywriting tends to be one of the smaller costs, overall, in a print job.
- *Photographer.* Particularly if photographs are being specially taken for the production, the photographer needs to understand the print item so that they know where the photograph will fit within the production and what impression

you are trying to achieve by using photographs. You need to detail availability of people/locations for photography, deadline, format in which you wish to receive the finished product, and whether or not this differs from the format in which the photos are to be sent to the printer.

Quotations

Each of the team members will need to give you quotations for the job. Check that the quotations actually meet the specification you outlined in the brief, and make sure that you are getting value for money.

Copy

When the copy is returned from the copywriter, check that it is what you were looking for. Ensure that it contains no jargon, is easy to read, and creates the right impression. If necessary, have the copy approved by senior management. Only when you are satisfied with the 'final' version should it go to the designer for inclusion in the print item.

Proofreading

When the final version of the print item has been sent to you by the designer/copy-writer, you need to proof it carefully. Spelling mistakes detract from any print item and reflect badly on your company. You have gone to a lot of time, trouble and expense to organise this item — don't let the small details ruin the production. You might also ask someone who is not closely involved if they would read the text for you. If they are not familiar with it, they may notice errors which you might not.

Allow plenty of time to proof the text. 'Typos' or errors in print make any publication look unprofessional. You should proof text three times:

1. *Syllable by syllable.* To make sure that you are actually reading the print and not what you expected to read;
2. *Layout.* Check that quotation marks have an opening and a closing; that apostrophes are in the right place; that all of the paragraphs are indented; that there is the same space between each paragraph, etc;
3. *Sense.* Finally, read each article from beginning to end to be certain that it makes sense (paragraphs are often omitted in the rush to typeset your text).

Realistically, no one risks a single proofing for spelling errors. Many PR people retain professional proofreaders to do the first proof, and read it again themselves before final sign-off.

You also need to check the layout, especially the point size of the text. If there is too much text, and the point size is reduced to 10 or lower, you will discourage readers rather than encourage them. The smaller the text, the more likely the reader is to leave it to one side to be read later.

Check photograph insertions against position and caption. Make sure that the right photographs actually appear in the right place, and read the captions carefully to make sure that the left-to-right caption really does reflect what the reader sees (i.e. that Mr Murphy is the first person on the left and not the last person on the right).

Finally, be totally paranoid about numbers. The loss of one digit can completely alter the message you are trying to convey. A winning prize fund of €250 isn't very appealing, particularly if it was supposed to be €2,500! Similarly, wrong figures for profits earned, or cost of product, or numbers of people who took voluntary redundancy, can completely change the sense of the message.

Quantity

Usually the designer will liaise with the printer for you and issue the instruction to go to print when the job is ready. Watch the quantity that you print. Printers are inclined to tell you, quite rightly, that you could run another 500–1,000 copies for the same price, or slightly more. It looks like good value. It is not. You should know exactly who this print run is intended for, and precisely how many copies you will be distributing. You will print some spare copies (max 10 per cent) but print does not store well. It becomes dog-eared (curly at the edges). It fades in sections depending on the way in which it was stacked and the amount of light getting at it. Print also dates quickly. Information that is correct in January 2004 will probably be out of date or subject to revision in January 2005. The chief executive who was pictured in the brochure may not be working with you in three months' time. Your office interiors may look completely different by summer of the same year because of the need to refurbish completely after a fire. Do not overprint. Print what you need and no more. Print is usually your biggest cost in the budget.

Circulation

You should know clearly how you propose to distribute the printed information. If the distribution is by post, the weight of the printed item is important for postal rates. You also need to determine who exactly is responsible for postage. Can it be handled from your own offices? Are there enough people with enough time (to produce mailing labels and fill the envelopes) and ensure that they are all posted on the same day? Should you sub-contract another group to handle the mailing for you? Should the postal items be sent for shrink-wrapping (in plastic) and mailed by a third party? If the print is to be distributed to branches, have the van drivers been notified? Will there be space on the day? If going to an exhibition, who will deliver? What are the delivery times allowed by the exhibition organisers? If the print item is a poster, you will need to roll it and post it in cardboard tubes. Is there an adequate supply?

You should always work to the rule that print is distributed within 24–48 hours of receipt. Otherwise, you set the wrong deadline for the printer! Get it out of the office and into the hands of your public as quickly as possible.

Budget Control

At all times, monitor costs to ensure that the job is coming in within budget. Agree, in writing, any cost over-runs or additional charges (these will occur, for example, if you change the copy after the text has been sent to the printer or if you needed additional photography). You began by estimating an overall cost of print, so that you could establish the cost per recipient. You should monitor carefully throughout the process to make sure that the costs still make the concept financially viable.

Corporate Identity

Finally, companies produce a very broad range of print, targeted to a variety of different publics. The look, size, shape and colours of print material will all differ one from another, but all should enhance the corporate identity of the company. The recipient should know, simply by looking at the print item, that it came from your company. This might be done by font type on the front of each brochure, or by the inclusion of the corporate logo on the bottom right-hand corner of the front page. There are numerous ways in which it could be done. The corporate identity, however, should always be retained.

The management of print is an essential element of public relations practice. From the initial brief to delivery of the printed item, you will manage the concept, the team, the budget, the delivery and the feedback.

The above gives you a broad outline of each of the factors involved in organising a print job. We will now look at one particular print item — the newsletter.

Newsletters

Newsletters are an increasingly popular way of keeping in contact with customers and staff. The pace of modern living can make good communications difficult to achieve and sustain. A newsletter allows you to create a regular flow of information to and from your target audience. (See sample newsletters on the next page.)

Introducing a newsletter requires decisions about:
- Readership
- Frequency
- Title
- Cover price
- Distribution
- Advertisements

Docklands News Issue 8 – May 2001; Issue 9 – August 2001; Issue 10 – November 2001.

- Contributors
- Response mechanism
- Production.

Readership

The first step to take when deciding to introduce a newsletter is to define clearly who your readers will be. Who is your target audience? Remember the rule about publics *v.* general public. Of course it is only natural that you would want everyone in the world to receive your newsletter. But newsletters are time-consuming and expensive to produce — so, back to the real world.

The decision about your readership helps to determine both the content and the style of your newsletter. If the newsletter is intended for staff only, it should contain information about other staff members — for example, who got married, had a baby, retired or won the golf outing.

A customer newsletter, on the other hand, would deal with new products launched, future seminars, or special 'end-of-line' bargains. A newsletter for customers differs from a staff newsletter in that it satisfies different needs.

Your company might be a high-tech manufacturer in the engineering field which wants to send its newsletter to engineers, professors of engineering and college students. If this is your audience, you need to give detailed technical information about your products, and the research and development that went into producing them. Your customers will also have an interest in your products, but they will want to know about the benefits and uses of the product, not the metal/alloy content.

Your readers might be salespeople or retailers, in which case they will need information that makes it easier for them to sell. They will need to be given statistics on the research you have done (e.g. eight out of ten people who were tested preferred this product to their old one). They will need information on the product cost (e.g. is your product bigger and cheaper than other brands? Or is it smaller but of superior quality?) Salespeople will also need to know about special offers you are planning for the customer, or incentives you are offering to the sales staff. If your audience is made up of salespeople and retailers, perhaps you don't need a newsletter at all — maybe a regular sales bulletin would be more appropriate?

Two things are vital when identifying your readers:

1. Be specific — know exactly who you are targeting
2. Do not try to be all things to all people.

If you try to combine too many publics, your newsletter will not be successful. Each public will receive irrelevant information. To be successful, and to compete with all of the other printed material landing on people's desks, the newsletter must be relevant and targeted. It is sometimes possible, however, to combine your audiences. For example, if you have a small staff, you may well decide to issue the customer newsletter to each employee. It is not an employee newsletter, but your staff will probably take pride in it and enjoy reading it.

Remember that newsletters are read by people who were not on your target public list. There is a natural cross-readership of newsletters. People bring home staff newsletters, or company visitors pick up a copy, or a journalist reads it. Your message, although targeted to one public in particular, must not alienate any other public.

National Irish Bank, and its parent National Australia Bank, advised staff, in an in-house newsletter, about how to deal with difficult customers. A customer who criticised the bank's healthy profits could be told that these were necessary to prevent a takeover by a foreign bank. 'This, said the newsletter, would cause the "assailant" to "slink off, silent and defeated"'.[1] As a customer, I would hate to think that staff thought of me as an 'assailant' to be sent home with my tail between my legs!

Frequency

Before you bring out your first edition, you must decide how often your newsletter will be published. This information should also be given to your readers. You want your readers to anticipate receiving your newsletter in the same way that they anticipate buying the Sunday newspapers, or monthly magazines. It should become a familiar sight and should be as 'regular' as any other publication.

If possible, you should also set a date for receipt. Your readers should know that the newsletter will be with them, for example, on the first Monday of every month, or the last Friday of every quarter.

The frequency of the publication may be determined by your budget. You might like to issue a monthly newsletter, but print and distribution costs might make that option prohibitive.

Remember also that the style in which your articles are written, and the topics you choose, will be determined by the frequency. If your newsletter is published every six months, and your next edition is due in June, you're hardly likely to need photos of the Christmas party or the February golf outing!

Title

The decision about what to call your newsletter is important because the title should remain unchanged for at least three years.

There are many options available to you. You might incorporate a company name. For example, Elton Communications called its newsletter *Elton News*. You might prefer to incorporate a brand name in the title — *Dairygold News* or *Kerrygold News*, for example.

The title might reflect the kind of business you are in. For example, With Taste Banqueting Services calls its newsletter *Banqueting News*. You always have the option of naming the newsletter in a newspaper style — the *Herald Gazette*, for example.

Remember that the title also reflects the content and the frequency of publication. If you call your newsletter the 'xx News', your readers will expect frequent publication. If you call it 'xx Review', your readers will expect to receive the newsletter perhaps twice a year.

Cover Price

In times of recession, companies are always looking for new ways to recover their costs. Charging a cover price is certainly an option. However, while some British companies sell their newsletters, the practice is not common in Ireland.

It is often said that people have greater respect for the thing they bought than the thing they were given for nothing. This may well be true, but you need to consider two questions:

1. Do you want to be one of the few companies in the country charging a cover price for your newsletter?
2. Will people buy it? (If your public is conditioned to receiving newsletters free, it is unlikely that they will pay to receive yours.)

Distribution

Before you issue your first edition, you must also decide how you are going to distribute.

If it is a staff newsletter, and your company has branches throughout the country, you probably have a distribution network already in place. You could distribute in bulk to each of your branches. Each branch could then arrange to leave the newsletter at reception or in the canteen for staff to collect. Both of these options have disadvantages though. The newsletter at reception will be read by visitors to the company (not your target audience); and the newsletter distributed in the canteen will have a very short shelf-life — it will be read over coffee and discarded. You might decide to distribute the newsletter with payslips. It is difficult to determine how successfully this system of distribution works. It would seem that 50 per cent of the companies who distribute in this way find it very successful, while the other 50 per cent find that it doesn't work for them at all!

If your newsletter is intended for existing and retired members of staff, you might prefer to post it to their homes. This would give the family an opportunity to read it, thereby increasing your total readership and broadening the profile of the target audience. If you distribute in work, the newsletter might not be brought home.

A customer newsletter should always be posted. Even if your sales staff call to customers every six weeks, it is unfair to expect one customer — who is the last visit on the list — to receive the newsletter six weeks after other customers.

Be wary of trying to distribute through your accounts system. Because you bill customers monthly, there is a temptation to save on the postage and enclose the newsletter. This system is ineffective for two reasons:

1. You cannot target your reader. If the newsletter is delivered to the accounts department, it may never leave it. The purchasing manager, your real target, may never receive it.
2. Your communication will be enclosed with bills or final demand notices. Do you really want to enclose your newsletter with a bill that has 'now in the hands of our solicitors/debt collection agency' on it?

Advertisements

You need an advertising policy for your newsletter. Will you allow advertisements to be included? If so, will you charge for them? How much space in the newsletter will you sell? Who will you allow to advertise?

If you intend to use the advertisements as a means of recovering some of your costs, then you need to take all of the above decisions in advance of publication. There is no point in reacting to requests as you get them. It is sloppy, inefficient and unprofessional. Design an advertising policy before edition one.

Your policy might be that manufacturers or sellers of complementary products would be allowed to advertise within your newsletter, but competing products would be banned. A bed manufacturer might encourage advertisements from people who produce duvets, sheets, bed-side lamps and furniture.

You might decide that you will allow advertising but not for the purpose of recovering costs. You might advertise new products, for example, or situations vacant within the company. If the newsletter is internal, you might include a 'Buy and Sell' section for staff. At no cost to employees, they could place an advertisement either selling something or looking for something.

Contributors

How are you going to fill the space? You probably will not have the time to write everything yourself. You may not have the time to travel the country (if you have branches nationwide) gathering stories. You might not even have the expertise to write some of the material yourself (if you are writing for a technical newsletter, for example).

You need a planned supply of editorial material, and should be aware of two important requirements:

1. *You need to identify the source.* If your in-house newsletter covers staff activities throughout the country, you need to identify someone in each location who can send you the relevant information. You may need to appoint 'regional correspondents'. Brief them on the length of article you need from them; the style the article should be written in (formal/informal); the type of photographs you will accept. Your regional correspondents also need to know the type of material you will not accept. In theory, it sounds easy; in practice, you may spend a lot of time training your correspondents in writing skills.

2. *You need to determine the format of the newsletter.* Look at any newspaper or magazine. Why do you feel so comfortable with it? Because you know where to find the home news, the foreign news, the women's page and the TV programmes. Every element of the newspaper or magazine is familiar because of consistency of style. The same topics appear on the same pages in every edition. Your newsletter should be exactly the same.

   Determining the format also allows you to decide if you will actually have enough information for each section for each edition. The first edition of a newsletter is always the easiest. You have not brought one out before, so the amount of information available to you is virtually endless. The second and third editions will not be the same. Your information will begin to dry up.

   This is particularly true, for example, if you are introducing a section on 'Our Products'. If the newsletter is new, and published monthly, you may find it very easy to fill this section for the first six months or one year. However, very few organisations introduce a new product each month and, if you discontinue the section, it may create the impression that your company is going into decline!

Response Mechanism

Every newsletter should contain a built-in response mechanism. If you are going to go to all the trouble of writing, producing and distributing a newsletter, you must have a way of finding out whether anyone is reading it.

There are many ways in which you can do this. For example:

- Have a 'Letters to the Editor' page and offer a prize for the best letter
- Include a crossword puzzle in every edition
- Have a children's page with a colouring competition
- Have a caption competition (but not on the back of an article that people will want to keep).

Production

Electronic Newsletters

There is a growing trend to produce newsletters electronically. Some companies produce a combination of both — a hard-copy on paper and an electronic version on the company's intranet system. Others use a 'bulletin board' type of newsletter — a regular up-date system which is e-mailed to staff or customers. And, of course, some companies make the latest edition of their customer newsletter available on their websites.

Production Cost Elements

Each of the different elements of production will affect your cost.

The newsletter size and weight will determine the cost of postage. Heavy paper may push you into a higher postage bracket. Most national postal systems have 'bulk mailing' offers which allow you to send specific quantities at a reduced postage cost, which can result in substantial savings. These bulk offers, however, apply to certain sizes and weights only.

If the newsletter uses a spot colour (e.g. black text with pink headlines), it will be much cheaper than printing in full colour, and you will require only black and white photographs.

The use of colour may be determined by what your competitors are doing. You might want to produce a monthly newsletter in spot colour, and your decision may be perfectly correct, based on the budget available to you. However, if your competitors have a full-colour monthly newsletter, your company might look like the 'junior partner'. In this instance, you might decide instead to produce a full-colour newsletter every three months.

What PR People Say about Newsletters

As professionals, we all know what should be included in newsletters, and the powerful impact they can have on readers. As PR people responsible for their production, our views differ greatly.

Poor Quality

Ifeanyi Mbanefo has studied the quality of in-house journals produced by PR depart-ments in Nigeria. 'Most of the journals — staff magazines, corporate magazines, annual reports...were unexciting and laborious to read,' he said. He did a quick inventory of organisations in major cities in Nigeria that offer quality pre-press (sub-editing, page planning, proofreading, etc) and post-press production facilities. The result, he said, 'was depressing!'[2]

Employee Participation

However, a fellow IPRA member, Ajit Menon, disagrees. His consultancy ran a research-cum-competition for one client to find out what employees wanted to read in their in-house magazine. In all, 1,800 of the 2,500 employees participated. The magazine is produced quarterly in three languages — English, Maraqthi and Tamil. Employees are involved in writing and photography for the publication. The quarterly magazine is so popular that the editors are receiving 'letters of complaint from employees' if some of their submissions are not published.[3]

Cost-Effectiveness

The Egyptian American Bank, with 31 branches nationwide, decided in 1999 to cen-tralise print production internally, and it proved very cost-effective. In the year 2001, the bank saved $3.5 million on print alone. Its publications (e.g. annual reports, newsletters and manuals) are all of a high quality, and most of the writers are external to the organisation (e.g. The Economist Intelligence Unit writes the annual report for the Egypt sector).[4]

Well Read

Northumbrian Water's house newspaper is produced for British staff, and there is also a worldwide newsletter (for 200,000+ employees) produced in several languages, from the head office in Paris. The editor, Alison Tipping, says that she found that although people would grumble periodically about the content, if the magazine (either the British or worldwide version) was issued late for some reason 'the phones would start ringing because people wanted to know where it was.'[5]

Misunderstood

Novartis Pakistan, a pharmaceutical company born of the merger of Ciba and Sandoz, produces an in-house newsletter. In one edition there is news of an award given by the company to one of its officers for 'industrial espionage' (a crime in the US, which can be investigated by the FBI). In all probability, the award was given for gathering information about competitors through contacts within the health community. But, as Zia ul Islam Zuberi says, 'The name of the award is almost self incriminating and shows how newsletters can become counterproductive'.[6]

THE PR VIDEO

It is said that we remember 10 per cent of what we hear, and 20 per cent of what we see, but we remember 60 per cent of what we see and hear simultaneously.

Purpose of PR Videos

Specially created public relations videos have an obvious advantage over print material: they incorporate moving visuals and sound and can, therefore, have a greater impact on the viewer.

PR videos can be created for private or public viewing. One company might produce a video to explain to staff the contents of the annual report. This would be for private use as the audience is limited. Another might produce a video to be shown on national television. This would be for public viewing.

A PR video for national broadcast is produced about a topic in which the broadcaster has an interest. The topic and its treatment are discussed with the broadcasting station in advance of production to establish whether there is an interest in showing the programme. The broadcaster retains the right to accept or reject the video on completion. The object of the exercise is to inform the public about an issue of interest, at no cost of production to the broadcaster, and without being heavily branded by the commissioning company. For example, the video might deal with changes in environmental awareness in Ireland (and deal with a range of issues from the use of coal to pollution of rivers). Although, in this case, the video would probably be commissioned by the relevant government department, the reference to the department would probably appear at the end of the programme. It would not be heavily branded throughout. As the commissioning PR person, you have content control as you would with a printed item.

The uses of PR video are limitless. They can be used:

- To demonstrate a product to distributors or customers
- To show how well the company handled a crisis situation
- To highlight the amount of coverage a launch achieved in media
- To instruct employees about safety equipment and precautions
- To introduce new employees to the company (as induction material)
- To enhance corporate image in presentations to conferences
- To attract potential employees at recruitment fairs
- To explain the company's annual report and balance sheet
- To promote a concept like investing in pensions.

Andec Media gives five examples of the uses to which its videos have been put:

- Staff training pack, comprising video and written resource material, for a large supermarket chain
- Corporate video for a multinational company, based in Limerick, specialising in the manufacture of baby nutritional products

- Video and resource material produced for the Money Advice Bureau, in association with the Department of Social Welfare
- The 'Stay Safe programme', an anti-abuse video, commissioned by the Child Abuse Prevention Unit, in association with the Department of Health
- Instructional video on coaching techniques, commissioned by Gaelic Athletic Association.[7]

Characteristics

PR videos are not sales tools — they should never be used to sell product. Their function is to inform, educate and generate interest.

Videos are a daily part of most people's lives, so it is a medium with which we are all familiar. PR videos must have realism and authenticity. Otherwise, quite simply, they will not be watched. If the video you produce has logos or signage prominently displayed at the back of each shot, the viewer will see it as propaganda and switch off — rightly so, in my opinion.

PR videos must be credible. You must put the same effort into creating a PR video as a film company will put into a Brad Pitt movie. If the video you produce is not well done, is not state of the art, is not credible, then you have succeeded in damaging your company's image instead of enhancing it.

The PR video must also have entertainment value. This is true no matter what the subject. If you look at any of the food programmes on television, you will find them to be filled with personality, little snippets to camera and lively interaction between people. You wouldn't watch them if exactly the same food were cooked in a sterile environment, where the presenter wore a white apron and hat, and spoke about the 'goodness' of eating your green vegetables. PR videos must be as professional as television programmes.

The opening sequence is vital in any video. Like the direct marketing people who have about 30 seconds in which to grab your attention, with video you have a couple of minutes after the opening credits, by which time you have either 'grabbed' the audience or you have lost them. The visual sequence in the opening section must make you believe that the programme will be a good one. The movement and the music are vital.

Video has a shelf-life of two–three years. You will spend a lot of money producing a video and your company should expect to get some years of value from it. If it is to be used for conferences, for example, it is reasonable to expect that the same corporate video could be used for a three-year period.

There are always exceptions to the rule. The training videos made by John Cleese nearly twenty years ago are still in use today. The clothes are dated; the furniture is old-fashioned; even the accessories are wrong. But the key message of the videos, and the way in which Cleese imparted those messages, remains as relevant today as it was when they were first made.

Videos generally run for approximately 27 minutes, so you have a lot of time, as a PR person, to get your message across. It can be easier, on video, to explain complicated issues by using graphs, inserted footage or cartoons. Text can be weighty and slightly boring. Video should always command your attention.

A video should always be made with a specific purpose in mind, and a specific target public. As with everything else you do in public relations, if your public is 'everyone', you will undoubtedly fail.

Remember too that videos can be co-operative ventures. They might involve two politicians from the same political party who want to explain their policies, or two complementary companies (make-up and clothes) who want to share the costs. In each case, they must share the same audience. With joint-ventures, you, as a PR person, will devote a lot of time (with a stop-watch) to ensuring that each gets an equal amount of time on film.

Finally, video productions can also attract awards, reflecting well on your company and the commissioning company, and bringing your message to the attention of a much wider audience.

Production

You will need to select a company to produce the video for you. Look at show-reels and see what the company has already done. Who are the members of the team and could you work with them? Are they creative? Can they produce the finished product within the required timescale?

While the rules for producing video are largely the same as those for producing print, there are some differences of which you should be aware at the briefing stage.

By the time you are ready to brief your production team, you should know clearly what the proposed length of time of the video is. If it is to be shown to a seated audience, probably the maximum time available to you is 30 minutes. If, on the other hand, your audience is standing (at a fair or exhibition) you have approximately 5–7 minutes.

You should know whether you want to use real people or actors. It might be better, if you are showing production processes, for example, that you would use real employees who are familiar with the machinery. Alternatively, no one might be willing to do it, or they might be brilliant at their jobs, but stiff as a board on camera! How many locations will you need to shoot in and how many visits will be needed? You might have branches around the country which you want to include, and timing is vital. You will need to arrange to be there at the appropriate time. Which do you need for the video — a quiet Sunday morning scene or mid-afternoon frantic Saturday shopping? And will you need the presenter in each location — or will you use voice-over? Should the store manager be there? All of these elements, as well as travel and set-up time for the crew, need to be carefully scheduled.

An example of getting the timing wrong is the Fine Gael party political broadcast of 1997 when the then leader, John Bruton TD, was standing on the fly-over of the Stillorgan Dual Carriageway, talking about Dublin being choked with traffic. The words he spoke were powerful, but the video was obviously shot either very early in the morning or mid-afternoon because there was hardly a car in sight. Watching it you thought, if that's his idea of choked with traffic, he should try to travel this dual carriageway at 5.30 in the evening!

Will you use a personality in the video? If so, who will you use and are they available? Or will you use voice-over only? Should the voice be well known or unknown? Will a well-known voice add credibility to the video, or distract the viewer? Should the voice be male or female — which will carry more authority? The general rule is that men's voices have more authority than women's, even when the subject is fashion or make-up. (Tell that to Mary Harney TD, Olivia O'Leary or Miriam O'Callaghan.)

The music you choose is vitally important. Will you use a well-known piece of music — in which case you need to get clearance for its use and pay copyright? Will you specially commission a piece for the video? What does the music add to the visuals — does it create a feeling of excitement, or a laid-back slow, easy-listening feel? It should link with the pace and tempo of the production. You should also check whether you need to pay royalties to the Performing Rights Society (PRS) or the Irish Music Rights Organisation (IMRO).

You need to decide if you should use animation, cartoons, graphics or special effects. Very difficult processes are often explained using animation or cartoon characters. Sellafield Nuclear Power Station uses a lot of special effects in its video presentations at its visitor centre. It helps to explain the splitting of the atom. In 1993, the Japanese Power Reactor and Nuclear Fuel Development Corporation famously used a cartoon character in a video it distributed to counteract negative feelings about nuclear power in general, and plutonium in particular. The cartoon featured 'Pluto Boy', wearing a helmet bearing the letters 'Pu', the chemical symbol for plutonium. In the video, a young boy is encouraged to take a drink of 'safe and drinkable' plutonium.[8] The video was criticised for its inaccuracies by the Nuclear Control Institute, Greenpeace International and US Energy Secretary Hazel O'Leary.[9] The campaign fell apart and the video had to be withdrawn.

Decide whether you will want a foreign distribution for this video. Could it be used by other branches in other countries or by head office? It might require two different voice-overs in different languages. Foreign distribution will also affect the way in which the video is shot. You will try, for example, to minimise interviews to camera because you cannot lip-sync the translation.

Finally, should the video be suitable for broadcast? Broadcast quality is very professional, but it is also very expensive. Unless you are sure that you will need to broadcast the video, or part of it, at some time in the future, you really should not be encouraging your employer/client to incur the additional costs.

Distribution

Your next big decision is how the video will be distributed. You have a key outlet in mind when you are deciding to produce it — let's say, for example, that the video is about the environment and has been produced for broadcast on a national station. Once you have achieved your main objective, you should swing into all of the other opportunities the video presents. You might choose to do one or more of the following:

- Seek to have it shown on local television stations;
- Hold a private screening, in advance of the national broadcast, for an invited audience of key customers or clients;
- Produce an information pack to be given to guests, which gives more information on the topic. This might also be made available to national viewers of the programme by incorporating a Freefone number at the end of the broadcast, and/or by placing an advertisement in *TV Now* and the *RTÉ Guide*, encouraging people to return the coupon and receive a booklet;
- Circularise schools, or place advertisements in educational or technical journals, offering a loan or a free copy of the video to interested parties;
- Arrange for the video to be distributed through one of the chains of video stores, and given as an 'extra' free rental to all customers over a specified period of time. This means that you will also need to produce point-of-sale material for each of the stores;
- Produce a much shorter version of the same video for use on exhibition stands, or to be shown in showrooms or reception areas;
- Distribute the video to journalists as part of a press pack;
- Have it distributed on CD-ROM or DVD;
- Organise a team of people to give talks to local community groups at which the video could be shown;
- Arrange a series of special viewing evenings in each of your branches for staff only — a special night for your employees to see the video in advance of screening.

Thus far, we have concentrated primarily on print and video, but this does not exclude the other tools available to you, such as CD ROMs, DVDs and cassettes, distributed by direct mail. Audio cassettes can be very successful if your target audience is likely to listen while travelling in a car (e.g. salespeople).

Don't forget the impact of a slide presentation, or a PowerPoint presentation (and the many ways in which they can go wrong). Graphics on the walls of exhibition stands, and scale models of buildings and plants also fall within your remit as a PR person.

Your true skill is in combining all of the tools available to you to achieve maximum impact. CD-ROMs allow investors to take an interactive visual tour of a proposed development thousands of miles away in America or Japan. Company websites can combine text, visuals, movement and sound, and often allow visitors to request that they be added to a subscribers' list for exclusive mailings. Other potential tools include 'free-phone numbers such as that of Hamilton Osborne King with an 1850 RING ROAD number for developments along the M50' or, in the case of the sale of the former Gateaux factory in Finglas in the early 1990s the distribution of brochures 'wrapped around a Swiss roll'.[10]

INTERNET

In the first instance, people probably recognised the benefits of e-mail quicker than they recognised the benefits of the net. We will look at e-mail first.

E-Mail

I believe that e-mail is one of the greatest technological inventions ever — I'm putting my bias on record from the start. The ability to respond to people, instantly, and with very short answers, has freed up time massively for busy executives. It also allows you a level of control. We will look at each of the elements in turn.

E-mail is an instant form of communication. Initially companies installed one e-mail address at which people could contact them. This made sense in the initial stages as no one was quite sure how much use the e-mail would get. Very quickly the idea took off and companies found that they needed to introduce systems which would allow all e-mails to be taken in on one ISDN line and distributed to separate e-mail addresses within the system. This meant that each section or each employee received e-mail directly. It was a far superior system. The relevant enquiry landed on the relevant desk. The system is similar to internal distribution of postal mail. The postal mail needs to be distributed by people; the e-mails are distributed electronically.

The efficiencies that this system offered companies were amazing. Think of consultancies, for example — clients could now directly e-mail the account handler with whom they were dealing. Photographers' and video and print quotes could be sent directly to the account director. E-mail also meant instant receipt. Even with internal distribution systems, e-mail will land on someone's desk within an hour. The mails can be 'flagged' so that the sender knows when the mail has arrived on the receiver's desk. This can be both a blessing and a curse.

If we look at e-mail as a time-management control tool, we have to acknowledge that it is wonderful. The control element is that you can look at the mail you have received, decide to leave it until later in the day (in some cases, you may leave things which require thought until the official close of business) and respond to them at a time of your choosing, knowing that the response will arrive instantly. Even if you were not to answer any e-mail until 9 o'clock at night, the answer would still be on the person's desk first thing the following morning. Previously, the only way that you could manage to get a response onto another person's desk by first thing the following morning was to send a fax. At best, the fax was a direct line into the section, so you still needed someone to distribute the fax to the person for whose attention it was marked, or you were hoping that by leaving a phone message for them, they would go to the machine and collect the fax. It was fast but not nearly as fast or efficient as the e-mail system.

Fax messages also need to be composed. They are marked for someone's attention, and begin with, for example: 'Dear Jeanette, Further to our conversation this morning....' With e-mail the system is greatly simplified. A client can send you a mail giving two possible dates for a meeting, and your reply is sent as a 'Reply to sender'. This means that their message appears beneath yours, so you don't need to repeat any of the information contained in it. Your response can be incredibly brief: 'John. Thurs 12th is fine. 3pm. See you then' — job done. You could not do this by fax.

You can take a quarter of an hour in a morning, and answer 15–20 mails. This would be impossible using any other system. You can also choose to answer later in the day — send a mail saying that you will deal with it later — and your response will still be received within a 24-hour period.

As a control tool, it gives you a record of all decisions taken, and on what day and at what time the communication/confirmation/refusal was issued. You have a record of all decisions taken with the client.

Irish governments have recognised that e-mail is a legitimate form of communication and, under the Freedom of Information Act (1997), e-mails are included in all of the information which you are entitled to request from most public bodies.

In the United States, Independent Counsel Kenneth Starr included e-mail messages from Monica Lewinsky as part of his supporting evidence in the presidential investigation. And although Oliver North erased 750 of 758 e-mails regarding the Iran-Contra affair, and National Security Adviser John Poindexter deleted 5,012 of 5,062 e-mails, all of those messages were recovered and used as evidence.[11]

However, there are also dangers within the system, and some of them are dealt with in the following paragraphs.

E-mail, by its nature, is immediate. As mentioned above, you can 'flag' a message so that the sender knows that it has been received. If someone got confirmation that a letter had been delivered by the postal service, or by courier, they would not phone you within 10–30 minutes, looking for an answer. They *will* if the message is sent by e-mail. Because of the immediacy of the delivery, there is a presumption that mails should be answered as they are received, so people get very shirty if they are left waiting for a response. As a way of running a business, this is bad time management — if you answer every mail as it is received, you have given priority status to any information arriving by e-mail, over and above all other forms of communication. This doesn't make sense. A lot of the mails could be dealt with later, and more important calls or meetings could be attended to during the same period.

The idea of flagging mail is presumably primarily intended as a comfort factor for the sender, who is happy to know that the mail has landed. But it also applies additional pressure to the receiver who believes that, as the sender knows that the message was received at 10.05 a.m., the response should issue before 11.00 a.m. Often the response is issued to prevent receipt of a follow-up mail asking if the first has been received. It is a silly pressure to put people under. It is particularly silly if the contents of the e-mail need thought and the sender is looking for advice in return. Something as simple as the time of a meeting can be dealt with in seconds — you either have a slot in your diary or you do not. However, a client mailing to seek advice about a particular situation is approaching you as a consultant for your expertise. The client is entitled to expect a reasoned, professionally thought-through and appropriate response, taking account of all of the implications of the advice you are giving. This simply cannot be done in the space of minutes. It is, however, exactly what clients will expect — and it is the nature of e-mail.

If the same issue were raised at a meeting, most clients would expect you to go away, think about it, do a little research, think through all of the options, and then revert to them. This might not take a lot of time — but you might need an hour or two. It is time which the client would willingly give you at a meeting, but will not give you if the query arrived by e-mail.

The difficulty for consultants is that the medium (e-mail) is squeezing their ability to provide the service to which clients are accustomed. If the service gets faster (and less thorough) the very industry itself will suffer. It is a live issue for PR people and one which has not, at the time of writing, been resolved.

Other, cross-industry, issues also arise with e-mail. How many companies have actually trained their employees in e-mail? How many have an established corporate style of response to e-mail? Think about a physical letter issuing from any organisation — the company will have a particular corporate style to be adopted by mail. There are rules about how far down the page the address should appear, whether titles like Mr/Ms should or should not be used, when people should be referred to formally or informally, etc. However, very few companies have the same rules about e-mail — and they should.

Employees respond to e-mail as they see fit. The nature of e-mail is that it is very informal — you would not begin a mail with 'Dear Mr....' It simply would not be appropriate to this medium. A colleague of mine, a journalist, was giving out one evening about PR people. His complaint was that he had sent a proposal for an electronic newsletter to a PR consultant, who had responded within ten minutes of receiving his mail, with a note rejecting his proposal. He was furious and believed that she could not possibly have had time to study the proposal and reach a decision on it. So he phoned her and outlined his complaint. To his surprise, she agreed, and told him that she had not even opened the attachment containing the proposal. She then proceeded to explain to him that his cover e-mail clearly showed that he was not familiar with e-mail (which he confessed he was not) and she therefore saw no point in opening the attachment as it was written for a medium he knew nothing about. He had to agree. He had asked a colleague to mail it for him. The cover e-mail was written in a formal style: 'Dear Ms Whelan. Attached please find, as requested, my outline proposals for an electronic newsletter....' The consultant was right. No one who was familiar with e-mail would send this note.

Older people within the organisation, and by that I mean probably anyone over 25 years of age, need to be trained in how to respond by e-mail. They are not familiar with the medium. Their training was in formal responses and some of their attempts at informal responses cross that invisible line and become too informal, and therefore unprofessional, when received as a reply.

The difficulty with employees under 25 years of age is that they are familiar with text message, and use the same language in e-mails. This is also an inappropriate use of the medium. To bL8 is perfectly acceptable on a text message. By e-mail you should tell someone that you will be late!

The same difficulties arise for companies. If every employee has e-mail on their desk, is it likely to consume their day? How much of that time will be spent sending mails to friends and colleagues? How much time will be spent sending or forwarding jokes? What jokes are actually being sent by your system? Are they inappropriate or offensive? Could the company be held responsible because, after all, they issue from the company e-mail?

Most large companies have introduced blocking systems which prevent moving pictures getting through as attachments, on the basis that these are usually jokes and not business communication, and many are virus infected. But it is impossible to put a system in place which blocks all jokes — how could they be identified? The issue, which is already causing problems for corporations, will only get bigger in the coming years.

And then there is the net.

The Internet

When companies initially developed a presence on the net, they put up a website because it seemed like everyone else was doing it. As the use of the net increased, so too did the level of investment by companies in their websites. They realised that it was not good enough to put the corporate brochure on the net (it was written for a different medium). So, websites now have specially written text, hyperlinks, video clips, mechanisms for checking the number of 'hits' the site receives, and e-mail addresses for comments. The sites have improved massively and are creating a corporate presence. Most companies, however, are anxious that they are not making money on the web. They are trying to use it as a selling tool.

Whether used for sales or communications, there is a problem with the net. Although companies can track how many people visited their sites, they have no idea who these people are, or what part of the planet they live on, or what exactly they were looking for. They don't know whether they found something of interest, or found the site in error.

With the exception of certain types of companies — *amazon.com* which sells books on the net, *irishacademy.com* which sells education courses on the net — the cost associated with the websites cannot yet be appropriated to one public or section of the public. Until that happens, companies will continue to spend money in 'splurge-gun' fashion — throw money at the web because they should, and hope that it hits someone. This is clearly not a very good commercial strategy.

The internet, however, is massively used by people. They use it to browse, to research, to see what's out there. There are literally millions of people using the net every day — it is a huge, and as yet untapped, market. These people 'live' in a virtual cyberspace. As with the e-mail, their demands are for instant information. They will excoriate a company which has not updated its website in six months. The medium is constantly changing and information on it should be live and current.

Governments have been among the first groups to recognise this. Possibly because the net is used by journalists a lot, governments now put crucial information on websites. When the Northern Ireland Peace Process negotiations culminated in the signing of a document which became known as the 'Good Friday Agreement', the British and Irish governments made websites available which contained the full document. This was of huge benefit to journalists who were not physically present, and it was also of benefit to interested parties, not involved in the media at all, who wanted to study the document.[12]

PR departments too were quick to recognise the power of the net. Many companies have a newsroom section on their website on which they post their press releases. When a release is issued by e-mail or in hard copy, it is also, instantly, posted on the website for open access (or in some cases restricted access by journalists only).

The net has also been enormously beneficial to PR people. It has allowed them access to a vast resource of information which can be used in client pitches, speeches, research, etc.

However, the net also has its downside. There is a lot of information on the net which could, at best, be deemed 'undesirable'. From a company's point of view, how do you monitor net access by employees? How do you know that people are not accessing inappropriate sites during their working day? There are logs which the IT department can check, password systems can be installed and machines can be programmed to shut down as employees leave their desks. But, this type of monitoring is time-consuming, and, really, how do you know that information accessed from a particular computer terminal was accessed by the person who sits at that desk? Could it have been accessed during a coffee or lunch break? Was another terminal down and someone simply swapped desks for a while? And how much time does it take to block access to these sites as they become identified?

Even if you password protect access to the net, how secure is your company's password system? In a lot of companies, passwords are common knowledge. Individuals like to access the net to get information on health issues or forthcoming concerts, and they see the introduction of a password system as management meanness — so everyone knows what the password is!

Intranet

There is also the intranet system, which cannot be accessed from outside the company. This is a system of internal communication by e-mail and website. It is a brilliant invention which, at its simplest, allows someone to forward information from one desk to another without the need to produce paper, make a call, or physically call into someone's office to brief them. The intranet is also used for electronic staff newsletters which can be sent by e-mail, by e-mail attachment, or posted on an internal website.

No research has yet been done on the success or otherwise of this system. My own belief is that electronic newsletters (e-letters or e-zines) are well received and well read in technology companies where the average age of employees is young and where their working day is spent online. For employees who travel a lot, and have internet access on their laptops through their mobiles, e-letters can be a great way of keeping in touch.

They are less successful, in my opinion, in older, longer-established organisations, which have a different age profile of employees. Employees as young as 30 years of age will tell you that they prefer to read from paper, particularly if they are working at a computer screen all day.

Xtranet

This is a controlled-access website, which may be password entered either internally or externally. The Xtranet is used by large international public relations consultancies. This site contains information on every client the company handles, in every country, and all of the details about each individual client. Company staff (depending on the level of access) may view the projects being handled, the agreed budgets, the outcomes achieved, etc.

The Xtranet is also available in a limited way, to clients, who are given their own individual passwords. Clients may, therefore, access their own portion of the site and find out what stage a particular job is at, whether or not invoices have been issued, or where a decision is 'jammed' (i.e. on whose desk it is sitting). They may also access a reference library of all cuttings which relate to them.

REFERENCES

1. *The Irish Times*, 21 August 1999.
2. Ifeanyi Mbanefo, *IPRA Digest*, No. 169, 2001.
3. Ajit Menon, *IPRA Digest*, No. 170, 2001.
4. Ihab Badran, *IPRA Digest*, No. 170, 2001.
5. Alison Tipping, *IPRA Digest*, No. 170, 2001.
6. Zia ul Islam Zuberi, *IPRA Digest*, No. 170, 2001.
7. Andec Media, 19/20 York Road, Dún Laoghaire, Co. Dublin
8. Eric Johnston, 'Monju ruling infuriates plaintiffs', *Japan Times*, 22 March 2000 (posted 27 March 2000), http://216.239.35.100/search?q=cache:8KIG5J1IeIEC:www.puinvestigation. org/english/othersnewsarchives/othersnews03_2000.html+Japanese+Minister+ and+Pluto+Boy&hl=en
9. TED Case Studies, Case No. 38, Japan Plutonium Imports, http://www.american.edu/TED/JAPANPL.HTM
10. Stephen McMahon, 'There's no such think as a free launch in a boom time', *Sunday Business Post*, 23 April 2000.
11. Justin Tyme, 'Think Before You Send: E-mail Security Problems', http://www.ideasandtraining.com/EmailSecurity.html 22.04.02.
12. Hillsborough, Good Friday, 1999.

Section 3
PR Events

CHAPTER 8

Organising Functions

Often, as a public relations practitioner, you will suggest holding a function for clients and media. You are probably trying to achieve two goals:

1. To reach the small but important audience attending the function;
2. To gain media exposure for whatever you are launching at the function.

Achieving both goals in one function makes sense, especially if the people you are inviting to your function are likely to attract media attention by their very presence.

However, whether you suggest the function yourself, or someone else asks you to organise it, bear in mind that a lot of preparation will go into it.

The secret of a successful function is that your guests remember the launch, the ambience, and the other guests they met. The second secret is for the media who attended to feel that they were well looked after, with a minimum of fuss and a maximum of efficiency, and that they got a good press release, interview and photograph.

If your guests and media focused on the purpose of the function — you've won. If they were conscious of things going wrong, or an air of panic or fuss, you did not do your job properly. Things will go wrong at the best-planned and best-executed functions in the world. There will always be factors beyond your control which can impact on the event. However, if you handle it properly, your guests and the media should not be aware of anything being amiss.

As the PR person, you are responsible for every element of planning in advance of the function, every element of its execution on the night, and all of the follow-up afterwards. You should begin planning as soon as possible.

There are numerous PR functions:

- Photo calls (to gain media attention)
- Photo shoots (to bring together key people for publicity shots for brochures)
- Press conferences (usually where media gather to hear a statement from a senior executive and to ask questions)
- Press briefings (often accompanied by lunch afterwards)
- Press receptions (usually evening functions with finger food and wine — mix-and-mingle occasions to generate society or personality shots)
- Annual general meetings (a gathering of shareholders and board to discuss history and future prospects of the company)

As has been stated, if things are handled well, guests and media will not be aware if something is wrong. For example, Elton Communications handled publicity for the opening of a new nightclub in the mid-1990s. For about three days in advance of the opening, we had been unable to gain access to the building because the carpet was being laid, or the painters were in. On the day of the opening, we were confronted with workmen hammering down carpet over pipes laid in trenches in the concrete floor. The lighting system on the dance floor consisted of a central area, out of which wiring cascaded to the ground — not a light in sight. The club was obviously not ready. With about half an hour to go, the function could not be cancelled. There was only one solution — proceed, and welcome guests and media to the 'newest nightclub in Ireland — so new, in fact, that we haven't yet finished building it'. Fortunately, everyone took it in great spirit, the launch went well and it attracted some marvellous publicity. One of the last journalists to leave called me aside and told me that I was one of the gutsiest PR people in Dublin — he couldn't believe that I would take the 'angle' of opening a club which was half built. I couldn't tell him that the 'angle' was never in the plans.

STEP 1: PREPARATION

Venue

Your first task is to select the venue. Where will the function be held? How many people will you be catering for? Will there be a bar? Do you need to keep the bar separate from the reception area? Are you looking for a city-centre location or somewhere slightly more distant? If the venue is in the suburbs, how will people get to it? Will you need to provide transport? What type of venue are you looking for? Will it be indoors or outdoors? Which type of venue is most appropriate to the function you are organising? What type of ambience are you trying to create?

You should make a list of no more than three possible venues, and then contact each, initially to establish that they can make the facilities available to you on the date you need them.

Visit each venue and do a recce. Study the rooms they are proposing to give you. Determine for yourself that there is adequate space for the number of people you are inviting. Is the lighting good? Are there sufficient sockets? Is there access for the disabled? Are there other rooms adjacent that you could spread into in case of emergency?

Check the costings carefully. Clearly establish what is included in the cost and what will attract extra charges. If you need the hotel to arrange extra lighting or microphones, you should state that on your first visit and get a costing.

Finally, confirm everything to the hotel in writing. Very often the hotel will send you a booking form, detailing the services they are providing, the special facilities you requested and the charges to be incurred. You should always check the booking form carefully to make sure that it is accurate in every detail.

Timing

The timing of any function is crucial. It must meet the needs of your guests and suit the deadlines of the media. You must give careful thought to a mid-morning function which could be very suitable if, for example, your guests were retired, but might be disastrous if your guests needed, but were unable, to leave their offices. A breakfast function is increasingly popular if you promise people that they will be away by 9.00 a.m. or 9.15 a.m. at the latest.

Lunch-time functions do not interfere with the working day. They operate on the same principle as a breakfast function — the days of leisurely lunches have long gone.

Evening functions immediately after work are popular, but watch the timing. Business people will not thank you for dragging them out to a function at 8 p.m., but voluntary workers for a charitable organisation might really appreciate it (they won't need to take time off work).

Guest List

This is the rock on which many PR people perish. Your job is to be ruthless. You are holding this function for a purpose — keep that purpose clearly in mind. You know who your target audience is and you know the budgetary allocation. No company nowadays has limitless 'entertainment' budgets. Target your guests professionally.

Do not over-invite. There is nothing more uncomfortable than attending a function that is overcrowded.

Invitations

When your guest list is complete, arrange to have the invitations printed. Study the style of invitation carefully. For some functions, the standard 'You are invited to attend...' is perfectly adequate. For others, you should leave a space for the person's name to be included. How will you include the name? Will you simply laser-print it onto the card (which affects your decision about the weight of the card) or will you employ someone to apply the names in calligraphic script?

Be aware of the impression the actual invitations will create. Do you want the 3-colour company logo to appear on the card? Or would black text on a gilt-edged card be more appropriate?

Finally, put RSVP on the card and give a date by which people must reply. Prepare a list of the names and telephone numbers of everyone you have invited. When the RSVP date passes, begin ringing everyone you have not heard from. Be thorough. Before the evening begins, you should have a very good idea of the numbers attending. It is important to do this for every function, but particularly crucial if you are booking meals for the guests.

Details in Advance

It is important that your guests receive as much information as possible in advance. In February 2002, I attended a conference which had been booked by fax in early December 2001 (the two booking options given were fax or post). The day before the conference I realised, to my horror, that I had received no confirmation. When I telephoned to check if it was still going ahead, I was told that it was, and that all information was contained on the website. This was the first time I had been made aware of the website and I wondered why I could not have registered online. The following morning, I learned that everyone had either phoned or faxed the organisation the previous day. Not one person I spoke with had received any form of communication from the organisation, and many spoke of the frustration of having to make that call and the lack of professionalism of the organisation. The conference itself was well managed and well run, and the supporting documentation was beautifully and expensively produced. The entire talk on the day, however, was of the lack of communication in advance.

Seeking Relevant Permissions

It is important to ensure that anything you are doing has the relevant permission. If you need a building to open early to facilitate a photo shoot, or if you plan to take photographs in Merrion Square in Dublin, or Fitzgerald Park in Cork, you will need to get permission in advance from the relevant authority.

Even if you believe that no permission is necessary, check. Some years ago, I handled a photo shoot. The photo accompanied a feature article about saving money. The client was photographed burning pretend money (i.e. we photocopied £50 notes, as they were at the time, and then had him burn the photocopies). It was a striking photograph which grabbed the attention of the reader. However, the Central Bank contacted the client when the photograph appeared, to say that it was illegal to burn money. When the client explained that we had burned photocopies, the Central Bank explained that it was also illegal to make photocopies of money!

Insurance

If your function is being held in a hotel, for example, insurance will not be an issue. If, on the other hand, you are hiring a boat or plane for a function, you will need to arrange insurance cover. This can be an extremely expensive element and should be carefully costed into your budget in advance.

Props

Remember that it is also important for any function that relevant props arrive and are available for use on time. Props might range from actors/actresses in costume, to a scale-model of the building; from a prototype of a new shoe, to a giant cardboard cut-out. Just think of the media coverage the Irish soccer team attracted when the players reached Saipan (World Cup, 2002) and there were no footballs!

Supporting Documentation

It is equally important that you ensure that any supporting documentation is delivered on time and has been checked before it is distributed to your guests. Decide whether documentation will be given to people on arrival or on departure. It is usually given on arrival if there is to be a long presentation which involves graphs, figures and statistics. Having the printed matter in front of you would ease your understanding.

Documentation is generally given on departure if the function involves a reception of any kind. It is more difficult for your guests to balance canapés and wine while also carrying bulky information packs.

Goody Bags

Many organisations give their guests 'goody bags' on departure. Particularly if you have launched a new product, it is a nice idea to send your guest home with a sample. The gift might also be chocolates, a toweling bath robe, or a branded travel clock.

Celebrity Participation

Would the function benefit from the presence of a celebrity? It might be that you should retain one of the RTÉ political or business correspondents to chair a meeting. It can add a certain weight and gravitas to the event. Or perhaps you should retain the comedian, Brendan O'Carroll, to perform the official opening because it will make the function a memorable one for your guests? Or you could have a guest speaker at the evening dinner — Mick McCarthy (Captain Fantastic), for example. The word 'celebrity' is used broadly here to incorporate anyone who is well known — whether they are drawn from the worlds of politics, arts, business, sport or modelling does not matter.

There are celebrity-speaker agencies and bureaus from which celebrities can be hired. Remember to make the celebrity relevant to the audience — there is no point in having Mick McCarthy address a group of people who have no interest in soccer. Similarly, in the world of music, the Bee Gees might appeal to the over-40s, but would be a piece of living history to under-25-year olds!

Dry Run

If you are using a new act or group, make sure that you have seen them perform. We handled a function some years ago in which a special performance was given for an open-air, mainly young audience. The performance had been seen by a member of staff. It was very manic and very comic — at one stage of the performance, a can of beans was split open using an electric cutting saw for steel. On the day, the chief executive expressed grave reservations about the use of cutting equipment in a public place, and the safety implications for those attending.

No Surprises

Try to ensure as few surprises as possible. Make sure that there are no competing functions happening on the same day. Brides, bridesmaids and particularly 'cute children' will distract your delegates from the work they are supposed to be engrossed in.

Make sure that everyone understands how thorough the check should be. I once sent a junior member of staff to recce a location in Cork. He came back and told me that the function rooms and accommodation were excellent, and that a rock band, which was performing in the city that weekend, would also be staying in the hotel — cool! What my junior had seen as an added bonus (nearness to super-stardom at his young age) would have horrified the senior business people for whom we were organising a conference.

Check and double-check everything. Most of the time (99 per cent), you will be going through the motions, wondering why you are bothering, but the other 1 per cent will convince you that it is worth taking the time and trouble.

Accommodation

Be careful to ensure that the accommodation you book is exactly what your clients will need. Many hotels, for example, will not serve food after 9 o'clock on a Sunday evening.

Ensure that the rooms your guests are given have internet access, or that the hotel has a business centre for guests. Make sure that the rooms are not above a nightclub area. Your selected hotel should be of the highest quality for your special guests.

See that people do not abuse your hospitality. You would be surprised at how over the top well-known and well-paid executives can be. If you are providing meals and accommodation, specify the quantities. For example, the meal is one meal per night, for the occupant, for each night of their stay. Is wine included? Who pays for the use of the mini-bar in the room? These kinds of details need to be worked out in advance, and communicated to the hotel and the guests (discreetly). No one minds what the rules are, as long as they know in advance.

An evening dinner the night before the function is always a good idea. It gives your speakers and chairpersons an opportunity to meet with each other, and to meet with the sponsoring company. These informal meetings can often clarify the different 'angles' each of the speakers is taking on a topic, and prevent an overlap in presentations on the day. Often the speakers are known to each other, and appreciate the opportunity to meet again in informal surroundings.

Transport

How will you transport your guests from one location to another? You might be hosting a conference at a hotel in the suburbs of Dublin, but the Lord Mayor could be hosting a reception for your guests in the Mansion House in the city centre. How will you move 50 or 300 people from the suburbs to the city centre? Have buses been arranged? Are the times clearly indicated in the information packs? Will the chairperson remind people as the conference ends? Will the buses be staggered? How will your guests travel (usually on the same bus, but you might need to make other arrangements for them). Have staff-members been rostered? Will some be in the Mansion House to greet and guide guests as the first bus arrives? How many will travel on each bus? Who is responsible for ensuring that everyone got away safely? And, of course, how do they get back to the suburbs after the function? All of the arrangements operate in reverse for getting them home again.

Special Promotions

If the marketing or advertising people are running promotions in advance of the function, to sell tickets or attract greater attendances, could you build part of your media publicity campaign around that?

STEP 2: THE FUNCTION

Flowers

When you were looking at the venue, you should have been conscious of decoration. Will you need a large spray of flowers in the fireplace; a high flower display for the base of the podium; perhaps smaller arrangements for the tables? Can the hotel organise the flowers for you? And is it possible that the flowers would be in the corporate colours (with a little forward planning, virtually any colour is possible).

Depending on the type of function, you might feel that balloons are more appropriate, or people in costumes to greet guests on arrival. Whatever you decide, check to see that the room is dressed.

Food and Drink

If your function is being held at 7.45 a.m., you will need to provide breakfast for your guests. Would a continental breakfast be sufficient or should you serve a full breakfast?

If the function is mid-morning, you could simply decide to have tea/coffee and biscuits. If it is going to run into lunch-time though, you might be wise to provide at least sandwiches at the end of the function.

For a lunch-time function, decide whether you need a sit-down three-course meal or a buffet. Your guests might prefer to stand and mingle while they eat, and would prefer the option of curry/chilli/stroganoff on rice with a glass of wine.

An early-evening function is perfectly suited to finger-food, possibly a mixture of hot and cold — sandwiches, cocktail sausages, cheese dips, canapés, meatballs, etc.

An evening function, unlike the others, presents a problem with drinks. Will you serve wine only or a full-bar? A wine reception should always offer guests an alternative to alcohol — either soft drinks or water. There are two difficulties with a full bar. The first is cost, which can be difficult to estimate because each drink is individually priced. The second is that a full bar is harder to control, because someone, inevitably, will tell the barman to keep it open for another 30 minutes (and your budget will go out the window). Long after the function has ended, when you are reviewing your budgets, you will take the blame for the overspend at the bar. The only way to avoid it is to make it clear that you will sign the bill at the designated time (say 8.30 p.m.) If the managing director or one of the partners wants to keep the bar open for another 30 minutes, they sign the second chit — not you. Consumption of drink will increase dramatically once your guests know that the bar is closing.

Microphones/Equipment

How many microphones will you need? If there is a podium, you will obviously need a microphone there. Are there to be questions and answers from the floor? Will you need roving microphones? And what of the presentation/speech at the function — you may require an overhead projector, or a slide carousel, a TV and video monitor, or facilities for a PowerPoint presentation. All of the equipment is your responsibility. Ideally you should have someone on stand-by in the room in case a fault develops in the equipment during use. Certainly if the people making the presentations are senior executives, you can almost assume that they will be unable to use the equipment comfortably.

Be aware of the pitfalls of clip-on mikes. They are popular at conferences, particularly if your speaker likes to stroll up and down the stage or platform while speaking. The problem with clip-on mikes is that people forget that they are live, and there are many examples of people cursing equipment — live to the audience — when they thought that they were speaking *sotto voce*.

Guest of Honour

Your guest of honour is an important person. This is someone who has been invited to lend credibility to your company and its product by their endorsement at this function. Depending on the purpose, your guest of honour may be a well-known scientist, the president of your institute, or a director of the local chamber of commerce. Your guest of honour will need to be booked in advance and may cost you a lot of money in attendance fees.

You might decide to invite a politician to be your guest of honour. Politicians are not paid for attending, and are always willing to oblige if they can. But remember that they may have to cancel their appointment with you, at short notice, because of government business on the day. Government ministers or their departments generally have press officers who will be very helpful to you.

If your guest of honour is the President, Taoiseach, Tánaiste, or a Government minister from Northern Ireland or Britain, you will have additional security. Sniffer dogs will check the venue before the VIP's arrival, and you will have accompanying detectives, security people and drivers. There are strict protocols attached to the speaking order and the way in which your guest should be introduced — always check with their advisers.

Make sure that the names and exact titles of all of the people being introduced as guests are correct. It is often a good idea to send them the chairperson's opening remarks — as they relate to them — and make sure that they are accurate.

A number of years ago, I attended a function at which the guest of honour was a minister of state with special responsibility in the relevant area. The company's French chief executive was also in attendance. He began his speech by saying that he had been expecting the minister, but he was glad to see that at least the junior minister could attend. This was seriously insulting! Moreover, the junior minister was the one who had originally been invited. Although colloquially we refer to people in this position as junior ministers, in press releases, and certainly in official speeches, they should always be referred to as the Minister of State at the relevant department.

John F. Kennedy famously said: 'I am the man who accompanied Jacqueline Kennedy to Paris, and I have enjoyed it.'[1] However, a lot of people are not comfortable with a public association with family. 'The well-known writer who is married to…' can give the impression that the writer is really well known only by association. Some women are comfortable with an introduction which says, in effect, that they are highly qualified nuclear scientists who like to bake their own bread in their spare time. Others would be horrified by any reference to domesticity. Check your facts with your guest in advance.

You should also have a stand-by arrangement in the event that the guest cannot make it. If the Taoiseach were delayed, for example, he would usually send a minister or deputy in his place — but it does no harm to check with the department if this is what is likely to happen.

Similarly, planes can be late arriving, buses and trains can crash or breakdown. You need to have either a stand-in to deliver the speech (if it has been sent in advance) or a stand-by person to deliver a different speech.

Entry and Exit

For press conferences, especially, you need to use a room with different entry and exit points. This is particularly important if you are dealing with a crisis where the chief executive, with the benefit of a briefing from corporate and legal teams, has a statement to read, and cannot take questions afterwards.

The idea of a press conference is that you make yourself available to media.

However, on some occasions, the press conference is called really to give television and radio a sound byte. The chief executive cannot say anything beyond what is in the statement. On these occasions, you need an entry and exit strategy. The idea behind it is quite simple. The chief executive enters by a door at the back of the room, and walks up the main aisle (with journalists on either side) to the top table. The PR person calls the conference to order and the chief executive reads the statement.

If the purpose of the conference was to give a controlled, legally approved comment, you don't want the chief executive to have to try to beat a path out again through the same exit, thus running the risk of cameras capturing any reluctance to respond to questions. You will, therefore, ensure that another door is used for departure. This would usually be situated at the top of the room so that, when the statement has been read, the chief executive can thank the media and leave by what has now become the nearest door — simple but effective.

Speeches

At every function there are speeches — someone must tell the guests why they have been invited! The length of the speeches will vary — an after-dinner address by the main speaker could run from 20 to 45 minutes. If the function is less formal, there might be three speakers in all — speaking for 5 to 10 minutes each.

Clearly establish in the early stages of planning who is responsible for writing the speeches. If it is your job, try to have them written in plenty of time to allow the speakers to make any changes they wish. If the guest of honour's speech is to be written by the guest of honour, establish how far in advance of the function you may be given the speech (you will need it for the press pack and press release).

Media

You will need a guest-book on the evening. Ask guests to sign in as they arrive. Someone should be placed at a desk by the main entrance door to welcome people and ensure that the signing-in runs smoothly. The media will collect their press packs as they sign.

The press packs will probably contain a copy of each of the speeches made on the night and a press release detailing the key purpose of the function. They might also contain leaflets or brochures about your company or the new product you are launching.

Be sure that you have a designated area available for radio interviews, away from the noise of the function. This area should be quiet, and should have a landline for telephone interviews.

Photographs

You will have booked and briefed your own photographer in advance of the function. No doubt, press photographers will also be present, and your own photographer will be keeping out of their way while they are getting their shots.

Check with photographers during the function that they are happy with the photographs they're getting. They might appreciate your setting up a special shot for them.

Podium

If someone is going to speak from a podium, you will have requested one in advance. If the function is in a hotel, the podium (which, in most cases, is an additional charge on your bill) will most likely have the hotel's name on it. You will need to add some sort of signage with your company logo.

If the signage is not already in existence, you need to have it made. If it already exists, you need to ensure that it is in the hotel at the appointed time, and that it fits the podium.

You may also need signage in the reception area, guiding your guests to your function room. This might be handled quite simply by listing your function on the hotel notice board, or you may need to erect your own sign.

Exhibition Area

If the function is attracting a large attendance, you may want to give attendees an opportunity to visit an exhibition about your company on their way into the function. Organising the exhibition is your job.

Alternatively, you might have to organise an area, complete with company backdrops, as a photographic location.

Seating/Standing

You also have the responsibility for deciding whether your guests sit or stand. The function may involve a presentation lasting 20 to 30 minutes. If so, you will have to provide seating for your guests.

Even if your function is a standing affair, you will need to provide a certain amount of seating on the periphery for the infirm, the disabled, the unwell, the pregnant or the aged.

Press Room

You will probably need to provide the press with a special area. If the function runs for several days, it might also be a good idea to provide pigeon holes with journalists' names on them. This ensures that, even if they are not present, all press releases and statements are available to them on their return to the area.

Signage

Think about where it is positioned in relation to the guests and, very importantly, the TV and stills cameras. How much signage? Too much can be overpowering; too little won't be noticed. What area gets most TV coverage? (People in this area pay most for the display of their signage.)

VIP Entertainment Area

You might also need to provide a special area in which you will entertain your VIP guests. This would happen, for example, at the Kerrygold Dublin Horse Show or the Budweiser Irish Derby. The invitation list of VIPs needs to be carefully drawn to ensure that you have included everyone. Groups need to be time-segregated so that you can physically accommodate them all.

You will need people to check the responses to the RSVP you included on the invitation and to give details of special parking arrangements, buses, etc.

You should also appoint people who will be responsible for meeting your guests on arrival, and walking them out when they are leaving.

Access to VIP Area

Access to the VIP area must be tightly controlled to ensure that only invited guests gain entry to the designated area. The people meeting your VIPs will need to be able to show some sort of security pass to validate the person they are bringing in. During the first Kerrygold Dublin Horse Show, the 'meeters and greeters' were issued with plastic wrist bands. These bands could not be removed until the function had ended. If they were removed, the seal was broken, and they could not be reaffixed to the wrist. It meant that a very simple system operated. 'Meeters and greeters' simply raised their sleeves slightly, revealing the wrist band, when they were accompanying someone to the VIP area — discreet and effective.

Press Access

There may be occasions when you need to control press access. Again, if you think of the Kerrygold Dublin Horse Show, how do you control the number of photographers who want access to the ring during the Aga Khan cup? It would not be possible to accommodate everyone without greatly antagonising the audience, the riders and the horses.

An accreditation system must be put in place which ensures that members of the media have as much access as they need, without intruding on the event. In this instance, some system of shared photography needs to be put in place. Perhaps you will allow photographers from national media (which could be Irish and foreign) to have access to the arena provided that they notify you in advance. All of the magazine photographers might be issued with photographs by one of your own retained photographers, and they would also be allowed to brief your photographers about specific shots which would be of interest to their readers.

STEP 3: FOLLOW-UP

Follow-up

Remember that the last part of the job you will do, with any function, is the follow-up afterwards. This includes sending releases and photographs to members of the media who could not attend, writing different releases for the magazines which will be published after national/local media and therefore need a different angle, and sending follow-up information to the guests who could not attend.

Evaluation

When the function is over, gather the team together and share information. Was there any feedback from guests? Was the service of food too quick or too slow? Were there long queues to use the toilets? Were there badges for everyone attending? Were there enough staff-members on the cloakroom? Was there sufficient seating? Who was a good or bad presenter? Was the documentation well produced and presented? Which media attended? What photo coverage did we achieve? What mix of newspapers covered the story? Did we get TV or radio coverage? How well did the chief executive perform when interviewed? What could we do better next time? Also evaluate in terms of budget — were you within budget? Where did the overrun occur? Could it have been prevented? Should you allow more money for the next function?

In the immediate days or weeks following the function, when the event is freshest in people's minds, you can analyse, evaluate and learn for the next time. No matter how well the function ran, there can always be improvements, however slight. Life is a learning curve and, as a PR consultant, you should be seeking to improve with each function.

Event Management — Checklist

- Venue — selection, recce, hire charges, lighting, overheads, etc.
- Relevant permission and notification
- Insurance
- Selection — celebrity participation/guest of honour
- Time — photo call, guests, media, interviews
- Guest list — invitations and date for responses to RSVP
- Advance details — conference packs, location maps, etc.
- Media invitations — photographers and journalists
- Dressing — flowers, balloons, bunting
- Props — mime artists, scale-model of building
- Food and Drink
- Equipment — microphones, overhead projector, PowerPoint, slides, video
- Guest of Honour — security, speech, travel, accommodation, special requirements
- Speeches — in advance, order of speakers, length of speeches
- Press packs — press release, speeches, company information
- Guest packs — conference information, annual report
- Goody bags
- Photographer — book, brief, recce
- Podium — book, corporate logo,
- Signage — podium and reception area
- Exhibition area — stands, backdrops, leaflets, product
- Seating
- Radio interview areas
- Press room
- VIP Entertainment area
- Accommodation — recce, book, confirm
- Transport — coaches, boats, limousine service

REFERENCES

1. President Kennedy's speech at SHAPE Headquarters, Paris, France, 2 June 1961 — reference archivist. John F. Kennedy Library, USA.

CHAPTER 9

Exhibitions, Workshops,
Seminars and Conferences

Exhibitions, workshops, seminars and conferences are tools of communication used by public relations professionals. The use of each of these tools will vary from one industry to another, and to meet different requirements. For example, the pharmaceutical industry will use seminars and conferences of invited medical guests to inform and explain, and to address issues of concern about new products — and ultimately to see a return in terms of prescriptions written. The software sector of the IT industry will use workshops which allow invited guests to sample and use their new products. The travel trade and motor industry use exhibitions to generate interest in new car ranges and holiday destinations, with the ultimate aim of selling. Each of these tools is used in conjunction with the other PR tools and is not a stand-alone solution to any communications situation.

The common thread which links all four is that they are all methods of reaching a target public. Your skill, as a PR person, is to decide which of these is the most appropriate, the most effective, and the most cost-efficient way of reaching a particular public.

You will need to go through the checklist for Event Management (e.g. recce the location, issue invitations, arrange catering). In addition, whichever of the four you choose, there is a list of decisions to be taken which is common to all:

- **Define the Objective**. Always the simplest and most basic challenge in public relations is establishing what you are trying to achieve. It might be that you want to build a closer relationship with your existing members (most professional associations' annual conferences fall into this category). You might wish to enhance your relationship with existing customers by holding a conference or seminar which looks at future trends within the industry. This might, in turn, enhance your profile as an industry leader. You might wish to provide a forum for discussion and exchange of information (this is done, for example, when new public initiatives are being introduced and the government, or relevant local authority, wishes to hear the views of the community). You might wish to create a forum in which you can sell more product (e.g. the annual Woman's World Show, held just before the Women's Mini-Marathon, provides a forum for selling to an audience of women interested in make-up, fashion, health, beauty, education, interiors, etc.).

You might use one of these to introduce an entirely new product onto the market (to sell a new holiday destination, for example), or to introduce your product into a foreign market (at the annual Showcase Fair in the RDS, perhaps). From the outset it is important to know exactly what you want to achieve because that, in turn, guides your budget, your selected publics and your key guests.

- **Target your publics**. You need a clear vision of who will attend your function. If it is by invitation only (to a conference, for example), you will be working from database lists. If it is an open exhibition, pay-as-you-enter, you will know only that those attending have an interest in the area covered by the title of the exhibition. You will be unable to target most of these publics in advance, but you should be working hard at the exhibition to build database records of the new publics you are attracting.

  A clear vision determines the type of speakers that you choose. If you are targeting chief executives, you will need speakers of their level; a technical audience will require speakers with technical expertise, etc.

  The audience may also determine the time at which the function is held. Technicians might be delighted with a full-day conference (Monday to Friday) while members of the voluntary sector might prefer a weekend or evening function.

- **Incorporate current topical issues**. For any conference or seminar, you should be aware of the issues currently under debate which might influence the discussion at your event, and you should also try to incorporate current issues to add relevance and interest to the topics under discussion.

  During the height of the foot-and-mouth scare in Ireland (spring 2001), most conferences geared to agricultural delegates were cancelled because of the fear of spreading the disease. In the immediate aftermath, most conferences dealt with the issue and its impact on the farming community.

  In the spring of 2002, with Élan, Enron and AIB in crisis, financial conferences incorporated topics and speakers addressing issues of internal controls and ethics.

- **Time your event**. Above and beyond choosing the most appropriate time or day, be conscious of all of the other events happening within the industry. Know the industry — its peak and slack times. A conference organised for a peak period of business is unlikely to attract many attendees, no matter how good the organisation and the speakers and the relevance of the topics. A conference organised for slack periods within the same industry would be much more likely to attract a full complement of delegates.

  The Learning Ireland Exhibition in September 2001 in the RDS, Dublin, suffered from, amongst many other things, the fact that there was a big match in Lansdowne Road on the Saturday afternoon. Unless you were attending the match, traffic restrictions alone would have put you off attending the exhibition. There was also a major concert in Slane the same day, so a lot of the young people who would be expected to attend were otherwise engaged. Dates for public events are either set annually, or are known months in advance. It is your job, as the PR person, to ensure that there is no clash.

However, public events cannot always be foreseen. In August 1997, Diana, Princess of Wales, died. The Aontas Adult Education exhibition in Dublin had been scheduled almost twelve months in advance, and her funeral was held on the Saturday of the exhibition.[1] The significant drop in attendance could have been anticipated only a matter of days in advance. The funeral could not have been foreseen at the time of organisation.

- **Tailor your material**. It sounds obvious, but make sure that the speaker's material is targeted to your audience. There are two great ways to insult your audience and ensure that people are left bored — either bring in speakers whose level of knowledge is far in excess of those attending the function, or bring in speakers whose knowledge is significantly less. You will switch people off either because you bamboozle them with facts and statistics which they cannot comprehend, or because you insult their intelligence with the simplicity of content.

- **Plan carefully**. Once the date has been set, work backwards and identify key decision dates. Then make sure that you stick to them!

- **Choose the venue**. This has already been discussed in Chapter 8: Organising Functions. However, there are some additional concerns of which you should be aware.

   If you are holding a small, private exhibition, you might well decide that your own offices are the most appropriate location. You will then need to check the simple things like access to the toilets, and where the toilets are located in relation to the exhibition area, and whether or not the area is capable of taking the numbers you wish to invite.

   If the exhibition is a mobile one, travelling the country in a self-contained unit, you will need to check mileage and service records. Ensure, in so far as you possibly can, that you have eliminated the possibility of breakdown.

- **Brochure**. Make sure that the brochure gives all of the information that a participant might need. The brochure should contain the name, address and contact details of the sender. Include brief biographies of the speakers, and a timed running order for the day. Incorporate maps showing access to the venue, and the location of train stations and bus stops. Lists should include bus numbers, embarkation points, approximate length of journey and relevant fare. Information about feeder buses serving the venue from the train stations would also be helpful. Finally, do not forget to give details of special rates of overnight accommodation.

   Request information from those attending. Find out whether they have any special dietary requirements (are they vegan or vegetarian, for example?) Are there any particular access issues of which you should be aware? Do they have flights to meet and, if so, can you arrange taxis for them?

   Be sure to include the cost, if any, of attending the function, or to highlight the fact that attendance is free. Costs in addition to the conference/seminar cost should be clearly outlined. Similarly with exhibitions, people attending should know in advance if, in addition to an entry fee of €10, there is a car-parking charge of €5.

- **Cross check the date and time**. A national advertising campaign on RTÉ television in February 2002 promoted a second concert by Neil Diamond and told viewers that tickets would go on sale on 'Valentine's Day, Wednesday, 14th February'. Valentine's Day was on a Thursday in 2002.[2]
- **Media**. Do not neglect the media. Send your press invitations well in advance. Have copies of speakers' scripts ready for the media on arrival. Clearly indicate the times at which photo calls will happen, or the times at which your guest of honour will be available for interview. Make pressroom facilities available if necessary. Be sure that all media have your mobile number for easy contact. Ensure that you have a local courier service on stand-by to send scripts or photographs. Organise a radio interview room.
- **Support staff**. Make sure that you have sufficient support staff to organise and attend the function. Ensure that they are all fully briefed.

  Take decisions early about whether or not your guests will wear badges. If so, will the badges be colour coded — e.g. yellow for speakers, green for delegates, blue for staff? Stick-on and pin-on badges will destroy leather and suede. Clip-on are perhaps the best.

The above points form a general guideline which is applicable to each of the areas under review. We will now look at each, in turn.

EXHIBITIONS

Companies normally participate in exhibitions for one of two reasons:

1. To sell their product/maintain a strong presence in the market, or
2. To educate and inform the public about what they do.

Thus, countries would participate in the Holiday Fair in order to sell you their country as a holiday destination. Likewise, universities would participate in an education exhibition because it makes potential students aware of the range of courses they provide. The objective of the country at the Holiday Fair is to sell the product. The objective of the university at the education exhibition is to inform and educate. The country is establishing a presence and the university is maintaining a strong presence in the market.

Essentially, the PR person can have one of two roles in an exhibition — in-house person working for a company participating in the exhibition, or PR for the entire exhibition. We will look first at the role of the in-house person.

In-House PR

Assuming that this is the first time your company has decided to participate in an exhibition, you need to begin by researching each of the important exhibitions in which you might participate. Find out how long the exhibition has been established. If the exhibition is well established, find out how many people visited it last year (if it is new, obviously, no figures will be available). Check the cost per square foot/metre to hire the space, and check what the cost includes — for example, is lighting included? Will a desk be provided? Are there shelves on your stand? Will there be power-points for a video? Are there any prohibitions in force? Can you, for example, have an entertainment area at the back of the stand or must you use the restaurant facilities?

Where exactly will your stand be located and how much are you willing to spend on its hire? Cost varies according to position. Often the smallest stands, at the cheapest cost, are the most difficult to find. You do not want to 'hide' at the exhibition.

You also need to decide, based on the attendance figures, how many staff you will need on the stand to handle the level of enquiries you anticipate. This will partly determine the amount of space you will need.

Once you have decided to participate in the exhibition, the fun really begins.

Dressing the Stand

You are responsible for the overall look of the stand. Your stand must look appealing in order to attract visitors. Are you going to incorporate the corporate colours? If your company colours are blue and green, will your stand be in the same colours?

Will you need additional shelving? If your product is something like crystal or jewellery, you might need glass-fronted cabinets with special lighting. Do you want your customers to walk around and through the stand? Or will you have a desk in front, blocking access to the rest of the stand, at which you will take enquiries?

You will also need to check for empty spaces left on the stand. It might be necessary, for instance, to bring in a floral display to take away the bare look of a corner. You will also need to decide about the walls of your stand — how will you dress them? You will probably use posters. What message should the posters carry? Will you need advertising posters which will name your products and state the prices? Or do you want your posters to build an image of the company which is not related specifically to your product?

You must also ask yourself whether your company or its product line particularly lends itself to video? If it does, will you show a video at the exhibition? You could reasonably anticipate that the maximum attention span of an exhibition visitor is 3–7 minutes. After that, they have moved on and you have lost them. Do you have a suitable video?

When dressing your stand, your company name and logo are very important. After all, you want the potential customer to remember who you are! You should always position your company name and logo at eye level, preferably on the back wall of your stand, facing the visitors.

Print Material

You will also be responsible for producing all of the leaflets, brochures and flyers that will be distributed at the exhibition.

Do not succumb to the temptation to use the corporate brochures you already have. They have probably been produced in full colour at a cost of €20 (or more) each. It would be very unwise of you to distribute them in their thousands, at an exhibition — far better to design a leaflet or brochure especially for the exhibition, which can be printed at a much lower cost.

Printing a special brochure also means that you can target your visitors more accurately, with the kind of information that is relevant to them.

The number of visitors the exhibition attracts will influence the number of brochures you print. The type of visitors you can expect (e.g. mainly foreign retail trade buyers or purchasing managers or the general public) will determine the content of your brochure.

Incentives

Be it an incentive, a give-away, or a gimmick, your stand needs something special to attract visitors. At an exhibition you are competing, in a limited space, with others selling a similar product — you need every advantage you can get! You may decide to provide free balloons for children or carrier bags for adults. If you are participating in a public exhibition, you should organise a raffle or run a competition at your stand, which requires people to fill in their names and addresses.

Exhibition Staff

You will obviously be conscious of the need to have staff on your stand throughout the exhibition. The number of staff you need will be based on the size of your stand and the numbers attending the exhibition.

Do not forget that, like anything else in life, people are seldom 'naturally' good on an exhibition stand. If you are exhibiting in order to sell product, your staff should be given sales training. Think about it. You will evaluate your success initially by the number of enquiries generated, and secondly by the actual sales made as a result of the sales leads gathered at the exhibition. You must have people on the stand who are capable of identifying good sales leads and gathering the relevant information so that your sales team can follow through. Staff on exhibition stands need to be trained, whether the purpose is to sell or to educate.

Bear in mind that if you take eight people out of the office for a 3-day exhibition, their work must continue in their absence. Someone in the office or factory has to do their job for them while they are at the exhibition. It would be foolish to have a well-manned exhibition stand and an office in turmoil! You might decide to roster staff, but this breaks continuity and can often backfire if things like travel time are taken into account. Instead, you might retain a company which specialises in providing exhibition staff.

The way exhibition staff look also enhances or detracts from the look of your stand. Even if your company does not have a uniform, consider purchasing uniforms for the people on your stand. It lends an air of professionalism and credibility to your company.

Finally, in terms of the number of people on your stand, be sure that you have enough people to 'cover' while some of the staff take coffee and lunch breaks.

The best motto is 'always be prepared'. You should notify participating staff, in writing, of the rules of your stand. The rules will mostly revolve around preserving the look of the stand. Where will staff hang their coats or leave their handbags? (You don't want them thrown in a corner.) Will you allow people to bring plastic mugs of coffee onto the stand? (They can look very sloppy.)

Decisions about all of these things have to be taken. It is unfair of you to expect people to be 'inspired' about the things that will detract from the look of the stand — far better to set out the rules clearly, in writing, before you begin.

Refreshments

You will also need to decide what refreshments, if any, you will offer your visitors and customers. Will you provide a glass of wine at your stand for visitors? It is an idea that's becoming increasingly popular — although the size of the glasses is decreasing rapidly! Will you install a coffee percolator so that you can serve coffee to any serious potential buyer? You will also need to check whether or not the exhibition organisers will allow you to have such a machine on your stand.

Will you require a refreshment/entertainment area at the back of the stand? You may need a private area in which to entertain your most important existing customers who will visit you at the exhibition. If you have a private entertainment area, you will need to keep it well out of sight of passing visitors and, of course, staff on duty could not be allowed to drink during the exhibition (although you may invite staff to stay back for an hour or so at the end of each evening).

Invitations

If the exhibition is an exhibition for the trade, you will want to issue invitations to your existing customers. There are benefits to your company in so doing — you are keeping in touch with your clients and informing them of your participation in the exhibition, and you are giving them an opportunity to visit your stand.

If your existing customers visit your stand, they may well become aware of products you produce that they hadn't previously associated with you. You will not be targeting them directly for sales (after all, they already buy from you) but you may get more business from them or they may refer new business to you because they have become aware of the full range of products you produce.

Media Interest

You should maximise your media exposure from the exhibition. You will obviously be seeking advance publicity in order to attract people to your stand at the exhibition. You will also try to secure publicity during the exhibition. How will you do it?

The exhibition organisers will (presumably) have arranged for a well-known personality to open the exhibition. You should liaise closely with the exhibition PR person and find out who has been invited and at what time and on which day the exhibition will be formally opened. Let us assume, for example, that the President has been invited to open the exhibition.

You should contact the President's office and request that she visit your stand after she has opened the exhibition. The President will be available for, say, one hour. After she has formally opened the exhibition, she will 'walk' the entire exhibition and stop at a maximum of six stands. The President will know in advance which stands she will stop at (these things are always pre-arranged). You should try to get agreement from her office that she will include your stand on her itinerary. Needless to say, if she agrees, you should have a senior member of the company (your Managing Director or Marketing Manager) present to greet her and you should have your own photographer on hand to record the meeting on film.

The President's visit will attract media attention (the exhibition's PR person will have taken care of this) — usually national media photographers and journalists. You will also have your own photographs which you may use later for local media, your company newsletter, trade press, etc.

You might also decide to have a personality visit your stand during the exhibition. You will need to book the personality well in advance and remember that your company will be responsible for paying their fee. You will obviously want to alert the media to the visit and you should also inform the exhibition PRO, who might be organising another media event which clashes with yours. The exhibition PRO will be happy to oblige because any publicity you secure will mention the exhibition, and you should also ensure that security staff are alerted to ensure that your personality moves swiftly and easily from the main door to your stand, and gets out again safely and easily when they are finished. After all, you don't want hassle but neither do you want your personality stopping at other stands along the way — that would not be the kind of media exposure you had in mind!

There are many other ways to attract attention to your stand. You might decide to launch a new product during the exhibition, or you could decide to have a robot on your stand, or belly dancers — whatever is appropriate.

Evaluation

Finally, at the end of the exhibition, you will need to evaluate your participation and see if it was worthwhile.

You will obviously examine the media coverage you secured, the number of visitors your staff spoke with, and the volume of sales leads you generated. Your evaluation, based on your original objectives, will determine whether or not you participate again next year.

PRO for the Entire Exhibition

As PRO for the exhibition, your job is broader than PRO for an exhibitor, although some of the steps will be common to both. There are five key additional functions of the Exhibition PR person:

- Inform potential exhibitors and visitors
- Organise the press office
- Arrange a special press day
- Handle the official opening
- Evaluate.

Inform Potential Exhibitors and Visitors

It is your job to generate interest from exhibitors and visitors alike. The first part of this task entails getting people interested in taking stands at the exhibition. You will use trade press, direct-mail material and possibly telephone calls. You will certainly include brochures in mailings issuing from professional bodies; you might include them with certain newspapers, and you will probably distribute them at other events in the lead-up to your exhibition, to attract exhibitors to participate.

You will also need to attract attendees. Target those people to whom your exhibitors want to sell. These may be Irish or foreign buyers, software designers or home-owners. It is your job to design a campaign that will entice them into the exhibition so that your exhibitors have an opportunity to sell to them.

You will generate stories about the exhibition, sometimes months in advance. The stories might revolve around the level of business done at this exhibition last year, the number of people who attended (record numbers?) or the number of new products that were introduced at the show. Your job is to link closely with the exhibitors so that they can give you the information from which you can generate stories. This is also in the interest of the exhibitors who are, in effect, getting free publicity.

Organise the Press Office

You will need to organise a press office for the exhibition. This room will be used exclusively by media. It will contain media information from the exhibitors (or those who were smart enough to put something together) and schedules of opening times, visits by politicians or celebrities, photographs of product (e.g. jewellery, fashion, furniture). The press office is a room in which the media can meet, exchange stories, gather information, send information to their editors and relax and have a coffee away from the madness that is going on outside.

The media will also have received a full schedule, in advance, of all of the things happening during the exhibition.

Arrange a Special Press Day

Very often, the exhibition PRO will organise a special press day in advance of the official opening of the show. This allows the press the freedom to mingle, without crowds, and speak with exhibitors and look at the products on display. In effect, it allows them to identify stories that they might use.

Handle the Official Opening

As the exhibition PR person, you will also be responsible for selecting and inviting the guest of honour who will perform the opening ceremony. The media will need to be notified of the time that the opening is taking place. Exhibitors will also need to be told. You will link with the guest to get a copy of their speech in advance, if possible, and to determine exactly how long they will be spending with you. The length of time will determine how many stands the guest can actually visit. Remember that the walk-about is also carefully planned. You will have told the guest, well in advance of their arrival, of the arrangements for their tour of the exhibition.

Evaluate

As with every other job in PR, you will evaluate, at the end of the exhibition, how successful each of your proposals has been.

Crisis PR

Remember that with any exhibition things can go radically wrong. The Baby & Kids Show in 1996 is a good example. As we saw in Chapter 6, publicity for the show in 1995 was very positive. In 1996, the organisers decided to boost the show's appeal by bringing along Barney 'the world's most-famous dinosaur'. Unfortunately, the organisers were unable to cope with the numbers — up to 20,000 people — who queued to see the TV star. Gardaí and fire brigade were called by the organisers because of fears of a serious crush. Print media carried photographs and text about the length of the queues and the disappointment of the children.[3]

Such was the level of disappointment among parents (who had broken promises to children) and distraught anguish among the children themselves that negative publicity continued after the show had ended. For days after the event, programmes on national radio were still jammed with parents complaining bitterly about the disappointment and anguish that their children suffered. Most of the children only caught a glimpse of Barney when he walked outside the RDS (but within the railings) and waved to them.[4] It was an excellent idea — obviously, since the level of interest was so high — but one that rebounded badly on BEC Exhibitions, the organisers.

WORKSHOPS

Workshops are generally confined to a maximum number of participants (usually 25). They are often break-out sessions from conferences, in which discussions in small group sessions can be held. These discussions would be led by the host company which would follow a fixed agenda of items to be discussed, or a particular aspect of a topic, and report back to the main body of the conference.

Alternatively a discussion document to be submitted to government might be discussed in workshops, each of which could be devoted to a different section of the report/document, thereby allowing delegates to make an input into the area of most relevance to them.

Workshops may also be used as opportunities for practical work, like seeing how the technology would actually be applied to certain situations. For example, accounts people will appreciate an opportunity to try your new payroll software package.

SEMINARS

Seminars are usually confined to a fixed number of people — generally a maximum of 50. Seminars can be a very effective way of spreading information, usually about one topic only. A seminar can be internal as well as external. A company might hold a seminar for employees, for example, to discuss the introduction of a new sexual harassment manual or a new policy on aids in the workplace.

Seminars are an effective way of spreading information because they allow for good interaction with the audience. They can also be used for external groups, sometimes with a formal programme of papers presented by individual speakers. A firm of solicitors, for example, might host a seminar for company directors to explain the introduction of new legislation and how it will impact on their industries. This 'positions' the firm as a leader in its field.

Exhibitions may also incorporate seminars on specific topics. These are an added bonus for those attending. During the exhibition, at specific times on each day, seminar sessions on different topics would be held. The programme for seminars would be included in the exhibition information sent or given to those attending.

CONFERENCES

Conferences are much larger gatherings than seminars — numbers are unlimited and attendance can be 600+ people. They do not concentrate on one single topic. Rather, they usually have an overall theme. Under that umbrella theme, several topics would be discussed.

Conferences usually allow you to select a panel of guest speakers, each of whom would address a different topic. Each of these guest speakers will reflect on the host company. Your guests will associate you with the guest speakers you present to them. It goes without saying that these speakers should not only have an established expertise in their area, but they should also be articulate. This is an important point. There is nothing worse than listening to an expert who is a poor communicator. A guest who cannot communicate effectively will lose your audience's attention. Try to book people you have heard before or people who have been recommended to you.

With conferences, the speakers will have prepared their speeches in advance. You may wish to make these speeches available to your delegates as part of their conference/seminar pack.

If you can secure copies of the speeches in advance, you may find that some of them contain interesting quotes which you could incorporate into a press release. You might even find that one of your speakers is going to be so controversial that you would want to invite journalists to attend that session and hear for themselves what the speaker has to say.

Remember too that, by their very nature, conferences are quiet affairs with delegates listening intently to what your guest speakers are saying. Under those circumstances, any noise becomes a distraction.

Be extra conscious of where the toilets are located in relation to your room. You do not want your delegates to be faced with a long walk when they want to use the ladies or gents — they might not return. Neither do you want the toilets positioned within the hall you are using. The constant noise of doors opening and closing, and the sound of electric hand-dryers is most aggravating for delegates.

Your chairperson (or rotating chairperson) has a pivotal role to play on the day. Preferably use experienced 'chairs'. They are responsible for ensuring that each session runs smoothly; that delegates have sufficient time to ask questions at the close of a session; that 'bores' are not allowed to make speeches from the floor; and that the sessions finish on time to allow your delegates their 15 minutes for coffee. If one session finishes late, it will impact on every other session that day, and very soon your timetable will be completely out of control.

Conference delegates are usually charged a fee for attending. The host company will expect that this fee will allow them at least to recoup their expenditure. In some cases, conferences are run with the express intention of making a profit.

Organising a conference is hugely time-consuming, and there are professional conference organisers who will perform the function for you. For large conferences especially, they are well worth the investment.

Finally, remember the golden rules: confirm all arrangements with the hotel and the speakers in advance; arrive early to test all of the equipment and ensure that the hall is as well presented as it possibly could be; and always be prepared — something will inevitably go wrong!

REFERENCES

1. Diana, Princess of Wales, died on 31 August 1997. Her funeral was held at Westminster Abbey on Saturday, 7 September 1997.
2. MCD Promotions. Neil Diamond Concerts at Lansdowne Road were held on Friday, 5 July 2002 and Saturday, 6 July 2002. Source: http://www.mcd.ie.
3. Fraser MacMillan and Tom Kerr, 'Kids wait in vain for TV idol Barney', *Star*, 29 April 1996.
4. *Gay Byrne Show*, RTÉ Radio 1, 29 April 1996; *News at One*, RTÉ Radio 1, 29 April 1996; *Gay Byrne Show*, RTÉ Radio 1, 30 April 1996.

Section 4
Structures, Roles
and Approaches

CHAPTER 10

Structure and Management
of a PR Consultancy

Every consultancy or, for that matter, PR department, needs to be managed.Management textbooks will tell you that there are four key functions of management: leading, planning, organising and controlling.[1]

There are five main reasons for adopting any management strategy. They are:

- *To get things done efficiently and cost-effectively*. This means that you are not wasting time. You are using your resources (people and technology) to benefit the consultancy and the client. Getting them done cost-effectively means that you are giving yourself the best possible chance of making a profit.
- *To have time to analyse opportunities and problems*. This is possible only if you are a good time manager. Everyone needs time to mull over a problem, to look at it from every possible angle, to analyse all of the potential long-term implications. Your job involves counselling and advising your client on what to do and what to say. Your role includes issues management, conflict resolution and negotiation. You are the eyes and ears of your clients. You need time to absorb and to analyse before you can make recommendations. Similarly, within the consultancy, you can quite easily miss good business opportunities if you cannot find the time to investigate them.
- *To find solutions to problems and take decisions*. The recommendation, which you put before your client, must be the best-possible solution to the problem. You must then, mutually, take the decision to act on the recommendation.
- *To get those decisions carried out*. This means allowing enough time and appointing the right staff to ensure the successful implementation of the proposals.
- *To do it all profitably*. Making a profit is crucial to the survival of the consultancy.

Clearly, there is a lot of management involved in consultancy work. Each account handler is handling approximately ten different clients, with varied proposals and mixed deadlines. You need to manage well in order to ensure that your people are not overloaded with work, burnt out, or creatively brain dead.

QUALITY CONTROL IN CONSULTANCIES

The application of good management strategies, people-management skills, budget balancing and profitability are all vital to a PR consultancy, and quality control is crucial. The following is just one example of how effective (and worthwhile) quality control can be.

The Danish State Information Service (DSIS) is a small government agency with a total of forty-five employees. It provides information services to citizens, government agencies and other public bodies. Customers pay for the service, and DSIS competes with other agencies for business.

By 1994, the agency had passed through a period of organisational and managerial disorder. The consultancy department with a staff of six was running with a large deficit, and the general reputation of the service was not satisfactory. A decision was made to introduce quality control measures.

There were six key objectives to be achieved by quality control:

1. Stabilise and then raise quality of service
2. Reduce failure costs
3. Increase business with established customers
4. Attract new customers through recommendations
5. Attract qualified staff
6. Increase Profitability.

Each of these objectives could be applied to any business. In the case of the Danes, they achieved the objectives by:

- Defining the customers
- Defining the needs of these customers
- Developing products to satisfy these needs
- Planning the process to produce these products
- Transferring these plans to employees.

Ongoing quality control is measured by quantitative compliance checks, as follows:

- Fast reaction to customer request
- Dialogue with the customer
- Compliance with deadlines
- Compliance with budget
- Checking of subcontractors
- Compliance with internal budget
- Customer satisfaction questionnaire
- Assessment and follow-up.

The consultancy service returned to full profitability in 1997. A focused, business-like approach to the management of the consultancy's business resulted in a loss-making service becoming a profit generator.[2]

MANAGEMENT AREAS

There are five key areas in PR practice which need to be managed: time, proposals, staff, clients and budgets. We will look at each in turn.

Managing Your Own Time

Each account executive needs to be a good time manager, and many consultancies send their account executives on time-management courses so that they can learn the skills. In public relations you are selling your skills, but you can only sell a maximum number of hours in each day. If you are a sloppy worker, easily distracted, unable to focus on deadlines, or devote too much time to minor areas, then, as an executive, you will find yourself under increasing time pressures.

Timesheets, whether computerised or manual, are used in all consultancies. As an account executive, you are expected to log every minute of the working day. From the time you arrive in the morning until you finish in the evening, everything you do is logged and accounted for. Each time sheet is dated. Each morning your first task is to log onto the time sheet. From the opening hour, you log everything you do in a day. You log by time, by client, and by the nature of the work. So, first thing in the morning, you might log 8.05 a.m. to 8.20 a.m. as administration. You might be scanning newspapers for client press cuttings and listening to *Morning Ireland* (RTÉ) for developing stories. At 8.20 a.m. you might begin drafting a press release, for ComCon Ltd. At 8.45 your release writing is interrupted by a call from a client. It becomes automatic and instinctive that you log 8.45 a.m. and the client name as you answer the phone. Each telephone conversation is usually charged as 15 minutes, assuming that it is a short conversation. It is estimated that even if the conversation is five minutes long, you need to allow time to switch off from the press release (and into the client problem), and time to switch back in again. You might also need to send a quick follow-up e-mail or ask your junior to make some follow-up calls in order to 'close' the client conversation. Some consultancies log all work in blocks of 15 minutes. If you are lunching with a client, and it is a business lunch, lunch is also logged on the time sheet. As you can see, with this level of detail, it would be impossible to keep an accurate sheet if it were not filled in as the day progresses.

The time sheets are evaluated on a weekly or monthly basis. The consultancy needs to know how much time you are spending servicing each client. Some clients will be on a monthly fee, which equates to a fixed number of hours per month. It is important to see if you are over-servicing or under-servicing a client. You might be under-servicing a client because other clients simply took over in that month — a series of mini-crises which could not have been anticipated. The analysis of the time sheet shows that you have neglected a client the previous month and need to move them to the top of your priority list for the coming month.

Similarly, if you are over-servicing your client, you need to analyse the reasons why this is happening. It might be that you have actually taken extra work from the client, which should be separately costed and not calculated as part of their monthly fee. It might be that the client is taking too much of your time discussing minor details of a proposal — in which case you need to train your client. Or it might simply be that you underestimated the time that you should have allowed for the contract. This is a difficult situation. After all — you set the fee! It can be hard to go back and tell a client that you got it wrong and need more money.

The time sheets are also evaluated to see how much time you are spending on administration each month. An executive who works eight hours a day, realistically, can sell a maximum of only six hours (allowing two hours for administration). Timesheets will tell you how well you are handling the administration and whether or not your 'system' needs to be re-evaluated in the light of the details showing on your time sheet. You may, for example, be doing administration that your junior could be doing for you.

It is in the consultancy's interest, and your own, to ensure that your work is as efficient as possible. Most people in PR will work more than an eight-hour day on average. Most will start early in the morning and finish late in the evening, often with a function that they have arranged. However, you should not be working late, on a regular basis, to finish administration. If you spend too much time in the office, you are in danger of burning out. Burn-out, in PR terms, is when you are recommending the same things to the same clients because your brain is actually too tired to spin laterally or creatively.

And remember to be honest in everything that you do, including monitoring your time. *The PRII Digest*[3] carried a tale of a PR director who died on his fortieth birthday and found himself at the Pearly Gates of heaven. St Peter himself shook his hand and said, 'Congratulations, my son, we've been waiting a long time for you…! We're celebrating the fact that you lived to be 160 years old! God himself wants to see you!' When the director explained that he was only 40 years old, St Peter replied, 'That's simply impossible, my son — we've added up your time sheets.'

Managing Your Proposals

When a set of proposals has been accepted, you need to detail each element: hire of venues, deadline for approval of press releases, dates of launch events. Each of these items needs to be recorded (again, either physically in your diary or by computer) so that no deadlines are missed. You are, after all, in a deadline business. Timescales, realistic ones, need to be determined for each element of the proposal, and you need also to establish who is responsible for doing what jobs. For example, if you are to issue a press release on a Monday morning, you might need to have the release approved by the previous Friday. In order to have it approved by Friday, you need to give the client company possibly 24 hours in advance — so it needs to go to the client on Thursday morning. In order for it to arrive on the client's desk on Thursday morning, you might need your junior to have it drafted for you (for amendment or approval) by Wednesday. In order to have it written by Wednesday, your junior needs to have the brief the previous Monday. Everything is worked out on a timescale so that there are no missed deadlines and, in theory at least, no last-minute panics. (There will always be panics but they should be kept to a minimum.) This type of scheduling relates to, for example, the launch of a new product, where the launch date has been set for weeks or months in advance. In many instances, press releases are drafted, approved and issued in less than an hour.

Managing Your Staff

If you are working as an account executive, you will have a junior executive and possibly a shared secretarial back-up working with you. You need to be sure that these people are aware of the deadlines to which you are working, and that their deadlines and skills complement the work you need them to do for you. You have to be satisfied that they are competent at their jobs. With ever-changing technology, you are constantly watching to see if training or up-skilling is needed.

Your back-up staff also need good communication skills. They need an ability to handle clients, printers, suppliers and others. Each of these may require a different skill. Printers and suppliers may need to be cajoled or sometimes harassed to make sure that they meet deadlines. Clients may need reassurance, or constant updating. Some will like to be treated informally and called by their first name (by your junior staff); others will prefer to be addressed formally. It is up to you to ensure that staff know how to deal with each of the different individuals.

They also need to understand your priorities clearly. They need to know when it is important to interrupt you, and when the interruption can wait. If they understand your priorities, they will naturally understand the pressure of your deadlines.

As an account executive, you need the ability to delegate and supervise. People cannot be expected to be inspired. You must clearly tell them what needs to be done, by when, and establish that they have the time, the skills, and the equipment to meet your deadline.

Your staff also need an ability to take concise and accurate messages. They should think of you as a 'one-page' person. Short, concise, accurate messages make it easier to establish in what order you should return calls or e-mails.

Managing Your Clients

Your clients will also need to know what kind of management structure or system you are using with them. Clients will need regular contact reports which update them on the current status of proposals and clearly signal the decisions that need to be made.

You will need to keep in contact regularly, by telephone, e-mail or in person, and they will also need to know what your understanding of the word 'regular' is — do you mean monthly, weekly, or every second day?

In most cases, you will arrange a monthly face-to-face meeting with your client so that you can confirm action taken since the last meeting, issues can be discussed, and new situations or potential opportunities brought to your attention or the attention of your client. In order to do this, you need to structure an agenda for each meeting.

The agenda needs to list clearly the items for discussion, in as much detail as possible. The worst meetings — the most unwieldy and the longest — are usually those which leave plenty of room for 'any other business'. Structure the agenda tightly so that the client knows exactly what is coming up for discussion. Send it a few days in advance of the meeting so that the client has the option to add additional items. Set a timescale for the meeting — clearly indicate that it is expected to last from 10.00 to 11.00 a.m., or whatever length of time you think is appropriate. And stick to your timescale — time is money, to you and to the client. I have never found anyone to be insulted by an efficient and tightly timed meeting! On the next page you will find an example of a timetable, which was also used as an agenda for the first meeting with the client.

After the meeting, you need to send a report — not the minutes of the meeting, but a short note of the key points covered under each item of the agenda, and the decisions that were taken. You should also indicate if follow-up work is needed, and who was assigned that task. Initials usually suffice.

Finally, remember that a lot of decisions will be taken outside the formal structure of a meeting. As you work through the proposals on a day-by-day basis, different issues will arise. For example, in discussion about a photo call, you might recommend that special costumes be hired for the occasion. If this is a change to the original plan, you need to e-mail, fax, or write a confirmation note to the client — a short note outlining the date and time that the additional expense was agreed, and with whom, and noting that a ball-park figure of €X was agreed for costume hire and that you are to revert with full and final costings before proceeding with the idea. This is necessary because you are constantly taking so many decisions, and making so many suggestions, as is the client, that it is easily forgotten at what point the decision was made to proceed or exactly how much money you had agreed to allocate.

Managing Your Budgets

Anyone in business will tell you that you must manage the finances carefully. There is no point in having plenty of really good clients if they do not pay you on time, or your system 'forgets' to bill them for certain items. As an account executive, you are responsible for managing the budget for the proposals you agreed with the client. This means that you must ensure that your proposals meet the agreed costs, or that you have confirmed any increase or reduction in the costs.

Everything that you do for the client has a cost implication. Meetings involve time and mileage to and from the venue, possibly coffee while you were there, and an hourly fee to be charged. Consultancies also recover the costs of faxes, e-mails, photocopying, telephone calls, postage, couriers, photographers (time and prints), hire of venues, travel, accommodation, entertainment, print and design. That is a long list of items to keep track of. We will now look at the budgeting element in some detail.

Media Relations Timetable for the Opening of a New Factory

Week 1: Friday, 16 April
(i)   Agree contract + initial fee
(ii)   Contact MGC, Fennel/Sheehan, and Ironside re photography
(iii)   Agree dates for interviews

Week 2: Friday, 23 April
(i)   Finalise key guest
(ii)   Background briefing material for releases & advertorial coverage

Week 3: Friday, 30 April
(i)   Issue invitations
(ii)   Background briefing to journalists (advertorials)

Week 4: Friday, 7 May
(i)   Interviews for Exam, SBP and B&F
           Completed & text agreed by Friday 7 May (x3)
(ii)   Book press cutting agency — May & June

Week 5: Friday, 14 May
(i)   Media invitations
(ii)   Brief photographers
(iii)   Media training — part 1
(iv)   Speech content information for press packs

Week 6: Friday, 21 May — launch week
(i)   Final (part 2) media training
(ii)   Agree press release
(iii)   Coverage (advertorial):
   Examiner — Sat 22 May
   Sun Bus Post — Sun 23 May
   Bus & Fin — Thurs 27 May

Week 7: Friday, 28 May
(i)   Run-ons from Bus & Fin
           How many? Method of distribution?

Other
   Invitations — look, name etc.
   Goody bags — Late Late Show — latest Friday 21 May
   Schedule of meetings with client

Perhaps the easiest way to look at each of the budget elements is to look at the ways in which the budget impacts on the client, and is reflected in your PR proposals. A PR budget has several elements:

1. PR fees — your own time
2. Those services that you are buying in
3. Those services that are provided in-house, but which attract charges
4. State taxes
5. Statement of billing procedures/charging policy.

1. PR Fees

For a PR proposal, a grand total is usually given. This may be divided by sections, to reflect the amount of work (time) you believe is involved in each of the proposals contained within the document. The hourly rate is fixed, and does not fluctuate per proposal.

Therefore, the budget your client receives might look like this:

Public Relations Fees		
a. Product launch	1,000	
b. Media liaison	5,000	
c. Sponsorship of trade event	10,000	
d. Print management	4,000	€20,000

In order to manage the proposals, within budget, your breakdown (estimated below at a student rate of fees) might look like this:

Public Relations Fees (all figures are approximate)		
a. Product launch		
15 hours @ €65	1,000	
b. Media liaison		
77 hours @ €65	5,000	
c. Sponsorship of trade event		
154 hours @ €65	10,000	
d. Print management		
62 hours @ €65	4,000	€20,000

(Note: €65 was the hourly rate applied to PR student projects (2002). The rate takes account of the fact that students would take longer to implement a proposal than a professional. The student rate is therefore considerably lower than the consultancy rate of €150–€250 per hour).

Levels of involvement within the consultancy also need to be factored into the management of the proposals. It is always possible that more than one account executive will work on any proposal, or will be needed to help implement the proposal. In this case, the fees would be further broken down. For example:

2. Those Services that You Are Buying In

You are also responsible for external budgets: agreeing a price, ensuring that it is not exceeded, and applying the mark-up. These mark-ups should be clearly indicated to the client in advance.

b. Media liaison		
Ms Maguire		
12 hours @ €250	3,000	
Mr Murphy		
30 hours @ €65	2,000	
Total Fees	5,000	

As you can see, the cost to the client differs substantially from the cost to you. The basis of the mark-up is that, if the print job finished on 2 February, the printer might expect payment from you by 28 February. At the same time (28 February) you would only be invoicing the client, who might take 60 days to pay you, the payment arriving into your office on 30 April. The 17.65 per cent is intended to compensate you for the cash-flow implication of handling the third-party costs.

Option 1 (Brochure)	
Design & layout	2,000
Text	500
Printing of brochure	6,500
(each of the above charges is liable to an addition of 17.65%)	

Option 2 (Brochure)	
Design & layout	2,353
Text	588
Printing of brochure	7,647
(each of the above charges is liable to an addition of 17.65%)	

Note: Postage charges are usually charged at face value, multiplied by two, to cover the cost of envelopes, franking, etc. Once again, clients are entitled to know that 1,000 envelopes @ 41c postage will cost them €820 (and not €410 as they might otherwise expect).

3. Those Services that You Provide In-house

Several in-house services cannot be accurately estimated in advance — you must recover all of your costs involved in handling any job.

Your pricing policy needs to be clearly identified. For example, even if you decide to charge for each fax, at cost, what is the cost? The cost includes rental of the telephone line, purchase, wear and tear, replacement of the fax machine, the telephone cost of sending the fax, the paper that is being used, and the time spent sending it through.

Similarly with telephone calls, you need to establish a policy. Will you charge for all phone calls? Will you charge only for calls made by mobile? (If so, how will you keep track of them?) Will you apply a flat fee for calls, per month? Will you charge only for international or long-distance calls?

4. State Taxes

Public Relations fees are liable to VAT at the standard rate, and all of the services you provide (whether internal or external) are similarly liable to VAT.

Many clients will ask you to provide a tax-clearance certificate (particularly if they are semi-state bodies) to establish that your tax affairs are in order.

5. Statement of Billing Charges

Statements of billing charges have become more detailed over the years. You have only to think of the 'small print' at the back of any form that you sign — to open a telephone or service account — to know this. For simplicity, the key purpose of a statement of billing charges is to inform clients of how you propose to invoice them. Important factors, which must be clearly stated, include:

Fees

Fees (in full) will be billed on conclusion of this project (seldom if ever done)
or
Fees will be billed, monthly, at €2,000 per month, for 10 months (i.e. the duration of the project)
or
Fees will be billed quarterly (in advance/in arrears) at €5,000 per quarter, commencing on x/x/07.

Handling Fee

State what the handling fee applies to, and at what percentage it is charged.

In-house Costs

These must be clearly outlined so that clients are (a) not surprised that they are being charged for these items, and (b) aware of the cost involved.

Terms and Conditions

These used to be covered in a single paragraph at the end of the budget page in your proposals. Nowadays, they may cover the back of the same page.

TYPICAL STRUCTURE OF PR CONSULTANCIES

Senior Account Executive

Senior account executives have a number of key functions: 'a mix of functional, managerial, organisational and negotiating abilities'.[4] They must look for new opportunities to pitch for contracts. They are often the link, at board level, with client companies. They are responsible for selecting the account executives who will work on particular projects, for choosing the team which will be involved in 'pitching' for new business, for monitoring how well their team and the client team are getting on. They also have ultimate responsibility for the satisfactory implementation of client proposals — the buck stops with the senior account executive. The account executive may be handling most of the client meetings, but if something goes wrong, it is ultimately the responsibility of the senior account executive. Finally, they are also responsible for the development of the consultancy. They recommend whether or not additional staff are to be hired, and if they should be full, part-time or contract staff. They oversee staff training and development for their own team. They monitor the IT requirements of their group to ensure that they have access to the best-possible and most cost-efficient IT systems. They also control staff holidays, maternity leave cover and the general flow of work in their area. In large consultancies, these responsibilities may be divided between Account Directors, Account Managers and Senior Account Executives.

Account Executive

An account executive works directly to the senior account executive. Ten to twelve clients will be handled at any one time by an account executive, whose job is to work directly with the clients, and attend meetings, functions and photo calls. Account executives are responsible for the implementation of programmes, and for budget control. They work from time sheets, and monitor deadlines, budgets and implementation at all times. They are also the people who write the proposals which will be presented to clients. This is often done after a meeting with the senior account executive (and possibly a think-tank with other account executives) to find the best-possible solutions to the client problem. They are front-of-house people who are also involved, as part of the team, in client 'pitches'.

Junior Account Executive

This is someone who has just completed a diploma in public relations and has a foot on the first rung of the ladder. Junior account executives work directly to account executives who delegate work to them. Junior account executives are the back-up people. They will ensure that briefing documents actually leave the office on time, and they will chase suppliers for quotes when they are tardy. They will write the first drafts of press releases, which will go to the account executive for approval/amendment. They

will handle a lot of research, either physically or on the internet, finding the information that the account executive needs in order to solve a problem, make a pitch or
incorporate a quote into a speech. They will work with photography companies,
notifying them of prints ordered, captioning and issuing the prints. They are often
the people who are given the ring-around job (contacting either journalists or photo
desks to see if media will be attending a particular function). They will attend functions with their account executive in a support capacity and occasionally attend client
meetings as a note-taker. They will not be contributing at these meetings, but will,
most likely, be asked to contribute at the internal think-tank meetings.

Secretarial/Administrative Back-up

Usually one person is shared among four executives. Everyone is expected to be
computer-literate — the days of giving something to a secretary to type are long
gone!

Salary Scales

The Achievers Group, a recruitment consultancy specialising in the placement of PR
people, provided a list of positions and salaries in 2002. The salary scales are as
follows:

PR Consultancies

Account Executive (1 year's experience)	€22,680
Account Executive (3 years' experience)	€38,600
Account Manager	€52,900
Account Director	€64,000

In-House Positions

Communications Executive (1 year's experience)	€21,500
Corporate Communications Executive (3 years' experience)	€34,000
Public Relations Manager (4 years' experience)	€36,500
Communications Manager (6 years' experience)	€50,000
Director of Corporate Communications (5 years' experience)	€63,500
Corporate Communications Manager (10 years' experience)	€70,000[5]

The salary quoted (in 2000) for a Junior Account Executive with six months'
experience was €19,000. Personally, I would think that €19,000 for a junior account
executive in November 2000 was high. The more usual salary within the industry
would be €15,000. A senior account manager with four years' experience should
command more than €36,500, and an account director at €64,000 is probably working
for a small consultancy.

It is interesting also to note the differences between consultancy and in-house rates of pay. While both are comparable up to account executive level, consultancy rates are higher (at fewer years' experience) than in-house rates. This may be, quite simply, because consultancy rates are negotiable, while in-house rates in the larger companies are usually tied to staff salary scales. It might also reflect the fact that there is more movement of consultancy staff generally than in-house.

What the figures clearly show, however, is that, having entered the business as a junior account executive at €19,000, within three years your salary could have increased by 70 per cent. How quickly you progress is down to hard work, good fortune, creativity and ability.

REFERENCES

1. S.P. Robbins and M. Coulter, *Management*, Prentice Hall International, 2002, (seventh edition); Gary Dessler, *A Framework for Management*, Prentice Hall, New Jersey, 2002.
2. Leon Ostergaard, Dire, Danish State Information Service, 'Quality Control in a Consultancy — Experiences', presentation to the CERP Conference, Copenhagen, October 1996.
3. *PRII Digest*, 14 January 2002.
4. J. White and L. Mazur, *Strategic Communications Management — Making Public Relations Work*, The Economist Intelligence Unit, Addison-Wesley, England, 1995.
5. The Achievers Group, Dublin, 26 March 2002, www.achieversgroup.ie.

CHAPTER 11

Preparing and Delivering a PR Proposal

Public relations consultancies spend a lot of time preparing and presenting proposals. After all, it is the way in which they secure business.

Although this chapter deals with the presentation of proposals, there is also a presentation of credentials by PR consultancies, of which you should be aware.

PRESENTATION OF CREDENTIALS

There are two types of presentation which a client may request. The first is a presentation of credentials. This involves calling a number of consultancies to a potential client's office, individually, and asking them to make a presentation about themselves. It gives the consultancy a chance to showcase its people, clients and achievements. It will show the impressive list of clients it has worked for in the past, and outline the range of issues it has handled for them. The consultancy will show the amount of media coverage secured, the improvement in staff relations, or statistics on attitude change by customers — in effect, the success of its proposals for previous clients. This meeting will also be used to introduce the potential client to the consultancy team — to show the quality of staff and service the company is likely to receive from the consultancy. Finally, the meeting will introduce the potential new client to the consultancy's key personnel, directors and senior account executives, and will make the 'pitch' that the consultancy is the best that could possibly be retained to handle the company.

For this type of presentation meeting, any number of consultancies may be invited. After the presentation meeting, up to three consultancies (usually) will be selected and briefed by the client, and invited to present proposals.

This type of meeting happens more with larger corporations and organisations. They will usually start with a pool of consultancies (up to ten) which are well known, have handled companies in the same industry, or have been recommended by other corporations. From this group, the client is trying to match not only the skills required, but also the people. The aim is to select the three best teams for the job — teams with whom the organisation can work successfully.

This presentation of credentials meeting is followed, for the chosen three, by a meeting at which you are briefed by the company. Your analysis of the brief and recommendations are presented at a subsequent meeting with the client. However, it does not always happen this way. Some of the smaller companies, in particular, will skip the credentials meeting entirely and invite a large number of consultancies to be briefed on their requirements and submit proposals.

CHARGING FOR PROPOSALS

There is debate within the industry about charging for proposals — some consultancies charge; others do not.

PR people are called into a meeting by a potential client seeking their services. Potential clients may call as many PR consultants and consultancies to the meeting as they wish. Each consultancy is briefed on exactly what the client is looking for. Each consultancy then prepares proposals which are presented to the client. The client decides which consultancy is awarded the contract.

Many of the smaller PR consultancies do not charge for proposals, so the time invested in their preparation and presentation is written off to 'administration' whether the proposals are successful or unsuccessful — in other words, costs cannot be recovered. When you look at the time spent preparing proposals, this is a sizeable write-off of time and creative effort.

The business of presenting proposals free of charge devalues the professionalism of the industry, in my opinion. Could you imagine any company briefing three or four barristers and asking them to outline their approach to a high-court case; explaining to them that the best approach will secure the business? They simply wouldn't wear it.

I believe that the business of presenting proposals, free of charge, also devalues the content. A client has been given a number of different approaches to solving particular problems. The client's understanding is that the consultancy has given the 'ideas, strategies, approaches' free. What will now be paid for is the implementation. This reinforces the client's perception that public relations is about tools rather than strategies. Moreover, if they were only ideas, presented free of charge, why not use a combination of all of the best ones? This is an ethical issue. As the selected consultancy, you are honour-bound to give due recognition to the author of the 'idea'. You should offer to recompense the consultancy for the time involved in designing the element of the proposals which you are now requested to implement.

This area is open to abuse by less ethical PR people and companies. The legal position is that it is virtually impossible to copyright an idea. The PR consultant can copyright the proposals and the presentation (the simplest way of doing it is to send yourself, by registered post, a copy of both in advance of presentation), but are you really going to sue the client or PR person afterwards? It is extremely unlikely that you will.

For unethical companies, the temptation to call a number of different consultancies, get all of their ideas, appoint none of them, and implement the best ideas is too great to resist. These companies — they are few, but they are out there — will then select 'other' consultancies the next time, and repeat the same process. As has been stated, if your strategies are freely given, it is difficult for the client to put a value on them.

Advertising agencies, although they reserve the right, in theory, to charge for presenting proposals, in practice seldom do.

Members of the Public Relations Consultants Association have adopted the 'advertising' approach. The PRCA states that 'a fee will be charged for the submission of creative proposals...this fee can be treated as a rejection fee and is only payable if a contract is not awarded to the consultancy in question'.[1] This, in my opinion, is a far more professional approach.

KNOWING YOUR PR COMPETITORS

Clients, traditionally, do not tell you which consultancies have been selected to pitch. Personally, I fail to see why you should not be told. After all, it is not as though you are going to phone the other consultancies and ask them what they are recommending. However, while PR is an expanding industry, it never takes long to find out who else is involved. If you are a small consultancy, it is always nice to know that you won a contract in a pitch against a larger consultancy — it is just good for your ego!

TAKING A BRIEF

Briefs vary. Companies that have used consultancies in the past are aware of the kind of information you require and are generally well prepared. They are structured in the way in which they impart the information to you, and let you know what the desired outcome of the PR work will be. Others, not accustomed to using PR, may give you a brief that wanders over the history of the company but fails to cut to the chase. Other companies again are reluctant to give you a full brief — particularly if the issue is a sensitive one. They want to let as few people as possible know that they have a delicate situation on their hands. This can be extremely difficult for a consultancy left trying to 'guess' where the real communications problems lie.

When taking a brief from any company or organisation, you are trying to establish as much as you possibly can about the company. All of the information will be used to help you build an accurate picture of the company, the industry it works in, the nature of its business. This, in turn, helps you to structure the most appropriate proposals to recommend.

Background Information

You should always begin by establishing as much background information about the company as possible (I will refer throughout to a 'company', but the same rules apply to voluntary bodies, charities, community groups, multinational organisations, etc). How was the company formed? How long has it been in existence? Has it always catered for the same market? Has it always produced the same product, or range of products? Who are the key people involved in the company, e.g. members of the board of directors? Is the company public or private? Has it any plans to go public in the future? How successful has the company been over the years? Where does it see itself going in the future? Is it Irish based? Irish owned? Foreign owned? Try to get as broad a picture as you can.

Attitudes

Establish the attitudes that the company believes are held about it. How is the company perceived by others (in its opinion)? How would it be seen by employees; customers; shareholders; other members of the same industry; suppliers; government or elected representatives? Who are its most important publics? What do these people think? Are there any current problems with any of the company's publics? If so, what are those problems, and do they form part of the brief? If not, how are they being addressed and resolved, and by whom? What follow-up is planned to see if the problems were actually resolved?

Why PR?

Why is the company now seeking the services of a PR consultancy? What does it want to achieve? Is there a specific objective (this is your starting point)? If there are no real reasons, why now? Why do it at all? The company might be seeking publicity because other competitors have been securing a higher profile in recent times. This is a perfectly valid reason. No company decides to retain a service that will cost them money, without having a reason for doing so. Get to the meat of the problem and find out why the company decided to do it at this particular time. Companies will not always tell you their real reasons.

My consultancy was retained by a restaurant some years ago. The brief was to raise the restaurant's profile locally. The owners sponsored a number of initiatives on their premises and wanted to gain media publicity for these events. As the events were of a local nature, we proceeded to target local media and secured good coverage for them. The owners' real aim, however, was to raise the profile of the business so that it could be sold. This is a perfectly valid objective, but one which they did not share with us. As a result, a lot of the publicity they secured was probably of little or no value to them. We would have structured an entirely different campaign, aimed at different media and different publics, had we known that the objective was to make the restaurant known to potential purchasers of the business.

Who are the Target Publics?

Who are the publics that the company is trying to reach? How is the company currently reaching them? What tools are being used? How much research has been done on these publics? Does the company know where these people live; what their habits are; how much they earn; what makes them different; what publications they read and respect; what they do with their free time? Basically, can the company provide you with a mental picture of the publics it is trying to target?

Who is the Competition?

Every company can identify its major competitor — ask the client company to identify the competitor for you and give you some information about that company. How long has it been established? How well respected is it? What is known about it? Is the market expanding or contracting? Is the competitor winning more market share or is it in decline? What is the client company's key advantage (or USP — unique selling point) over its major competitor?

Previous PR Experience

What is the company's history of previous involvement with PR? Has it used in-house PR? Is your consultancy being introduced to work with the in-house department? Is there a representative of that department present at the briefing meeting? If the company no longer has an in-house department, why? Has it worked with a consultancy before? Was this on contract or project basis (i.e. a once-only job) or was it on a retainer (on-going) basis? If so, for how long did the relationship last? Has that consultancy also been invited to tender for this contract? What was the company's experience with PR in the past — was it positive or negative?

If the experience was negative, you have an uphill battle. The negative experience could have been caused by many factors — the selection of the wrong consultancy; a mismatch of personalities; too high an expectation on the part of the client; perceived high costs. The more you can establish at this stage, the better. The most difficult clients in the world are those who feel that they have been 'burned' by PR in the past. Your job is not to establish the truth or otherwise of their belief, but it is important that you establish what the belief is based on.

Finally, you should also find out whether the company has had any PR involvement through its customers or clients. Has it participated in functions organised by others? Has it sponsored events for customers? How much does it feel it benefited from the involvement?

Budget

This is almost an impossible question for clients to answer. How much money are they prepared to allocate? What is their total budget? Clients are always reluctant to tell you how much they are thinking of spending. They live in mortal fear that, if they give you a figure, you will spend it and probably a little more. It is important, however, that you establish some sort of ball-park figure. There is no point in spending time designing a brilliant programme which will cost, say, €32,000, if the client really felt that €6,500 would cover the job. It may be that you could tell the client instantly that the problem could not be solved for that amount of money, or that you can begin to temper the client's expectations about what could reasonably be done within that budget.

Establishing some sort of figure is also treating yourself, and your creative team, with respect. You don't want to waste their time and energy either. Bear in mind that the proposals you would write for €32,000 will take an entirely different approach from those you would write for €6,500. You cannot simply 'shrink' the €32,000 recommendations down to €6,500 — you would need to begin all over again. Time is money. Get the figure right before you start.

Tools of PR

Try to establish the tools the client company is currently using, or has used in the past. Has it had any involvement with sponsorship / exhibitions / press, radio and TV coverage / education / lecture panels / promotions / national or regional competitions / direct mail? What was the level of involvement? Did the company feel that it was successful?

Company Structure

Find out as much as you can about the way in which the company is structured. How many employees are there? Is the company centralised or does it operate from different regional bases? What is the internal structure? With whom would you be liaising? (Are they at the briefing? Could you meet with them?) Are there any others (internal/external) with whom the company believes you should speak? Again, be aware that potential clients are usually very reluctant to let you speak with members of staff or key customers while they are still in these initial stages of selection.

Revert

Establish whom you should contact if you need to revert to the company for clarification. Also establish the information you will need to know for your return visit. What is the deadline for presentation of proposals? Does the company want detailed or outline proposals? (This establishes if there will be a follow-up pitch with more detailed costings, etc.) How many other consultancies will be invited to pitch? Companies may be reluctant to tell you who is pitching, but they should be able to tell you how many. It is important that you establish this figure. Are there three consultancies involved? Or are there ten or fifteen? You need to decide, based on the numbers, whether or not you are prepared to pitch for this contract.

Numbers differ depending on the contracts. When the Dublin Transportation Initiative was being launched,[2] virtually every consultancy in Dublin attended the briefing meeting and a large number of consultancies submitted proposals. The size of the contract being awarded, and the challenge it presented, were too tempting for most consultancies to pass up.

On the other hand, if the company is an SME (small to medium-sized enterprise) with a low PR budget, you might decide that it is not a productive use of your time to prepare and submit proposals against ten or more consultancies. You might also decide that the company is on a fishing exercise — the potential client might, in fact be simply fishing for any PR ideas that are out there. It is something you need to be conscious of because disreputable potential clients exist.

A colleague of mine pitched for a contract, in detail, and was told that she had not secured the job. She checked within the industry (as you would) and failed to find anyone who had won the contract. About a year later, she phoned to tell me to look at the coverage for a particular group — it was exactly, down to the idea for the photo call, the proposal that she had put to the group twelve months earlier. The group had taken her ideas and implemented them itself. She neither got paid for her creative input, nor was she recognised in any way as the 'author' of that approach. So, be careful out there.

Finally, try to establish, on your return, how many people will be at the presentation. What are their roles within the company? Can they provide video / overhead / Power-Point / slide facilities for your presentation?

Having established as much as you possibly can at the briefing stage, you then need to begin to research the company, its industry and its competitors in greater detail before you begin to prepare your proposals.

RESEARCH FOR PR

Existing Literature

Look at the range of literature the company currently produces. Study its corporate brochures, posters, letterheads/compliments slips and advertising flyers. Try to establish the company style, at least in printed material. Also look at the competitors' literature. This is always useful for comparison. The competitors probably produce the same range of literature, but a comparison will tell you what their style is — more upmarket; better designed; greater use of colour? Also study the websites of both the potential client company and its competitors.

Press Coverage

Study past press coverage that the company has secured. Go back three years. Look at the nature of the coverage — was it favourable or unfavourable? What topics were covered — an annual award ceremony, an industrial dispute? Check the spread of coverage — it can tell you a lot. If the coverage appears primarily in one newspaper or magazine, it may simply be that someone in the company has a good connection with a journalist in that particular organ. If there is a wide spread of coverage, did the company secure it itself? Did a PR consultancy handle the coverage? Was the PR consultancy working for the company or for the event it sponsored? Study the coverage that the competitors secured and do exactly the same analysis (the nature of the coverage, the spread and the topics). This type of study might also reveal that the competitors have become more pro-active with the media of late, or that the competitors secure regular annual coverage, or that the competitors concentrate on one medium only. You can access the press coverage through the business libraries (by company, industry, and location) and on the internet.

Attitude Research

Note your own attitudes to the company before and after the briefing session (your attitudes may have changed because of the information you learned during the brief). Then try to see if the attitudes the company told you were prevalent actually reflect the attitudes out there in the real world. Speak with customers, media and opinion leaders, and ask them for their impression of the company. Speak with friends. You can get some great information this way. Do not tell people that you are pitching for a contract for the company, or indeed that you have any connection at all with the company. Simply throw in a question over a pint some evening to see if anyone knows anything about this company or its products. Some people will remember only industrial disputes; some will have had a bad experience of the product or the company follow-up service; some will know nothing at all about the company; and some will think that it is a wonderful employer. It is amazing what you can learn.

Outside Factors

Look also at the exterior factors which may impact on the company in the future. Look at the trends within the industry — are companies decentralising, downsizing, recruiting in huge numbers, privatising or going public? All of these areas may impact on the company for which you are preparing proposals. Also look at national and European legislation for the industry, and the future trends in legislation. Look at things like changes in working hours, or environmental restrictions which might impact on the company's profitability or business practices.

What You Saw and Heard

You can learn a lot by observation when you visit the company's premises. Look at the reception area and how it is presented. Watch the way in which visitors are received. Be mindful of the attitude of the receptionist or the telephonist when you phoned to make an appointment. Look at the way in which staff-members interact with each other as they meet. Look at the building itself — is it well presented; in need of a coat of paint? Observe!

Financial Check

Can you run a financial 'health check' on the company? If not, speak with others within your own professional circle. Has any other consultancy, ad agency, marketing or print organisation worked with this company before. Is it reliable? Does it pay on time? Is it in financial trouble? Does it have a reputation for settling disputes in the courts? You are trying to be sure that you are not buying trouble for yourself. You cannot recover time spent on a contract, and if the company is in financial difficulty, or has a bad reputation, you may find that you never get paid for the work done or that it takes so long to get paid, it doesn't justify taking the contract.

My consultancy was involved with one client company in the mid-1990s. The client was a new company which could not be financially checked through the normal routes. Admittedly we were somewhat nervous about the company from the start. In fact, everyone involved in the project — direct marketing people, printers, and advertising agencies — was a little nervous. As an insurance policy for ourselves, we insisted that the contract be paid 50 per cent in advance, 50 per cent in arrears. The client agreed but, on the first day when press releases were to be issued, we held the releases and had to send a courier to collect the first instalment of our fees. The company went bust within weeks, and left each of the agencies seriously out of pocket. We never did get paid the other 50 per cent, but at least we had not lost completely. Other agencies were very badly burned by the experience.

Recce

Do as much homework as you can — on foot! Visit the company outlets and ask questions. You can learn a lot from what sales staff will tell you — an ordinary customer. I have used this method in the past, and it works extremely well.

By visiting a number of different shops, I found out that a jewellery manufacturer's sales were in decline. Sales staff told me that the earrings they manufactured were, in fact, too heavy. People never bought that brand of earring a second time because it hurt their ear lobes to wear them.

THE PROPOSALS

You have now taken the brief and conducted additional research. You are able to categorise what you already know about the company. You have established information on the current situation in the industry and the market, and have conducted a SWOT analysis (strengths — weaknesses — opportunities — threats). You have studied the company's publics and know who they are. And you have looked at the company's objectives, and know what it is that your potential client wants to achieve. All of this information will point you towards the PR opportunities available to you.

You are ready to begin preparing the proposals. Make them clear. I am indebted to my school-friend, Ursula Forde (who always e-mails me with PR-related goodies), for the following dire warning about preparing proposals:

> And then came the Assumptions. And the Assumptions were without form and the Plan was without substance. And darkness was upon the face of the Workers. And the Workers spoke among themselves, saying, one to another, 'This is a crock of shit, and it stinks.' And the Workers went unto their Supervisors and said, 'It is a pail of dung,

and we can't live with the smell.' And the Supervisors went unto their Managers, saying, 'It is a container of excrement, and it is very strong, such that none may abide by it.' And the Managers went unto their Senior Managers, saying, 'It is a vessel of fertiliser, and none may abide its strength.' And the Senior Managers spoke among themselves, saying one to another, 'It contains that which aids plant growth, and it is very strong.' And the Senior Managers went to the Directors, saying unto them, 'It promotes growth, and it is very powerful.' And the Directors went to the Chief Executive, saying unto him, 'This new plan will actively promote the growth and vigour of the company with powerful effects.' And the Chief Executive looked upon The Plan and saw that it was good. And so The Plan became Policy...And that, my friends, is how shit happens.

Structure of Public Relations Proposals

PR proposals work to a defined structure, always. The structure follows a logical sequence, for both client and consultancy.

(a) Title Page

Proposals always contain a title page which gives the following information:

- The title of the proposal
- The name and address of the company to which the proposals are submitted
- The name, address and logo of your own consultancy
- The date on which the presentation was made.

(b) Table of Contents

The table of contents simply acts as an easy reference for clients to follow your proposals, or look back in detail at a particular element.

(c) Background Information/Brief

This section deals with the brief, as you were given it. It states the problem or opportunity identified by the company. It outlines the information you were given at the briefing meeting and sets the scene for the recommendations to follow.

(d) Additional Research

This is the information you established in addition to that given to you at the brief. This section should show that you have done your homework, and that you have developed a good 'feel' for the business, its competitors, and the market in which it operates. It might also highlight information you unearthed which in some way impacted on the proposals.

(e) Key Objectives

These are the objectives for the proposals — the key items you have identified which will be addressed over the period of the plan. Remember to make your objectives specific. The tighter they are, the tighter your proposals will be, and the better will be your evaluation.

(f) Relevant Publics

This is a detailed list of the publics you have identified who are relevant to the objectives you have set. Note that you might also list other business publics who were not addressed within the proposals. This might be because of the time-span the client dictated, or because of lack of client resources. Or you might just 'flag' the fact that there is a particular public which has been consistently overlooked and for whom separate proposals should be written at some stage in the future.

(g) Proposals

This part contains the proposals themselves — your creative strategy for ensuring that the objectives are met, the coverage is secured, the problem is solved, or the issue is resolved. Highlight the word 'creative'. You are making a competitive pitch against other consultancies. If you have done your preparation properly, each consultancy will have identified the same objectives and publics. What differentiates one from the other is the creativity of approach to the problem, and the breadth of understanding.

Your proposals will be divided into sections for easy comprehension. These sections might include corporate identity, internal relations, staff morale, company newsletter, external relations, dealing with media, launches, lunches, exhibitions, sponsorships, etc. — all of the tools of the trade which you feel are relevant to achieving the objectives of the proposals.

(h) Evaluation

For decades, PR practitioners paid little attention to evaluation until 'calls for accountability sparked greater interest in tools for measuring the effectiveness of media relations'.[3]

Industries worldwide spent £20 billion a year on public relations throughout the 1990s. Surveys have shown that these industries (our clients) rate the ability to evaluate second only to creativity and consultancy attributes. While 90 per cent of international PR consultancies thought evaluation necessary, only 20 per cent actually did it! The industry still has a long way to go to meet the needs of our clients.[4]

Evaluation is the stick you give to the client to beat you with. It is not enough to be creative — you must be able to show that your creative strategies will achieve the desired outcomes for the company. The evaluation section shows the client how the effectiveness of your proposals can be measured.

Evaluation is usually measured quantitatively or qualitatively, or — ideally — both.

- *Quantitative* (relating to quantity) means measuring by number or percentage — e.g. more job applicants; higher percentage response than anticipated to the launch of a new product (PR in advance of the campaign); or more frequent mentions in the press/media.
- *Qualitative* (relating to quality) means focusing on content, not numbers — e.g. job applicants are better educated, or press coverage is more favourable in tone. Qualitative measures are effective for research among leaders of activist groups, government officials or journalists.[5]

So, how is this evaluation actually established? There are seven useful methods:

1. Self-evident results
2. Analysis of media coverage
3. Structured research
4. Media enquiries
5. Direct statistical feedback
6. Changes in attitude or behaviour
7. Relationship change.

1 Self-evident Results

These are results that need no formal research. It is always useful, however, if the client company nominates one or two people in addition to your own consultancy to monitor the 'self-evident' changes. Self-evident results include things like company salespeople being better received in stores after the introduction of a new retailer newsletter (this feedback can come from the sales staff); or that the introduction of the newsletter created greater interest in the company — retailers told salespeople how interesting the newsletter was, or that they never knew the company was so big, or it never crossed their minds to think of how long it actually took to produce a product. Again, feedback from sales staff might show that existing customers had broadened their range of purchases from the company. Or it might be obvious that there was a better atmosphere among the staff as a result of the introduction of an awards scheme.

2 Analysis of Media Coverage

If the proposals were aimed at securing greater media coverage, analysis of the amount of column inches secured or airtime achieved will show an increase in coverage. The analysis might look at the fact that the business secured coverage in newspapers with greater circulation figures (creating more OTSs). Likewise, the company might have secured coverage on TV programmes with high Nielsen ratings.[6] The quality of the coverage might have improved. There might be no increase at all in the quantity, but the tone of the coverage could be more favourable. There might be a greater national spread of media, or vastly improved local radio coverage. Whatever media coverage the proposals set out to achieve should be evaluated and analysed.

3 Structured Research

Structured research, usually carried out by opinion polls, is an expensive but accurate way of determining two key areas: (a) opinions and attitudes towards your company, and (b) the level of name recognition your company has achieved. This is a highly specialised skill which involves structuring questions so that people cannot anticipate the answer you are looking for, and will, therefore, give you an honest opinion. Research is used to determine, for example, whether more people know about the company now than knew about it twelve months ago — presuming, always, that you had done initial research to establish the level of knowledge about your company before the PR programme began. Research could also be used to establish whether the company name, unprompted, was listed as one of the top companies, or a brand leader in a particular field. This type of research would usually be undertaken after a company has entered a sponsorship deal, for the duration of the sponsorship, to see if the name recognition has improved.

4 Media Enquiries

This is certainly not one of the key evaluation tools, but is a very useful one none the less. It is done by tracking within the company the number of people who phoned about the company or product because of media coverage. If you build in a question into each call, it is easy to establish where people heard of you or saw a reference to you. It should be noted that this relates to news coverage, not to advertising.

5 Direct Statistical Feedback

This refers to the kind of statistics that would be available within the company and simply need to be compared with the figures/statistics for the previous year. You can analyse things like greater attendance at an exhibition, or more sales leads generated. You can study any increase in the number of job applicants. You might look at an improvement in the share price, or the successful uptake of a new share issue. You can learn a lot from responses to questionnaires issued with all products purchased, or issued to everyone attending an event. You can also monitor feedback about a seminar or conference — did people say it was better than last year? In what way?

6 Changes in Attitude or Behaviour

Has there been a change in attitude from negative to positive, which shows that your message has been received and understood by your target public? Ideally, this would result in behavioural change as well.[7]

7 Relationship Change

This entails measuring the relationship between an organisation and its publics. This is a new but rapidly developing area of PR interest. Still largely in the academic research/theory phase, it will, no doubt, become more relevant in future years.[8]

(i) Timescale

Every PR proposal should include a timescale. It is important that the client knows over what period of time you propose to implement the proposals. It is also important for the PR practitioner. You need to work out the length of time involved in implementing the proposals in order to structure a budget and determine whether or not you have the capacity to handle the proposals within the given timeframe.

The timescale should detail, on a month-by-month basis, exactly what work will be undertaken by the consultancy. And, of course, the timescale covers all proposals contained within the document. This allows you to be sure that you are actually doing everything on time, and allows the client to get a handle on the work to be done in each month. Very often the work is 'unseen' in the initial stages (e.g. the appointment of printers, graphic designers or video production teams). It is all legitimate work which needs to be undertaken in order to reach the final goal, and the client should know the background as well as the foreground work being undertaken on behalf of, and at a cost to, the company.

(j) Budget — Fees and Expenses

The budget is a vital area of the proposals. You will have sought estimates for each of the items you are proposing, and you will give details of exactly how much you estimate everything will cost. The budget consists of four elements:

1. Your own time
2. Services that you are buying in
3. Services that are provided in-house by the consultancy
4. State taxes.

1 Your Own Time

This is calculated at a fixed hourly rate. You may bill on an hourly basis, on retainer, or by project fee. If billing on an hourly basis, you need to estimate the number of hours which will be involved in the proposal, and give the client an estimate of costs. The invoices for your time will show the number of hours worked monthly.

A retainer establishes a fixed fee and is usually paid monthly. Retainers are sometimes paid not for work done, but to ensure that the consultant is available, should the company need advice. You are 'retained' to advise the company as the need arises.

You may also bill fees on a project basis. This means setting a fixed fee for doing a particular job (e.g. the launch of a new product). Payment could be by instalment, or in arrears on completion.

2 Services that You are Buying in

You will be responsible for external budgets — for agreeing a price and ensuring that the price is not exceeded. External budgets include things like: photography, print, room hire, food and wine charges, video production, and advertorial space. External items attract a mark-up, which is designed to compensate your consultancy for handling the payment of the invoices, in advance of billing to the client. Mark-ups are generally of the order of 17.65 per cent. They should be clearly indicated to the client in advance. Bear in mind that the application of a mark-up brings legally binding responsibilities with it. In applying a mark-up, you are acting as an agent or intermediary for your client. You contract directly with the service-provider. So, whether the client pays you or not, you are legally liable to pay the service-provider.

3 Services that are Provided In-house by the Consultancy

Several in-house services cannot be accurately estimated in advance, but you must recover all of your costs involved in handling any job. Clear pricing policies need to be established for recovering the cost of such items as photocopying, faxes, telephone calls (land and mobile) and post. Larger consultancies monitor in-house costs by means of client numbers — every time you photocopy or make a call, you prefix the client reference in advance, and the computer adds up the total charges at the end of the month. Smaller consultancies still monitor manually. In-house service charges are usually billed on a monthly basis, in arrears.

4 State Taxes

Public Relations fees are liable to VAT at the standard rate. With the notable exception of photography, which is charged at the lower rate, most other services are billed at the standard rate.

(k) Consultancy Details

The consultancy details are often more irreverently referred to as the 'brag list'. This is an additional section which details the clients you have handled or are currently handling, the nature of the work you have done for them, and the breadth of success of the proposals.

It also contains details of the members of the consultancy who would be handling this account, with a brief biography of each. Potential clients, therefore, have a handle on the team they will be working with. This is the same team which should have been present at the 'pitch' for the contract.

(l) Appendices

The final section of the proposal, this is sometimes used to provide mock sketches of concepts which the client might have difficulty visualising.

PRESENTATION OF THE PROPOSALS

Proposals are presented to the client at a pre-arranged meeting. The consultancy puts together a team, consisting of the people who would actually be handling the account (should you win it), usually a consultancy director, and possibly a specialist in a particular field who will match the expertise at the other side of the table.

Your team, on the consultancy side, should match the team skills on the client side. Therefore, if the client has the head of the financial department attending, there is a very good chance that detailed questions of a financial nature will be asked. Your team should have someone on it with matching financial skills.

Ideally, your team should consist of the same number of people as the client side so that you neither drown nor intimidate each other.

Presentation of the proposals is a performance. You will bring the written proposals with you, and leave them after you for the client to study. The nature of the presentation, however, is to pitch the proposals to the client, arouse interest, generate lively debate, and bring the concepts to life. It also gives the client an opportunity to meet with your team and see if the personalities fit together.

I once attended a presentation, by an advertising agency, to one of our clients. The agency's presentation was pitch perfect — lively, interesting, and to the point. The client asked me afterwards for my opinion. I told him honestly. There were eight people on the agency side — seven men and one woman. The seven men all spoke; the woman never uttered a word. Yet, at the close of the meeting, one of the directors of the agency stated that the woman would be the main link with the client. I felt that the client could not accept the team as we had no idea if she could even speak! The presentation had created the impression — no doubt unintentionally — that the woman was the junior on the team, and it was the junior who would be looking after the client. The agency did not win the account.

Presentations can be expensive. Not only do consultancies invest time in research, analysis and pitch, but money may also be spent on preparing PowerPoint presentations, mock-ups and scale models.

Finally, after every presentation, you should analyse the strength and weaknesses of your pitch. Remember, in the PR business, you are continually learning.

REFERENCES

1. www.prca.ie/fees.html.

2. In 1988, the Minister for the Environment appointed the Dublin Transportation Review Group, with representatives from the relevant government departments, local authorities and Córas Iompair Éireann (CIE) to review transportation planning arrangements for the Greater Dublin Area. From 1988 to 1995, the Group worked on the best transportation strategy for Dublin. The entire process is called the Dublin Initiative Transportation. For further information see http://www.epe.be/workbooks/tcui/example10.html

3. Bruce Jeffries-Fox, 'Toward an Understanding of How News Coverage and Advertising Impact Consumer Perceptions, Attitudes and Behavior', Insight Farm, a Burrelle's/VMS Company, on Institute for Public Relations (Florida) website at www.instituteforpr.com

4. IPRA World Congress, Helsinki, 1997.

5. James E. Grunig, 'Qualitative Methods for Assessing Relationships Between Organizations and Publics', on Institute for Public Relations (Florida) website at www.instituteforpr.com

6. Nielsen ratings are viewer figures for television programmes. They are produced daily. Nielsen replaced the older TAM ratings in the late 1990s. Information supplied by Padraig Guilfoyle, Media Guilfoyle, Blackrock, Dublin.

7. Dr Linda Childers Hon, and Dr James E. Grunig, 'Guidelines for Measuring Relationships in Public Relations', on Institute for Public Relations (Florida) website at www.instituteforpr.com

8. Ibid.

CHAPTER 12

Role of the In-house Press / Media Officer

Press or Media Officer is a position found only outside PR consultancies. In consultancy work, every account executive is expected to combine at least some of the roles of the media officer within their own job.

Press or Media Officer is an in-house position. Large organisations, sports bodies, departments of state and governments all have press officers. Their backgrounds often differ from those of PR consultants. Many press officers are former journalists retained because they have worked on the 'other side'. They know the main players, the constraints, the 'ethos', and the deadlines of the media.

Although the term 'Press Officer' survives to this day, particularly in government circles, the job is really that of media officer. The press officer deals not only with the printed press (newspapers, magazines, trade publications) but also with television and radio.

Increasingly in Ireland, the impact of non-Irish media is being felt. British newspapers have decent circulation figures in Ireland and are quite widely read. Similarly, Sky News, UTV, BBC and Channel 4 are all accessible in most parts of the country, and are therefore included in the media for which press officers are responsible.

There are some in-house departments where the role of press officer is not singled out exclusively — where, for example, press officers would deal also with sponsorship or the in-house newsletter. In this chapter, we will look at the role of the press officer as an 'exclusive' position, a dedicated position, which rests in the hands of one person.

Press officers may or may not have a team of people working with them. If the organisation is small, the press officer may have one person providing administrative back-up. If the organisation is large — e.g. government, the Garda Síochána, or the Defence Forces — the press officer may be backed by a team of up to ten people.

The role of the press officer will be looked at under the following headings:

- Function of the Press Officer
- Skills Needed to Perform the Job
- Infrastructure
- Created Back-up Systems
- Tools of the Trade.

FUNCTION

A press officer is usually a specially nominated member of a company's in-house public relations department. Within a PR department, certain staff members are given specific tasks to perform. A press officer's job is to deal with the press or, more properly, the media. The job involves responding to enquiries from the media and generating favourable coverage/exposure for the company. Within the company, the press officer is the media expert. Press officers may also be called media officers or media liaison officers.

The press officer's role differs, in one significant way, from that of a consultant who is handling media relations. In the case of consultancies, the rule, generally applied, is that consultants are background people — advising, liaising, monitoring, but, crucially, training spokespersons and making them available (as the public face of the organisation) to media.

A press officer's job usually entails being the 'face' of the organisation. They too liaise and monitor and advise, but they also, usually, take 'front of house' and are interviewed themselves by radio, television and print media. The press officer becomes publicly identified with the organisation. You have only to think of someone like Superintendent John Farrelly of the Garda Press Office. If there is a murder, rape, robbery, or any kind of serious incident, he is the one that we expect to see being interviewed and putting the Garda position on TV, radio and in print.

Press officers need to inform the media of their appointment. They should contact the media, introduce themselves, give their home, mobile and work telephone numbers, and let the media know that they are available to deal with any queries they may have. They become the conduit through which all media enquiries flow.

The third element of a press officer's job is to generate favourable coverage/exposure for the company. To do this, it is necessary to have a constant flow of information from all sections within the company. The press officer needs communication flows to senior and junior members of staff, across all departments, on an on-going basis.

Press officers also require an ability to identify news or create a good story from the germ of an idea. The key requirement of journalists is always for news that would interest their readers, and the press officers try to satisfy that need. They have a 'nose' for a good story. They would often do a lot of research to develop an angle suitable for media — for example, a new product might have been suggested by the youngest person in the factory, or it might combine two chemicals for the first time. The actual product may not provide the story, but something in its development might.

Press officers also need to know where to issue the news. Different magazines and newspapers have different interests. One story may have the potential to be told in four different ways by coming at it from four different angles. The press officer has to know which newspaper or magazine would be interested in what angle — there's no point in approaching the right magazine with the wrong angle!

Press officers must also be able to select the best way to issue the news — not every story is issued by press release! They choose whether to issue a release, or to look for feature coverage. They might choose to hold a press conference, press reception or a management/media briefing. They might decide that the story is visual and organise a photo call. They might offer an exclusive interview on radio or television. Press officers must be conversant with all of the possibilities in order to select the option that offers the best chance of media coverage.

Many press officers are former journalists and some find it surprisingly difficult to 'swap horses' and move to the PR side of the fence. Former journalists know the workings of media well — it is how they previously earned their living.

If you are really interested in the role of the journalist turned press officer (turned journalist again afterwards), read Sean Duignan's book, *One Spin on the Merry-go-round*. You won't find a more elucidating account anywhere.[1]

Press officers understand the way in which stories develop; the likely interpretation which a story will attract; the deadlines for publication or broadcast of a story; and the 'ideal' time to break a story.

However, you do not need to be a press officer to know how the media works. Seán Doherty TD gave a press conference in 1992. At the conference, he stated that the then Taoiseach and Fianna Fáil leader, Charles Haughey, had known that journalists Geraldine Kennedy and Bruce Arnold's phones were tapped, and had seen the transcripts.[2] The conference was held in the Montrose Hotel, which was very convenient for RTÉ (TV3 had not yet arrived on the scene). The conference started at approximately 8.15 p.m. — perfectly timed for the 9 o'clock bulletin as a 'breaking' news story. The telephones were tapped in 1982. The topic, the choice of venue and the timing of the press conference virtually guaranteed coverage. (Seán Doherty, in an interview on the RTÉ *This Week* programme later revealed that journalist Vincent Browne's phone had also been tapped.[3])

SKILLS NEEDED TO PERFORM THE JOB

A press officer obviously needs writing skills — an ability to write information in a format acceptable to newspapers, radio and TV stations. This must include the ability to write press releases and feature articles.

The press officer also needs to be familiar with every journalist who is important to the company, and needs to be familiar with their work, and their deadlines.

Press officers should have interpersonal communication skills. Part of their job involves building a rapport with journalists. They build a rapport because it is important that journalists are familiar with their style of work. Journalists need to know that their enquiries will be dealt with efficiently; the information will be relevant; and the response will arrive in plenty of time to meet their copy or broadcast deadlines. Press officers must be professionally respected by the journalists. They also need to build a rapport so that approaches to journalists with stories, press releases or 'angles' are welcomed. The press officer needs to understand, above all else, that the journalists' need is for news in which their readers will be interested.

Good interpersonal skills should not be confused with an outgoing, gregarious personality. Press officers are of differing personality types. Some are indeed outgoing and gregarious; others are quiet, thoughtful, careful and analytical in their responses. All, however, have an ability to communicate with people.

Press officers have to be respected by senior management. They can do their job properly only if they are taken into senior management's confidence and fully briefed on all situations (and their backgrounds) before they, in turn, brief the media.

Finally, press officers need excellent time-management and organisational skills. More than any other PR professional, their job involves 24-hour-a-day, 7-day-a-week accessibility. Excellent management skills are required in order to ensure that all media enquiries are handled thoroughly, management is kept fully briefed, and the press officer doesn't burn out!

INFRASTRUCTURE

The press office should be a repository of information, which is easily accessible.

Computer Systems

Nowadays, it is understood that anyone, in any line of business, has at least basic computer literacy. Press offices couldn't function without the standard software packages that allow press officers, or their staff, to input press releases and speeches in draft form.

In the past, speeches and releases were typed. Any error found meant a correction with Tipp-Ex, and changing the order of paragraphs meant going to a complete re-type. Nowadays, we take it for granted that we can draft and re-draft on screen as easily as answering a telephone.

The computer has much wider uses, however. Modern systems mean that day, week or month schedulers enable people to schedule for imminent deadlines and meetings. Many of these systems allow access, sometimes on a controlled basis, to the diaries of others, so that meetings can be arranged even in someone's absence.

Computerisation has also meant that faxes can be delivered much more speedily. All systems have address books which can store names — by journalist, by newspaper, by subject — which can be accessed either as individuals or by group. Modern faxing is done by modem. If paper is produced, it is merely as an aide-mémoire for someone. Sending a fax is a paperless process, with the message sent from screen to receiver.

Computers in press offices also need e-mail, intranet and internet systems. E-mail is one of the greatest time savers (and time wasters) ever invented. The group e-mail must be one of the fastest and easiest ways to disperse information.

Most computers nowadays have internet access capability. In public relations generally, but in the role of the press officer in particular, it is difficult to imagine people being able to do their jobs without it. Many press officers use the net as a resource tool — they find useful information and research, particularly for inclusion in speeches and feature articles. It is also necessary to monitor the websites of others — in particular, checking chat rooms which might be discussing your organisation or product. And virtually every press office has computers with ISDN capability for faster transfer of information and visuals. Moreover, most large companies put press releases onto their websites at the same time that they are issued to media.

Television and Radio

It goes without saying that each press office has television sets and radios. It would be difficult to imagine press officers being able to do their job if they could not watch the TV news, or listen to a breaking debate on radio. The larger press offices will have several radios, each tuned to a different (usually national) station. They are on 'in the background' with someone monitoring content, in case it should relate to their organisation.

Filing and Tracing Systems

No press office could work without excellent filing and tracing systems. Photographs are constantly being taken, statements are regularly issued on different topics, and press releases are distributed daily. On a daily/weekly basis, press cuttings, audio and video tapes are being received, which relate to the organisation. Each press office needs to have a system in place which allows for the immediate tracing and retrieval of information. This is sometimes better done by consultancies than in-house.

Some years ago, I dealt with a large organisation, which had an in-house PR section. In the early days of our relationship, I was told that there was no need to retain a press-cutting agency as there was a staff member responsible for cuttings. I agreed that, under those circumstances, it would be unnecessary for the organisation to retain a cutting agency. I asked if I could have all relevant cuttings on the topic under debate, for the previous three months, and was keen to establish by what time each day senior members of the organisation received the relevant cuttings. I was then informed that the system did not work like that and, in fact, there was a three-month backlog in processing the cuttings. There's not much point in having a system if it doesn't work. The nature of media is that news should be read, listened to and watched on a daily basis, and the response must be immediate. Could any organisation respond to a three-month old cutting and retain credibility?

The difficulty with a press-cutting function is that it is seen as something 'worthy' which should be done, if only time were available. In consultancies, this function is better handled (although it still falls behind occasionally) because the consultancy understands that an inability to retrieve information, instantly, results in an additional cost. Quite simply it will take someone longer, cause more stress, and increase the cost (either to the consultancy or the client) if the system doesn't work.

Finally, don't forget the vital role that press-cutting agencies play. For a fixed fee each month, and an additional fee per cutting, agencies will monitor all press mentions of your company, product or competitor. The newspaper cuttings can be sent to you daily by fax or e-mail, or weekly by post. Press-cutting agencies will also monitor and provide audio and video tapes of radio and television interviews, and transcripts.

CREATED BACK-UP SYSTEMS

Reference Material

Press officers should assemble as much reference material as possible about the company, including all of the annual reports, brochures, flyers, induction manuals, leaflets, posters and corporate videos. They need to reference them by year and by topic. This material gives a good overview of the development of the company over the years and may provide useful information to incorporate in a feature article at some point in the future.

Historical Material

As much historical material as possible should also be gathered — like old photographs of the original factory, the first employees (whom the press officer should try to identify), or the delivery carts. The press officer should gather information about the founder of the company, and possibly keep a copy of the minutes of the first company meeting. If the company is long established, there should be a sizeable amount of material available. The problem is usually that such material is scattered — held in different offices throughout the company. At short notice it could be very difficult to find the one piece of information or the particular photograph you are looking for.

This material should all be housed and catalogued in one area for ease of access by everyone. The press officer may want to use the material for feature articles, or may wish to make reference to the founding of the company in the chairman's address to the AGM. The material has many uses for other members of the PR team. Old photographs may be used as part of an exhibition or for the corporate Christmas cards. The uses for historical material are endless.

Scanners have made life simpler in this regard. Material can be scanned onto computer and archived for access by all, removing the need to retrieve the paper. The press office, however, should house all of the original material and act as a resource for the entire company.

Press Material

The press officer should also have a library of press cuttings, audio and video tapes. Press officers should have immediate access to anything ever published about the company in a newspaper or magazine. They should have audio tapes (and transcripts) of any radio interview given, and video tapes of any TV interviews or references to the company.

Tapes should always be requested in transcript and audio form in order to analyse not only what was said, but the speed and clarity with which it was said.

Spokespersons

Key personnel in the organisation should be identified, who, in addition to the press officer, would act as spokespersons. As a general rule, there should be more than one spokesperson. The chief executive or managing director may know absolutely everything about the company, but what if they are away on holidays, or ill in hospital, or not contactable because they are on a flight to Bahrain? There should be at least two. Each organisation will decide, depending on the nature of its business, where these spokespersons should be drawn from. If you begin by assuming that the chief executive will be the overall spokesperson, you should then establish which department your second spokesperson should come from.

If you are a publicly quoted company, it might be crucial that you train a spokesperson from finance. Similarly, if your company produces a food product, there should be one spokesperson from this area who can answer questions about product content, or food hygiene policy. If your company employs a large number of people, it might be wise to select someone from Human Resources to put the management position in union negotiations.

Each organisation is different. The key rule to remember is that one spokesperson only is generally a mistake. At a minimum, there should be a 'deputy' who can take over in times of crisis. The nature of any crisis is that it will be intensive for the first 48 hours or so, then, generally, will begin to abate. No one can stay on top of everything that is happening, and speak with clarity, authority and calmness for a 48-hour period. Exhaustion takes over. There must be a 'deputy' who can step into the breach.

Each of these spokespersons needs to be media trained. It is not part of their daily jobs to give media interviews. The press officer must ensure that they are familiar and comfortable with all media. The press officer will also use these training sessions to look at the strengths and weaknesses of each individual. Some may be extraordinarily good at radio interviews, but very weak on television. Not all media suit each individual. The press officer will seek to enhance the company strengths by selecting the right people who will be the best-possible spokespersons for the organisation.

Press officers should also ensure that spokespersons are given regular refresher courses. It is a bit like riding a bicycle. If you have been taught to do it, you will remember. But you will not necessarily wish to start riding a bicycle again in public, after a gap of four years, without first having a test run. Media interviews are exactly the same. The press officer owes it to those being interviewed, and to the company, to ensure that they receive regular refresher courses.

Background Information on Spokespersons

When press officers have been with an organisation for a long time, they naturally collect, in their mind, all sorts of information about the company spokespersons. A new press officer needs to gather this information.

The information allows the press officer to give background information about the spokesperson to the journalist before they meet and, often, vice versa. It is nice to be able to tell a journalist that the person to be interviewed also has a deep abiding love of golf; or spends most of their free time at classical concerts in the National Concert Hall; or takes extravagant foreign holidays. It is a nice touch — and a professional one. The press officer knows something about the journalist and spokesperson which they each have in common. All it does, quite simply, is act as an ice-breaker, but it can often set both at ease with each other, resulting in the journalist getting a better interview and the spokesperson being more at ease.

How this information is gathered varies. As mentioned above, press officers who have been a long time with the organisation instinctively know the link between both. New press officers must ask questions; pick it up as they go along (always assuming that they have the luxury of time); or approach each spokesperson and ask for details. A structured questionnaire seldom works because people fail to understand why you are looking for the information, and may feel that you are looking for irrelevant or personal details. Bear in mind that these are, inevitably, very senior people.

Instead of a questionnaire, the press officer could ask spokespersons to write a brief biographical note about themselves. The result will be similar to the entries in *Who's Who in Ireland*.[4] The information will certainly vary, but it is information willingly given for your use. Think about the variety of responses possible. Some people are comfortable telling you the name of the person they married and the names and ages of each of their children. Others will be more comfortable giving you details of their academic achievements. Some will list their hobbies; others are workaholics who would have difficulty identifying a true hobby. Whatever the type of response received, the press officer will now have a better 'handle' on their spokesperson and where they are coming from.

Deep Throat

Behind each spokesperson, the press officer also needs to identify what I call a 'Deep Throat'. Anyone who has watched the film *All the President's Men*[5] will know that Bob Woodward's mystery source was known as 'Deep Throat'.

In this instance, a deep throat is someone who has a deep knowledge of a specialist area. This person is often the first point of contact for the press officer. It is the deep throat who will tell the press officer why the media might be pursuing a particular angle; which of the product contents, if inappropriately used, might cause illness; or why the share price has dropped so dramatically. The deep throat gives the background briefing to the press officer, providing vital background information in a particular area. The press officer, in turn, uses this information as the basis of the advice to be given to the spokesperson who will be interviewed. The skill of press officers is as communications experts. They are not expected to know everything about the company (although they will know quite a lot).

Finally, press officers need all possible contact numbers for the deep throats and the spokespersons. They will already have the work number and the direct line number if there is one. They will also need home, mobile and bleeper. Senior people usually have fax and e-mail numbers at home, and might also have personal mobile numbers. We have all become so accessible — 24 hours a day — that it is possible to find someone, at any hour of the day or night, provided that you have all of their contact details.

The press officer is senior enough not to abuse the access, but has enough savvy to know when is it important to disturb someone at home, to clear a statement for immediate release.

Photographic Library

The press officer also needs to compile an up-to-date photographic library of spokespersons, products and company premises. (See Chapter 6 on photography.)

Media Information Documents: Product and Production Process

The press officer should accumulate written information on each of the products, the processes and the company itself. These become Media Information Documents. These documents include how the product was developed, and what elements go into the production (this is not always available in the case of pharmaceuticals, for example, where ingredients or quantities of ingredients are seldom disclosed because this information is regarded as competitor-sensitive). The information document also includes the volume of sales, the retail price, the distribution channels, the outlets, the number of people employed on this particular product and the international sales figures. It may even include information on the rationale for the product (e.g. pre-prepared meals as a response to changing lifestyles).

The process briefing will explain in detail what happens from start to finish — how the ingredients are combined, how many different heating or cooling processes they go through, health and safety measures, packaging and distribution of the product. In essence, the information document contains details of everything that happens from delivery of ingredients to shipment of products.

Finally, the company profile will give details of the history of the company from its formation to its current status; the number of people employed; the range of products produced; the annual turnover; the market share for each product; international sales; and future plans for development.

All of this information needs to be updated regularly. The information documents are designed for use by the media. This could be in response to an enquiry; as part of a press pack; or as an advance briefing before an interview. The document is at its most useful, however, in a crisis situation where the company needs to issue immediately some form of information about itself while trying to get to grips with the crisis. It is a good service to provide to journalists who will have a lot of space/air-time to fill and it allows them to get started. It also gives a certain amount of breathing space to the company itself (very little but very necessary) to try to begin to establish how the crisis occurred and what the implications of the crisis are.

Knowledge of Key Media

Press officers have to build up as much information as possible about the media they are working with.

They need to take a subscription with a press-cutting service, on an on-going basis, and instruct the service to send regular cuttings of every reference to their company that appears in print, and tapes and transcripts from radio or TV. Press officers will, of course, know to which magazines and papers they are issuing stories. However, it is possible to miss coverage. You might have bought an early edition of the evening newspaper and coverage appeared in a later edition; your company might have been mentioned by someone in an interview or an article might have appeared in a magazine which you would not usually monitor.

Press officers should also subscribe to media directories (Irish, European and American), particularly if they are handling international media relations. These directories list all of the publications and stations; name news and picture editors, correspondents, producers and commissioning editors; provide contact phone, fax and e-mail numbers; and give publication dates and deadlines for receipt of information.

In addition to national media, press officers should take subscriptions with all of the magazines relevant to their industry. They should also make sure that they receive a copy of the publications produced by groups or institutions to which their company is affiliated (e.g. magazine of the Chamber of Commerce, or newsletter of the Surveyors Institute); and they should monitor the web — in particular, their own and competitors' websites.

The press officer's position is a highly specialised one. Because press officers deal exclusively with one company, it is their business to know each of the key media who report on their area of interest. They will read all of the cuttings, but they will also be familiar with each magazine and newspaper. This is necessary so that they can target a specific section of the paper/magazine with a story; or pitch a press release written in the style of a particular journalist; or identify a gap in coverage across some sectors of the media.

TOOLS OF THE TRADE

Off-the-Record Briefings

The very mention of an 'off-the-record briefing' will cause an immediate reaction. Some people will react with delight — at last, the real story or at least a fuller explanation. Some will be utterly disgusted — is it ethical to issue information to which you will not attach your name? Many will react with scepticism — how trustworthy can the information be?

As a general rule, practitioners avoid off-the-record briefings. It is their job, after all, to make information available to the public from an identifiable source.

However, off-the-record briefings happen because of custom and practice, for reasons of spin, in response to media queries, or to give sensitive background information to journalists.

We will deal with each in turn.

- *Custom and Practice.* Press officers are hugely influential. They are responsible for a lot of 'off-the-record' briefings which give journalists a 'steer' on how the organisation is thinking, or what moves are being planned.

  Off-the-record briefings are most noticeable (if that is the right word to use) in government circles. Government press officers brief on a daily, often more than once a day, basis. They speak with journalists who are part of the lobby system. The journalists and the press officers become quite close to each other, which sometimes leads to a 'confusion' in roles.

  During the 1983–4 period of political unrest in Fianna Fáil, the then Government Press Secretary, P. J. Mara, well known for his witty turn of phrase, found himself quoted by the media. The quote has since become legendary. At a government press briefing, in response to a question about his leader, Charles Haughey, he famously adapted Mussolini's slogan and said '*Uno duce, una voce*. In other words, there'll be no more nibbling at my leader's bum'. He may well have understood that he was speaking off-the-record and would not be quoted.[6]

- *Spin.* Off-the-record briefings, however, can also be used to influence improperly. Politicians, in particular, set great store by public opinion (even if they all love to deny the value of opinion polls). No politician wants to be publicly seen to be out of step with their electorate, and no government wants to do it either. So off-the-record briefings can also be used to 'plant' stories, which are not attributed to the source, and which, consequently, carry a 'total deniability' sticker when the public reacts negatively.

- *Media Queries.* Off-the-record briefings can be extremely useful, for both the press officer and the media. The press officer gets to confirm or deny a story without having the organisation attributed as the source. You will often see in articles statements attributed to 'sources close to…' or 'a source, who did not wish to be identified…', or it might say 'an inside source said….' In many cases the source is the press officer who has given an off-the-record briefing. Briefings are very useful if properly handled. The press officer confirms or denies without attribution. The reporters know that they are on the right or wrong track with a story.

- *Sensitive Information.* An off-the-record briefing could provide media with useful background information, which cannot be used, but which explains the paucity of on-the-record comment. For example, the briefing might be used to explain the legal difficulties of commenting publicly.

  Or it could be something as simple as 'common decency'. A journalist enquiring about a chief executive/politician/high-ranking official, who had not been seen publicly for a while might be quite satisfied to know, off-the-record, that the person in question had a drink problem which was being addressed by detoxification. In a lot of cases, Irish media (unlike their British counterparts) would not report the fact. If they did, they might allude to 'personal matters'.

Off-the-record briefings are an area in which there are no hard and fast rules. You are walking on shifting sand. Suppose that your client is a highly respected anti-drugs campaigner. What if the same anti-drugs campaigner had told a journalist, off-the-record, that he was a recreational user of cocaine? Should the journalist feel obliged to respect the privacy of this off-the-record comment or would it be in the public interest to disclose it?

Unless you know how to use off-the-record comment, steer clear of it. The purpose of an off-the-record briefing has been outlined above. However, many people confuse it with telling journalists information that they will not use. That is like putting a bowl of sweets in front of a three-year-old child, and telling them not to touch. It is inhuman! What is the point in telling journalists 'the real story' if they are to do nothing with it? They are in the information business, and if you tell them something, you must expect that it will be used, in some form, in print or voice-over.

Press Conferences

The press officer decides when it is appropriate to call a press conference, which is usually called at short notice because there is an issue that requires debate. A press conference might be called because it is necessary to make the chief executive available in person, to the media, to be seen and questioned. A press conference might be necessary because news is breaking so fast that the press officer believes it is the only way to keep the media abreast of developments. In a crisis situation, a press conference is almost always called — for example, Michael Buckley made himself available to media, at a press conference, when the story of All First Bank and the Rusnak affair broke in 2002.

Press Briefings

A press briefing should not to be confused with an off-the-record briefing. The purpose of a press briefing is often to tell media about future plans — to let them know the direction the company is planning to take. Usually, a press briefing will be held with a small number of journalists, in an informal atmosphere, with a senior member of the company available

For example, I worked for a semi-state organisation which introduced a competition for transition-year students. The details of the competition were scheduled to be issued to schools in May, so that the teachers, on their return in September, would have the event in their calendars. The education media were invited to a lunch briefing in a city-centre hotel in March/April. The purpose of the briefing was not to attract coverage but simply to pay them the courtesy of explaining how the concept came about, why the semi-state organisation was getting involved, and how the scheme would run. They understood, and we understood, that there was no publicity value in the meeting. Rather, as people reporting in this area, it was necessary for them to know of imminent developments. The publicity campaign began only in October/November when schools began to return their application forms. The relevant media, however, had known about the initiative for six months at that stage.

Press Releases

Press releases are one of the most basic tools in the armoury of a press officer. A press release allows the company to give a short, tightly focused piece of information, to the relevant media and, through them, to their readership. The volume of press releases issued depends on the organisation itself. Many of the larger companies issue literally thousands in a year; other organisations, like the Garda Síochána, issue very few because the entire nature of their business is crisis management (breaking crime stories would never be covered by release).

Photo-Call Opportunities

Press officers are also responsible for ensuring that their company receives adequate visual coverage in the media. It is their job to maximise the potential of naturally occurring situations, and maximise photographic coverage of them. Schools, for example, have a naturally occurring photo opportunity at the beginning of each year. It is a staple of the media diet that photographs of young children (and their distraught parents!) will appear on the day of or the day after their first day in school. (Evening newspapers and television coverage will appear on the day. Daily newspaper coverage will appear the day after.) Schools are competing with each other for the coverage, (and only one or two schools in each area will be visited by media photographers), but it is a naturally occurring opportunity for photo coverage.

The press officer also creates opportunities for coverage. The story itself may not be a strong one, but a photo might bring it to life. For example, if you had sponsored a mountain climber and your company was responsible for the boots the climber wore while tackling Mount Everest, a press release or press conference might attract very little publicity. However, if the same climber participates in a photo call, and can be photographed abseiling down the front of Liberty Hall, the photo opportunity becomes too good to pass up. The story, from a media point of view, is a weak one (a company making footwear sponsoring a climber, who probably had fifteen other sponsors), but the photo can bring this otherwise weak (but worthy) story to life.

CREATED MEDIA OPPORTUNITIES

A press officer who did not also try to create opportunities in the wider field of media would be remiss in their duties. Press officers are constantly thinking about ways of generating publicity. Is there an opportunity to pitch a feature article to a magazine? The press officer can research the article, retain the journalist to write it, and have complementary photographs taken to go with it. The opportunity would not have existed without the pro-active involvement of the press officer.

With television, there might be an opportunity to broaden the media profile of the organisation by putting someone forward as a spokesperson on an arts show to explain their involvement in an artistic endeavour. *The Late Late Show* might be interested in interviewing the key speaker invited to your annual conference (the researchers might not be particularly interested in the possibility of interviewing the managing director, but the guest speaker, if well known, might prove a great attraction). If you are involved in the promotion of a film, you could offer some of the actors for interview on radio.

In each of these cases the focus is on a person associated with the company — not on the company itself. However, if the link is made (that the actor is involved in this film, or the speaker is over to attend your conference), it enhances the profile of your company by association.

Success in the Field

At the end of each year, the press officer should be able, in theory, to point to two different 'bundles' of coverage. One bundle is the coverage that was re-active (the media approached the press officer and, as a result of the press officer's competence and speed in dealing with the enquiry, coverage resulted). The other bundle should be pro-active coverage (the photo calls, feature articles and generated opportunities which would never have happened without the initiative of the press officer).

Finally, it is worth noting that many press officers do not have an annual plan to which they work. If a consultancy is retained to work with a company, for whatever length of time, it begins by putting forward a proposal. This document identifies the issues likely to arise in the coming months, the way in which those issues will be tackled, and the method of evaluation which will be used, on completion of the proposals, to estimate their success. Many in-house press officers still fail to do this.

Partly, their job is a busy one, and senior managers do not see the need for an annual plan when they are already satisfied that a good and necessary job is being done. Partly, in-house people themselves feel the need to put together a plan only when they are undertaking something new — like a major sponsorship.

REFERENCES

1. Seán Duignan, *One Spin on the Merry-go-Round*, Dublin: Blackwater Press, 1995.
2. Mark Hennessy, 'Doherty seeks advice on Ahern apology', *The Irish Times*, 12 October 2001.
3. *This Week*, Sunday, 14 October 2001 — RTÉ Radio1, RTÉ Interactive News, http://www.rte.ie/news/2001/1014.thisweek.html
4. Maureen Cairnduff (ed.), *Who's Who in Ireland — The Influential 1,000*, Dublin: Vesey Publications, 1984.
5. *All the President's Men*, Warner Home Video, original release date: 1976; Video/DVD release date: 29 October 1997.
6. Louis McRedmond (ed.), *Modern Irish Lives: Dictionary of 20th-century Biography*, Gill and Macmillan, Dublin, 1996.

Section 5
Specialist Areas

CHAPTER 13

Sponsorship

WHAT IS SPONSORSHIP?

Sponsorship surrounds us. Just about everything you can think of is sponsored nowadays — television broadcasts, television programmes, weather reports, sports events, books, concerts, awards, programmes of education, charity events, exhibitions. The list is endless. Major companies and corporations invest huge sums of money in sponsorship, usually of a high-profile nature, which attracts national media coverage. Many smaller companies, with smaller budgets, invest in sponsorships which are either locally based or targeted to a specific group.

We begin by looking at what sponsorship actually is. Sponsorship means supporting an activity or individual for a commercial return. Modern sponsors are rarely interested in giving money away. Rather, they are seeking a return on their investment. The individual or activity is carefully selected to match criteria set by the company. The investment is generally substantial. The return must be quantifiable. In essence, a company is investing money with the clear intention of getting a return for it, and in the certain knowledge that it has identified precisely what that return will be.

Sponsoring an individual is generally regarded as more 'risky' than sponsoring a team, organisation or activity. When the Irish Permanent Building Society (IPBS) sponsored Barry McGuigan, the boxer, it did not anticipate that the coverage would be short term. McGuigan was sponsored by IPBS when he won the world title in June 1985.[1] He successfully defended his title twice — against Bernard Taylor in September 1985 and Danilo Cabrera in February 1986 — before losing to Steve Cruz in June 1986.[2]

In 1986, Pepsi-Cola entered a sponsorship deal with Michael Jackson; the deal was worth $15 million.[3] At the time, it was believed to be one of the biggest sponsorship deals of its kind. Seven years later, however, allegations of sexual abuse damaged Jackson's image and Pepsi-Cola decided to pull out of its contract with the world superstar.[4]

Any corporation sponsoring an individual is investing in the success of one person. If that person fails to achieve their maximum potential, does not succeed in progressing to the next round of the competition, has a financial/drugs/personal scandal attaching to them, then these negatives might also attach to the sponsor. It also means the end of the 'exposure' value to the sponsoring organisation. The risk is very high.

If, by comparison, you sponsor a team event and one member of the team attracts negative publicity or is involved in a scandal of some sort, the team will continue to be well regarded. Think of any match that the Irish football team failed to win. Viewers and fans might comment that the manager should have made a different selection of players, or that one player was 'brutal', but the team, in general, will not be thought of negatively. The players 'did their best' but were let down by other factors. The corporate sponsor is still linked with national pride, sporting endeavour, and a team of players willing to 'give their all'. Failure of one individual in a group endeavour like a team sport, an orchestral recital, or the performance of a play will not, necessarily, attract negative publicity to the sponsoring organisation.

Lombard and Ulster Bank in Ireland introduced a competition, originally known as the 'Lombard & Ulster/Late Late Show Music Foundation'. (It later became an Ulster Bank sponsorship.) The first competition was held in 1986. The sponsorship was in the form of a bursary of €19,000 (£15,000 at the time), which was usually spread over three years, but on occasion was used for a single item such as the purchase of an instrument. The competition ran until the last season of *The Late Late Show* presented by Gay Byrne in 1999. The sponsorship was a showcase of young, musical high-achievers. Not all of the winners would achieve high-profile careers in music, but it was clearly intended, over the years, that the bursary would provide assistance to at least one future maestro. Lombard & Ulster, therefore, would not be judged by the failure of some to achieve. Rather they would be judged by the success of one of many.[5]

Thus, sponsorship is a business decision, to support an individual or organisation, for a quantifiable commercial return. The sponsoring organisation must be able to identify and cost the benefits of its investment.

PATRONAGE

Sponsorship is often confused with patronage and charity. So, let us look at these two separately for a moment. Patronage is the very old-fashioned idea of 'being a patron'. It still applies mostly to the visual arts and the performing arts. Individuals and corporations like to be associated with something that is perceived to have a 'cultural' value, to be on a higher plane than merely investing for a return. It is an investment for the general good of society.

There are numerous patrons or friends of the Abbey Theatre, the National Concert Hall and the National Gallery. The financial investment is not nearly as great as a sponsorship, and the return is not evaluated in the same way. The benefit of being a friend or patron is that you might receive tickets to the opening night, or to selected performances of a play or orchestra. You are entitled, usually, to two tickets. By any criteria, this could not be regarded as a commercial return.

The patron, however — either an individual or a company — has an interest in these 'higher' things and would like to be seen to be supporting cultural endeavours.

This is not in any way to denigrate patronage. Most cultural institutions would not survive without their patrons, many of whom bring valuable contacts to the organisations, and some of whom become sponsors in time. It is merely to separate the role of patronage from that of sponsorship.

Patronage is supporting something you are interested in or would like to have an association with. Patrons make an annual donation to preserve their association with a cultural institution. Although their names are printed on programmes, there is no real publicity associated with their involvement. The benefit they receive is not a commercial return, but rather an association with a prestige cultural institution.

Likewise a company that has the catering franchise for a golf club may be asked to 'sponsor' a member's tournament. The catering company is not really sponsoring — it is giving patronage. It is its way of saying 'thank you' to the members for their business. There is certainly no commercial return attached.

Finally, there are well-known figures, from the world of business, politics, the media and other areas, who lend their names, as patrons, to an organisation. This is a different type of patronage. Usually these people will allow their names to be attached to a worthy cause with which they have an empathy or sympathy. The only condition they attach is that they first establish for themselves that the charity is legitimate and well managed. They know that the use of their name on headed notepaper will enhance the charity's chances of securing donations.

The role of these patrons is unique. They are senior people, working under extraordinary time constraints, who may confine themselves to attending one meeting a year — possibly the AGM. They do, however, usually participate in at least one fund-raising function annually where they would host, for example, a table at a fundraising dinner, at a cost to themselves, or their companies, of €1,000 or more.

The greatest benefit to the charities is the use of the names. The association of a charity with high-profile or celebrity personalities gives an endorsement to its work. The endorsement, through the use of the celebrities' names, or their participation in photo calls or press conferences, encourages members of the public to give donations.

The most high-profile and highly regarded of all sponsors is the President of Ireland. Her patronage of charities is keenly sought. The President is patron of the Irish Red Cross Society, which is made up of staff, voluntary members and government nominees. She is kept abreast of issues and developments on an on-going basis. Once a year, the President hosts a reception in Áras an Uachtaráin for members. The function gives members an opportunity, which they might not otherwise have, to meet the President and have a good look at the Irish equivalent of the White House. More importantly it gives the President an opportunity to thank members for their good work in the past and to encourage all present to continue to serve. The President also highlights initiatives that will be undertaken in future years and points to challenges ahead for the organisation.

CHARITY

The other element of confusion is the confusion between charity and sponsorship. Companies are seldom confused by the difference. The general rule with corporate charitable donations is that they should be given without seeking publicity or reward. The donation is given to support the work of a worthy cause. It is a charitable donation for which no return is requested or expected.

Many of the larger corporations set aside an annual charitable budget and form committees composed of management and staff representatives who decide, often on a monthly basis, which charities will receive donations. Others donate goods, and their employees donate time to charitable events.[6] An old rule, which applies to charitable donations, is that seeking publicity for a donation may well have negative repercussions. A photo call or press release to publicise a donation of €5,000 from a large corporation may result in the donations being viewed as 'very little' or 'mean'. On the other hand, the same donation, given quietly, will be welcomed as genuine.

Once again, there is an obvious exception to the rule of giving quietly. The one time people give publicly in Ireland is during the Telethon when virtually every organisation in the country gets involved. The RTÉ Telethon raises money for people in need. It takes place every two years.[7] It is an opportunity for companies, internally, to build staff morale, team leadership and a sharing spirit. It is also an opportunity to achieve national publicity for what, relatively speaking, might be a small donation.

Charities, on the other hand, often confuse charitable donation with sponsorship. Charities are always seeking money — they could not survive without it — but they often apply to companies for 'sponsorship' of an event when they are really seeking a donation. The event might be something worthwhile, for which they require funding, but which would not be seen by corporations as 'sponsorship' because there is no return on the investment.

Charity is donating money or goods to a worthy cause. With rare exceptions, donations are given, away from the glare of publicity, with no return expected other than the 'warm glow' of having done something good.

PURPOSES OF SPONSORSHIP

Sponsorship is used primarily for five reasons:

- To generate name awareness
- To position the company accurately
- To provide corporate entertainment opportunities
- To demonstrate social responsibility
- To enhance and complement an advertising campaign.

All are equally valid reasons but, in my opinion, the two most successful are name awareness and company positioning. All rely on your ability to target the right public.

Name Awareness

Sponsorship is great at creating name awareness. In order to evaluate your success, however, you must be prepared to spend money on research. You have to begin from a position of knowledge. What percentage of the population (or specific target audience) can spontaneously name your company or product? What increase would you hope to achieve over a 1-year period; over a 3-to 5-year period?

Televised sponsorships, which command huge budgets and have massive audiences, are mostly undertaken by companies with mass-market products such as cars, electrical goods, beers, soft drinks, snacks and chocolates. Media coverage of sports, and football in particular, attracts such large audiences that sponsors pay huge fees to have their branding carried on football jerseys or Formula One racing cars.

Positioning

Sponsorship is also a very good medium for positioning a company — for example, as the producer of mass-market products; or exclusive products; or products geared to a particular age group. The Dublin International Piano Competition is an excellent example of how GPA, through sponsorship, positioned itself at the exclusive end of the market.

Sponsorship can also help to re-position a company or brand that has undergone change. You have only to look at advertising to see how successfully a brand can be re-positioned. Think of how ice-cream advertising has changed over the past number of years. Ice-cream used to be promoted as a summer product — primarily aimed at the younger market. That market has been expanded with the introduction of brands like 'Romantica'. Ice-cream is now promoted as an adult, year-round indulgence. Using sponsorship of the Coronation Street programme, Cadbury's has achieved the same effect of promoting its product as an adult indulgence.

Creating Corporate Entertainment Opportunities

Many companies do not need the profile of sponsoring an entire event, but they do need a corporate entertainment opportunity to reward their customers and maintain loyalty. The corporate entertainment market is enormous — from tents at rugby matches to flights and accommodation abroad for the World Cup. Companies are constantly seeking new sponsorship opportunities which fit their financial budgets, their corporate image, and their customers' interests.

Demonstrating Corporate Social Responsibility

One of the best examples of demonstrating social responsibility is sponsorship of advertisements which encourage socially responsible behaviour. The National Road Safety Campaign (1997–2002) used advertising on television to encourage both the use of safety belts in cars and slower driving by young people.[8] Part of the campaign was sponsored by AXA Insurance. Its message was one of social responsibility — by all means drive cars, and take pleasure from them, but use them in a responsible way.

Another example was Bank of Ireland's sponsorship of the advertising campaign for the Special Olympics in 2003. It is hard to tell whether this particular initiative should be categorised as sponsorship or patronage, but the bank was definitely showing corporate social responsibility to certain members of the community.

The Electricity Supply Board (ESB) and the Irish Energy Centre (IEC), amongst others, are involved in the organisation of a national Energy Awareness Week which takes place in September of each year. The ESB organised the week in 1993 and 1994. Since 1995 it has been co-ordinated by the Irish Energy Centre.[9] Whilst it is in the interest (and is part of the remit) of the IEC to encourage energy conservation, it is not necessarily in the interest of the ESB. It is a producer of electricity and a seller of electrical products. Its involvement in Energy Awareness Week shows its corporate sense of social responsibility. The message is simple — use our product (electricity), but demonstrate your awareness of the environment by being efficient in your use.

Enhancing and Complementing an Advertising Campaign

The strongest marketing campaigns combine all of the tools available to a corporation, by linking advertising, public relations, direct marketing, publicity and sponsorship. The use of all (or a combination) enhances the messages from each.

Opel used public relations and advertising together when it sponsored the Irish national soccer team (1985–99). Coca-Cola mixes its advertising and sponsorship in a very different way. Whilst its advertising reflects the global nature of the brand, its sponsorship has a very Irish focus which adds balance nationally. Coca-Cola's sponsorship activities include the GAA's schoolboy hurling festival, Féile na nGael, the National Ploughing Championship, and the Galway Arts Festival.[10]

Opel and the Irish National Soccer Team

When Opel decided to sponsor the Irish national soccer team, it could hardly have foreseen the massive level of interest that the team would attract. Its sponsorship coincided with a change in players and the introduction of a new manager, Jack Charlton. This, in turn, led to better fortune for the team, which generated an upsurge in national interest.

The Opel decision was a very clever one for a number of reasons. Opel produces a mass-market product: its cars are in the low-to-middle-income range and are therefore, in theory, available to be purchased by most people. Football attracts a wide cross-section of fans, most of whom would be in the low-to-middle-income bracket, and most of whom would be car drivers.

Opel combined its sponsorship of the team with a national PR and advertising campaign. The campaign highlighted the 'investment' Opel made in Ireland (i.e. the value, in money terms, of the Irish-manufactured products it bought). It also introduced the slogan, 'Opel Ireland's No. 1 supporter', which was widely used in advertising and editorial coverage, and which was applied to the back windows of all of its vehicles before they were sold.

When Opel began sponsoring the Irish soccer team, its target market was soccer supporters. The success of the team, however, broadened that market to encompass every man and woman in the country who took a national pride in the team's success. It was a bonus which Opel could not have anticipated or foreseen.

Opel's managing director, Arnold O'Byrne, believes that the sponsorship decision was a wise one. 'There is no doubt but that it created a massive awareness of the name Opel,' he said. That awareness, in turn, created a commercial gain: 'It is difficult to ascertain how many cars we sold from the sponsorship but the goodwill it generated certainly got us onto several shopping lists.'[11]

The *Irish Times* columnist, Kevin Myers, wrote that Opel's investment in the team was 'the shrewdest investment in the entire history of the automobile industry'.[12]

The sponsorship made Opel 'Ireland's greatest fan'. The sponsorship gave the company great name awareness (you could not fail to notice that Opel was sponsoring the team), and it positioned Opel, in market terms, exactly where it wanted to be — the sponsor of a low-to-middle-income sport, by a low-to-middle-range car company.

Since 1999, the national team has been sponsored by Eircom, at a cost of €7.5 million for a 10-year period.[13]

The Kerrygold Dublin Horse Show

When An Bord Bainne (as it was then — now the Irish Dairy Board) decided to sponsor the Dublin Horse Show and call it the Kerrygold Dublin Horse Show, it chose a sporting occasion with broad appeal. The association with the Horse Show linked Irish products to clean, green countryside and healthy outdoor pursuits. The Board's public relations manager, Aidan McCarthy, said that when it first sponsored the show, it was 'in the belief that this world renowned event would lend itself admirably to the further development of Ireland's only international food brand in the markets of the world'.[14]

The horse show itself was greatly enhanced by the involvement of An Bord Bainne. The show achieved broadcast coverage in Ireland, Britain, throughout Europe, and in the US. It was, and is, a massive market to reach with a single brand name — Kerrygold. The sponsorship also allowed Bord Bainne to entertain corporately some of its biggest customers and influencers, including the co-operatives, government ministers and opposition spokespersons. An Bord Bainne achieved a number of key objectives with this sponsorship. The Kerrygold Dublin Horse Show attracted national and international coverage; attendance at the show was increased; a corporate entertainment opportunity was provided for customers and key influencers; a link was formed between an outdoor pursuit and its mostly rural public; and an interest in a 'national event' was re-generated and renewed.

Brown Thomas Ladies' Day

Brown Thomas, which sponsored Ladies' Day at the Horse Show until 2000, invested much less money in this single-day endeavour, but it too was very successful.[15] It would not have made sense for Brown Thomas to sponsor the entire show, but the sponsorship of Ladies' Day achieved everything the company would wish for. The highlight of the day was the 'Best-Dressed Lady' competition.

The competition was a high-profile event with thousands of women dressing with the intention of entering. Most of these women probably visited BTs at least once to check what colours were in fashion, what hem-lengths, what styles designers were pursuing this year, etc. Objective one: attract more potential customers into the store. Objective two: publicity. Ladies' Day attracted considerable publicity each year, more often than not achieving front-page national media coverage as well as television coverage. The sponsorship linked the store with well-dressed women — one of its primary markets. The prize was often awarded to someone dressed from another store, or to someone who had made her own clothes. BTs, however, lost nothing by this, as the coverage was always of 'Brown Thomas Ladies' Day'. This sponsorship achieved a commercial return on a sponsorship within a sponsorship. Neither the Kerrygold Dublin Horse Show nor Ladies' Day competed with each other — in fact, both were complementary.

Active Age Week

Sponsorship can also be used to demonstrate social responsibility and to show that your organisation is interested in the community of which it is part. There are many examples of companies showing social responsibility.

Many years ago (1984), I formed a committee to host the first Active Age Week in our area. The initiative was launched by Dublin Corporation as a special week for senior citizens. It was a great idea, but the Corporation provided neither assistance nor money! I approached many companies and organisations and asked them if they would sponsor functions for the elderly. There was, in most cases, no financial return for these organisations. Their involvement depended on their sense of social responsibility. All rose to the challenge.

The local yacht club took senior citizens for trips on the river, the Garda Síochána hosted a social night, and the local bank gave an afternoon of music and merriment. We had a special trip to the Zoo, a bingo night and even a ballroom of romance (see next page)! The very positive outcome at the end of the week was the formation of a senior citizens club in the area.

The Garda Síochána used the evening to remind people that they were welcome to call into the Garda station for any reason, at any time. Senior citizens were advised about security of their persons and their homes, and the opportunity was cleverly used to introduce local gardaí by name, which made them much more approachable. The local bank had a new product for the over 55s, and it showed a promotional video at its function, before entertaining everyone to a sing-along (again including members of the bank) and a few Irish Coffees.

The dedication of these organisations to the community in which they operated, and their sense of social responsibility, is reflected in the fact that now, twenty years later, those same organisations are still actively involved.

Ringsend Active Age Week, 1984 — Programme of Events

Sunday, 7 October

3.00 p.m.: Special Opening Mass said by Fr J. Stone PP. Tea will be served immediately afterwards in the Community Centre. Names and addresses will be collected for a Free Raffle.

8.00 p.m.: Sing-A-Long & Dance in the Community Centre

Monday, 8 October

10 a.m.–5 p.m.: Information Caravan in Ringsend all day to tell you what you are entitled to

8.00 p.m.: Golden Oldie film in the Community Centre

Tuesday, 9 October

8.00 p.m.: Special 100-Year History of Ringsend (1884–1984) in the Community Centre

Wednesday, 10 October

3.00 p.m.: Afternoon Tea will be served in the Community Centre – there are some surprises in store!

8.00 p.m.: Traditional Irish night in the CYMS – there'll be plenty of singing, dancing and craic!!

Thursday, 11 October

3.00 p.m.: Mystery Scenic Tour. Bus leaves from Ringsend Church. There are only 30 places available – tickets must be booked.

8.00 p.m.: Ringsend Concert Band will give a special performance in the School Hall.

Friday, 12 October

3.00 p.m.: Special trip to the Zoo. Bring your pass card. Admission is free. The bus leaves from outside the church.

7.30 p.m.: Senior Citizens' 'Free Bingo' in the CYMS with surprise prizes

Saturday, 13 October

8.00 p.m.: A special concert in the School Hall given by the Cambridge Concert Band

Sunday, 14 October

8.00 p.m.: Senior Citizens' 'Ballroom of Romance' in the Community Centre — a special night to end the week with a bang.

The organising committee comprises:

Ellen Gunning (Co-Ordinator); Michael Whelan (Society of St Vincent de Paul); Eddie Flynn (CYMS); Noel Miley (Ringsend & Irishtown Res. Assoc.); Ted Whelan (Shelbourne Park Res. Assoc.); Jimmy Geoghegan & Simon Weafer (Poolbeg Yacht & Boat Club); Joe Carroll (Ballroom of Romance); May Kane (Ringsend Ladies Club); Nurse M. Fallon (Eastern Health Board); John Kane (Ringsend Concert Band); Mary Byrne, Brendan Nugent; Mary O'Toole; Kay Whelan.

Dublin International Piano Competition

Companies also create events in order to provide themselves with corporate entertainment opportunities; or position themselves at the mass or exclusive ends of the market.

When Guinness Peat Aviation (GPA) introduced the Dublin International Piano Competition (now sponsored by AXA) the company was looking for a unique sponsorship opportunity. It needed a vehicle which would allow it to entertain customers — people with budgets of millions of pounds — who had the power to decide to lease/not lease an aircraft from them. The competition was created by Dr John O'Conor,[16] who approached GPA with the concept which would link the company with excellence. The competition attracted 'quality' entrants and large audiences who wanted to hear the competitors perform, and it gave GPA the black-tie, corporate entertainment opportunity it was seeking. The winner of the competition was given the opportunity, as part of the prize, to play in several national concert halls throughout the world. The benefit of GPA's sponsorship, and its corporate entertainment opportunities, were thus spread to each of the locations relevant to its audiences.

When GPA withdrew from the sponsorship, the new sponsor became Guardian Insurance. At the time, Guardian had just merged with PMPA and its involvement was mainly altruistic — it wanted to put something back into the community. It continues to sponsor now, as AXA. The company believes that the main benefits it derives from this sponsorship are:

*   The opportunity to make contact with the key influencers in Irish society
*   AXA's global brand is complemented
*   A corporate hospitality opportunity
*   Live TV coverage for the final and associated concerts, which generates positive PR for AXA.[17]

Background to the International Piano Competition

The concept of holding an international piano competition in Dublin was developed by John O'Conor and friends during many games of bridge around Dublin. Much of the banter at the card table had been music-related. One evening someone asked Ann Fuller and himself, 'So what are you doing next?' to which one of them replied, 'Running an international music competition', and the other added, 'which must be for piano.' To this day neither of them can remember who said which!

During 1986, the concept was further developed. Through Brian Coyle (of Adam's Auctioneers), Tony Ryan of GPA became interested. A meeting was arranged between John O'Conor and Niall Greene at the GPA Headquarters in Shannon, and then with Maurice Foley who loved the idea.

The competition was being developed at a time when many people had inferiority complexes about how good music could be in Ireland. It was felt that there were many locations throughout the world where fine music was played but John O'Conor thought that the National Concert Hall in Dublin was as worthy a venue as any.

A committee was formed with John O'Conor as Artistic Director, Ann Fuller as Administrator, Laurie Cearr as Public Relations Officer and Ida Delamer in charge of attracting volunteers.

Important help was secured from Bill Maxwell, Public Relations Officer of Aer Lingus. Free flights were provided for the committee to visit other important international piano competitions abroad. The committee members also visited the Headquarters of the World Federation of International Music Competitions in Geneva.

Vincent Finn, Director General of RTÉ, promised support which included the (then) RTÉ Symphony Orchestra, as well as radio and television coverage. Des Ryan of Carroll's gave them some 'seed' funding to get themselves going, whilst Dublin Corporation provided them with free offices which relieved them of the expenses of rent, telephone, electricity and heating bills.

GPA was, according to John O'Conor a 'wonderful' sponsor. With the enthusiastic support of Tony Ryan and Maurice Foley, GPA sponsored not only the first competition in 1988, but also the subsequent competitions in 1991 and 1994.

After the failed GPA flotation, John O'Conor found himself without a sponsor. With the willing help of presenter Mike Murphy, he announced his need on the National Lottery show, *Winning Streak*, saying, 'If there's anyone out there watching with a large chequebook, we would love to hear from you.'

Gerard Healy of Guardian Insurance heard the call and offered sponsorship for the 1997 competition. The company became AXA Insurance and the sponsorship has continued. John O'Neill, head of AXA, and his associate, Paul Moloney, keep in close touch with Ann Fuller and John O'Conor and travel to New York and London to hear and support the winner's recitals. The AXA sponsorship of the Dublin International Piano Competition will continue until 2006 — or maybe longer.

The competition is run every three years and an age limit of 17–30 applies. There is a screening process where about sixty musicians are selected from over two hundred entries. Most are prize-winners from other international competitions. From the field of participants usually fifty-five are from overseas.

In Ireland, a qualifying competition is held six months in advance. The five best pianists are admitted to the international competition. These five talented musicians are awarded a Foley Scholarship of €1,250 (generously provided by Maurice and Marie Foley).

The musicians can use this money to attend concerts, enhance their skills or get extra music lessons in Ireland or abroad before the main competition. They are also awarded approximately ten concerts around Ireland and a broadcast on RTÉ's Lyric FM. This certainly is a very attractive package to any aspiring and talented young musician. A young Irishman, Finghin Collins, then aged 20, was a semi-finalist in 1997. Two years later, he won a major international competition in Switzerland.

The competition has a total prize fund of over €56,000. The first prize consists of a cash prize of €12,000 plus about fifty concerts throughout the world. This includes a recital début in New York (which costs about $20,000) and a recital début in London (which costs about stg£7,000). The finals are broadcast live on RTÉ television and the prizes are presented by the President of Ireland.

It is a stipulation of the competition that foreign entrants pay their own fares to and from Ireland. However, once they arrive at Dublin Airport, they are picked up by a volunteer and taken to a host family which looks after them for the duration of their stay.

There are over five hundred such volunteers in and around Dublin. Some host families welcome the musicians as guests to their homes while others allow their homes to be used for practising music. Volunteer drivers transport the participants from homes to practice pianos, and to the competition itself. There is an incredible amount of organising involved, but everyone enters into the spirit of things with great enthusiasm.

'We wouldn't be able to achieve this without the enlightened vision and generosity of our sponsors, and they deserve all the publicity they can get from their hard work and commitment,' according to John O'Conor.[18]

John O'Conor and Alexei Nabioulin, first prize winner,
AXA Dublin International Piano Competition 2000

TYPES OF SPONSORSHIP

It is possible to sponsor almost anything. In recent years, sponsorship of awards (by AIB, Cothú and others) has increased in popularity and recognition. Education has also been the recipient of sponsorship (e.g. the Esat Young Scientist, O'Reilly Hall and Smurfit Business School). The main types of sponsorship, however, could probably be divided into five key areas:

1. Sport
2. The Arts (high and not-so-high)
3. Literature (of all kinds)
4. Public Exhibitions
5. Media (especially television).

1. Sport

Sport is perhaps the highest profile of all sponsorships, particularly if it achieves television coverage, attracting an audience in millions. Look at the brand OTSs (opportunities to see) for Marlboro, Duckhams, Goodyear, Compaq, Yahoo! and Shell, all of whom are involved in Formula One. Think of the audience of millions who are exposed to the branding of Carlsberg and Amstel through English soccer.

Media coverage of football means that sponsors pay huge fees to have their branding carried on jerseys. The exposure that sporting events receive in a European market more than justifies the sponsorship costs, and the sponsors are all producers of mass-market products. Sports teams (football, hurling, Gaelic games, basketball, rugby, etc.), league and cup competitions, and even stadia attract sponsorship. In Ireland, we almost saw the creation of the first sponsored national stadium when the FAI negotiated a deal for Eircom Park. Plans for the Park were abandoned in 2001 when the FAI decided, instead, to become an anchor tenant at Sports Campus Stadium Ireland.[19]

On the international scene, we see sponsorship by soft drinks companies of the World Cup and the Olympics. The theory is simple: the more often a company can remind you of its product (particularly if the reminder carries an association with something you enjoy), the more brand-conscious you are likely to become.

The Department of Health and Children entered a sponsorship arrangement in 2001 to take over sponsorship of the Irish Open Snooker Tournament at Citywest. The sponsorship is part of the national 'quit smoking' campaign — the previous sponsor was Benson & Hedges.

We have already mentioned two Irish sports sponsorships: Opel and the Irish soccer team and the Kerrygold Dublin Horse Show. Three other Irish sponsorships worthy of note are: the Murphy's Irish Open, the Nissan Classic and the Budweiser Derby.

Murphy's Irish Open

Murphy's stout took over the sponsorship of the Irish Open from Carroll's in 1993.[20] At the time, Carroll's (a cigarette manufacturer) had gone through a period of diversification and had decided to re-focus the business, and cease its involvement in sponsorships. To the credit of the company, it spent a number of years ensuring that events which they had sponsored in the past secured other sponsors for the future. Throughout the country, the company's involvement in sponsorship was wide ranging, and most national or community groups speak highly of the company's efforts to find replacement sponsors.

When Murphy's entered the sponsorship deal, the Irish Open was already attracting European and international coverage, and Murphy's was expanding the market for its product. Unlike Carroll's (the brand), Murphy's stout was sold — or it was planned that it would be sold — to an international market. The sponsorship of the Irish Open created two opportunities for Murphy's. It allowed the company to raise its profile considerably in the Irish market. In addition, it allowed the company to create name awareness — throughout Europe and the US — in advance of the introduction of its product. Murphy's ended its sponsorship in 2002.

Nissan Classic

Similarly, when Nissan sponsored the Irish cycling race (1985–92), it did so in order to create an awareness of its change of name from Datsun to Nissan.[21] The sponsorship was undertaken at a time of great international wins for Irish cyclists Stephen Roche and Seán Kelly. The heightened national interest in the sport at the time (the Taoiseach travelled to Paris to see Stephen Roche win the Tour de France) ensured that Nissan's objective was successfully achieved.

Budweiser Irish Derby

The Irish Derby had been declining in audience, impact and appeal for a number of years when Budweiser decided to step forward as a sponsor. Budweiser, a newly introduced brand in the Irish market, was seeking to create brand awareness. There is a natural link between the Budweiser horses (widely used in advertising campaigns) and an Irish horse derby. The investment was sizeable and probably could not have been justified had it been targeted at the Irish market alone. However, the fact that the Derby was also broadcast in the US made it not only justifiable, but very cost-effective. Through its involvement in this sponsorship Budweiser secured national and international brand coverage; attracted a new audience of attendees to the derby; re-invigorated a national event; and even managed to change the pronunciation of the name from 'der-bie' to 'dar-bie'! The sponsorship was in its sixteenth successful year in 2001.[22]

2. The Arts

The arts, visual and performing, have always attracted sponsorship. In the past decade, however, this sponsorship has grown significantly. The growth results from changes in both the artistic and corporate worlds.

The arts have become much more professional in creating linkages, adopting a strategic approach, and delivering their product. In fact, Jerome Hynes, Chief Executive of the Wexford Festival Opera, has attributed at least part of the festival's phenomenal success to a 'partnership between artistic excellence and business excellence which is fundamental to the running of an arts organisation'.[23]

The second change has been in the corporate arena, with a growth in companies seeking to sponsor the arts. This corporate 'willingness' to sponsor, has been attributed by John O'Neill, Chief Executive of AXA Insurance to 'a more enlightened arts community today'.[24] The organisation Business2Arts (formerly Cothú) is dedicated to matching arts events with suitable sponsors.

Some of the most prominent Irish arts sponsorships would include the Murphy's Cat Laughs Festival, the Heineken Green Energy Festival, the AXA Dublin International Piano Competition, the Texaco Children's Art Competition, the Guinness Jazz Festival and the Vodafone (previously Eircell) Press Photographer of the Year awards.

3. Literature

Books are almost forgotten as a sponsorship tool, but where would we be without the excellent guides sponsored by Michelin, Shell and the AA? There are also awards for literary endeavour — the IMPAC Literary Awards, for example.

4. Public Exhibitions

Exhibitions are regularly sponsored either by national media or by national organisations. The Irish Times Higher Options Exhibition, the First Active Our House Exhibition and the FÁS Recruitment Fair are three prominent examples.

5. The Media

There are numerous forms of sponsorship within the media. There are the competitions in newspapers, magazines and on radio, which are sponsored by companies promoting a product, encouraging participation in an event, or, in the case of semi-state bodies, encouraging us to change our habits.

2FM has the hugely popular 'Roadshow' which is massively sponsored. Companies sponsor the Roadcaster for a day or a week. These companies (through their PR people) determine where the Roadcaster will be sited, and what competitions and prizes will be handled on the show. The Roadcaster provides a physical presence in a location and encourages participation by the public in the area (to be interviewed, or play a request). The show puts a focus on whatever the company is doing (opening a new store, for example) and creates an understanding of the organisational ethos or product range or message (through competitions and prizes). Finally, it provides a national platform for media coverage.

Television programmes — or their broadcast — have become an increasingly expensive, high-profile and successful form of sponsorship. When Telecom Éireann (now Eircom) began sponsoring *Weatherline* on RTÉ in 1990, the company undoubtedly had deregulation in mind.[25] It needed to create a better awareness of itself and the changes it was implementing to provide the customer with a better service. It chose a programme with one of the highest viewership figures — it is practically a national pastime to watch and discuss the weather!

The programme *Friends* has been sponsored by Bailey's since 2000.[26] Bailey's has re-branded the drink from an older person's after-dinner alternative to brandy, to a much trendier drink, aimed at the younger market. Its advertisements also enhanced the image change by portraying Bailey's being consumed by young trendies in a New York apartment. The 'young' theme is continued in present advertising.

Sponsorship of television broadcasts is particularly attractive to companies producing for the mass market. Favourite sponsors include manufacturers of cars, electrical goods, beers, soft drinks, snacks and chocolates.

Although it is not a part of sponsorship, it is important to be aware also of the role of product placement in television shows and movies. That particular can of beer, the washing powder in the background, the brand of chocolate bought in the corner shop, the advertising hoarding in the background, the cars being driven — none are sponsorship, but all send subliminal messages to their audiences.

Lastly, there are the sponsorship opportunities which arise on television. The old 'one for everyone in the audience' opportunity was traditionally provided by *The Late Late Show*, and was widely used by PR professionals. Kathy Sheridan of *The Irish Times* has referred to them as 'hidden' sponsorships, 'involving cars and holidays given away by presenters spouting blatant advertising blurbs, on shows already built around plugging new books, bands and movies'.[27] In 2001, *The Late Late Show* itself provided a sponsorship opportunity for Renault cars.

Hibernian and Crimeline

In addition to sponsoring the broadcast of programmes (which have already been purchased by TV stations), companies create programmes for broadcast. Perhaps the best example in Ireland is the association between Hibernian and *Crimeline*, (1992 to present) and, of course, the Garda Síochána.[28]

When *Garda Patrol* ceased broadcast, it had probably reached the end of its useful life. Its format — a speech to camera, from a desk, using props — had not kept pace with modern television formats, and it was, consequently, losing viewers.

Hibernian Insurance saw an opportunity to reach an audience with a trendy, crime-focused programme. *Crimeline* uses CCTV (closed circuit television) footage, creates dramatic re-enactments of crimes, and shows interviews with the detectives and superintendents who are leading the investigations. In addition, the programme encourages interaction with the public through dedicated phone lines, and updates the viewers on how their assistance has provided leads which might help to solve crime.

This sponsorship by Hibernian, an insurance company, has enhanced that company's name awareness, and positioned it by creating a link between solving crime and insuring against it. A report in 2002 stated that 'Hibernian's *Crimeline* sponsorship helped over 200,000 Irish adults to think a lot more positively about the brand as a result of the sponsorship'.[29] Now that is a quantifiable return!

ETHICAL, MORAL, SOCIETAL AND IDENTITY ISSUES

As with every other tool used in public relations, there are ethical issues in sponsorship. There are also moral, societal and identity issues. The issues are not black and white. However, they should always be factored into any decision to sponsor.

For example, should the makers of low-fat/low-calorie meals sponsor the 'Slimmer of the Year' competition? It would link nicely with their product — but is it encouraging overweight people to believe that by using a particular product they will lose pounds?

Is it ethical for drinks companies to sponsor late-night concerts when patrons attending have probably already spent some time in a pub? Is it ethical for the makers of baby products to give 'goody bags' to new mothers as they leave hospital?

Will the selected sponsorship alienate some audiences? Is it ethically and ethnically sensitive across national and cultural barriers? If you sponsor fox hunting in certain rural areas, your sponsorship will be received favourably, but urbanites will be much more inclined to think negatively of you. If you sponsor bull fighting in Spain, you are sponsoring a national pastime (like football in Ireland), but how will it be viewed in other countries in which you sell your products?

If your audience is tightly defined, you may well take the decision that whilst others will disapprove, the target audience you are seeking will completely approve. Some years ago, at the National Ploughing Championships, the National Ploughing Association renamed one women's ploughing class category the 'Farmerette' category.[30] I thought at the time that the term was a new one, but it actually originated in the early 1900s.[31] When I commented that the name was a derogatory one, I was told, in no uncertain terms, that it was not seen as derogatory by those using it. I am equally sure that some disapproved of the term 'Housewife of the Year', while others disapproved of its re-naming as 'Homemaker of the Year' when it was sponsored by Centra (1996–8).[32] However, if the audience is clearly defined and supportive of the sponsorship, it matters little what you personally think (we are all products of particular backgrounds). What matters is that the sponsorship 'fits' the company and that you are conscious of audience reaction from a group wider than your target audience.

The key points are that sponsorship should be viewed from the perspective of the company in the first instance, the participants in the second, and your wider public in the third. When Smirnoff sponsored the 2001 UCD Freshers' Ball at the Point Depot, it sponsored an evening, which, by student accounts, was a great success. Smirnoff even filmed the occasion for an event to be held later in the student bar. On the night, however, an RTÉ *Primetime* camera crew arrived. It was doing a story about teen drinking and violence. Smirnoff removed its name from the exterior of the building and the camera crew was refused admission to the Point Depot. Smirnoff had prevented an association in the minds of the wider viewing public between teen drinking, student nights and its product, but it was happy to promote its association to a smaller target audience.[33]

Sponsorship should also enhance your corporate image and do nothing to detract from it. Could you imagine a women's business group hosting a fashion night or a make-up party? It would hardly complement the women's image as serious entrepreneurs and managers.

Be mindful that your hard work is not undone by some silly (and often very catchy!) slogan which is used as part of your campaign. There are numerous examples of slogans alienating women, young people, senior citizens, the disabled or particular ethnic or religious groups. You have only to look at the billboard advertising campaign for Scrumpy Jack cider in 1996. It showed an apple with what could have been water or juice or a tear running down it, and the caption read, 'She was sweet, tender and juicy so we flattened her'. It caused great offence to women (and men), who took their complaints to the Advertising Standards Authority of Ireland (ASAI). There were two key complaints, namely: (1) by using the female pronoun, it appeared to validate and endorse violence against women; and (2) the advertisement seemed to create an association between alcohol and violence — particularly worrying in that the advertisement was apparently targeted at the young male drinker. The ASAI upheld the complaint.[34]

In so far as it is humanly possible, cross-check in advance, with as many people as possible, particularly those outside the circle making the decision. No one has a monopoly on wisdom — and mistakes can be very costly.

Finally, bear in mind that not all decisions or factors affecting your sponsorship are within your control. Outside factors — poor weather, the collapse of the government, a breaking story at one of the tribunals, an outbreak of foot and mouth disease — may affect the running of the event, the attendance figures, or the media coverage you would have expected to achieve. As part of your planning process, however, you should make every effort to cross-check that no other similar function is taking place at the same time. Most major functions happen on an annual basis — sporting fixtures, conferences, opera festivals, etc. — and, as a professional, you should be aware of them.

SEEKING A SPONSORSHIP OPPORTUNITY

For companies seeking a sponsorship opportunity, there are several steps to be taken, namely:

1. Define your objectives
2. Define the target market/audience
3. Set your budgets

4. Study the potential strategic development of the sponsorship
5. Undertake a competitive review
6. Develop a detailed programme
7. Implement the sponsorship
8. Evaluate the successes and failures.

Looking at sponsorship from a corporate perspective, we will deal with each in turn.

1. Define Your Objectives

Do not begin by looking at what you want to sponsor (golfers always want to sponsor golf; motor enthusiasts want to sponsor racing cars). *The Irish Times* has been critical, in the past, of the Smurfit sponsorship of the European Open in the K Club, asking 'What business does a manufacturer of a commodity product like cardboard boxes have in expensive golf sponsorship — except to indulge the whims of its golf-loving chairman?'[35]

Look instead at the reason why you are considering sponsorship, and what you hope to achieve. Sponsorship is at its most effective when the object is to create name awareness or to position the company.

2. Define Your Target Market/Audience

You need to be very clear about who you are trying to reach. If your company or product sells to a mass market, fine. But what if it does not?

It would not make sense for Mercedes Benz or Volvo or BMW to sponsor a national soccer team, because 80–90 per cent of the audience could not afford to buy their product. It would make sense, however, for any of these car companies to sponsor an annual conference for company directors, or an annual budget briefing for industry leaders. It would create good name awareness among key influencers and earners, and position their product nicely as a suitable vehicle (excuse the pun!) for senior management.

Sponsorship must be capable of reaching the target audience with a minimum of waste.

3. Set Your Budgets

In the first year particularly, sponsorship budgets can be difficult to quantify. A broad rule of thumb is that, if you are buying into an existing sponsorship, you should back the cost euro for euro. If, for example, you were taking over a tennis tournament from a previous sponsor, and you were being charged a fee of €150,000 per annum, then you should allow another €150,000 per annum to cover the communications costs, including promotion, PR, advertising, and literature.

4. Potential Strategic Development

If you are entering a new area of sponsorship — for example, wind surfing — you need to look closely at the potential to develop that sponsorship over a number of years. What kind of research and forecasts are available? How many people participate in the sport? How many have an interest in it? Are the numbers likely to grow in future years? Is it just a fad? For large sponsorships, it is advisable to consult an expert group, such as Amárach Consulting, whose specialty is accurately predicting lifestyles, spending patterns, etc., over the coming years, taking a lot of the guesswork out of the decision.

When entering into a sponsorship arrangement you should be looking at a three- to six-year involvement. You will not create the level of name awareness and positioning you desire (and which will show a reasonable return on your investment) in one year. You need to select your sponsorship carefully — it must have the potential for growth.

You also need to determine, carefully, the stage of development of your potential sponsorship. Ideally you want to enter a sponsorship arrangement at the bottom of the mountain (when interest is beginning to grow) and leave at the top of the mountain (when interest has peaked). You want to put your money into a developing and not a declining interest.

Ideally you should also be able to forecast the benefits to the sponsored organisation, which will accrue from your involvement. Will the money you invest lead to the provision of more services for the underprivileged, or allow clubs to increase the numbers of players, or give sponsorship to a child prodigy, or provide a new centre for the charity?

A good corporate sponsor will provide sponsorship which enhances the reputation of the sponsor and the sponsored.

5. Undertake a Competitive Review

It is important that you don't get carried away with the idea of sponsoring, just because that is where you started from. You should take time to review the decision, and all possible alternatives, before deciding to proceed.

Take time out and look at the audience you are reaching and the amount of money, per head, that this sponsorship is costing you. Is there another way to reach that same audience, just as effectively, at half the cost?

Before you proceed, you need to be absolutely sure that the sponsorship you are embarking on is the most cost-effective way of reaching your public and achieving your objectives.

6. Develop a Detailed Programme

You must now begin to plan every element of your sponsorship. How will it be announced? Where do you intend to advertise and for how long? Will it attract television coverage? Will you run a poster campaign? Are you willing to offer special concessions to students, the unwaged and senior citizens? How are you going to attract foreign media interest? What signage will you require — and where will you put it? Will you be entertaining corporate clients? How will you entertain them? How many staff do you need to manage the sponsorship successfully? Have you sufficient manpower resources within your company or will you need to bring in extra people? Do you have a panel of experts in the field available to you (e.g. someone who understands hockey or Beethoven)? If not, how will you assemble them?

The detailed programme involves teamwork. The PR person will work closely with the people from advertising, marketing, and direct marketing. The finished programme will include such items as the advertising campaign, use of tee-shirts, badges, balloons, carrier bags, direct-mail campaigns, and celebrity endorsements. Every single element needs to be planned in detail, including its timing.

The detailed programme also allows you to prepare a budget, incorporating all of the above costs, and allowing an additional percentage to cover unforeseen opportunities and threats.

7. Implement the Sponsorship

The day or the week has arrived. All of the preparatory work and publicity have been completed. The team is in place, with clearly defined responsibilities. The sponsorship is finally 'live'. This is the busiest and most demanding phase because you are not only implementing the sponsorship, but also keeping a watchful eye as it progresses to see if minor (you hope not major) changes need to be made during the life of the event.

8. Evaluate the Successes and Failures

You now have your first opportunity to evaluate the successes and failures of your sponsorship.

You should gather everyone involved, shortly after the event is over, certainly within six weeks of it. The purpose of the meeting is to gather observations, feedback and opinions about the sponsorship, including things like staffing levels, facilities for children, peak times when long queues formed, car parking, and corporate entertainment. All of this information will help you to do an even better job next year.

You should establish the amount of interest shown by staff and their families. If the sponsorship was well handled, staff should have been involved not only as employees at the event, but as participants in their free time. Sponsorship should provide an opportunity to improve internal communications.

You should critically analyse the budget you allowed, and the area of over- and under-spend that you encountered over the period of the sponsorship.

Media coverage also needs to be studied to determine whether or not you secured the level of exposure you were seeking. You will study coverage for frequency and prominence of mention of your name as a sponsor. You will evaluate both the quantity and the quality of the coverage and seek to identify areas for improvement in the coming year. Bear in mind that some newspapers have a policy of not mentioning the sponsor's name.

Finally, if you conducted research before the sponsorship began, you need to conduct follow-up research to see how the position has improved.

SEEKING A SPONSOR

If you are an organisation, local group, or charity seeking a sponsor, you should apply the same rules. This is, sadly, often not done, and results in voluntary bodies losing potential sponsorship.

When approaching a sponsor, you are seeking a financial investment in your function or event. You must expect that that body will look for a return, and your proposal or pitch must be geared to answering the questions that they will pose.

Your charity might do good work for the elderly, or young people, or victims of rape; or your community group might provide a vital outlet for young people in the summer months, or meals on wheels for the elderly. This vital information should be included in your proposal, but the document should also answer sponsor's questions. Broadly they can be divided as follows:

Who are the Organisers?

The age of your organisation (when was it formed?), the number of staff and volunteers involved, your patrons, the voluntary expertise available to you, and the work that you do should all be detailed.

What is the Purpose of the Event?

You need to explain the rationale behind the function: that it will promote the work of new and emerging artists; or raise awareness of depression; or highlight the achievement of athletes; or promote better community relations.

What is the Benefit to the Sponsoring Company?

What will the sponsoring company gain by its involvement with your organisation? You need to establish that the audience you are reaching is an audience that is relevant to the sponsor.

What is the Cost?

There are two parts to this question really — what is the cost of mounting the event, and what is the cost to the sponsor?

Many charities try to recover 100 per cent of the cost of a function. This can often be a mistake. The charity should allow a budget to 'service' the sponsor. In addition to branding the event with the sponsor's name, a budget should be allocated for PR initiatives, photo calls involving the sponsor, posters on which the sponsor's name and logo will appear. The sponsor will need to establish that there is a total 'package' on offer.

The sponsor needs to know that you are bringing resources to the event which will ensure its success, including man-power, know-how, and media ability.

Why this Particular Sponsorship?

Think like a corporate body. Does it fit with the aims and objectives of the organisation? Will this sponsorship reach a market that the company is trying to influence? Will the sponsorship address a 'gap' in the company's publics? You should also determine whether the company is already addressing this particular public — does it already sponsor something in a similar vein; has it been involved in sponsorship of this type in the past, but is no longer involved? You will need to do a lot of research in order to make the pitch worthwhile.

Who is Involved?

The sponsor will need to know if there are other sponsors involved. The general rule of thumb is that corporations prefer to be the sole sponsor. The involvement of several sponsors (and their many PR consultants) means a dilution of the message/association for each.

The exception, of course, is something like the World Cup or the Olympics. These events are far too costly for one corporate body to sponsor, and are designed to give publicity and return to each of their many sponsors, commensurate with the level of their involvement.

Some years ago, I was involved in a charitable sponsorship which my client had agreed to enter into. The cost to the company was €5,000. The charity was seeking four sponsors in total (i.e. €20,000). My client, naturally, wanted to maximise the benefit of the investment to his company. I, therefore, launched a publicity and media relations blitz. The result, for my client, was excellent. The company was associated in the public mind with sponsorship of the event. The result for the charity was disastrous as it found it impossible to get the remaining three sponsors. Every company it approached mentioned that my client had already secured coverage as a sponsor, and there was little room for them to achieve the profile they would wish. The charity ran the function, no doubt at a loss, with a single sponsorship of €5,000. Had the charity involved approached the situation differently, I believe that, instead of securing an investment of €5,000 for one year, it could have obtained a much greater financial commitment over a longer period — possibly 3–5 years.

Is it Existing or New?

If the sponsorship already exists, it is possible that you have had one sponsor for a number of years, or possibly a different sponsor each year. Your new sponsor will need to know the details.

If you are constantly changing sponsors, are you willing to allow your potential new sponsor to contact the old ones? Could you be satisfied that their experience was a good one and that they will positively recommend and endorse involvement with you?

If a sponsoring body is leaving after a number of years, it is quite possible that that body has achieved its objectives in that time, and it might reflect positively on your organisation. On the other hand, the sponsor may decide that the previous sponsor has branded the event so well that a totally new idea might be a better investment.

If it is a new idea, can you demonstrate to the sponsor that you have the necessary resources and ability to launch this event, successfully and professionally, in its formative year?

Has the Sponsor the Budget for this Year?

You will need to establish the business year of the corporate you are approaching. Timing is everything. An accurately timed proposal, when budgets are being set for the coming year, has at least some chance of success. An approach when budgets have already been decided is patently a waste of time, effort and energy.

What Platform will the Company be Given?

Is there an opportunity for the managing director or chief executive to address a meeting; participate in a photo call; present an award? The sponsoring body will want to see how much effort you are prepared to invest in forming a partnership with it.

Be mindful that you may also have to advise the sponsor. I was involved in a function for senior citizens some years ago, to find the 'glamorous granny'. I had sought sponsorship, but neglected to offer advice to the sponsors. The sponsoring cosmetics company sent a stunning, glamorous eighteen-year-old female model to present the prizes. The model reminded people of how they used to look.

The sponsor would have achieved a better return on its sponsorship, I believe, if a stunning, glamorous, 50-or 60-year-old had been sent to present the prizes. A glamorous, but more mature, model would have been more uplifting, inspirational, and appropriate.

Is the Sponsor Interested in the Subject/Topic?

You should try to establish a natural link between the sponsor and the function. The links can be quite obvious: a food company and a celebrity chef visit; a public house and a darts competition; a men's retail outlet and a 'snazziest dresser' award.

Will it be a Suitable Vehicle for the Sponsoring Company?

If there are any negatives or downsides to the sponsor's involvement, you should have anticipated, explained and dealt with them at an early stage.

How Many People are Likely to be Reached by this Sponsorship?

Every company will try to evaluate, and one of the critical evaluators is money. The company will need to establish the cost, per head, of reaching a quantifiable number of people, and satisfy itself that the cost is justified.

There is no simple rule of thumb in this case. A large investment in a small group of people may be an excellent return on an investment if the group is otherwise difficult to reach. On the other hand, a small cost per head for a divergent group may not be cost-effective.

The numbers will vary depending on the type of function, but you should be calculating with two groups in mind — those attending, and those likely to see the publicity arising.

Who is the Target Public?

You should be almost able to sketch a photo-fit picture of the people who will be attending your function. As part of your pitch, you should be telling the sponsor the age level you will be attracting, or the disposable income of the audience, or the locality from which it will be drawn. The target public is a key factor in the decision to sponsor.

Is this an On-going Sponsorship or Once Only?

If it is once only, there may be a very good reason — to commemorate a centenary year, for example. On the other hand, the sponsor may fear that your organisation is taking a short-term view, and missing the big picture — always a worrying sign.

How Much Involvement Will be Needed from the Sponsoring Company?

In addition to the investment of money, the organisers will need to know the full level of the sponsor's involvement. Will you need the use of company meeting rooms; the advice of financial executives; or the input of staff? Is your organisation willing to work with the sponsoring company's PR people? Must a company representative attend meetings?

The company needs to be assured that it will not be drained of resources while it tries to manage a function it is sponsoring. The company will, however, seek a level of involvement which allows it to protect its investment.

What is the Return?

Quantify it. The sponsor will need to know the number of people targeted; the extent and breadth of media coverage anticipated; the level of involvement by professionals and volunteers from your organisation; and the 'endorsers' (e.g. Lord Mayor, a minister or a celebrity) that you propose to use.

How will it be Evaluated?

Finally, and crucially, you will need to show the sponsor that there are evaluation methods in place to establish the success of the sponsorship. The evaluation might include media coverage, prominence of sponsor's name, feedback from media, or questionnaires completed by participants. The method of evaluation will depend on the event being sponsored, and the 'package' you have offered to the sponsor.

Sponsorship, whether large or small, is an investment of money, time and goodwill in an event which will yield a quantifiable return to the sponsoring organisation. Whether you are deciding to enter a sponsorship arrangement, or seeking a sponsor, the same thoroughness of approach is necessary.

REFERENCES

1. http://www.rte.ie/news/1999/0716/moriarty.html
2. http://www.clones.ie/htmfiles/vtour/famous/mcguig1.htm
3. http://eightiesclub.tripod.com/id8.htm
4. http://www.soulwalking.co.ukMichael%20Jackson.html
5. Information provided by Nuala Heatley, Assistant Manager, Communications, Ulster Bank, Retail Marketing.
6. Smurfit-Stone Container Corporation (Chicago) was involved, with others, in the 2001 'Message from America' project, which helped Americans reach out to US servicemen and women stationed abroad. Employees at the company's Bentonville, AR, Packaging Solutions Center volunteered to design the backdrop, and Smurfit-Stone's Humboldt, TN, corrugated container plant produced and shipped the corrugated panels free-of-charge to military bases around the world. See http://www.smurfit-stone.com/content/news_105.asp
7. http://www.rte.ie/ace/2001/0918/telethon.html
8. http://www.ireland.com
9. Information provided by Orla Thornton and Brenda O'Brien, Corporate Marketing Executives, Irish Energy Centre.
10. Colin Kerr, 'Coca-Cola marketing has the patented formula for success', *Irish Independent*, 20 April 2000.
11. Róisín Ingle, 'Why big business is now seeking the Midas touch', *The Irish Times*, 17 November 1997, Finance section.
12. Ibid.
13. Colm Keena, 'All-in one offer swings it for Telecom', *The Irish Times*, 29 July 1999, Sport section.
14. Seán MacConnell, 'RDS revamped for horse show', *The Irish Times*, 22 July 1998.
15. Since 2000, Ladies' Day has been sponsored by SEAT. Information received from Deirdre O'Reilly, Marketing Executive at RDS. The sponsor is not specified on website: http://www.rds.ie/kerrygold/index.html

16. Irish pianist John O'Conor has garnered international praise for his impeccable technique, eloquent phrasing, and mastery of keyboard colour. Through his recitals, concerto appearances, and critically acclaimed recordings, he has earned a reputation as a masterful interpreter of the Classic and early-Romantic piano repertoires. He has performed throughout Europe, North America, and Asia and has appeared with such orchestras as the Royal Philharmonic, the Czech Philharmonic, l'Orchestre National de France, and the Stuttgart Chamber Orchestra in Europe and the orchestras of Cleveland, San Francisco, Seattle, Dallas, Detroit, Montreal, and Washington, DC, in North America. His concert tours have also taken him to Japan, Korea, Hong Kong, Singapore, Australia, New Zealand, Israel, and the countries of Eastern Europe. John O'Conor is deeply committed to, and is well known as a key figure in, the development of young musicians, not only in Ireland, but throughout the world through his role as director of the Royal Irish Academy of Music and as artistic director of the AXA Dublin International Piano Competition, which he co-founded. He often gives master classes and lectures in the cities where he performs. www. trawickartists. net/acts/oconor.html

17. Information provided by Paul Moloney, AXA Insurance.

18. John O'Conor was interviewed by Ita Glavin on 16 April 2002. I am indebted to her for conducting the interview and writing the report. I am also grateful to John O'Conor for giving us the benefit of a wonderful insight into the stress and pressure (and fun and glory) of running an international piano competition.

19. Gillian Ní Cheallaigh and Emmett Malone, 'FAI abandons Eircom Park plan', *The Irish Times*, 10 March 2001.

20. Dick Hogan, 'Cork tourism grateful to golf', *The Irish Times*, 28 June 2001.

21. Nissan sponsored the Nissan Classic Cycle Race of Ireland from 1985 to 1992 inclusive. Information provided by Jeanne McGann, Communications Executive, Nissan Ireland.

22. Information provided by Sharleen O'Reilly, info@curragh.ie

23. Jerome Hynes, Chief Executive, Wexford Festival Opera, quoted in Business2Arts brochure, seeking nominations for the Business2Arts Sponsor of the Year Awards, 2001.

24. John O'Neill, Chief Executive, AXA Insurance, quoted in Business2Arts brochure, seeking nominations for the Business2Arts Sponsor of the Year Awards, 2001.

25. Information provided by Eilish Ruddle, Eircom Corporate Advertising

26. Information provided by Tracey Atherton, Senior Brand Manager, Bailey's.

27. Kathy Sheridan, 'A cut too deep', *The Irish Times*, 4 March 2000.

28. The Hibernian Insurance/*Crimeline* programme started in September 1992 and Hibernian has been in the sponsorship seat since inception. Information provided by Garda Jerry Moroney, Garda *Crimeline* Office.

29. Carmel Killoran, 'Sponsors help pay the bills at RTÉ', *Irish Examiner*, 12 April 2002.

30. There is no particular sponsorship for the ploughing class 'Farmerettes'. Women

who participate in this particular class are known as Farmerettes. However, women may also participate in other ploughing classes, subject to age verification etc., but they would not be referred to as Farmerettes in those categories. You do not have to be a farmer to enter the ploughing competitions — it might, for example, be a part-time hobby. The term 'Farmerettes' applies to one specific Ploughing Class Category, among many other categories, in which entrants participate at the National Ploughing Championships. The term was reactivated only some few years ago. Information provided by Anna Marie McHugh, PRO, National Ploughing Association.

31. The 'Farmerette' movement was started at the women's colleges, Bryn Mawr, Barnard, Smith, Vassar, Wellesley, etc. in the US. As early as 1918, in New York state, plans were made for 200 working units of Farmerettes. Arthur L. Frothingham, *Handbook of War Facts and Peace Problems*, 'Chapter 6: New Activities of the Citizen', http://www.ku.edu/~libsite/wwi-www/WarFacts/wfacts3.htm

32. Information on Centra sponsorship provided by Nicky Crichton, Senior Account Executive, Fleishman-Hillard Saunders — International Communications.

33. Thomas Geoghegan, 'Freshers' Ball makes £9,000 profit', *The College Tribune*, UCD (undated).

34. Advertising Standards Authority of Ireland, Case report, Batch No. 98 (Ref: AC/966/11), Product: Scrumpy Jack Cider. Advertiser: Beamish & Crawford. Agency: O'Connor O'Sullivan. Medium: Billboard.

35. 'Time to pack in golf', *The Irish Times*, 26 May 2000, Current Account column.

CHAPTER 14

Corporate Image and Corporate Identity

The Institute of Public Relations (UK) website states that 'public relations is about reputation — the result of what you do, what you say and what others say about you'.[1]

Corporate reputation, like personal reputation, is hard earned. A company's reputation is its badge of good character. It is made up of many elements including: the company's mission statement, the quality of its products, the way in which it treats its employees, the value of its shares, the company's ethics, and the care it shows towards the environment and the community.

Reputation is enhanced by the strength and reliability of the company's corporate identity, which is often reinforced by sponsorship arrangements. It is influenced by attitudes, perceptions and experience.

Corporate reputation is a valuable asset. On balance sheets, it is calculated as a financial asset called 'goodwill'.

It is also easily lost. As Alexander Pope said, 'At every word a reputation dies'.[2]

Two of the many elements of corporate reputation — identity and image — are dealt with in this chapter. From the outset, it is necessary to make a clear distinction in your own mind between 'identity' and 'image'. The two expressions are inclined to be used interchangeably. While both are connected, and one can enhance or detract from the other, they are two entirely separate things.

Organisations are complex, but corporate identity must be simple. Identity is physical. It is made up of the things that can be seen and recognised, like corporate logos, uniforms, letterheads, brochures and websites.

Corporate image is literally that — a mental image held in the mind. Marianne Henry has defined image as 'the net result of the interaction of all the experiences, impressions, beliefs, feelings and knowledge that people have about a company'.[3]

My learned colleague and dear friend, Professor W. R. Spence, believes that in order to understand the concept of 'image', it is necessary to examine briefly two related topics. The first is the idea of 'the social construction of reality'.

In essence, this proclaims that since we can perceive what we call the real world only by means of our basic sense, we actually live in an individual world which is personal and subjective, rather than impersonal and objective. There is, it is claimed, no objective reality. What is real to us is simply what we see, hear, taste, smell and touch for ourselves. A rainbow is therefore 'real' for us, even though nothing physical exists, because a mental sensation arising from refractive dispersion of light waves causes us to 'see' it.

The second topic concerns perception and cognition. In basic terms, perception is what we see or become aware of; cognition is what sense our brains can make of it or what understanding we can produce concerning it. It can easily be demonstrated, however, that we all operate a process (conscious or unconscious) of selective perception. In effect, we choose what we want to become aware of! As with the first topic, it follows, therefore, that no two persons can actually be sure that they have identical information or similar understanding about anything.

This may seem somewhat academic, but public relations practitioners have to cope with issues concerning brand image and corporate image. If imagery lies in the eye of the beholder, how can it be created, polished or projected? And how do we determine what is a 'favourable image'? How does it relate to identity, including corporate identity, which has an observable physical dimension?[4]

CORPORATE IMAGE

Image is in the mind. It is closely linked with what is often called corporate personality. The image of a company is that instant reaction in the mind when the company is named. So, for example, it is often said that the image of Brown Thomas is exclusive, expensive, intimidating and snobby. The image of Roches Stores, by comparison, is friendly, welcoming, good quality. While this is linked with the physical appearance of the store, you can hold the image of the company without ever visiting one of its outlets. How many people think that Brown Thomas is snobby, and, so, never cross the threshold? For them, the image is the reality.

The computer industry has an image of young, lively, techie, sloppy people. Think of Bill Gates of Microsoft — he almost single-handedly created the image of computer-software companies. The image is of a casual style of dress, somewhat dishevelled because of dedication to solving the problem; staff members are all young — in their thirties at the oldest; they work hard, and play hard. It is a mental image that would probably persist even if the reality changed.

Think of the image of people working in different industries. What is your mental image of an advertising person; a PR person; a marketing person? The images are very different. In the case of a male working in advertising, we expect someone who looks somewhat artistic — bow tie, long grey hair in a ponytail, eccentrically coloured shirt or neckerchief. For a female PR person, we see a blonde, immaculately dressed, thin person, driving a top-of-the range sporty-type car, constantly talking on a mobile phone. The image of a marketing person, on the other hand, is more solid: three-piece suit, sensible, clean-shaven, solid corporate citizen.

Think of the last two presidential campaigns in Ireland. Mary Robinson deliberately cultivated a new image for the 1990 presidential campaign.[5] She changed her image — as indeed most in her position would have done — which caused people to perceive her differently. She was no longer just the hard-working, liberal, campaigning lawyer — tough, reliable and driven. While she remained all of these things, our image of her softened with the change in her physical image. She looked more like someone who could represent us abroad, her language softened and her look became more feminine.

For the 1997 campaign, remember the appearance of the presidential candidates on *The Late Late Show*[6]? Think for a moment of the women only — Adi Roche, Mary Banotti and Dana all wore perfectly nice suits; they looked like job applicants for the position of president. Mary McAleese, on the other hand, wore a purple knitted dress/suit with shiny purple boots. The boots were the talk of the country for days afterwards. She looked like a woman who was comfortable in her own skin. Yes, she too was an applicant, but she was bringing her own personality with her. Here was a woman who would not conform easily to the public perception of what a president should be. Here was a woman who would change the perception.

Finally, if you think internationally, look at the image of Catholics and Protestants in Northern Ireland, Israelis and Palestinians, Americans and Afghanis. The images are based on information received and expected patterns of behaviour.

Image is a very important element of PR. We all have mental images of companies, organisations, products, brands. These images influence our decisions to buy, to invest, to support a charity.

A company's image is based on what we know about it, how it presents itself, how management deals with crises, what relationships with staff are like, how tribunals of enquiry are treated, how the company delivery vans look, the layout of the company premises, the attitude of staff, the presentation of literature. The image is mental, but is formed, at least in part, by physical elements of the company.

Bear in mind that the company might also have a bad image. The bad image could be the result of poor industrial relations, dubious practices, poor interim results on the stock exchange, rude or stressed staff. In other words, it might be perfectly justified.

On the other hand, a bad image for a company might result from the poor image of the industry generally. Revelations about illegal dumping of toxic and hospital waste in Co. Wicklow (December 2001) undoubtedly tarnished the reputations of all companies involved in the waste-disposal business. Even if your company was not involved, the public perception might be that 'they are all at it', 'there's no smoke without fire', or 'no one turns down that kind of money'. In this instance, the company has to work very hard indeed to restore public confidence — not in the industry, but in its particular business — so that people's mental image will change.

Instead of 'they are all at it' the public image needs to change to 'there were some amazing cowboys in that industry — and some good operators as well'. Once a bad image has been applied to an industry it is extremely hard work for individual companies to try to change it.

The public relations task in all of this is to increase people's knowledge and experience of the company. The more we know about a company; the more often we visit its premises — or its website; the more often we deal with its staff, the better understanding we have of the industry. The greater the understanding that a PR person can create, the better are the chances of the public having a real and correct image of the company or the industry.

Look at the image that PR people and the media have of each other. PR people will tell you that journalists are lazy — they need everything written for them in the form of a press release and they expect you to do all the research for them. Journalists, on the other hand, will tell you that PR people are buffers — they merely prevent you from getting at the main players to interview them; they issue silly press releases; they are never on top of their brief, and they serve no useful purpose.

Some years ago, I did research into agenda setting. Who sets the agenda — PR or media? As part of this research, I interviewed people on both sides of the fence to establish their perceptions of each other and whether or not perception reflected reality. All of the attitudes above were reflected in the interviews when the question was asked broadly — i.e. 'What to you think of PR/media people?' When, however, you tied it down to specific people — 'So X journalist is a lazy git?' or 'Y PR person is useless?' — the responses were very different. Once it was tied down to an individual, the response inevitably was that X or Y was the exception. They were dedicated, hard working, on top of their brief and, usually, overqualified for the job they were in.

Each journalist who linked with an individual PR person found them helpful, insightful, on top of their brief, willing to assist in any way possible. Each PR person found an individual journalist to be well informed, insightful, conscious of the power of their writing, anxious not to exacerbate a tense industrial relations situation. The image remained unaltered, despite the fact that the experience was the exact opposite of the image.[7]

A clear image will not make you change your attitude completely. If you are a Christian who never liked Moslems, or a Protestant who never liked Catholics, you will not suddenly embrace them with love. But you will, as a result of a good public relations campaign, at least understand them better. You will not move from one end of the spectrum to the other, but you will develop a tolerance based on knowledge — and that is a massive shift in image.

It is important to remember that everyone who deals with a company or a charity may hold a different image.

As an employee, your image of the company is based on your experience of dealing with it. So, your image might be of a good company, or a tight company (badly paid employees), or a difficult company (because there are poor staff relations), or a headless chicken company (never enough time to get everything done).

Your image as an investor is based on the return on shares and the vision of management. The company, from an employee's point of view, might be under-resourced and stressed. From an investor's point of view, it might be a tightly run organisation with good profit margins.

Your image as a distributor may differ again. It will be based on smoothness of the working arrangements (from your perspective). Simple things like all trucks being asked to deliver at 8 a.m. (very poor scheduling), which means that you inevitably sit in a queue of trucks for 2–3 hours, will have a huge effect on your mental image of the company. Similarly, the length of time it takes the company to pay you for the goods — and how that affects your own cash flow — will have a huge impact.

As a member of the local community, your image might be based on the only thing that you know about the business — that it holds a senior citizens' party each year. It looks after the old folk well. The company's own staff-members participate in the day and really enjoy it. There's a great atmosphere in the company when you attend the dinner. It's a great company. (You might know this without really understanding even what it is that the company actually does.)

Your image as a customer is based on the quality of the product and the level of after-sales service that you receive. If you have been well looked after, the mental image is of a good company. If, on the other hand, the after-sales service was extremely poor, your image is of a company that does not deliver — it can talk the talk, but it doesn't walk the walk.

Finally, your image, as an opinion leader, is based on what you know about the company and how its people treat you. If you are the chairperson of the local residents' association or the local TD, your image is based on the amount of effort that the company makes to explain to you what it does, who it is, what its future plans are. Your image is based on the level of inclusiveness afforded to you, and the level of respect with which the company treats you. It is easy to see how an opinion-former would see a company as arrogant or distant purely because its people have never taken the time to consult.

Corporate image is easier for companies involved in one product range only, but there are relatively few of these. Even if you are involved in one product, the differences in the product range will affect the image. The following are some examples:

- Bord Gáis is involved in one product only — selling gas. The public image is of a clean fuel which is environmentally friendly and has helped dispel the fog (after the banning of solid fuel) from city-centre areas. If you are an environmentalist, however, you might well argue that gas is a clean fuel at the point of use by the consumer, but it is not a clean fuel if you study the production processes.
- Jurys Hotels are involved in one product only — hotels. Yet the product divides into Jurys hotels and Jurys Inns hotels. Your mental image will be based on your experience of either one, or the comparison between one and the other. And the physical identity of the two differs as well. Jurys Hotels are middle-market, middle-management hotels. They have conference and, in many cases, leisure facilities, plush carpeting, and a semi-exclusive feel to the bar areas. Jurys Inns, by comparison, attract the lower end of the market. There is more wooden seating, the bars have more the feel of an outside bar (not a hotel bar) and the atmosphere is different from the time you come through the front door.

- Corporate image is much easier for Ryanair. It is a low-fares airline. Do you remember the first set of ads Ryanair introduced? I remember attending a conference which was addressed by Catherine Donnelly, the copywriter, who gave a brief history of the introduction of the strapline — 'the airline with absolutely nothing going for it'. She explained how management, as part of the brief, told her that breakfast, coffee, or any of the other in-flight services that people expected would not be provided. The airline would, however, be flying at the lowest possible cost to each of its destinations. She decided to highlight the 'no frills' element and practically brought the board meeting to a standstill! She felt that, instead of downplaying the lack of in-flight services, the company should highlight it as a positive. Yes, you could get breakfast on other airlines, but it would cost you considerably more to fly with them and, heck, if you wanted to pay that kind of money for breakfast — do it! It firmly established Ryanair in the minds of consumers as no frills but good value. It is an image which has lasted through the years. When customers complained to RTÉ's *Liveline* programme, and others, that they had been stranded in Beauvais Airport, on a bank holiday weekend to Paris (2001) and that Ryanair had done nothing for them, the company's chief executive, Michael O'Leary, came on air to say that of course the company did nothing for them — the passengers had paid very little for their flights. They had to overnight — tough; they flew low-cost. The airline was under no obligation to give them accommodation. Almost incredibly, this approach was well received by the public.

Corporate image is very often based on one person — the high-profile chief executive who is publicly associated with the company. These are usually dynamic and energetic individuals who are the 'face' of the organisation. If you think of any of the Smurfit companies, you think of Dr Michael Smurfit. Virgin Airlines immediately brings Richard Branson to mind. Superquinn's name conjures the immediate mental image of Senator Feargal Quinn. The image of Esat was Denis O'Brien, and the image of Budget Travel, even though she sold the company, is of Gillian Bowler with her trademark sunglasses on her head.

The difficulty with an image revolving around a person is that if that person moves jobs, or gets involved in a scandal, or dies, then the company, in the minds of the consumer, is somewhat lost for direction. The company appears to be in a vacuum without this person and instantly loses its image. If the chairman who is publicly associated with your company is found guilty of fraud, all of the good work of building an image for the company is lost. People believe that they have been duped and will associate the behaviour of the chairman with the image of the company (even if the fraud was not connected to the company).

If, therefore, image is closely related to experience and information, you need to ensure that the experience is a quality one, and that the flow of information is relevant and timely. Basic rule of PR: image is different depending on your experience of the company and your relationship with it. Target each of the different groups — shareholders, employees, opinion leaders, etc. — with information that is relevant to their needs. It will enhance the image of the company/organisation in their minds.

A colleague sent me, by e-mail, this note about Microsoft and General Motors. It might be true and, for that again, it might be cyber-myth and legend. It is, however, a witty way of explaining what image is all about.

> Microsoft's head honcho, Bill Gates, reportedly said that if General Motors (GM), the world's largest car manufacturer, had kept up with technology like the computer industry, we would have $25 cars that go 1,000 miles to the gallon.
>
> Naturally this prompted the following response from GM: If cars were like the computer industry for no reason whatsoever, your car would crash twice a day. Occasionally, executing a manoeuvre such as a left turn would cause your car to shut down and refuse to restart, in which case you would have to reinstall the engine.
>
> Occasionally your car would die. You would have to pull over, close all of the windows, shut down the car, restart it, and reopen the windows before you could continue. For some reason you would simply accept this.
>
> Macintosh would make a solar-powered car that was five times as fast and twice as easy to drive — but it would run on only 5% of the roads.
>
> The oil, water, temperature and alternator warning lights would all be replaced by a single 'general protection fault' warning light.
>
> Occasionally your car would lock you out and refuse to let you in until you simultaneously lifted the door handle, turned the key and grabbed the aerial.
>
> The airbag system would ask 'are you sure?' before deploying.
>
> Every time GM introduced a new car, car buyers would have to learn to drive all over again because none of the controls would operate in the same manner as in the old car.[8]

CORPORATE IDENTITY

Corporate identity, on the other hand, is the same for everyone. It is the physical manifestation of the company — its offices, showrooms, staff uniforms, company vans, letterheads, logos, etc. A good corporate identity should be instantly recognisable by all. If you were parachuted, blindfolded, into Dunnes Stores, you should instantly be able to identify the store based on store layout and staff uniforms when the blindfold was removed. Similarly, you should be able to recognise instantly if, although you were told you would be parachuted into Dunnes Stores, you have, in fact, landed in Superquinn.

Corporate identity is most obviously created by corporate logos and branding. The slightly crooked shamrock of Aer Lingus is well known (in Ireland at least) and the tail fins of British Airways planes make them instantly identifiable.

Logos and branding, however, need to be professionally communicated to customers, staff and the general public so that they are, indeed, identifiable. The introduction of a new logo will do nothing if time, effort, energy and sizable quantities of money are not put into its promotion.

Logos create an identity for the business and are seen as valuable by boards of directors, investors and PR people. They are seldom seen by the media as having any worth.

There are numerous examples of companies that changed or amended their logos over the years. The Guinness beer bottle has changed through the years, but so subtly that it is hardly noticeable. Enable Ireland launched its new yellow branding, and when Eircell became Vodafone, red became the new purple (to paraphrase the advertisement).

The logos must also be appropriate to the business you are in. A brightly coloured letterhead from a firm of solicitors would definitely look wrong and probably make you nervous about the company. By comparison, a nice respectable headed notepaper from a design company would not enhance its image or inspire confidence. Nor would you expect to find dark colours used on the letterhead of a pre-school group.

Corporate identity is important for any company, and cannot remain static. This is not to suggest that it will change on a regular basis; it will not. However, it needs to be reviewed every decade or so to make sure that it still reflects the ethos of the company. Companies, after all, change and so should their corporate identity.

Before we look at some of the big-budget identity changes, note the advice from Fiona McLoughlin, Head of Corporate Marketing, Enable Ireland. She advises that organisations or companies should:

- Think BIG
- Think the change through
- Build the case for change
- Engage senior management — they must engage staff
- Champion the champions of change
- Make the process consultative
- Involve the resisters to change — don't ignore them
- Listen and persuade
- Thank everyone for their contributions
- Communicate until everyone feels they own the brand.

When Cerebral Palsy Ireland and the Lavanagh Centre (as the organisation was known in Cork) changed their name to Enable Ireland, the concept had been nine months in gestation. As a charity, money was scarce. Radio advertising campaigns were sponsored, the goodwill of journalists (developed over years of communication) was harnessed, and champions of their cause willingly gave their time to endorse and attend functions. For an outlay of approximately €5,000 on the launch, Enable Ireland estimates that it achieved €203,000 worth of coverage — a great return on investment (ROI) by any standard![9]

Practitioners generally dislike this method of evaluation, known as AVE (Advertising

Value Equivalent). Editorial carries the weight of independence and perspective of the journalist, while advertising is bought space into which you place your message. So, in real terms, the value of the coverage Enable Ireland achieved was probably at least ten times greater than the €203,000 advertising equivalent. However, while practitioners may frown upon this method, charities and corporate bodies continue to use it as part of their evaluation of the value of their investment in PR.

At the other end of the scale, although not strictly a corporate identity change, by far the largest product and identity change in Ireland was the change in currency in 2002 from the Irish pound to the euro. The scale of the undertaking was enormous. According to John Collins, President of the Institute of Bankers in Ireland:

> As a logistical exercise the introduction of the euro was a credit to everyone involved, the Government, the Central Bank, the financial services sector and retailers. It really was like a military exercise. Computers and ATMs had to be adapted and there was the physical distribution of vast amounts of cash...The ease with which the euro was introduced surprised everybody — but also reflected the scale and thoroughness of the preparations made by all involved.[10]

We will now look, in some detail, at the key steps involved in implementing a corporate identity change.

KEY STEPS INVOLVED IN IDENTITY CHANGE

1. Background to Identity Change

Rationale

You need to establish clearly a reason for the change. A change in corporate identity is a very costly undertaking which should not be entered into lightly. Most companies change their identity to reflect changes in their business. A little over a decade ago, AIB changed its identity from the old Mercedes-type logo to a newer Dove and Ark logo.[11] The change was introduced as the bank began to expand into foreign markets (notably Poland and the US), and introduce new technology which would provide easier access to services for the customer. Enable Ireland changed its identity in the millennium year (2000) because its old name, Cerebral Palsy Ireland, was dated and associated with affliction.[12] The charity wanted its new identity to reflect the fact that its job was one of enabling people to achieve their best. You might also change your identity if you were moving into new markets which either would have difficulty translating your name, or in which the translated name meant something entirely different.

Changing corporate identity means changing the logo, the offices, the areas for the public, the vans, the letterheads — everything.

Benefits

You need to establish clearly the benefits of the change, and you need to bring each of your stakeholders along with you. Everyone should 'buy into' the change. Establish what benefits the company expects to achieve by the change. Enable Ireland wanted to change public perception and its corporate identity change formed part of that. AIB was trying to do the same thing. Aer Lingus wanted to portray a much more vibrant image — perhaps in an effort to attract suitable airline partners?

Buying into the Change

Make sure that all of the stakeholders buy into the concept, from board of management to employees and stakeholders. The Tourism Brand Ireland logo changed three times in four years. The first logo was introduced under a Fine Gael government (1996); it was changed a year later (1997) under a Fianna Fáil government (who did not buy into the concept); and changed again (1999) because an entirely new entity was created to manage the brand. The background is explained below.

In 1995 the Tourism Council recommended the development of a Brand for Ireland Tourism. The Tourism Brand Ireland (TBI) initiative was officially launched in November 1996, following nearly two years of research and development in the derivation of the brand. Bord Fáilte was charged with the responsibility of making the concept a reality. The Northern Ireland Tourist Board was a full partner in the whole branding initiative.

The need to develop a visual identity to support Tourism Brand Ireland led to the appointment of an Irish design agency, DesignWorks, to handle this aspect of the project. The visual identity system included a brand mark or logo for Ireland. The visual identity comprised a series of 'building blocks' including the mark, colour, typography and a system for application. The colour palette concentrated on the use of purple and two shades of green. This colour combination, when juxtaposed with strong use of photography, created a distinctive look for the identity that transcended the mark. The visual equity established in the initial phase of the brand's creation has been retained and evolved throughout the various developments of the mark.

The brand mark has undergone significant change on two occasions since the original version in 1996. The original mark brought together a number of elements: the two forms which can be interpreted as two human beings about to embrace, the shamrock, the distinctive colours and the typography of the word Ireland.

In 1997 there was a change of government. The new Minister for Tourism requested the creation of a brand device that gave more prominence to the shamrock. This was undertaken by DesignWorks and introduced in the same year.

In 1999, an all-island tourism marketing company, Tourism Ireland Ltd, was incorporated. The company, which was created under the Good Friday Agreement, became fully operational on 1 January 2002. Its principal function is to carry out strategic all-Ireland destination marketing in all markets outside the island of Ireland.

The new company has responsibility for Tourism Brand Ireland. A new identity system for TBI incorporating a brand mark or logo was developed by DesignWorks at the request of Tourism Ireland Ltd. It was introduced in November 2001.

The new Tourism Brand Ireland visual identity system, including a brand mark or logo, is a normal evolution of the original system. It was decided to contemporise the design for a dynamic industry which operates in a highly competitive international marketplace.[13] The evolution of the logo can be seen in below.

The Three Varieties of Irish Tourist Board Logo

Selection of Designers

The selection of designers to look after the introduction of a new identity has been a contentious issue in Ireland almost since corporate logos began to change. Although Irish companies have been used to design corporate identity schemes — notably those for Tourism Brand Ireland[14] and Eircom[15] — it is British companies that have secured the lion's share of corporate identity design in Ireland. Irish companies complain that they should be getting much more of the work as they are just as capable of handling it as their British counterparts are.

Design companies should be asked to tender for the work — select from a large pool, view their work, hold tentative meetings, and then brief three companies to tender. You are looking for a mix of people, concepts and ability to deliver.

Corporate identity changes cost a lot of money. They are often accompanied by large tomes explaining the rationale behind the change. This can be difficult to communicate to shareholders and employees, and others not directly involved — especially the media.

When Aer Lingus launched its new logo, the press savaged it. The new logo, according to *Sunday Independent* journalist Jonathan Philbin Bowman, 'was part of a reinvestment in the brand — the biggest asset Aer Lingus owned, they told us.' 'Funny,' he added, 'I would have thought that was the aeroplanes, but what would I know?'[16]

Design Concept Approval

Once the final design has been chosen, it requires the approval of the board of directors. The final design, its rationale, and the cost of implementation should all be put before the board for approval.

Putting Together the Project Team

At this stage, the really hard work of the PR person begins. It is now necessary to put together a project team — people who will oversee the change in letterheads, stationery, printed material and brochures; corporate logos on videos, offices, reception areas, sales areas, exterior signage; livery on vans and trucks. The undertaking is enormous and the logistical skills required cannot be underestimated.

2. Doing it — Using Project–Management Techniques

Analyse Requirements and Objectives

Try to determine exactly what is required and when. It is important that you understand at the outset, particularly if you are a nationwide organisation, that it will not be logistically feasible to implement a corporate identity change in one fell swoop. Objectives therefore need to be identified. Which are the most important locations that must be ready on launch day? By what date will customers be informed that a change of identity is on its way? What will the roll-out period be? How many media events will be held? The list goes on.

Agree Activity and Tasks to be Performed

Divide the project-management team and assign responsibilities to each member. Each member in turn should schedule the items for which they are responsible.

Computerised Time-Management System

Whether the team meets on a monthly, weekly or daily basis, some form of time management and control system will have to be implemented. This system also needs to be overseen to ensure that there is no slippage. One deadline missed will affect all of the other elements of the roll-out.

By the time that the launch day has arrived, there are a number of things which must be complete. Before the launch day:

- Shareholders, employees and media should be told that the identity is changing. They should also know the date on which the change takes place, and you might do a campaign around the 'count-down' to the launch of the new look.
- Supporting literature will need to be printed, explaining the reason for the change, showing the new look that will be adopted (this will not be distributed until launch day), and explaining the rationale for changing the identity, and the phased (or un-phased) nature of the roll-out. The literature needs to build confidence and support for this new initiative.

Staff Involvement

It is vital that you explain to your staff the rationale behind the change, and harness staff enthusiasm and support. When Telecom Éireann changed its identity to Eircom, management adopted an internal communications strategy which recognised the value of staff input into the 'old' company, explained the vision of the 'new' company, and encouraged support. As part of the strategy, 112 staff workshops called 'Building Eircom' were held for its 11,000 employees. The workshops were held over a five-week period and reflected the Eircom values of a professional, progressive and friendly company. The workshops achieved high levels of staff involvement and interaction. Research at their conclusion revealed that 91 per cent of all staff-members who attended the workshops felt well informed about the change in the corporate identity.[17]

3. The Launch

Stationery

The relevant stationery, compliments slips, envelopes, etc. will need to have been delivered to each of your branches in advance of the launch day, so that they can immediately begin to use them. Any delay will cause a loss of impact with the receivers.

Invitations

Invitations will have been sent to guests and media to attend the launch functions. There may be only one function, at company headquarters. However, if the company has a national spread of branch networks, or charity offices, or retail outlets, you will probably have more than one launch. These might be arranged to happen simultaneously.

At a minimum, you will probably have divided the country into regions, and arranged for at least one outlet in each region to be formally 'launched' with the new look.

Each of these functions requires the same attention to detail. Depending on the company, you might have a government minister at the 'national' launch at headquarters, and the local Lord Mayor at each of the regional launches. Company personnel will need to be spread throughout the country to ensure that there are board members at each launch. Separate invitations, by region, will need to be issued to guests.

Staff Invitations

Selections will need to be made of the employees to attend (especially if the launch occurs on a working day and in one branch only). It is important that all employees feel that they were a part of the launch, even if it was in Cork, for the Munster region, and they were based in Tralee. A system will need to be found to ensure that representatives from every outlet attend the Cork function. The same format will be repeated in Galway, Athlone, and wherever else you have chosen for your regional launches. Internal communications will need to be excellent to ensure the smooth launching of the new identity.

Signage

The change in identity will most likely involve a change in exterior signage, whether it is a change of logo (AIB) or a change of name (Enable Ireland). Who will unveil the new signage? Will it be a cord pulling and curtain exercise? How will the formal unveiling be handled in each location?

For the selected locations, the interior look of the premises might have changed, as might the staff uniforms. From the guests' point of view, they should feel like they are participating in the launch of an entirely new venture by your company.

Reception

Decide what type of reception will be held. Should the new identity be launched with champagne and strawberries; or tea and biscuits? How long should the reception last? What kind of memento will people receive on departure (in addition to the literature they will be given)?

Media (print, radio and TV)

For the 'national' launch, you will be trying to attract national cross-media coverage. For each of the regional launches, you will be trying to achieve at least print and radio coverage.

Different media lists will be involved, as local media will be crucial to the success of the local launches. Staff and customer newsletters will also need to carry coverage of each of the events, nationwide, so possibly freelance journalists and certainly photographers will have to be retained for each location.

The Actual Event

The launch will probably include celebrity involvement, but you will also try to involve the local community. You might create razzmatazz by using balloons, face painters, clowns, jugglers, musicians or search lights.

Celebrities, board members and politicians should also be encouraged to participate in the celebrations.

4. Implementation and Roll-out

Phases and Timescales

You will have clearly determined in the early stages how many phases will be involved in the roll-out. The phases might, for example, mean that all branches had the new identity letterheads, compliments slips and brochures on day one, and all staff wore the new uniforms from launch day. There might be a corporate decision that invoices which are issued on the last day of the month would be held until the second of the next month, so that every customer in the country would receive an invoice showing the new identity. The exterior signage, however, and the internal changes might not be made for several months. The phased introduction of these changes — and a clear plan about which areas or locations are involved, in what order, and whether interior and exterior changes are to be made at the same time, etc. — will mean that the team will be involved in the implementation phase for probably eighteen months after the launch day.

5. Maintaining and Monitoring a Consistent Identity

Corporate Identity Manuals

Corporate identity manuals need to be produced and issued to all relevant departments handling sales, public relations, advertising, marketing, direct marketing, sales promotion, exhibitions — anything, in fact, that involves the use of the new logo. The manual must clearly give details of the logo — the size, the font type, the pantone references for colour, the place on the brochures on which the logo should appear. The corporate manual must leave nothing to chance. Vast amounts of money have been spent in re-launching the identity; it would be shameful if the identity were not consistently applied across all media and in all locations throughout the country.

Setting up a Corporate Identity Unit

In addition to the corporate identity manuals, it might be necessary to set up a unit with special responsibility for monitoring the implementation of the requirements of the manual. The unit would monitor each advertisement placed, or each brochure produced, to ensure that there is no dilution of the logo and its application.

This unit might also be responsible for monitoring feedback after the introduction. How well received was the new look? Were there different reactions from the different groups consulted? How did shareholders feel? How did employees react? What was the tone of media coverage?

This unit would remain in existence until the full roll-out has been completed and thereafter would be scaled down. Its members would then meet less frequently, but continue to monitor at a distance to ensure that there was no slippage.

REFERENCES

1. www.ipr.org.uk
2. J. M. and M .J. Cohen, *The Penguin Dictionary of Quotations*, Penguin, 1980.
3. Marianne Henry, lecturer in PR Theory and Practice with the Irish Academy of Public Relations in conversation with the author.
4. Professor W. R. Spence, presentation at Irish Academy of Public Relations course entitled 'Public Relations Skills for Practitioners', at Skull Kommunikációs Iskola, Budapest, 1997.
5. Ciarán Swan, 'Red Roses for the President', *CIRCA Art Magazine*, Back Issues CIRCA 89, www.recirca.com/features/index.shtml
6. *The Late Late Show*, RTÉ1 television, 14 October 1997.
7. Ellen Gunning, 'Agenda Setting: A Study of the Blue Flu', thesis submitted in part fulfilment of the requirements for the awarding of the degree of Masters in Communications and Cultural Studies, Dublin City University, August 1999.
8. Received by e-mail from Ursula Forde.
9. Fiona McLoughlin, Head of Corporate Marketing, Enable Ireland, presentation at the PRII forum, 'Changing Corporate Identity/Image', Cork, 23 February 2001.
10. John Collins, President of the Institute of Bankers in Ireland (2002–2003), 'The challenge of Change', *Banking Ireland — the Journal of the Institute of Bankers in Ireland*, Spring 2002.
11. Jacqui McCrum, Group Corporate Identity Manager, AIB Group, presentations at the PRII forum, 'Changing Corporate Identity/Image', Cork, 23 February 2001.
12. Enable Ireland changed its identity on 24 October 2000. Fiona McLoughlin, Head of Corporate Marketing, Enable Ireland, presentation at the PRII forum, 'Changing Corporate Identity/Image', Cork, 23 February 2001.
13. Information provided by John Brown MPRII, Marketing Department, Bord Fáilte.
14. The original design and subsequent development/re-launch of the brand/logo for the Irish Tourist Board was commissioned to the DesignWorks design studio in Dublin.
15. The Identity Business handled the change of logo which accompanied the name change from Telecom Éireann to Eircom. Philip Barlow, Brand Consultant, The Identity Business, presentation at the PRII forum, 'Changing Corporate Identity/Image', Cork, 23 February 2001.

16. Jonathan Philbin Bowman, 'Crooked shamrock's launch fails to soar', *Sunday Independent*, 18 February 1996.
17. Philip Barlow, Brand Consultant, The Identity Business, presentation at the PRII forum, 'Changing Corporate Identity/Image', Cork, 23 February 2001.

CHAPTER 15

PR for Charities and Voluntary Organisations

Public relations for charities (or voluntary bodies) involves primarily three areas:

1. Building awareness and credibility for the charity
2. Promoting the overall image of the charity
3. Promoting the product brand.

PR for charity almost inevitably has a fundraising element — there are few charity PR people whose position does not include at least an element of fundraising. In fact, few charities have dedicated PROs. Although some have, most incorporate the role and functions of PR into the wider role of Development Officer.

Do not be confused into thinking that PR for charities is somehow woollier or less professional than PR for a corporate body. It is not. The charity market is (partly) voluntary, highly competitive and utterly professional.

COMPETITIVE MARKET

The charity market in Ireland is believed to receive in excess of €300 million annually from public contributions. In 2000, Concern raised €22.86 million in donations, while Trócaire raised €22.79 million.[1] These charities operate in a very competitive market. In 2001, there were almost 5,500 organisations registered with the Revenue Commissioners for charity exemption status.[2]

Each charity competes with every other charity. So Goal, Trócaire, Concern, Irish Red Cross, Chernobyl Children and others are all competing for your donation. The public has only a limited amount of disposable income (no matter how wealthy the economy) and only a percentage of that income will be given to charity. Charities, therefore, need to work hard to ensure that it is they who receive your donation, and not their competitors.

They compete in sectors. We are all, by design, by upbringing, by choice, by life experience, more inclined to give to one type of charity than another. It is quite simple really — we mentally pre-select those areas in which we are interested. I am therefore, because of my background, interested in the Society of St Vincent de Paul (SVP). My father worked as a local volunteer and was president of the local branch throughout my childhood. I worked with the society as a volunteer myself for a number of years subsequently. This is a close relationship. I have seen the work of the SVP from the outside and inside, and I believe wholeheartedly in what the SVP is doing. Family members have fought and lost battles with cancer, so the Irish Cancer Society and its work will always receive my support. I had the privilege of serving two terms on the board of the Irish Red Cross as a government nominee. I saw at first hand the tremendous work that body does, and I became a lifetime supporter. I'm sure that children's charities are worthy of support — but I don't have any children, and there is, therefore, no natural connection for me.

So, we select the broad categories of charity in which we are interested. If the category was 'relieving the plight of people in the developing world', the choice would include Trócaire, Goal, Concern and the Irish Red Cross. These four would compete with each other to gain my attention, my loyalty, and my donations.

People will not buy a brand with which they are unfamiliar, and neither will they contribute to a charity about which they know little. Why should they? Instead, they will contribute to a charity with which they are familiar, and whom they trust.

So the first thing to keep in mind is that charities are in a competitive market. They compete with each other for funding. Without funding, after all, there would be no good works and no charity. And without publicity, their good works would be unknown.

VOLUNTARY NATURE

The perception is that charities are populated by well-meaning volunteers. While these people do exist, they are becoming the minority. Think of the changes in lifestyles over the years.

In the 1980s, large numbers of women worked full-time in the home. They had free time while the children were at school. This free time was devoted to looking after elderly members of the family and, very often, involving themselves in community and charitable works. It was primarily from this pool and those of retired people and part-time workers that charities got their volunteers. How else would it be possible to keep charity shops open during working hours? This group has been declining over the years, and its numbers are smaller than ever before.

In the 1980s, people in full-time employment also worked as volunteers for charities, doing good work in the evenings. It seems like a lifetime ago (not a couple of decades) since people actually had reasonable amounts of free time. The stresses and strains of modern life are such that people find themselves with less and less free time. What free time they have involves caring for children, their parents, shopping, studying, working — very little time is left for voluntary work.

In the 2000s, time is at a premium. It is noticeably easier to get money from people than it is to get them to donate their time.

PROFESSIONALISM

Charities have become more professional in their outlook, their approach, and their communications. They had to. Members of the public expect professionalism from any group with which they are involved. This has meant that charities need to employ full-time staff members to provide services and communicate with their donors. However, the public does not like to see money spent on administration staff or PR people, and there are loud objections when it is revealed that a disproportionate (in the opinion of the public) percentage of donations is spent in this way.

Charities have a great difficulty with this. If they do not communicate professionally, they will lose donations. If they are seen to spend money on communications, they also lose money (because of disapproval). PR for charities, therefore, is tied into fundraising. Charities, in my experience, never retain outside consultancies — they could not be seen to do so, and could not afford the fees. They gain the services of external PR people when a corporate body agrees to become involved, and the corporate body, in turn, involves its own PR people. They also gain the services of PR people (individuals and consultancies) who offer their time and expertise to selected charities each year.

Charities must, however, advertise. Even with sponsored ads, the cost to charities is quite high. Trócaire spent €1.64 million on advertising in 2000. Concern spent €5.7 million on advertising in the same period.[3]

KEY PUBLICS FOR CHARITIES

The key publics for charities are donors, potential donors, patrons, corporate bodies, volunteers, government and those in need of help. Each of these groups needs constant communication and this communication needs to be sophisticated and tailored to each group, in order to catch its attention.

Donors need to be told where their money is going. Their donations must be receipted and their contribution recognised. They should be informed of the uses to which their donations were put, and thanked for the valuable contribution they have made to the cause.

Potential donors need to be attracted to the charity, in ever-growing numbers. A charity which fails to attract new donors constantly is a charity doomed to die. These might be donors of goods (transport, food and drink, for example), donors of time (solicitors, PR people, accountants) or donors of money.

Patrons are crucial to the success of a charity — it is by celebrities lending their names for use by the charity that ordinary members of the public accept the bona fides of the organisation. One way of generating confidence in a new charity is by reference to its patrons. If it has patrons who are well known and respected, the public is much more likely to become involved.

Corporate bodies can provide valuable funding through sponsorships. They need to be kept informed not only of the work of the charity, but of the potential to get involved. Many charities liaise with PR consultancies, knowing that if there is a good sponsorship opportunity, the consultancies will bring it to the attention of their clients. Others constantly liaise with the larger companies and corporations through their public relations or marketing departments.

Volunteers are always needed. People are needed to make door-to-door collections. Others are needed to address meetings where the audience is asked to consider bequeathing a donation to the charity in their last will, or to act as ambassadors for the charity, promoting the good work of the organisation. People are needed for bucket collections, to visit sick people in their homes, to deliver meals, and to provide accommodation.

Government needs to understand the work of the charity and how it can help. Over the years, charities have become very good at lobbying government and successfully harvesting their assistance.

The charity family — the community of people it is trying to help — also needs to be communicated with. There's no point in having a charity which provides services to the disabled if the disabled have never heard of it. There's no point in providing assistance to AIDS patients if their families don't know where to go to look for help. And there's no point in providing family budgeting services if the financial community, the banks and the credit unions don't know that the service is on offer.

BUILDING AWARENESS

In order to communicate with each of these groups, various PR tools need to be employed. Charities employ the full range of PR tools to help them build awareness of their cause. They use media (photo calls, press releases, media visits), newsletters, meetings, fundraising extravaganzas and a variety of functions to reach their audiences.

Printed Material

Newsletters are regarded, rightly in my opinion, as a vital tool of charity PR. They are a way of keeping in touch with donors and letting them know how much funding has been raised, how it was spent, the number of volunteers involved, and the number of lives saved (or quality of lives improved). Newsletters for charities are, however, caught between a rock and a hard place. They must be professional in their presentation or no one would read them. But if they look too professional, too glossy, too much colour, the donating public is inclined to believe that this is how all the money is being spent. There is a constant balance to be struck between keeping people informed and not raising their hackles! The newsletter must be professional, but it must be reasonable to produce or sponsored. Even if the product is sponsored, a full-colour glossy newsletter for a charity instantly sparks the thought that some of that sponsorship money could have been used for the 'cause'.

Newsletters cost money to put together, write, print, and post to donors. Yet, without them, people would lose touch with the charity and move their donations elsewhere.

Changing Attitudes and Habits

Other forms of literature produced by charities are intended to change attitudes and habits. In the early 1990s, the Irish Society for the Prevention of Cruelty to Children (ISPCC) ran a nationwide billboard campaign to stop adults slapping children,[4] while the Irish Heart Foundation runs a number of health-promotion events during the year, including a restaurant campaign, Happy Heart Eat Out, and Irish Heart week.[5]

Celebrity Endorsement

Third-party endorsement is also important for charities. Chernobyl Children must benefit (financially and in terms of awareness) from the involvement of Ali Hewson (Bono's wife). Similarly, the Irish Kidney Association's Organ Donor Week had the endorsement of Andrea Corr for its appeal in 2001, and pop group Six in 2002. Their appearances on television, posters, ads and photographs raised awareness nationally.

Lobbying

Lobbying is another PR activity in which charities get involved. Charities successfully lobbied government to make charitable donations tax-deductible for corporations and companies. The introduction of tax-deductible donations meant that charities could reach a wider audience, give people an incentive to donate, and take in more funds. In 2002 any company, corporation, or self-employed person who made a donation in excess of €250 (minimum amount) received a tax credit (calculated at their relevant tax rate) relative to the amount donated.[6]

In addition, charities encourage supporters to lobby organisations on their behalf. When Trócaire launched its 'Campaign to End Slavery', its website urged people to contact the United Nations (UN) and International Labour Organisation (ILO). It also provided online postcards which supporters could complete and send to the Minister for Enterprise, asking for the issue to be raised with the ILO. In 2001, as part of this campaign, Trócaire highlighted bonded labour; in 2002, the focus was on children who were involved in armed conflict.[7]

Irish overseas development charities also work together on common issues, in an umbrella group called Dóchas, and occasionally an ad hoc lobby group will be set up by various charities to deal with a specific issue (e.g. the problem of VAT).[8]

Media Coverage

The power of media in promoting the work of charities cannot be overstated. Media, especially photographic and television, are crucial to a charity's success. If we see, with our own eyes, children dying of famine, or wasted with disease, or animals which have been horribly abused, we are roused much more quickly to give donations.

This also brings with it a certain number of problems. The visuals must be striking and the starker they are, the better the response from the public in terms of donations.

Charities compete with each other to ensure that it is they, and not their competitors, who bring the TV crews to a disaster area to get footage which will be shown back home. From a branding and fundraising point of view, it makes sense. The charity which brings over the crew will ensure that all of its people are wearing branded tee-shirts which reinforce the message that this charity is providing relief. The branded charity, in turn, receives most of the donations for that situation, so it is well worth its while to ensure that it is the one to bring over the TV crews.

The images must also be stark. Everyone can remember pictures of Ethiopian children dying — their emaciated bodies held lovingly by their mothers, their bones protruding under taut skin, their eyes covered in flies. In 1984, the world was alerted to this famine, of biblical proportions, by BBC correspondent Michael Buerk. Pop-star Bob Geldof decided that he could not sit back and watch the suffering; he organised the 16-hour Live Aid phenomenon. Live Aid took place on 13 July 1985 and was held simultaneously in London and Philadelphia. Throughout the world, viewers reacted by sending donations, and the event raised more than £60 million. Despite this huge international effort, 1.2 million people still starved to death.

Credibility

Those harrowing scenes are undoubtedly successful in encouraging donations. However, they raise two critical issues: respect for victims, and donor fatigue. The first of these issues is dealt with below. Donor fatigue will be discussed later under the heading 'The Charity Brand'.

Respect for Victims

There must be a respect for the victims themselves, and this can be overlooked in the headlong rush to make the world aware of the tragedy and secure funds for its relief. It can be forgotten that these are real people, with dignity, who have lost real members of their families, who are suffering real trauma, who need a seat and a drink of water and not the cameras of the world in their faces, when they finally flee oppression or arrive at a feeding station. There is a growing debate about the way in which these images are used without the consent of the victims, and often portraying them in a way that they would not choose to be portrayed. How often have you heard, in this type of coverage, people speak of themselves as a proud nation? How often have you seen reference to that fact that these are a self-sufficient people, perfectly capable of looking after all of their own needs, except for this fire/flood/famine which has left them needing assistance? It is seldom how things are portrayed and even more rarely the public perception of how they are.

We have moved a long way from the 'little black baby' syndrome of the 1960s and 1970s when an entire generation of schoolchildren grew up believing that they were helping poor, ignorant, helpless, black babies in Africa. But sometimes you would wonder how far we have really progressed.

Is there still a belief that we in the west know best? The stories abound of organisations trying to teach people how to do things the western way (when their own way was fine for generations). There are stories of charities that went into developing countries and provided machinery — tractors and the like — and believed they were doing a power of good. What they overlooked was the fact that there were no spare parts available in the event of a breakdown, and no infrastructure — no trained mechanics — on which to rely. So, when the machinery broke, it stayed broken, and the locals went back to cultivating in the way that they had always done for centuries.

There is also a debate about schemes which encourage the public to 'adopt a child', which is closely linked to the above point. Someone in the west donates money, by standing order/direct debit, and that money goes to help a particular child. The child, in turn, is encouraged to write to the donor. It is a great idea for the charities — guaranteed income in return for a couple of letters. It also creates a bond between donor and recipient which will probably last for 10–15 years, if not for a lifetime. It provides a feel-good factor for the donors — they are physically receiving the gratitude of the person to whom their funds are going. It is a great fundraising idea — but what does it do to the recipients? Does it make victims of them? Do these children who receive western money grow up believing that there are plenty of rich benefactors in the west who will help them? Does it propagate a dependency culture (the belief that there are people out there willing to give handouts)? Does it make you turn against your own people (believing that you are worthless, slow, backward, if you can't look after yourselves)? Does it propagate western values (and encourage children to want to live in the west when they grow up)?

What does it say of your parents who allow you to accept this money? How does it change your relationship with them; your relationship with your community? These are huge ethical issues for charities, which can only be touched upon here.

Good News is No News

Charities also have a problem with good news — to twist a well-known saying: good news is no news. Thin emaciated little bodies which need our help are news. Fattened bodies doing very nicely are not. The positive stories of the on-going good work of charities generally get little media attention and no donor response in terms of money. A famine site revisited three years later, and the story told of a recovered, self-sufficient community, actually encourages us to move our donations elsewhere. They're doing fine now, we think, but there are plenty of starving people somewhere else out there still to help.

It is a constant problem for charities and one that will change only when we, the donors, change our patterns of donation.

The 'good news' stories or the follow-up stories are broadcast on fund-raising programmes like *Comic Relief*, but they are not generally covered as news items.

Media Coverage

If you accept that media coverage is vital, bringing media to the scene of a disaster is crucial, and that having branding prominently displayed by volunteer workers affects donations, then it follows that the fight for media attention is a serious one. When disaster strikes, one charity each, from every 'developed' nation, tries to achieve coverage back home. This means that large numbers of media people converge on the scene of a disaster.

Different media representing different national interests cover the story from different national angles (e.g. Goal in Ireland, and Médecins Sans Frontières in France). The media themselves are beginning to question their role. Is it really necessary to have twenty-five television crews reporting on a famine? Each of these crews needs transport, accommodation, water and food. Would it not be better to send one crew, and allow that crew to share its footage with all television stations, and free up the transport, tents and food to help the victims? Has famine become a 'business' in which the media are necessary to 'sell' the product? And, if so, should they be willing participants?

When catastrophic flooding hit Mozambique in March 2000, presenters on *Five Live Drive* (BBC Radio 5 Live) told of many callers who phoned to complain about radio and film crews taking up space on helicopters — space which should have been occupied by rescued people. The programme's hosts admitted that there had been considerable soul-searching at the BBC on this issue.[9]

It is a loaded situation. If media adopted a shared approach to coverage, it would require a similar, shared approach by the charities. It would no longer be necessary, desirable or even viable to compete for coverage. Donations would be proportionately divided among all of the national charities, in each country, which were providing famine relief.

In Britain, the Disasters Emergency Committee (DEC) is an umbrella organisation of fourteen charities, formed to co-ordinate national appeals to major disasters overseas.[10] No such approach exists in Ireland that I am aware of. If it did, some charities might lose donations, some might close, and others might amalgamate. These are serious issues for both the media and the charitable organisations.

Administrative Costs

There is also the issue of how much of the funds raised are actually used for the cause. Some charities have administrative costs which absorb up to 50c of every euro donated. There must be professional administration in every charity, but donors object to giving money for this purpose. They expect that 90 per cent of their donation will go to the cause for which it is given.

The full euro (i.e. 100 per cent) donated to the Irish Red Cross[11] and Trócaire[12] for all overseas projects goes abroad entirely without any deduction of costs. In addition, Trócaire has a Donor's Charter which was introduced on the charity's twenty-fifth anniversary in 1998.[13]

It is an issue that charities need to address. They need to agree jointly on an administration percentage, and have that percentage independently audited. Either that or they each, individually, should issue an annual statement stating clearly how much of the funding raised went to the causes for which it was given. In the absence of either of these options, the government might need to introduce legislation capping the percentage that can be spent on administration. It is an issue for donors and, therefore, an issue for charities.

Fundraisers

Charities are obviously concerned with the behaviour of their fundraisers (their integrity and their approach). In addition, there are two other issues of concern: presentation and payment.

- *Presentation.* If the organisation were a bank or an airline, everyone working for it would wear a uniform which would make them immediately identifiable. Even if they worked for a company with no uniforms, there would be a corporate dress code. This could vary from casual (for a technology company) to flamboyant (for an advertising agency) to suited (for a firm of solicitors). Volunteers, however, come from every walk of life and don't have uniforms. How does any charity encourage its volunteers to project a particular image? It cannot buy uniforms for them, nor can it refuse their willing help. Often, the 'face' of the charity is the person who collects on its behalf. How does any charity control its image among such a diverse group of people?
- *Payment.* Because of the changes in lifestyle, and the difficulty of getting enough volunteers, charities have to recruit and pay people (usually a percentage of funds collected) in order to have a presence on the streets and raise sufficient funding. This approach also impacts on the donors.

Is it reasonable for a charity to pay 40–50 per cent of all monies collected to the collector? The collector has become an employee (not a volunteer) who needs to earn a living and should be paid accordingly. But should this be a percentage of what was collected? Or should it be an hourly fee? And, of course, if it is an hourly fee, does it remove the incentive to collect money seriously? If collectors are paid the same amount of money whether they collect €5 or €500, the donations to charity might actually decrease. The situation is fraught with difficulties.

THE CHARITY BRAND

The charity 'brand' has also changed. No longer is it enough to know that the charity is doing good works; the charity and its works need to be branded, just like Coca-Cola, to attract donations.

Donor Fatigue

Donor fatigue is a real issue for charities. There are so many charities doing good works, and only so much money to go around, that we, the donors, actually get to the stage where we are switched off by tragedy — harsh but true.

We see so many people on television dying of AIDS, famine or cancer that it no longer has the impact it once did. We are seeing too much of it and, as a result, are more hardened, fatigued, exasperated, and less inclined to give money immediately.

Receiving Something for Your Donation

One of the biggest changes charities have seen over the years is the identified need by people actually to receive something in return for their donation (excluding crisis/famine relief).

Sales of work were one of the earliest examples of incentivised giving. People attended looking for a bargain, or something handmade, or just something different which could not be bought in a chain store. They were willing to pay for it, and felt that they had helped a local group or a charity in the process.

Instead of simply giving funds for the on-going good works of charities, donors need to be incentivised. They prefer to receive something in return. So, charities are now involved in the Christmas card market. The sales price, or a portion of it, goes to the charity, and the donor gets the cards, with the charity's name on them, to send to friends with Christmas greetings. Similarly, donors attend fashion shows, at €100–€150 per head or more. The money goes to the charity, but the donor has been given a good night out. The same holds true for fundraising dinners, golf tournaments, whist drives and sponsored walks.

Another example of this trend is the growth in 'adventure holidays' to raise funds for charities. Usually, individuals are asked to raise a set sum for the charity, which varies between €2,500 and €4,000. In return, they are offered the opportunity to go parachute jumping, walk the Great Wall of China, trek among glaciers in Iceland or the rain forests of Peru, cycle across America or go white water rafting on the Zambesi.

Even shopping online can provide charities with an income. One such site, www.charitymall.com, contains over 200 retailers. Every time a purchase is made, a donation is given to the charity chosen by the shopper. The shopper chooses to donate to a particular charity from a very wide range, including children, AIDS, leprosy, deafness, cancer, animal welfare, medical research and the environment.

Donating Corporate Monies

Finally, one of the cleverest ideas I have come across is on the web — a charity site at www.quickdonations.com. The purpose of the site is to allow visitors to make quick donations, to worthy causes, at no cost to themselves. The donations are sponsored by corporate bodies. Each site of this type has a different policy but, as a general rule, the value of the donation is fixed, and only one donation per site, per day, is allowed. The visitor selects from three main categories — hunger, environment, health — and makes a donation which comes from corporate funds. The site also lists and provides links to other 'click and donate' sites and encourages people to list these sites as favourites, and visit them daily to make donations.

An Irish variation of this idea, equally clever, is www.goodspider.com which makes donations to Concern. In April 2002 Concern launched its 'Tipping for Charity' campaign. There are a number of (specified) websites which offer quality content free. Tipping for Charity asks the internet user with a credit card to 'tip' these websites a small amount in appreciation of their content. All money raised by these sites will be received by the Good Spider website and channelled to Concern.[14]

Slogans Can Make Giving Easy

Charities also use advertising techniques very successfully to reinforce their corporate aims or carry simple messages. The Salvation Army ran a very successful appeal which carried the slogan 'For God's sake, give us a quid'.[15] It made it easy for the public to donate because they knew exactly how much was expected of them. One of the fears that charities had when Ireland changed over to the euro, in January 2002, was that people would give one euro where they used to give one pound. Instead, early indications (March 2002) suggested that the public increased its donation to a minimum €2, thereby increasing the charity 'give' by 50 per cent. By June 2002, a gap in donations was appearing at the upper end of the scale. UNICEF stated that 'ever since the introduction of the Euro, UNICEF Ireland, along with so many other Irish charities, has experienced…a falling off in the actual value of donations…in the past, where we might have anticipated a contribution of £20 we are now, in many cases, receiving €20…the value of donations that we have received in recent months has been reduced by as much as 25%'.[16]

Lengthening the Donor Year

Trócaire is famous for its Lenten campaign, and raises approximately one-third of its annual income from the Trócaire Lenten Campaign.[17] Boxes are distributed through schools to children who are encouraged to give up something for Lent and put the money into the box for charity. It has been an enormous success for Trócaire down through the years. In 2001, the Trócaire Lenten Campaign raised €10 million.[18]

In November 2000, Trócaire introduced its Christmas Global Gift Campaign. This was cleverly tied into the Christmas time of year when people give gifts. It offered the public an opportunity to give a gift to a family in a developing country. So, donors bought a pig, a roof for a house, or a wind-up radio for a family in need. They were given a certificate of purchase, which in turn was given to a friend as a Christmas present. It tied in with the Celtic tiger economy, then still at its height. People believed that there was very little left that you could buy anyone. The economy was doing well and most people who wanted something simply went out and bought it. Trócaire gave people a chance to do a good deed, support a charity, and still give a gift — very clever. The Global Gift campaign for Christmas 2001 offered donors a choice of a clutch of chickens (Colombia), a vegetable patch (Sudan), fruit trees (El Salvador), a village goat (Angola/Ethiopia) or school and art supplies (Central America). The campaign raised €1.6 million, and 50,000 gifts were purchased.[19]

Interestingly, Bóthar had been doing something similar since 1991. Formed by a group of farmers, businessmen, and community and church leaders, Bóthar establishes micro-farming units in deprived areas of Africa. It sends pregnant dairy heifers and goats, breeding pigs, hens, bees and rabbits to families to help them to become self-sufficient. Its campaign is geared to rural communities in Ireland. It is a very similar idea certainly, but, from a national perspective, much less well known and perhaps less well promoted than the Trócaire option.[20]

PROMOTING THE BRAND — CREATIVITY

Charities constantly need to be creative. There are numerous ways in which charities try to separate us from our money. Some of the most successful include:

- *Incentives*: raffle tickets
- *Physical purchase*: charity shops, Christmas cards, sales of work, daffodils
- *Attendance*: dinners, auctions, fashion shows, golf days, film galas
- *Collections*: door-to-door, church gate, bucket collections
- *Donations*: bric-a-brac, old clothes, antiques
- *Direct appeal*: on radio or TV, or by letter
- *Return for investment*: corporate sponsorship
- *Realisation of a dream*: sponsored parachute jumps, 'adventure' holidays
- *Effortless*: use of a designated credit card, donations online
- *In remembrance*: donations given through your last will and testament.

This list is not, by any means, exhaustive, but it does give a good idea of the breadth of fundraising options in which charities are engaged. Note that sponsorship can include corporate sponsorship of ads appealing for funding. These ads, on radio, TV or in the press, are expensive and the cost of production and space is usually sponsored by corporate bodies.

Door-to-door collections are declining because of societal change. The introduction of security systems in people's homes (notably the simple spy hole in front doors) allows people the choice of opening their doors only to people they know. Similarly, apartment living makes it difficult for the collector to gain access.

Raising funds in a competitive market is challenging, and charities are becoming more and more creative in their approaches.

Sightsavers International and Concern are both involved in what Paul Cullen calls 'face-to-face' fundraising. Young collectors stop members of the public on the streets, seeking commitments from them that they will donate by standing order to the charities. 'Typically, the collectors are paid £8 to £9 an hour (€10–€11) and the fundraising company receives a fee from the charity, plus a commission based on the number of "hits",' says Cullen.[21]

The Trócaire Christmas campaign is an excellent example of creativity. And the Irish Heart Foundation runs an annual Skipathon for Schools campaign to raise funds.[22]

Although the idea originated in Canada, the introduction of Daffodil Day to Ireland, by the Irish Cancer Society in 1988, was also very creative. The Cancer Society raised €406,300 in the first year of Daffodil Day. In 2002, this annual fundraiser exceeded its own fundraising target of €2.25 million for the charity, and needed 5,000 volunteers to co-ordinate it.[23]

However, if you look at the number of similar days now — yellow ribbon day, pink ribbon day, wear a bonnet day, sheaf of wheat day, happy heart day — you wonder whether charities are killing the goose that laid the golden egg. Daffodil Day is well established, and generates a healthy profit for the charity. But how much money is actually made by each of the other groups? And how confused are the public? Do they know, any more, which charity they are actually supporting?

Credit cards generate income for charities as they do, indeed, for third-level institutions. The idea is a simple one. The donor chooses to use a particular credit card. Each time that card is used to purchase something, the charity receives a fixed donation. The system benefits the issuing credit-card institution and the charity. Donors are doing good simply by continuing their normal spending habits. It is another example of the way in which charities have adopted creative ideas in order to generate ongoing income.

Bill Cullen's book, *It's a Long Way from Penny Apples*, was another clever and creative idea. All of the royalties were donated to the Irish Youth Foundation.[24]

ISPCC holds a 'Childline' concert every year which attracts enormous publicity, raises funds, and is targeted at those children who use Childline. Many international and domestic 'stars' of the pop world perform at this concert and Six (the band created by Popstars) actually made its début at a Childline concert in 2002.

Concern Worldwide received a lot of negative media publicity in November 2001 for a new fundraising venture into which it had entered. Concern gave its mailing lists of supporters to a broker, who then used the lists for a banking client (GE Capital). Concern Worldwide, unusually, did not sell the lists — instead it gave them to the marketing broker. Receivers got a direct-mail message offering them a bank loan. In return, GE Capital offered Concern an average of €190 for every loan taken out under the offer. Members of the public complained about the practice, and the Data Protection Commissioner investigated.[25]

From a legal point of view, the charity argued that, because the lists had been passed to a third party (and not directly to the banks), there was no breach of the Data Protection Act of 1988. From a moral point of view, the decision was questionable.

The concept received mixed reactions and was widely discussed on radio. Some people felt that, as there was no obligation on the recipient to take the loan, there was no harm done. Others felt that it was an invasion of their privacy to give their names in this way (even if the names were not given directly to the banks). They felt that they had already done their good deed by donating to the charity, and saw no reason why they should be inundated with junk mail. It also raised the spectre of the letter from a bank being followed by a similar offer from a building society, an insurance brokerage or a book club.

Direct marketing people will tell you that they are not in the business of junk mail — that the list, in this case, reflected the interest (in the charity) of the person concerned and, if that person were in need of finance, their natural inclination would be to take that finance with an organisation which would benefit the charity. Most of the people on the receiving end of these letters regard them as junk mail!

CHOCaid and its charity partner, Gorta, are a wonderful example of Irish shopping on-line for charity. At Gorta's annual conference on World Food Day, October 2001, CHOCaid.com launched its new Chocolate World e-gift.[26] The concept is a simple one. Chocolate is one of the world's favourite indulgences, on which consumers spend an estimated $25 billion per year. This site allows the purchaser to buy handmade Irish chocolate on-line and donate to charity at the same time. Almost one-third of the purchase price (30 per cent) is donated to specific, named and budgeted projects of the purchaser's choice. The chocolates are made by CHOCaid.com in Kinsale, Co. Cork. By April 2002, €5,200 had been dispatched to hunger relief projects.[27]

REFERENCES

1. Paul Cullen, 'Inquiry call into charity "mailing list"', *The Irish Times*, 22 November 2001.
2. There were 5,477 organisations registered for charity exemption with the Revenue Commissioners in April 2002. Information provided by Mary Bergin, Revenue Commissioners, Nenagh.
3. Paul Cullen, Op cit.
4. Information provided by Emma McKinley, Senior Administrator, ISPCC Head Office.
5. Details of health-promotion initiatives provided by Maureen Mulvihill, Health Promotions Manager, Irish Heart Foundation.
6. Information provided by Charities Section, Revenue Commissioners, Nenagh.
7. Information provided by Patricia Breen, Lenten Campaign Office, Trócaire; www.trocaire.ie

8. Ibid.
9. Harry Browne, 'Media witnesses take precious helicopter places', *The Irish Times*, March 2000.
10. www.dec.org.uk
11. Information provided by Siobhan McGee, Irish Red Cross.
12. Information provided by Patricia Breen, Op cit.
13. Ibid.
14. http://www.thegoodspider.com/tipping.htm
15. This campaign is thought to have been specific to Dublin. No date available. Information provided by Pamela Neill, PR/Fundraiser, The Salvation Army, Belfast Office.
16. UNICEF circular letter (21 June 2002) appealing for donations to ease the food shortage in Zimbabwe and neighbouring African countries.
17. Information provided by Patricia Breen, Op cit.
18. Ibid.
19. Ibid.
20. Bóthar, 99 O'Connell Street, Limerick. www.bothar.org
21. Paul Cullen, Op cit.
22. Information provided by Maureen Mulvihill, Health Promotions Manager, Irish Heart Foundation.
23. Information provided by Don Delaney, Communications Department, Irish Cancer Society.
24. Bill Cullen, *It's a Long Way from Penny Apples*, Cork: Mercier Press, 2001.
25. Paul Cullen, Op cit.
26. http://www.gorta.ie/wfd2001.htm
27. http://www.chocaid.com

CHAPTER 16

Crisis PR

Every company, every organisation, has a crisis waiting to happen. Some can be anticipated; others seem to strike out of a clear blue sky. One thing is certain — even when you are prepared, a crisis can damage a company. If you are not prepared, long-term damage is unavoidable.

Doug Newhouse suggests that crises can be divided into three types, and that each type has a violent and non-violent form.[1]

Source/Type	Violent	Non-Violent
Act of Nature	Earthquake/Forest Fire	Drought/Famine
Intentional	Terrorism/Product Tampering	Hostile Takeover/ Insider Trading
Unintentional	Leaks/Fires/Accident	Product Problems

Although companies are very conscious that a crisis will strike at some stage, most, incredibly, seem ill-prepared. Perhaps people are putting off the evil day. Perhaps, like pensions, we think that it is not appropriate now — sometime in the future perhaps? Maybe we even believe, like Cinderella, that it won't happen to our company?

Think about the multitude of crises which have befallen companies and you will realise that it is something which should be to the forefront of a business agenda. In 1984, when poisonous gas escaped from a Union Carbide factory in India, 2,000 people died and over 200,000 were injured.[2] In 1988, 167 people died when the Piper Alpha oil platform caught fire in the North Sea.[3] In 1998, two people died and eight were injured when part of an Esso oil refinery exploded at the Longford Gas Plant in Victoria, Australia.[4] In 1999, two people died and more than one hundred became ill after visiting a newly built aquarium in Melbourne, Australia (Legionnaire's Disease was found in the air conditioning system).[5]

More recently, in 2001, the South African government took on the might of the pharmaceutical giants (causing a crisis in the industry), in an effort to import cheaper generic copies of patented drugs to deal with the country's AIDS crisis.[6]

A year later, activities attributed to John Rusnak, an employee of All First bank in the US, cost AIB (the parent company) an estimated €770 million.[7] Who would have expected that the firm of Arthur Andersen and its offshoot, Andersen Consulting, would be 'going bust. Its name…in tatters…its clients…leaving in droves' because of its behaviour in the Enron case;[8] or that the Campus Stadium Ireland Development — the Bertie Bowl — would be in crisis by 2002 with the resignation of its executive chairman, Paddy Teahon, and the fees of Magahy and Co. (executive service providers) questioned by a Dáil committee?[9]

Crises fall into two categories:

1. Those you can and should anticipate
2. Those which cannot be foreseen.

You could not be expected to foresee, for example, a block of frozen toilet waste, expelled from a travelling aircraft, crashing through the roof of your home, wrecking your favourite chair and then shattering into little pieces, could you? It seems far-fetched, doesn't it? It actually happened to a woman in New York.[10]

You could not be expected to foresee that staff and customers of your Galway store would be mauled by a wild lion (the animal might have escaped from a travelling circus). Nor would you reasonably anticipate a swarm of locusts in Cork, or staff in Mullingar succumbing to African sleeping sickness. There are many crises which cannot be foreseen.

On the other hand, the foreseeable crises are immediately evident to a company and should be tackled. The company could anticipate severe flooding, sabotage, the spread of an infectious virus among staff members, or the hospitalisation or death of a member of staff from AIDS.

Any company in the food industry has a number of potential crises. A cessation in supplies (because of crop damage or industrial action) would be a crisis. Contamination of the product while in production is an internal crisis, if identified swiftly. The crisis becomes external if the product contamination was not identified on time, or happened after the product had left the factory and appeared on shop shelves. Serious food poisoning arising from one of your products is a foreseeable, if undesirable, crisis. And a campaign by environmentalists to ban a product because of its contents could also put the company in crisis.

An airline company has to anticipate aircraft failure, aircraft crash, serious injury to passengers or loss of life, pilots having heart attacks, terrorists taking over a plane, and airport closures. The company would be remiss if it did not. When a Concorde flight blew a tyre on departure from Charles de Gaulle Airport in Paris in August 2000, 118 people lost their lives and the crisis brought Concorde to its knees.

When Richard Branson sued British Airways in 1992, arising from an article published in an internal publication — BA News — a dirty tricks campaign against Virgin Atlantic was revealed. The 'world's favourite airline' found itself in crisis.[11]

A computer software company must anticipate virus infection of its software. Often, it is how these crises are handled that determines the damage to the company. The Irish Academy of Public Relations received an e-mail from a software company promoting its products. It did not get through our virus screening because it was infected. We immediately e-mailed the company, notifying its people of the problem.

It took six hours before they sent an e-mail to everyone on the list telling them that their original mail was infected. This would not inspire confidence in the company.

International companies should not forget that a crisis in one country can result in not only media coverage throughout the world, but consumer reaction on the same scale. Nor should they overlook the safety of their employees. Andrew J. Duffin, of Pinkerton Consulting and Investigation Services in Miami, believes that companies should also be prepared for kidnap. 'Colombia has the highest rate of kidnapping in the world...5,000 kidnappings a year....High on the list of victims are employees of energy or oil companies,' he says.[12]

Every company, irrespective of the range of procedures it puts in place, must live with the possibility of a crisis arising from fraud, sexual harassment, discrimination, sabotage or industrial action. Companies publicly quoted on the stock exchange are in crisis when the share price falls for no apparent reason.

Charitable organisations are not immune either. Think of the on-going damage done to the ISPCC when a newspaper reported that collectors were not being paid the right commission.[13]

Remember too that rumour can put a company into crisis. In the 1990s, one of our clients asked if we had heard anything about a video production company that they were thinking of retaining. We told them that there were rumours within the industry that the company was losing money heavily and might close in the future.

However, we advised the client to request a meeting with the production company and challenge its people about the rumours. This they did. The production company's people thanked the client for confronting them. They welcomed the opportunity to explain the background (disastrous financial results some years previously) and used the opportunity to show the client how their company had survived and thrived in the intervening years. They were awarded the contract.

Rumour can be malicious or it can arise from poor external or internal relations which 'feed' the rumour machine because of a vacuum in real communications. A survey of seventy-four PR professionals revealed that the majority of rumours they dealt with were 'internal in nature and were most likely to be about personnel changes, job security, or job satisfaction'. External rumours affected 'the organiza-tion's reputation' and were about either product or service quality. The worrying aspect of the survey was the very real impact that rumours had on companies, resulting in bad press, lowered staff morale or increased absenteeism.[14]

HANDLING CRISES

There are four key elements of crisis PR:

Anticipation
Homework
Activity
Aftermath　　　　　**AHAA!**

ANTICIPATION

So, how do you prepare for a crisis? You begin by conducting an audit of the company and all of its practices. When the *Herald of Free Enterprise*, a Townsend Thoresen ferry, capsized in February 1987 after loading doors had been left open, 187 people died.[15] The company referred the world media to an office which had just two telephone lines — blocked communications and a worsened crisis. While the company was cleared in the courts for the accident, the public relations issues remained unanswered. PR consultant and author Roger Haywood believes that if public relations had been central to the company, and they had undertaken an issues audit, 'there would have been a lot of senior people concerned with their safety standards.... Public relations would have brought those issues to the surface so that the experts could deal with them'. If the safety issues had been raised at an audit stage, the tragedy which followed later might have been avoided.[16]

Therefore, you begin with a thorough review of all of your practices. How is product delivered to your site? Are there best-possible procedures in place? Are they implemented? (When someone is injured, or dies, on a building site, the first question always relates to safety issues.) There's not much point in having procedures in place if no one knows what they are, or — worse — no one pays any heed to them.

It takes time to explain to staff why procedures have been introduced, but a clear explanation leads to a clear implementation policy. Although not specifically required by legislation to do so, the food industry, as a best-practice measure, introduced the wearing of hairnets and caps for people dealing with food.[17] I'm sure it took a lot of time to explain the importance of the measure to people, some of whom would have felt that they looked foolish.

My brother applied for a job several years ago. He had just grown a beard which, he had no doubt, made him the coolest thing ever! At the end of a very successful interview, the interviewer told him that it was company policy that there should be no facial hair, and he would have to shave his beard. My brother — horrified — asked for an explanation. The interviewer then explained that as he was an engineer, dealing with machinery, facial hair could get caught in the machinery and cause injury or death. There was a logical reason for the rule. He understood it, complied with it, and has never grown a beard since, but he still looks cool!

My nephew recently gave up a part-time job in a supermarket chain. He was regularly asked to attend early so that he could help unload vegetable deliveries. He regarded this as 'utterly stupid' since no one bought vegetables at 8 o'clock in the morning! His logic was simple but it was poor management. He failed to understand the logical sequence of delivery, preparation and presentation for the customer. No one had explained that this has an impact on sales, which, in turn, affect profit margins. He was convinced that the managers were just spoilsports who wanted to drag him out of his bed early each morning.

The first preparatory step for any company is to look at its internal systems. Are there any faults apparent? Where are they? How could they be fixed? Companies need to look at delivery systems, production processes, staff health-and-safety issues (both regulatory and best practice), financial safeguards, and reporting procedures.

Anticipate the things that could go wrong: pollution of lakes or rivers, strikes or industrial action, embezzlement, fire or fatalities. Each department within the company should be able to provide the PR person with a list of possible crises which might befall it.

Crisis always means coping with bad publicity. There is no such things as a 'good' crisis (although there can be a good recovery). In addition to coping with the bad publicity, you are also trying to limit the damage to the company, its reputation and its products.

HOMEWORK

Once you have accepted that crisis is as inevitable as death or taxes, you can begin to prepare for it. There are several steps involved.

You need to make friends in advance. It is virtually impossible to make friends in the middle of a crisis — no one has the time. If you are working in-house particularly, you should be very familiar with the media who cover your particular area of interest. You need to keep them abreast of developments within the company. Constantly supply them with information. Build up a rapport with them. Your company should be respected and trusted, even if it is not liked.

If journalists reporting a crisis know that the in-house PR person is trustworthy and information is always factually accurate, they are much more likely to give you some kind of breathing space when the crisis happens. This is not to say that they will treat you with kid gloves. They will not. They would not be doing their jobs if they did. But they are less likely to react badly if you ask for a further 30 minutes to clarify information before you issue it.

When you brief the media, brief them as thoroughly as possible. Be very careful that you cross-check all of the facts that you are issuing. This sounds simple and is easily done when issuing, say, a regular press release about a product launch or the opening of a new building. In a crisis, however, everyone is under pressure. People are reacting quickly to the situation — and to the questions you are posing to them. It is vital that you check and double-check the accuracy of your information. The media will be prepared to wait a short while for the information but, no matter how quickly you communicate it, they will not make any allowances for inaccuracies.

Have factual material prepared in advance and ready for immediate issue. Every business should have a standard crisis pack ready to issue. This pack will be in several parts, depending on the nature of your business. (See Chapter 12 on the role of in-house press officer.)

Crisis Management Team

The company should form a crisis management team made up of the chief executive, members of the board, spokespersons, senior management staff with responsibility for each area of the business, PR people, and legal advisors. This team should have a clear plan of action in the event of a crisis. Each member should know exactly what their responsibility is.

There are a number of rules about crisis management teams. Each member of the team should have home and mobile contacts for all of the other members. They should be immediately contactable in the event of a crisis. There should be one person designated with responsibility to contact all. This person should also be aware, at all times, of where people are (e.g. if they are on annual leave, or if a parent is dying).

The team should have a primary location and a fall-back location at which they meet. It is all very well deciding that the team will meet at headquarters but what if the crisis occurred at headquarters — a petrol tank crashed into the building and the fire is still raging? There must be a second area where people will meet, and its location should be known to all team members.

Each team member should have 24-hour access to both meeting places. There is little point in people arriving for a crisis meeting if there is no security guard on the main gate, or the security guard cannot be found (because he is investigating something in another area of the plant/building). Crisis management team members should have access codes and keys for all locations in which they will meet.

The locations should also be carefully chosen. They need to have all of the facilities you would expect to have to hand in a crisis — telephone lines, ISDN for e-mail, press releases and photos, etc.

The nerve centre where the team meets is also the location to which the media will be invited for press conferences and briefings. It is important that the media briefing room is a little distant from the team meeting room. Crisis meetings should be handled away from the glare of the media. You need that control. So the press conference room or briefing area should be somewhat separate from the room in which the management committee is meeting.

Watch also that blinds on windows are drawn. Photographers and cameramen are looking for visuals and footage. You cannot blame them if they know that a meeting is being held on the second floor, there are lights on, and it is possible to get footage of the meeting using the zoom facility on their cameras. People at the meeting will not be conscious of cameras outside the building, and the visual may be of someone highly stressed, furrowed brow, hands running through their hair. The impression created is of serious crisis. The crisis may well be of a very serious nature, but you also want as much control as possible of the visuals and you should not be giving hostages to fortune. A little forward planning goes a long way.

The press office information, particularly the crisis packs, should also be stored in both locations. There is no point in the crisis team meeting in location Number 2 if all of the media information is in location Number 1 only. The terrorist attacks on the World Trade Center, New York (11 September 2001) are a case in point. Those companies which had all of their data backed up at a location outside New York city were the quickest to resume business after the disaster.

In both locations you should have up-to-date media lists of the newspapers, radio and TV stations which are most likely to have an interest in this crisis. You should have contact names for the journalists who report your area and the editor of each paper/programme. You should have current phone, mobile and e-mail contacts for each of them.

You should also have press releases prepared for each eventuality. These releases are written well in advance of any crisis when you have time to look carefully at the wording. The releases will contain necessary blanks (the date on which the crisis occurred, the exact time if relevant), and the precise location of the press conference. The first few hours of a crisis are crucial. Your job, as the PR person, is to ensure that all media are informed swiftly, by phone or e-mail, of the fact that a crisis has occurred. They must be given information which they can immediately begin to use (the crisis pack). There should also be a clear indication that the company will be making someone available, and when and where this will happen (an arranged press conference).

The crisis management team is responsible for ensuring that everyone who might have a role to play in the crisis is trained. Who is responsible for contacting tele- phonists and getting them to the building to field calls? To whom are the calls referred? Have all of these people been trained? The strain of dealing with a crisis is enormous and takes a great toll on people. These telephonists work with the people who might be involved in the crisis — people trapped in the building, possibly feared dead. There is a close relationship. Staff dealing with crisis calls may also know the families of some of the victims, and these are the people they will be speaking with on the phone.

Companies which take potential crises seriously have mock crisis training days on a regular basis, which involve all members of staff. The telephonists, spokespersons, and back-up staff are all brought to a location and given details of a scenario of what has happened. With the help of specially trained outsiders, who take the role of dis- tressed relatives or journalists, they 'live' the crisis for a day. Crisis training systems, like Crisisport, are used in these situations.[18] Companies have found over the years that these days take a huge toll on their staff. Research showed that most people involved went out for a drink that night and ended up footless (often on very little drink) because of the stress. Now, coping with stress sessions and de-stressing sessions are included at the end of these mock days.

Even government departments have crisis management teams and hold mock training days. For example, the Department of Public Enterprise (DPE) organised a training day to test the National Plan for Nuclear Emergencies with the Radiological Protection Institute of Ireland in November 2001.

The DPE retained Emergency Response Management (ERM) Consultants to assist them. All relevant state departments and services were involved on the day, as were DPE staff and selected journalists (who were involved in this mock emergency).

There were negative and positive outcomes. The negative outcome was the publicity the day achieved. Although not intended as a public or media event, journalists arrived to cover the 'emergency exercise' from a news perspective. This seems to have been unanticipated. Media were upset that they were not given access to control rooms, etc., and coverage of the event was unfavourable.

On the positive side, the test was necessary in order to see how the plan worked, and from that perspective, the day achieved its aim. Since November 2001, a National Emergency Committee has been formed under the aegis of the Minister of Defence and involving all other relevant departments. This committee covers all aspects of national emergencies, including the National Plan for Nuclear Emergencies.

The ERM consultants issued a report, which was published, and dealt with all aspects of the plan, including the management of media, monitoring the internet, and monitoring public response to information. The original National Plan for Nuclear Emergencies (1992) was updated in spring 2002.[19]

ACTIVITY

Before the first briefing with media, ascertain all of the facts — the five Ws and H.

Be as careful as you possibly can in establishing the veracity of the information you are about to impart. Be especially careful about names and numbers. You cannot assume/presume that because someone was scheduled to work that day, they actually worked. Nor can you assume that someone who should have been beside a machine was actually there. Or that someone who should have been on their tea-break had actually gone to the canteen. You cannot even be categoric about the numbers of people. It is possible that 230 people were due on site that night but, if the crisis happened overnight, how many of those actually came into work? All 230?

Were some sick? Did some deputise for others in a local arrangement? You do not want to worsen the crisis. The company staff, the media and the relatives are all depending on you for information. You do them all a disservice if you do not check and cross-check the information you are issuing.

This is not to underestimate the difficulty of the task — it is enormous. When the World Trade Center towers collapsed in New York (11 September 2001) initial estimates of the people feared dead were high. These estimates were reduced as it became clear that some people had been late leaving for work, or had phoned in sick, or were at meetings somewhere else in the city.

Brief staff and spokespersons as completely as you can, and as regularly as you can. Let them know what the position is, and how they should handle enquiries. And keep them up to date, as developments break. They are as entitled to be informed as the media.

Before issuing information, write out all of the facts and copy them to the relevant people. This is important. People often think twice when they see something in writing. Everyone is under pressure. A written note may be more carefully checked than a verbal confirmation. As the PR person, you may need to nominate someone to keep a diary or running notes of the event as it unfolds. This may be necessary in the event of a political or judicial enquiry later. The note-taker should record all of the facts, the name and title of the person who confirmed the information, the place at which it happened, and the time and date of the confirmation. By its nature, crisis is fast-moving. If you do not take notes or keep a log at the time, it will be virtually impossible to remember later who told you what, and when — and even what information was available to you at that time.

Anticipate that even when you, and your spokesperson, have gone home exhausted to get some rest and sleep, you will receive media calls. The media get used to dealing with one person. However, no one can be good in a crisis for 24–48 hours without rest and — exhaustion takes over, mistakes happen, and the crisis deepens.

You might also consider having a rest room on the premises — somewhere that pressurised and stressed staff can go, for a few minutes, to lie down, have a cup of tea or just take a few moments' relaxation.

One of the advantages of the mobile phone is that you can physically transfer it to another person — thus, the person who has taken over from you carries your mobile while you take a rest. In a lot of cases, PR people carry two mobiles — their work mobile and their personal mobile. Provided that you have not given out your personal mobile number at any time (to a journalist friend to call you for a pint, for example), you can, with reasonable safety (if it is an ex-directory number), take calls on your personal mobile. Another piece of advice for home phones (landlines) is that you should have two facilities — caller ID (so that you can monitor calls in a crisis) and the good old-fashioned answering machine. When in doubt, do not answer. Wait for the message. These are important because, although you are involved in the crisis management directly, your family is also involved. Relatives and friends will want to call you to see how you are? How are you coping? Can they be of any help? It could be very good for you, psychologically, to take these calls. But if you are not 'working', these are the only calls you want to take. Find a way of filtering the non-business calls.

The same rules apply to a lesser crisis as to a major one. It is worth considering that a minor crisis may not attract any media coverage at the time. However, the media might become aware of it several months later. If they do, and you had not told them at the time, they are perfectly entitled to think that you will give them information only when you have to. It is far better to put the information out there as it happens. It might not be picked up but if the media decide to report on it at some time in the future, you can honestly point to the fact that the information was put into the public arena at the time when it happened.

Dealing with Journalists

When dealing with journalists, you should always be honest, and you should give as much information as you possibly can — provided, always, that it is in the public interest. A constantly recurring crisis for the gardaí is when people are killed in road traffic accidents. They issue information about the nature of the accident, whether there was more than one vehicle involved, whether anyone died/survived, and the sex of those people. They do not, however, issue the names of the people until the relatives have been informed. This is an example of giving honest information which is in the public interest, but not giving all of the information at a particular time. You will be doing exactly the same in a crisis.

Never speculate. Never guess. Never presume that the information 'sounds right'. If you do not know the answer to a question — check it. Take the journalist's number, the query, and the deadline by which an answer is needed. Give yourself time to check the facts. If you fail to confirm the facts by the journalist's deadline, phone and explain why you cannot answer the question within the deadline.

There should be a specific area of the building set aside for journalists. This area should be away from the crisis management team meeting room, and away from the reception area where calls are being taken, experts/other directors are arriving, relatives are congregating. Keep them separate.

In all crisis situations, you are trying to establish what the journalist already knows. This is helpful to both of you. If the journalist has not gained access to the scene of the crisis, you can actually arrange for a photographer and camera crew to gain access. This is an old rule of PR — we looked at it earlier when we looked at Ivy Ledbetter Lee and the railroad crisis of the early 1900s. It is not in your interest to prevent visual footage of the crisis. There may be an issue of gaining access to people escaping the crisis (making their way out of a building) or safety concerns (if the fire is still raging) but, in most cases, you can arrange the footage without interfering with the rescue effort, and you should.

In addition to sending information to journalists by e-mail or courier, you should also have physical press packs available at the press conference. The pack should contain all of the background information already issued, and a copy of the statement which the company is issuing.

As mentioned earlier, there should be a legal representative on the crisis committee. Ensure that this person fully understands their brief. The nature of legal people is that they will advise you to say as little as possible, which will be of benefit to you in the event of a court case arising. The nature of PR people is that we encourage as much communication as possible in a crisis. If possible, sort out this dilemma in advance. The legal person is not there to rewrite the statement. This person has a valuable role to play in protecting the company — but so have you. Neither of you should lose sight of the fact that you should both be working together.

For example, legal advisors may tell the company that it should accept no liability and issue no public apology. This may be good legal advice, but it is a poor form of communication. A company that has seen one of its workers die will be expected to show some empathy, sympathy and remorse for the situation. PR advice will be to communicate. It is simply a case of the legal people agreeing a wording which is not totally legalistic and with which everyone can live. It is possible — it just takes understanding. PR might also advise the company Chief Executive to visit the family of the dead worker.

Damage Limitation

The best way to limit damage to your organisation is to issue factual information — usually very short, sharp bites of news, on a regular basis. Set up a system whereby the media will be updated at a press conference — hourly or every three hours, for example. In this way, they know that the flow of information will be constant. Explain that even if there is nothing more to tell, your spokesperson will be present, in the conference area, for a briefing, questions and answers, or statement on a regular basis. The amount of control you need is determined by the stage of the crisis. In the early stages, you might be in a position to issue a statement only. At a later stage, when more information has emerged, your spokespeople will be in a position to take questions and answers at the press conferences.

Remember to keep a record of everything that happens and, where possible, to issue written confirmation to media of the facts, as you know them, at that time.

Handling Bad News

Do not attempt to cover up — it is guaranteed to backfire on you. Silence can be acceptable (think of the *sub judice* rule — the silence is enforced because of fear of influencing a court case), but lies never are.

Do not apportion blame or responsibility. No matter how strong the evidence that human error caused the crisis, you cannot apportion blame to an individual. You can, of course, state that you think the cause was human error. If you apportion blame, however, it will rebound on you. People will ask questions. If he got it wrong, who put him into the job? What kind of training was she given? Why hadn't a supervisory grade noticed that something was wrong? The corporate buck stops with you.

Remember that your appointed spokesperson should be trained and confident in dealing with the media — discreet, tactful, slow to anger, capable of handling difficult questions, and available to media at all times. Most of all, your spokesperson must speak from a position of authority — don't send a boy on a man's errand.

Crisis Management

Be thoroughly prepared for all eventualities. Know the kinds of crisis that can befall your company and have crisis packs in place to deal with them. Do simulation training and rehearsals annually with staff and spokespersons to keep their skills in peak condition. Apportion responsibilities within the team and outside the team. Do not apportion blame. Gather as much information as possible. Be pro-active in your approach to media — tell them before they have a chance to contact you. Use the contacts in media that you have built up in advance — you need friends in a crisis. Test the effectiveness of your communications constantly. Ensure that your messages are clear and capable of being understood by people under stress.

Consider having a team of specially trained people who will call to the homes of victims and explain what has happened.

AFTERMATH

After the crisis has subsided, you need to begin to rebuild faith and confidence in your company.

Corrections

As a general rule, you should correct factual inaccuracies immediately — even if the correction is not in your favour. Clarify, for example, if it was not three people who died, but five, and indicate that there is a possibility of more in the coming hours. Similarly, a statement that you employ 2,400 people when you employ 1,400 should be corrected.

Minor corrections — misspelling someone's name for example — do not need attention. Such errors will happen several times over the course of coverage of the crisis.

A letter to the editor may serve as a clarification. If the letter is issued for publication, this should be clearly stated. If it is not, it should be clearly marked as 'Private Correspondence — not for publication'. However, private letters, like off-the-record comments, are not always treated in the way you would expect. Again, there are no hard-and-fast rules in this area.

Finally, at the end of a crisis, if the press has reported inaccurately, you always have the right to legal redress. This, however, is seldom resorted to — probably because the journalists, like the company and its PR people, were doing their best in difficult circumstances. Legal redress also holds open the certainty that, by your action, you will bring the crisis to the attention of the public again in the future, and this may not be desirable.

Publics

Consider placing ads to thank people after the crisis. Thank them for their patience and forbearing, for their help and their sympathy. Put a human face on the corporation and show that you are a caring company.

Learn from your mistakes. Are there additional health, safety or security measures which should be introduced for staff? Is there any additional training needed? How do you thank your own staff for their support?

Public Image

Rebuild the public image of the company. Let people know (through the media and using all of the PR tools available to you) that your company has not only survived the crisis but has learned from it and is a better company as a result.

Dubarry Crisis

Dubarry, the Galway-based shoe manufacturer, found itself in crisis in 1993 when shoe moulds, vital for production, were impounded by workers in a supplier company in Spain. Dubarry at that time made up 80 per cent of the shoe industry in Ireland.

The Spanish company, Solano, had been seized by the workers. The moulds were needed to make soles for Dubarry's boating shoe. The company was in danger of losing the entire season, its export markets were threatened, and staff were worried that short-time working would be introduced.

The company needed to resolve the crisis as quickly as possible and also needed to be sure that its message was clear. The Ministers for Enterprise and Foreign Affairs, the Irish Embassy in Spain, the Spanish Embassy in Ireland and the IDA were all making valiant efforts to resolve the situation.

When the story broke, Dubarry called a press conference and issued a press release. In the release, titled 'Dubarry Jobs Crisis', the company explained the situation, called for immediate intervention to secure the release of the moulds, and thanked everyone for their help. The story was widely covered by national media (television, radio and newspapers) as well as Galway newspapers and radio.

Various crucial publics were watching the press conference and reading the coverage, including the Irish government, the IDA, local politicians, members of the Urban District Council (UDC), Dubarry workforce and unions, and the workers in the Solano factory in Spain.

There were several danger points for the company. Management did not want to get involved in commenting on the Spanish workers' action — it was not Dubarry's dispute. The company did not want to encourage a negative reaction towards state organisations which were doing everything in their power, as was the Spanish Embassy, to resolve the situation. Management did not want to comment on inter-union issues (Dubarry and Solano workforces were both unionised).

Dubarry knew that it would need to explain why the moulds were being sourced in Spain (Solano had relocated its business from Mayo to Spain some years previously). Management was conscious of Dubarry's image as the makers of Irish hand-made shoes and was aware of the damage that the Spanish dispute could inflict on Dubarry's reputation. The Solano factory was located in Agreda, in the sometimes volatile Basque area of Spain, and the necessity to

---

Dubarry Crisis (continued)

translate all communications (from English to Spanish) meant that the true meanings of words written or spoken might be lost.

The company sent one of its managers, with SIPTU representatives, to Spain to enter negotiations with the workers. Meanwhile, replacement moulds were ordered from another source and Dubarry reluctantly started talking about shortening staff working weeks or layoffs. The company continued to lobby government for intervention.

By May 1993, some two months after the situation had arisen, the IDA had stepped in with an offer of training schemes for employees while the company awaited delivery of new moulds.

Dubarry had handled the crisis well. Its lobbying and public relations approach ensured a successful resolution of the company's problems. TV, radio and newspaper cuttings were later used to explain to distributors how the problem had been handled. The company also introduced a newsletter for retailers.

Consider introducing newsletters for the community, employees or suppliers. Look at the possibility of entering a sponsorship arrangement to enhance the profile of the company. Essentially, go through the check-list of tools available to you and utilise them to the best of your ability.

Make people aware of the policies and procedures you have put in place since the crisis occurred.

REFERENCES

1. Doug Newhouse, *Topology for Anticipating a Crisis*, Northwestern University, USA.
2. Bhopal <../case_studies/study1.htm>; http://business.unisa.edu.au/cobar/corpresp/default.htm
3. Piper Alpha <../case_studies/study4.htm>; http://business.unisa.edu.au/cobar/corpresp/default.htm
4. Longford <../case_studies/study2.htm; http://business.unisa.edu.au/cobar/corpresp/default.htm
5. aquarium <../case_studies/study5.htm>; http://business.unisa.edu.au/cobar/corpresp/default.htm
6. Charlotte Denny and James Meek, 'Drug giants made to swallow bitter pill', *Guardian*, 19 April 2001, http://society.guardian.co.uk/hivaids/story/0,8150,475077,00.html
7. Siobhán Creaton, 'Rusnak's activities wipe out 60% of profits', *The Irish Times*, 7 February 2002.
8. David McWilliams, 'Andersen emperor has few clothes', *Sunday Business Post*, 24 March 2002.
9. Frank McDonald, 'Pool crisis shines light on woman whose advice does not

come cheap', *The Irish Times*, 23 March 2002.

10. A large block of frozen green material crashed through the roof of the home of Esther Kochanowicz in Alden, New York, in 1992. It was identified as human waste from the toilet of an aeroplane. Information received from http://216.239.51.100/search?q=cache:gVwfRtfwWYwC: www.visi.com/~rodsmine/reading/humor/truefact.html+frozen+block +toilet+waste&hl=en

11. Maol Muire Tynan, 'From secret taping in the Tickled Trout to tying up Trimble', *Sunday Business Post*, 2 April 2000.

12. Steve Macko, 'Companies should prepare for kidnapping situations', ENN Daily Intelligence Report, 15 May 1997, at http://www.emergency.com/co-kdnap.htm

13. 'Ex-ISPCC chief's request to curb press denied', *The Irish Times*/ireland.com, http://scripts.ireland.com/newspaper/breaking/printable.cfm?id=41291

14. Nicholas de Fonzo and Prashant Bordia, 'How Top PR Professionals Handle Hot Air: Types of Corporate Rumors, Their Effects and Strategies to Manage Them', Institute for PR website (Florida) at www.instituteforpr.com

15. Colin Boyd, 'Case Studies in Corporate Social Policy' in Post, Frederick, Lawrence and Weber, *Business and Society*, New York, 1996.

16. Roger Haywood interviewed in *Actions Speak Louder than Words*, video by PRTV Ltd. London, c/o The Institute of Public Relations (UK), 1991.

17. Neither Section 31 of the Food Hygiene Regulations, 1950, nor the Hygiene of Foodstuffs regulations, 2000, specifically states that a worker must wear a hair net/cap. Information provided by Susan Lally, Food Safety Authority of Ireland.

18. Paul O'Shea, 'God Gave us Bantry, We Gave it to Gulf Oil', in F. X. Carty (ed.), From *John Paul to Saint Jack*, Dublin: Able Press, 1995.

19. Information provided by Mary Sheerin, Press Officer, Department of Public Enterprise.

CHAPTER 17

Environmental PR

Fleishman-Hillard conducted a survey of senior public relations executives in large corporations in 1993. Eighty PR people in the United States and 113 PR people in Europe participated. They were asked to list the top ten areas of concern for the coming decade (1993–2003). Environmental issues were ranked second — after global competition (US) and technological innovation (Europe). How right those PR people were![1]

The late twentieth century saw a heightened awareness of the environment on the part of Non Governmental Organisations (NGOs), citizens, consumers, corporations and governments. This awareness will continue to grow in the twenty-first century.

ENVIRONMENTAL INITIATIVES

Ireland began to go 'green' in the 1990s and early 2000s, with:

- The election of representatives of the Green Party
- Solid-fuel burning bans in our major cities
- Widespread use of unleaded petrol
- Smoking bans in most public buildings
- Refuse charges to pay for recycling initiatives
- Plastic carrier bags attracting an environmental tax
- Formation of the Irish Energy Centre
- Strengthened power for the Environmental Protection Agency (EPA)
- Agricultural initiatives to help reduce pollution of rivers and lakes
- A National Car Test (NCT) for older vehicles
- Bus and cycle lanes in major cities
- Initiatives which encouraged greater use of public transport
- Recycle bins for paper, bottles and clothes
- Celebration of the millennium by planting a tree for every family in Ireland.

There have been other global and industry initiatives as well, including the Earth Summit in Rio de Janeiro, the Kyoto Protocol, and the formation of government /activist/industry committees on the environment in Australia, China, Britain, and Brazil.[2]

ENVIRONMENTAL ACTIVIST GROUPS

In her book on activism, Denise Deegan offers the following definition: 'Activists, also known as pressure groups, advocacy groups, activist groups, interest groups and citizen groups, are formed when two or more people organise on behalf of a cause to exert pressure on an organisation to change the way it functions'.[3]

Over the past decade, environmental activist groups became less predictable, more global, more diverse, much more media savvy, and consequently more powerful.

The groups are less predictable because they can form virtually overnight. Companies can still 'list' activist groups for inclusion in discussions, but they can no longer be sure that they are dealing with all of them. Some activist groups are formed only in response to a company initiative, and disappear when they have won/lost the battle. They are single-issue, self-selecting publics.

Activist groups are also more global with international appeal. Greenpeace is perhaps the largest environmental group in the world, and certainly one of the most active. E. Bruce Harrison said of Greenpeace, that its members 'play "chicken" with whalers in the Arctic, shadow the Japanese plutonium ship in the South Atlantic, picket a French pesticide industry group…and erect billboards in Delaware protesting the pace of CFC phase out — all more or less simultaneously'.[4] That makes them a very powerful lobby indeed.

The groups are more diverse because the issue of environmentalism attracts a broad sweep of people who are mobile and can re-locate — county, country or continent — to support a cause. One Irish example of this trend was in the Glen of the Downs in Wicklow (2001), where the tree people comprised Irish residents and non-nationals who came to support the protest.

Environmental activists have also become much more media savvy. They know how to maximise publicity for their cause, and put their issue on the media agenda — and companies are suffering as a result. The 1995 case of Ken Saro-Wiwa in the Ogoni region of Nigeria[5] led to a global boycott of Shell products.

News creation has been defined as 'an unending battle between a multitude of differentially powerful parties over the definition of reality'.[6] Activists are extremely professional when it comes to providing media with footage and visuals to accompany their 'reality'. The media, by using the supplied material — as you would expect them to — give prominence to activist issues. These issues, in turn, 'come to occupy prominent positions on the public agenda'.[7]

Once an environmental issue has reached the public consciousness, it lingers for years. For example, on 24 March 1989, the Exxon Valdez struck Bligh Reef in Prince William Sound, releasing 11 million gallons of crude oil into the sea. It was 'only the thirty-fourth largest oil spill at that time'[8] but it is one of the most remembered corporate crises.[9]

Don't be misled into thinking that it is all about good use of media to highlight a cause. Denise Deegan talks about the darker side of activism, including 'hoax bomb threats, death threats, arson, damage to property…home addresses and telephone numbers of directors (have been published)… shareholders…have been warned to sell their shares and prove that they have done so or run the risk of demonstrations outside their homes…employees have had property attacked, have been followed home and have received threatening letters telling them to leave the company or face arson or physical beatings'.[10]

CREDIBILITY

Companies invest large sums of money in environmental PR. As Denise Deegan said in an interview with Pat Kenny, 'It's not about white-washing…it's not about quietening down the groups — it's about working with them'.[11]

Companies treat Environmental PR as a specialised area. They need to, because all of the research shows that, no matter what strides companies take, the consumer treats information from corporations with great suspicion. One of the greatest difficulties which companies have to overcome is their perceived lack of credibility in the eyes of their publics. Deegan says that 'activists claim to be motivated by a desire to correct apparent injustices (e.g. abuse of the rights of workers, animals or humans) and perceived dangers (e.g. damage to the environment, health, etc) for the greater benefit of society. This places them in a morally superior position to those that they target'.[12]

More than a decade ago, the Wirthlin Group (US) asked more than 1,000 adults which of three scientists — from the federal government, industry and an environmental group — they would believe the most regarding an environmental question. Sixty-six per cent said that they would believe the environmental scientist, 11 per cent would believe government and only 7 per cent would believe industry.[13] There are large numbers of environmental groups and a huge public respect for them. The public is much more inclined to believe the environmentalist than the industrialist. Despite the best efforts of companies, little has changed over the decade.

For example, British Nuclear Fuels Ltd (BNFL) runs the Sellafield Nuclear Reprocessing Plant which has been a cause of concern to Irish governments and citizens for years. Sellafield, as you would expect, has a large public relations department with a sizeable budget, dedicated to creating an understanding of its industry. It also has a BNFL public relations representative in Dublin, Veronica McDermott.[14] Despite a massive investment in communications, public cynicism remains high.

According to Martin Forwood of CORE (Cumbrians Opposed to a Radioactive Environment), when Sellafield introduced its Open and Honest Policy in 1986, 12 per cent of the public thought that the company was honest. By the 1990s, after spending millions of pounds on public relations, that figure had dropped to 10 per cent.[15]

When BNFL announced that it was reducing its workforce by 500 people in 1999, Patricia McKenna MEP responded that 'BNFL should cut its PR budget' instead.[16]

In an article in the *Irish Examiner*, in 2002, Michael O'Farrell pointed out that Sellafield's workers 'joke that they are great in discos because of the way they glow and that the lamb and fish from the area comes ready-cooked'. And he was completely unimpressed with the public relations section. '"We are doing our best but we can guarantee nothing. Yes, we've messed up in the past but now you can trust us," is the central message Sellafield's PR department has for Ireland,' he wrote.[17]

PR GUIDANCE IN THE TWENTY-FIRST CENTURY

So, how do we, as PR practitioners, provide guidance to our clients? The International Public Relations Association addressed this issue when it adopted its Charter on Environmental Communication, better known as the Nairobi Code.[18] It contains nine points of guidance for practitioners:

- IPRA members accept that they have a responsibility to ensure that the information and counsel which they provide, and products and services which they promote, fall within the context of sustainable development.
- Members shall endeavour to encourage their organisations, companies or clients to adopt policies which recognise that careless use of resources and disregard for the environment can lead to severe limitations for economic growth, grave social disruption and serious health hazards.
- Members shall, where appropriate, counsel their companies, clients or organisations to undertake regular environmental assessments of products and operations and to produce and communicate environmental codes of practice or guidelines for their employees and other publics.
- Members shall not publicise or promote products, organisations or services as having environmental benefit unless these benefits are demonstrable in the light of current science and knowledge.
- Members shall endeavour at all times to promote openness and dialogue which fairly handle both facts and concerns related to the environment and development.
- Members shall not seek to raise or respond to unrealistic environmental expectations but shall generally support organisations, products or services which are provably taking steps to improve environmental performance in a time scale which takes account of community concerns and government requirements as well as technological and economic constraints.
- Members shall seek to develop programmes which counsel and communicate on the benefit of a balanced consideration of environmental, economic and social development factors.
- Members shall provide a free flow of information within and through IPRA concerning environmental and development issues on an international level.
- Members should be familiar with, and encourage the organisations they work for to support, and abide by, Codes of Practice of other internationally recognised organisations such as the United Nations and International Chamber of Commerce.

CORPORATE RESPONSE

According to David Morgan Rees, 'the outside world intrudes increasingly upon the conduct of a company's affairs, questioning motives and judging performance from levels of understanding which may vary from the expert and informed, to the cynical, ignorant or prejudiced'.[19]

Denig and Wesink point out that companies adopt either buffering (defensive approaches) or bridging (two-way symmetric communications) strategies in response to activism.[20] And research suggests that companies which are led by managers with backgrounds in marketing, research or product development, have a more open attitude to external stakeholders.[21]

Industry has responded to this wave of environmental awareness compulsorily — because of the introduction of national legislation; with assistance — from government bodies; or with vision — because companies believe in the future of their industry. For an example of a company with vision, see the Tetra Pac case study.

Assembly of Tetra Pak Environmental Reports

Tetra Pak — A Case Study

Tetra Pak Ireland Ltd is part of the international Tetra Pak group. Tetra Pak develops, manufactures and markets systems for processing, packaging and distributing liquid food like milk, juice, soup, etc. The company employs 20,150 people worldwide. Its products are sold in more than 165 countries, and in 2001, it achieved net sales of €7.6 billion.

The company, which is Swedish, has had a corporate ethos of respect for the environment since its inception. The company's mission statement 'is to contribute — together with our customers and suppliers — to the safe, efficient and environmentally sound production and distribution of liquid foods to the consumers of the world'.*

Worldwide corporate environmental policies are centrally decided and communicated to each national Tetra Pak company, which has the autonomy to organise the implementation of those policies within national guidelines.

Throughout the 1990s, with a growing concern for the environment, an increasing level of environmental awareness among consumers and a surge in environmental legislation being imposed on companies by governments worldwide, companies were under tremendous pressure to improve and report on their environmental performance.

Tetra Pak responded to this by taking action, and devised a strategy to evaluate and improve the environmental impact of all its processes. In 1999, Tetra Pak published its first Corporate Environmental Report which was produced with the assistance of international consultants Environmental Resources Management (ERM).

KEY APPLICATIONS OF THE ENVIRONMENTAL POLICY**

Corporate Structures

Tetra Pak formed an Environmental Council, consisting of senior management representatives from different markets and business areas within the company, to design policies, and a Corporate Environmental Affairs Group to ensure that the Council's decisions are implemented.

Compliance Measures

Tetra Pak meets the requirements of all relevant environmental legislation, regulations and guidelines in each of the countries in which it operates. For example, in Ireland, the company operates in full compliance with national Packaging and Packaging Waste regulations, and is a member of Repak, a company set up in 1997 under voluntary agreement between government and industry to meet Ireland's recycling targets.†

Employees

One of Tetra Pak's environmental goals is to ensure that employees are aware of the company's environmental policies and goals. In September 2001, Tetra Pak launched an employee environmental awareness programme called 'Eco Drive' to inform employees about its activities and increase commitment to reaching environmental goals. Each market company had an 'Environmental Day', consisting of presentations, discussions, environmental quizzes, tree planting, etc.

Sourcing Policy

Tetra Pak encourages all its suppliers to implement and maintain environmental management systems and to reduce the environmental impact of their operations. Suppliers of paperboard, for example, are being asked to ensure that the fibres Tetra Pak buys from them come from sustainably managed forests and that they adopt performance standards for sustainable forest management such as those of the Forest Stewardship Council (FSC) and others. Tetra Pak has a comprehensive evaluation system for suppliers, and environment forms a part of the overall score.

Recycling

For Tetra Pak, contributing to the recycling capabilities of the packages it produces is part of its responsible approach to the environment. As part of this approach, Tetra Pak Ireland works closely with some of its suppliers, recycling companies, paper mills and local entrepreneurs to find recycling capacity. Cartons are currently being recycled in many countries worldwide to produce paper products like paper bags, tissue paper and panel boards.

Energy Reduction

Every Tetra Pak manufacturing plant and market company worldwide sets energy-reduction targets each year. Actual measures Tetra Pak plants undertake to achieve these targets range from simply encouraging employees to switch off lights and computers when they go home, to more sophisticated initiatives such as investing in more energy-efficient equipment and recovering hot air from one process to reuse elsewhere in the operations.

Building Awareness

In Ireland, the company is actively promoting the environmental benefits of cartons through its schools programme. In conjunction with Séamus O'Neill of We and Us Ltd, the programme encourages primary-school children to produce maths materials (counters/pie charts, etc.) from used cartons.‡ Tetra Pak also supports other educational initiatives — for example, Tetra Pak Ireland has sponsored participants who attended the International Children's Conference on the Environment, in Canada.

Dealing with Consumers

In each Tetra Pak company there are specified staff-members responsible for environmental affairs, keeping consumers informed of environmental policies and practices and answering any queries they may have such as: what cartons are made of; how they can be recycled; etc.

Environmental Planning and Reporting

Tetra Pak produces a full environmental report every two years. The report is published and distributed to stakeholders — customers, government departments and key interest groups — throughout the world.

In the interim year, between reports, a progress report is published.

The report contains detailed feedback on the company's environmental performance and is a true reflection of what goals were achieved and what goals need to be improved on in the future.

Website

The 1999 Corporate Environmental Report and the 2000 Environmental Progress Report are published on the Tetra Pak website (see Visual 13).

References

* Source: www.tetrapak.com
** An interview by the author with Marie Kiernan, Communications and Environmental Affairs Director, Tetra Pak Ireland, conducted on 24 April 2002.
† Source: www.repak.ie
‡ Source: www.weandus.com

Annual Reports

Some companies already include in their annual reports a statement of their environmental policy, or an environmental audit. Annual reports are a documented record of what the company has done, and what it is planning to do. In addition to the vital financial information (historical and projections) it provides, the annual report has become a vehicle for explaining and expanding the corporate ethos of the company.

The inclusion of this section clearly tells investors, employees, competitors and suppliers that the company is responding to their concerns.

Energy Awareness

Companies are becoming more aware of their energy use. This is partly driven by environmental concerns, partly by cost savings. Major companies now have energy-saving systems for lighting, heating, and computer use at office level, as well as energy-saving initiatives in their plants. But there is still a long way to go. According to Andrew Parish of the Irish Energy Centre, industry still needs to play a part 'in taking steps to achieve energy savings...[and to play] a leadership role for other energy consumers'.[22]

Recycling Policies

Many companies combine environmental awareness with good business sense. They can foresee a time, in the not-too-distant future, when they will be required by legislation to reduce packaging, or facilitate customers who wish to return packaging.

Working with Environmental Groups — Pro-active Initiatives

Companies need to go beyond compliance with national and international regulations in order to impress the public. Some have already started.

Shell has introduced consumer panels in the Netherlands. These panels meet annually to discuss issues of concern to the broadest possible range of consumers — individuals, business organisations, environmental groups and representative bodies. They compile a report at the end of each annual meeting and, at the beginning of the next one, the company reports on how it has adapted or changed to take account of the issues raised at the previous forum. They are trying to be seriously pro-active in their approach to the environment.

Staff Recruitment and Retention

Future trends for companies include predictions that employees will 'choose to work for organisations which take an affirmative approach to ethics, environmental and social responsibility'.[23] If they are environmentally proactive, corporations will win and retain staff.

Community and Local Environment

Companies also encourage and support local environmental initiatives. Through sponsorship, for example, they can encourage environmental awareness in schools, enhance the quality of life of the community by providing a parkland area, involve their own staff in a clean-up and re-stocking of local rivers or sponsor 'Clean our Town' initiatives. Companies, for relatively little investment, can show that they are good environmental neighbours.

Shareholder and Consumer Influence

Finally, there are investment groups which will recommend only stocks and shares in companies that are ethically or environmentally conscious. Any company will gain by inclusion in this group. Consumers, particularly when economies are buoyant, exercise their power of influence by refusing to purchase products from companies with a poor environmental record.

The Internet

The internet is one of the most powerful tools of activist groups. One of the key findings of a report called 'Putting the Pressure on' was that 'Modern day pressure groups have become a major political force in their own right, and are here to stay. They manifest themselves in the use of powerful communication techniques, and they succeed in attracting wide attention and sympathy, projecting their case with great skill via the mass media — they understand the power of PR and of the media 'sound-bite.' And now increasingly, they do so over the global telecommunication networks'.[24]

According to Peter Verhille from the Entente PR agency, the greatest threat to the corporate world's reputation comes from the internet, the pressure groups' newest weapon. 'A growing number of multinational companies — such as McDonald's and Microsoft — have been viciously attacked on the Internet by unidentifiable opponents which leave their victims in a desperate search for adequate countermeasures....One of the major strengths of pressure groups — in fact the leveling factor in their confrontation with powerful companies — is their ability to exploit the instruments of the telecommunication revolution. Their agile use of global tools such as the Internet reduces the advantage that corporate budgets once provided.'[25]

Any review of the Shell/Brent Spar situation (see Chapter 3) shows that Shell was completely unprepared for the impact of the internet. The company has learned its lesson since, however, as evidenced by the appointment of an internet manager, Simon May, and the retention of specialised, external consultants who scout the web daily, inventorying all possible ways Shell is being mentioned on the net, and in what context.[26] How many other companies could show that they are this well prepared?

THE FUTURE

The purpose of public relations is to develop, build and sustain credible relationships with all relevant publics. The challenge for environmental PR, in addition, is to seek to overcome the enormous credibility issue which attaches to corporations. It will not be easy.

Harrison's **QUALITY** model[27] provides an outline of the process necessary to change opinion and overcome the credibility issue. He recommends a seven-step approach:

Quantify your publics
Understand what they want
Ask questions
Listen aggressively
Interpret
Take charge, and
You — yes, you — have a role.

The future for corporations and their public relations people is challenging. Research shows that the reaction of those targeted determines, to a large extent, how aggressive or co-operative activists will be.[28] The corporations must become more environmentally pro-active because their shareholders, consumers and employees are demanding it. The public relations people need to find new ways to meet the communications challenge, establish credible relationships with environmentalists, and succeed in having their voice heard — and believed!

REFERENCES

1. Jon White and Laura Mazur, *Strategic Communications Management — Making Public Relations Work*, The Economist Intelligence Unit, England: Addison-Wesley, 1994.
2. The Australian Manufacturing Council's Industry and the Environment Committee, China's Council for International Cooperation on Environment and Development, Britain's Advisory Committee on Business and the Environment, and Brazil's National Council for the Environment.
3. Denise Deegan, *Managing Activism, A Guide to Dealing with Activists and Pressure Groups*, Institute of Public Relations, UK: Kogan Page, 2001.
4. E. Bruce Harrison, APR, MIPRA, in 'Green Communication in the age of sustainable development', *IPRA Gold*, paper No. 9, January 1993.
5. David Shanks, 'The accidental activist', *The Irish Times*, 15 March 2002.
6. J. Turow (1989), 'Public Relations and Newswork, A Neglected Relationship', in David Deacon, 'The Voluntary Sector in a Changing Communication Environment — A Case Study of Non-official News Sources', *European Journal of Communication*, Vol. 11, No. 2, 1996.
7. Rainer Mathes and Barbara Pfetsch, 'The Role of the Alternative Press in the Agenda-Building Process: Spill-over Effects and Media Opinion Leadership', *European Journal of Communication*, Vol. 6, No. 1, 1991.
8. Allen H. Center and Patrick Jackson, *Public Relations Practices — Managerial Case Studies and Problems*, New Jersey: Prentice Hall, 1995 (fifth edition).
9. PR Reporter, 12 July 1993, in Allen H. Center and Patrick Jackson, Op cit.
10. Denise Deegan, Op cit.
11. Denise Deegan, author of *Managing Activism*, and Clare Watson, environmentalist, were interviewed on the Pat Kenny radio show, RTÉ Radio 1, 2001.
12. Denise Deegan, Op cit.
13. E. Bruce Harrison, Op cit.
14. Full text of the letters regarding Mildred Fox's inquiry about Sellafield', *The Irish Times*, Special Report, 4 March 2000.
15. Martin Forwood interviewed by Matthew Parris in 'P.R.-ISM, Bad Ideas of the 20th Century', *Without Walls* series, Channel Four.
16. Rachel Donnelly, '500 Sellafield job cuts a threat to Irish coast', *The Irish Times*, 1 April 1999.
17. Michael O'Farrell, 'Cloud of secrecy does little to allay safety fears', *Irish Examiner*, 12 April 2002.
18. The IPRA Charter on Environmental Communication — Nairobi Declaration, 1991, in *IPRA Codes and Declarations*, England: Alpha Publishing, 2001.
19. David Morgan Rees, 'Public Relations in a Large Industrial Company', in Wilfred Howard (ed.), *The Practice of Public Relations*, Oxford: Butterworth-Heinemann, on behalf of the CAM Foundation and the Chartered Institute of

Marketing, UK, 1992 (third edition).

20. Eric Denig and Anita Weisink (eds), 'Challenges in Communication — State of the Art & Future Trends', *IPRA Gold*, paper No. 13, October 2000.

21. A. S. Thomas and R. L. Simerly (1994), 'Market Information Processing and Organizational Learning', *Journal of Marketing*, in Eric Denig and Anita Weisink (eds), Op cit.

22. 'Energy Claim', *Irish Examiner*, 12 April 2002, Money and Jobs section.

23. Tom Cannon, 'Welcome to the Revolution — Managing Paradox in the 21st Century', London: Pitman Publishing, 1996.

24. Entente PR agency report, 'Putting the Pressure on' presented to a conference devoted to pressure groups' growing influence, Brussels, June 1998. http://www.ex4all.nl/~evel/brenteg.htm

25. Peter Verhille, Entente PR agency, presentation to a conference devoted to pressure groups' growing influence, Brussels, June 1998. http://www.ex4all.nl/~evel/brenteg.htm

26. 'The Brent Spar Syndrome — Counterstrategies against online activism', http://www.ex4all.nl/~evel/brenteg.htm

27. E. Bruce Harrison, Op cit.

28. Larissa Grunig (1992) 'Activism: How it Limits the Effectiveness of Organizations and How Excellent Public Relations Departments Respond' cited in Denise Deegan, Op cit.

CHAPTER 18

Financial PR/Investor Relations

Financial public relations is a highly specialised area. To handle financial PR, a background in finance is a huge benefit. A deep understanding of the stock exchange (stock exchanges), shareholders and financial media is necessary. So too is an understanding of the impact of financial communications on shareholders and stakeholders — share prices can be affected by a single press release. And the publics of financial PR are small, identifiable, and volatile — they react instantly to rumour.

Although there is a financial aspect to every business, large or small, financial PR relates primarily to companies that are launching on or quoted on the stock exchange.

In Ireland, Murray Consultants was the first consultancy to specialise in financial PR. The consultancy was formed by two former journalists whose background was financial/economic journalism.

Because financial public relations has such an impact, nationally and internationally, on share prices, this area of communications is heavily legislated for and regulated. The 'Yellow Book' of the stock exchange, for example, covers client–company communications, and the ways in which information must be imparted to the stock exchange and to shareholders. Before we begin to discuss the public relations aspects, however, we should first look at the stock exchange and how it operates.

IRISH AND INTERNATIONAL STOCK EXCHANGES

At one point, between Ireland and Britain, there were seven stock exchanges. In 1971, the Dublin and Cork exchanges amalgamated and, in 1973, Dublin, Belfast, Glasgow, Birmingham and Manchester merged with the London Stock Exchange.[1]

The Stock Exchange Act of 1995[2] required the Irish Stock Exchange to incorporate separately and, on 8 September 1995, the Irish Stock Exchange formally separated from the London Stock Exchange. Until then, the Irish exchange had operated as a branch of the International Stock Exchange of the UK and the Republic of Ireland.

The Central Bank approved the Irish Stock Exchange and regulates it on an ongoing basis, in three key areas:

1. The Central Bank assesses stockbroking firms for authorisation to carry on investment business and regulates them on an ongoing basis;
2. It monitors the adherence of stockbroking firms to requirements imposed on them by the bank;

3. It reviews and approves any proposed changes to the rules of the Exchange (see reference 5).

Internationally the so-called 'golden triangle' of stock market cities comprises London, Tokyo and New York. In April 2002, there was talk of London and Frankfurt merging.

WHAT IS THE STOCK EXCHANGE?

The main function of the stock market is to bring companies and investors together. Investors put risk capital into companies by purchasing shares, and realise their investment by selling those shares on the market. Companies, in turn, benefit from the capital injection, which allows them to grow and invest in new projects. The stock exchange also deals in government securities which are known as 'gilts'.

The Central Bank approves and monitors the Irish Stock Exchange. The exchange, in turn, is charged with regulating the market, to ensure that all dealings are fair. The Irish Stock Exchange:

1. Operates the stock market
2. Admits stockbroking firms to membership (once authorised by the Central Bank)
3. Regulates stockbroking firms dealing with each other and with the clients
4. Assesses applications for listing
5. Supervises quoted companies and ensures that they make full and correct disclosures to the market
6. Sets the rules within which the market and firms operate. (see reference 5)

The Irish Stock Exchange regulates three markets:

1. Domestic Equities
2. Bonds and Company Fixed Interest Securities
3. Offshore investment funds operating out of the International Financial Services Centre (IFSC).

A company that wants to have some or all of its shares listed on the stock exchange must agree to obey the stock exchange rules. For companies with a listing on the main market, these rules are contained in the 'Admission of Securities to Listing' agreement, commonly known as the 'Yellow Book'.[3]

Yellow Book

There are ten separate sections in the Yellow Book. Of particular interest to financial PR people, are:
*   Section 2: the application procedures and requirements regarding publicity;
*   Section 5: the ongoing obligations that a company must satisfy, in relation to public announcements and annual and half-yearly reports;

- Section 6: the rules regarding takeovers and mergers, which includes what is known as the City Code.[4]

'Floating' on the Stock Exchange

A company is said to be 'floated' when its shares are offered for sale. A company can be floated in a number of ways.

Offers for Sale

This is the most common type of issue for shares coming onto the official list. It involves the use of an intermediary (usually the issuing house) who buys all the securities that are being sold, either by the existing shareholders or from the new capital created.

These shares are then offered for sale to the general public at a slightly higher price. The issuing house will ensure that the issue is underwritten by paying a commission to other merchant banks (usually around 2 per cent) in return for their agreement to take some of the share issue if it is not fully subscribed

Offers for Subscription (prospectus issue)

This method of issue is distinctive in that it is an issue made direct to the general public, and does not involve the use of an intermediary such as an issuing house. The most common examples of such an issue are those made by the National Treasury Management Agency where no issuing house is involved. It is rare for ordinary shares to be issued in this manner, since it would involve a different type of underwriting operation from the normal. Shares in investment trusts are usually issued by this method. However, the Emerald Investment Trust plc issue in December 1995 was both an offer for subscription and a placing.

Selective Marketings (or placings)

Offers for sale (or for sale by tender) are the most democratic way of introducing new shares to the market. However, the less costly concession of a selective marketing is available for smaller new issues.

The mechanism involves the issuing house placing shares with its own or another ISE firm's clients. The concession is permitted provided that at least 25 per cent of the shares are placed either with the other firm's private clients, or with the public, but not with the institutional investors. The remaining shares are usually placed with the issuing house's own clients (including the institutional investors).

To ensure that this is still a form of public issue, placed shares must not fall into too few hands; therefore there must be at least 30 shareholders per €1.27 million worth of shares placed and a total of at least 100 private shareholders.

To ensure that the investing public is aware of the placing, a box advertisement giving formal notice of the transaction must be placed in at least two national papers.

Introductions

This is the second type of listing which does not involve the offer of sale to the general public. It is a concession granted by the ISE and is frequently used when an overseas company, which is already quoted on an established exchange in its own country, seeks a listing in Ireland to increase the sources of capital for that company. The company will already have a wide spread of shareholders, but to ensure that the market makers can create a market in the shares when trading commences, some of the major shareholders (i.e. the directors) will be asked to make some of their shares available to the market makers. Introductions must be notified in the press by a formal notice (box advertisement) similar to that required for selective marketings.[5]

Mergers and Takeovers

Mergers and takeovers of companies whose shares are quoted on the stock exchange are covered by the 'City Code on Take-overs and Mergers', commonly called City Code, which is an integral part of the 'Yellow Book'.[6]

Secondary Markets

Many companies find the requirements of a listing on the main market too onerous in the initial stages, and they often, therefore, begin by seeking a listing on the second-tier market (the junior market), progressing to a full market listing after a few years of growth.[7]

In 1981, the London Stock Exchange created an Unlisted Securities Market (USM) to cater for companies which could not satisfy the stringent requirements of a full listing.[8]

Alternative Investment Market (AIM)

However, during the 1990s there were concerns that the complexities in meeting USM requirements, which were hardly any less demanding than those for a full listing, were causing stagnation in the growth of junior markets for smaller companies. So, in June 1994, after extensive review and consultation, the UK launched the new Alternative Investment Market (AIM).[9] Many smaller Irish companies have chosen to go directly to AIM.

There are certain entry requirements to the AIM but they do not involve the company having to be a specified size, or to prove its trade history. One condition is that the company must at all times retain the services of a Nominated Adviser and a Nominated Broker. In order to be listed on AIM, the company must publish a prospectus showing full descriptions of the securities to be listed.

Developing Companies Market

The Developing Companies Market (DCM) is the Irish Stock Exchange's answer to the Alternative Investment Market. It is directed at small to medium-sized companies.

The free float of shares is 10 per cent, the requirement is for one year's audited accounts, and the directors and key personnel must have been with the company throughout the period covered by the accounts.

AIM and DCM are both designed to provide a diverse range of companies with the opportunity to raise capital and trade their shares without the need to be subject to the rigours of official list regulations.

Market Operators on the Stock Exchange

Since 1986, all stock-exchange member firms are now *broker/dealers* and deal by telephone, using the computerised price-display system, rather than on the trading floor. The broker/dealer can apply to register as a *market maker*, dealing on its own account in certain securities. These market makers are allowed to trade in a *dual capacity* — i.e. acting as *principals* by dealing on their own account, and acting as agents by dealing on behalf of clients. Brokers/dealers who deal only for clients on a commission basis and not on their own account are known as *agency brokers*.[10]

Safeguards and Penalties

The stock exchange monitors activity on the markets closely, and penalties are severe for breaches of the regulations.

Disregard of stock exchange regulations by company directors can constitute evidence of improper and unlawful motives on the directors' behalf. Breaches of some of the requirements in the European Union (EU) Directives concerning stock exchanges amount to criminal offences. When the stock exchange acts under the EU Directives, it exercises public powers which can be the subject of an application to the High Court for judicial review.[11]

People who have suffered loss and damage as a result of any untrue statement in a prospectus are entitled to recover compensation from people connected with the issue, such as the promoters and the directors. A prison term or financial fine, or both, may be imposed on conviction.[12]

Until Ernest Saunders was sent to Ford Open Prison in Essex, company directors or managers were rarely jailed for breaking the Companies Acts.[13]

In the case of the controversial Guinness takeover of Distillers, the Panel on Take-Overs and Mergers directed Guinness to pay very substantial compensation to the Distillers' shareholders when it found that Guinness had contravened several requirements of the Code.[14]

Even the intranet — internal, employee communication — has been the source of stock-exchange investigation. In a ruling issued on 22 October 1999, 'the Amsterdam Stock Exchanges came to the conclusion that the prestigious Dutch airline, KLM, had contravened their Listing and Issuing Rules when it disseminated announcements via its own Intranet entitled "Prognosis of KLM's operating results: disappointing results call for measures"'.[15]

The Amsterdam rules, like the rules of other stock exchanges, state that information that might have a significant effect on share prices should be published to all parties at the same time. Although KLM argued that the information related to internal budgeting, the stock exchange ruled that the announcement (the intranet message) 'qualified as price-sensitive as defined by Article 28 of Amsterdam's Listing and Issuing Rules....They went on to say that, given this fact, the widespread circulation of the message among KLM's employees, some of whom were assumed to be KLM shareholders, implied that shareholders were not given equal treatment as defined by the Rules'.[16]

In January 2002, fruit importers Fyffes instigated a civil action, the first in the state, alleging insider dealing by DCC. The case involves the sale of shares weeks ahead of a profit warning. 'Fruit importers Fyffes claims DCC chief executive Mr Jim Flavin and his company were aware of crucial price-sensitive information when they sold 10.2 per cent of Fyffes two years ago, at the height of the dotcom boom'. The hearing is scheduled for the High Court.[17]

In January 2002, Philip Byrne, the former managing director of property firm Dunloe Ewart plc, was cleared of insider dealing by a jury at the Dublin Circuit Criminal Court. Philip Byrne 'had pleaded not guilty to two counts of insider dealing, contrary to the Companies Act 1990'.[18] What was described as a 'nightmare' for Philip Byrne and his family, had started 'in November 1997 with a stock exchange investigation'.[19]

FLOW OF COMMUNICATIONS

The stock exchange and its primary and secondary markets are highly regulated for companies and their advisors. The role of financial PR, while operating within the regulations, is primarily one of communications. Good financial PR is highly dependent on a constant flow of communications. People, corporations and institutions who have invested in a company constantly monitor developments and progress within that company which could affect the share price, and, by logical extension, the quality or otherwise of their investment.

Investors: Black/White Knights

In the 1990s, there were many stories in the media of black knights and white knights. These were financial terms which tripped off the tongue easily. The film, *Trading Places* (with Eddie Murphy), also served to bring financial dealings to the forefront of people's minds — people who might otherwise not have had the slightest interest in stocks and shares.

Hostile takeover bids for companies (made by black knights) happened where an organisation identified potential in a listed company. This organisation, the black knight, then approached the shareholders in the listed company and offered to buy out their shares for a premium. Often the aim of the buy-out was to acquire the assets of the company and strip them — i.e. sell them off in sections thereby effectively closing the companies, causing massive redundancies, and generating huge profits for the new owners.

The appeal of the black knights was one of financial return. If you were an investor in the company, why should you not sell your shares, at a good profit, and let the new owners do whatever they liked with the company after you had sold to them? Black knights could operate only among shareholders who had invested in a company, but not grown close to it. If you had made the investment on purely monetary grounds (which is quite legitimate) and you owed no debt of loyalty to the company, or felt no closeness to your investment, it made perfect sense to dispose of it and realise a good profit on your investment.

Companies have resorted to aggressive responses to help them in their defence against a takeover. They have engaged in advertising campaigns to promote their independence. (This activity has been greatly curtailed in recent years under the Takeover Panel's regulations, but it still takes place.) With the consent of the Takeover Panel, the company may sell off some of its key assets or subsidiaries, making it less attractive to the hostile bidder. And, of course, companies have sought out what is known as a white knight.

White knights, which were also external to the listed company, were actually invited, by that company, to offer a counter takeover bid. Essentially the listed company knew that it was in trouble, and was likely to be taken over anyway, but tried to involve a takeover company of its choice. This involved selecting and approaching another company to counter-offer to purchase the same shareholders' shares. The white knights generally shared a common vision of the company with the existing directors and were therefore given the blessing of the company. The directors, naturally, would have preferred no takeover but, once the battle lines were drawn, they needed to be pro-active in order to keep the company alive.

The white knights appealed to the shareholders to sell to them instead on the basis of loyalty, shared vision of the future of the company and, of course, a good return.

The corporate vision of the black knights was to make profit, at any cost. The corporate vision of the white knights was to help preserve and grow industry.

The French drinks company, Pernod Ricard, rode in as a white knight to rescue Irish Distillers from the British company, GrandMet, in 1988.[20]

Lessons Learned

Companies learned a lot from the rash of hostile takeovers in the 1990s. They suddenly realised the value of their shareholders and began to pay much more attention to them. They started to spend more money on them, communicate with them more frequently and try to convert them into company visionaries loyal to the ethos and future direction of the business in which they had invested their money.

POWER OF RUMOUR

Shareholders are also very responsive to rumour. The slightest rumour on the market can encourage people to sell or buy large quantities of stock, driven by what Tom Goldin of the *Sunday Business Post* has called 'a herd mentality'.[21] 'Rumour' on Friday, 14 April 2000, caused a 25 per cent drop in the value of dot.com shares on the NASDAQ market. That Friday, individuals and corporations decided (all on the same day) that technology shares were overvalued, and began to sell.

The collapse of the dot.com companies was as spectacular as their rise. Investors had originally decided that the future was with the dot.coms. They poured huge amounts of money into shares in these companies, many of which launched, with small numbers of employees and a vision (but no product), at phenomenal ratings. The market decided that their potential was much more valuable than a simple addition of their assets would suggest.

The market similarly got 'scared' about the rise of the dot.coms, changed its mind and decided that there wasn't as much potential out there as had been thought. Shareholders got nervous about the number of viruses appearing on the net. There were rumours that the net was not the great new medium it had been cracked up to be (and might, in fact, have to be withdrawn). So, shareholders simply sold their shares, resulting in the collapse of many of the dot.com companies.

Many of these companies, when they were launched, had created (paper) millionaires and billionaires overnight. Directors who had formed companies with their original vision suddenly found themselves worth huge amounts of money (in shares). Just as suddenly, they found that, when the market changed its mind, they were worth half — or less than half (on paper) — of what they had been worth the day before.

There are different types of investors on the market, each of whom needs to receive constant communication, but all of whom have different needs and consequently need to be communicated with in a different way.

It can be difficult to follow or anticipate the 'logic' of investors. When, in April 2000, Yahoo announced robust growth for the first quarter of the year, in which revenues more than doubled over the same period the previous year, its share price fell more than $5. In the weeks previous to this announcement, NetJ.com had seen its share price double to nearly $4. It doubled 'despite the fact that the company plainly disclosed in Securities and Exchange Commission documents that it not only had no profits, but no revenues, and in fact that it did no business of any kind. The company told the SEC that it might begin doing business soon, but maybe not. It if did, it had no specific idea about what kind of work it would do'.[22]

FINANCIAL PUBLICS

Investors

The primary public of financial PR is the investor. Investors are individuals, syndicates, major corporations or institutions. It is important that companies build strong relationships with these investors. The investors need to know what is going on; they need to have faith in the company, its policies, its directors and its vision for the future.

The National Investor Relations Institute (NIRI) of the United States describes Investor Relations as: 'A corporate, strategic, marketing activity combining the disciplines of communication and finance, and providing present and potential investors with an accurate portrayal of a company's performance and prospects. Conducted effectively, investor relations can have a positive effect on a company's total value relative to that of the overall market and a company's cost of capital'.[23]

Peter Smith, one of the founders of the investor relations movement in Britain, said: 'The central purpose of investor relations is…to communicate to the market up-to-date information relevant to the valuation of a company's shares by existing and potential investors, their advisors and those who influence them'.[24]

Many investors will not remain loyal to a company they know little about — a company that has not taken the time to develop a relationship with them. Investors crave information, much of which is now available on investor websites which are an important source of professional advice. Among the best are sites like the Motley Fool (www.fool.com), the British Investor Relations Society's site (www.ir-soc.org.uk), and the American National Investor Relations Institute site (www.niri.org).[25]

Institutional Investors

There are major institutional investors on the Irish market including Irish Life and Bank of Ireland Asset Management (BIAM), which manages (amongst others) the New York Police Department Pension Fund! These investors are the life blood of major organisations. They are the investors who control pension funds, with millions and billions of euro at their disposal; the investors who seek to invest in a broad portfolio of companies — some high earners in the short term, some simply reliable government stock, some with potential for the future. Their portfolios are always balanced, at least in theory, to cover their pension fund's liability.

The major institutional investors are:

- Pension funds
- Insurance companies
- Investment trusts (companies which invest in the securities of a wide range of other companies)
- Unit trusts (small investors who join together to create sufficient funds for a portfolio)

- Venture capital organisations (high risk investments, usually in return for equity in the company, and at an expected high return).

Of these, pension funds and insurance companies have the largest amounts of funds to invest.[26]

These investors are, in fact, a small group of very powerful people. They exercise great influence on the stock exchange by the sheer volume and value of their purchases and sales. They are influenced by each other and are therefore inclined all to arrive at the same investment decisions at the same time.

Institutional investors are dealt with mostly by face-to-face communications. They need to meet with the company on a regular basis, in groups and individually. They need to be kept abreast of trends and developments — they do not like surprises. They expect companies to predict accurately a downturn or an increased profit margin in the next quarter. It causes major problems on the exchange when companies release figures which were, particularly, lower than anticipated. The major investors feel scalded.

These investors are also quite open in expressing their opinions and reservations about companies, often through the media. When Michael Smurfit retired as chief executive officer of the paper and packaging company, the decision was influenced, at least in part, by the views of major corporate investors. 'Smurfit the company has been dogged...by complaints that Smurfit the man had too much influence and was overpaid....Smurfit's €6.6m pay package angered investors so much that four large Irish institutions abstained from a number of key votes at last May's [2001] Smurfit annual general meeting'.[27]

Those same institutional investors were quick to welcome publicly the announcement of Michael Smurfit's decision to step down. Ann Fitzgerald, the secretary general of the Irish Association of Investment Managers (IAIM), said that the association, which was the industry body representing the major investment institutions in the Irish market, had been seeking Dr Smurfit's retirement as chief executive for some time. 'We are very pleased with the announcement. We had been looking for it for a long time,' she said.[28]

Financial Journalists

Financial journalists are an important public of the financial PR specialist. The financial journalists, like the investors, hold great power of influence. It is their columns, their pages in the newspapers, after all, that the investors read. It is crucial, therefore, that they too are kept abreast of developments.

Most of the dealing with financial journalists is done on a one-to-one basis. Communication is by telephone call or meeting — either individually between PR and journalist, or company executive and journalist, or by briefing for a number of financial journalists if there is an issue of which all should be made aware.

Like the investors, financial journalists do not like surprises. They like to be kept abreast of developments as they occur. The link is closely kept. Financial journalists are like the corporate investors — they move in packs. Information given to one is soon known by the others. Planted 'scoops' never happen. All are given the same information. That is not to say that one journalist making an enquiry would have the enquiry answered to all, but important information emanating from the company is given to all financial journalists at the same time.

It is necessary only to look at the way in which the National Irish Bank story about Deposit Interest Retention Tax (DIRT) was broken on RTÉ by George Lee (financial/economic editor) and Charlie Bird (1998) to understand the power of journalists who write in this area.[29]

Individual Investors (internal and external)

The profile of investors on the stock exchange has changed radically since the mid-1980s. Before that, investing on the stock exchange, if you were an individual, meant that you were seriously wealthy, financially clued in, and moving probably in the upper circles of society.

The move by governments, in particular, to sell government entities to the man-in-the-street, meant that the profile of individual investors changed forever.

In the United States, 'the majority of middle-class Americans now fall into the category of equity investors in some form. In the last 20 years, the average working American has shifted his savings away from bank-sponsored certificates of deposits (CDs) and passbook savings accounts in banks....Small investors realised what the rich had always known; real money is made in the stock market, not in savings accounts. Since the crash of 1929, the stock market's average return has been at least 10 per cent a year'.[30]

And there is another important point to bear in mind — human psychology. 'Most professional and managerial workers in the US aged under 40 have little practical experience of recession. Do the sums: someone born in 1961 and entering the workforce at the age of 22 would have started work in 1983. The only recession they will have known was that little one in 1990–1. By contrast, someone who was 40 in 1960 would have experienced four recessions in their working life'.[31]

In Ireland, we had been watching the trend in Britain, where shareholder numbers had been experiencing huge growth from 1986 onwards.

It was really only in 2000, however, that the Irish market opened to new investors with the sale of Telecom Éireann. This sale was the first time the government in Ireland had decided to sell what had previously been a 'national asset'. It was also the first time that the ordinary person was targeted, by television, radio and newspaper advertising, to invest on the stock exchange.

The government's intention was that this privatisation would be followed by others, notably Aer Rianta. However, consumer and individual investor reaction to the sale of Telecom led to cabinet opposition to the flotation of the airports authority.[32]

The growth of ordinary investors is a blessing and a curse for companies. The 'blessing' lies in the fact that there are more investors willing to support your company, possibly willing to invest more should you need to issue special share offerings, etc. The 'curse' is that these people are not the 'polite upper classes'. They expect a return on their investment and will complain loudly about the company, its directors, its policies and its dividends, if they are not happy.

In the early 1980s, it is fairly true to say that if you attended the AGM of a publicly quoted company you met mostly retired people — senior citizens who had invested in the company, wanted to meet the directors, have a nice day out, and satisfy themselves that they were up to date with what was happening in the company. Company directors also found these meetings much easier to control — they ran to the agenda the directors had outlined.

All of that changed in the 1990s. Following their hostile takeover by Vodafone, Klaus Esser, chief executive of German company Mannesmann said that 'the shareholder is king'. In doing so, he heralded what is, for many, a new and 'unwelcome, concentration on the rights of one stakeholder group over others such as employees, customers and the community'.[33]

Linked Circles — Media

Investor information comes from a linked circle. Investors read the press (corporate image/general news). They listen to interviews on general news programmes with Colm Rapple or Dan McLaughlin.[34] They watch specialist financial programmes. They are influenced by the views of knowledgeable analysts and other investors.

They speak with journalists, who are a direct link to those same analysts and investors, to get an 'inside' feeling for how a company is developing. And, like every other public in the world, they are influenced by any inconsistency in the company, and hear every rumour — true and false — which circulates about it.

The problem with rumours is that people seldom repeat them to the company so that it can have an opportunity to deal with them. Worse — people make decisions based on the rumours.

Corporate Behaviour

Investors monitor the media to gather information from general news items as well as the financial pages, so it is important that they are receiving the same messages from all sources. They are conscious of the profile of the company, the presentation of its corporate image and the way in which the media report on it.

Share prices today 'result from a composite interaction of forces which are put into play by four actors of corporate life: shareholders (and their intermediaries in financial institutions), consumers (or, more generally, clients), society (and its representative institutions), and companies themselves (meaning mostly their management)'.[35]

In 1993 Dragon International Consultancy published research based on interviews with brokers, analysts, fund managers, venture capitalists and financial journalists.[36] The report highlighted four areas of importance to investors:

- Trust is a major issue. The City felt badly misled during the late 1980s and early 1990s;
- Management is being scrutinised with a new level of intensity. Corporate ethics are crucial to success. Honesty, openness, and the quality of information are important;
- Brand performance (i.e. consumer purchasing power) is a measure of success;
- The quality of information being communicated is vital. Sixty per cent of those interviewed felt that the level and quality of information supplied by companies was inadequate.

Jean-Pierre Beaudoin, has written about an 'image composite' — the four components of opinion, crucial to a company's success. He identified them as:

1. The results that a company brings to its shareholders
2. The success it has in meeting demand
3. The ethical behaviour it displays
4. The image it communicates.

'Whenever public opinion perceives any imbalance among the four components of its attitudes, damage will result for the company's financial performance,' according to Beaudoin. In addition, brand consistency is vital. 'With brands becoming a key element of any company's assets, and therefore also of its financial value, "goodwill" is a component of companies' balance sheets which financial analysts watch more and more closely. A component to which communication contributes most significantly'.[37]

Working Closely with Financial Director

Working in financial PR means that you are inevitably working closely with the financial director at all times, and you have access to sensitive information — information which could affect the value of a share price.

This raises all sorts of ethical issues. As the PR person involved with the company, you should not hold any shares in the company, nor should any members of your staff. If they do, or if they did at the time you won the contract, you should make the shareholding known to the company. You should name the people, including yourself, and declare the value of any investment. You should also offer to sell those shares before you begin to work with the company. The company may agree that you should do so, or it may simply note the shareholdings for its files. If the company agrees that you may retain the shares, you may not, of course, increase your shareholding or dispose of your shares without notifying the company first. The best option by far, and the one which is most transparent, is simply not to hold shares in companies that retain your services, or to dispose of any shares you hold in a company as soon as you secure the contract to handle the company's financial public relations. There should never be the slightest doubt about the ethics of what you, as a PR person, are doing.

Information that is Important to Investors

It is important that you understand the sorts of information that are important to investors — the quality and strength of management, financial status of the business, and ethical positions.

Investors who have put money into a company will carefully monitor the quality and strength of the management team. The management team, after all, is responsible for running the company. If the team isn't good, strong, well balanced, capable, and mixed in age and experience, the company may suffer as a result.

Investors, naturally, will look to the financial status of the company. What are its borrowings, profit levels, product portfolios, assets (land, machinery), etc?

And, of course, investors are also ethical creatures. They will carefully monitor the ethical positions adopted by the company. No one wants to 'admit' to holding shares in an unethical company. Investors and consumers are the two biggest driving forces in encouraging companies to behave ethically.

Retaining Shareholder Loyalty and Attracting New Investment

The overall objective of financial public relations is to retain shareholder loyalty and investment, and attract new shareholders/investors. These objectives can be achieved only by ethically run, well-managed, commercially conscious companies which communicate with their publics. Those publics include shareholders, investors — corporate and individual — financial and economic journalists, employees, consumers and the stock exchange.

PR TOOLS

The PR tools of financial public relations include all of the PR tools available in every other form of PR. In addition, however, they also include annual general meetings, annual reports and briefings of journalists and analysts.

Annual General Meeting

The Annual General Meeting (AGM) is probably the one occasion each year when shareholders have an opportunity to meet with the directors and applaud or deride their policies for the company. Individual shareholders are beginning to dominate news media coverage of AGMs. The change in investor profile over the years means that, although statistically small, the sheer number of individual investors in companies has increased, and they are not only attending but also voicing their opinions at company AGMs. Most of the coverage of the AIB AGM in 2000 was dominated by shareholder comment from the floor: 'rebel AIB shareholder and former employee,

Niall Murphy, positively poured forth invective, some of it cringe-inducing, against the nine man team of directors on the podium'.[38]

Individual Briefings

Briefings of journalists, investors and analysts — individually or in groups — to keep them abreast of developments within the company are crucial. When the web education provider, Riverdeep, floated in March 2000, it was the most successful market début by an Irish company ever, making Barry O'Callaghan, its chief executive, an internet millionaire at 30 years of age. 'We did 77 meetings in 10 days (prior to the flotation) and 65 of those were one-to-one with institutional investors,' said O'Callaghan. In total, he believed he addressed '250 institutions in Dublin, London, New York and Paris during the period'.[39]

Press Coverage

Financial press conferences to announce new directions the company is taking, or explain a change in management, or give advance notice of a new development will influence investors. Corporate image, as portrayed in media, industrial relations activity, research and development, and a company's ethical policies, will also influence shareholders. Not all of these areas are covered by financial PR — many fall into the categories of media relations or product PR, but all have an influence on investors and, ultimately, the company's share price.

The Annual Report

The annual report is, perhaps, a company's biggest undertaking in print each year. The annual report, by its very nature, is something which people keep. It will survive in their libraries as reference material for years. The annual report has changed over the years from a dull, figures-oriented production to a lively, colourful production which not only gives you the financial projections and year-end figures for the company, but also seeks to tell you about broader policies regarding the environment, sponsorship, employees or equality.

The annual report will still, for the foreseeable future, be produced in full-colour, glossy hard copy. The report is one of the most expensive print items in a company's armoury. The estimated annual cost of investor mailings in the US (2000) was $17 per shareholder.[40]

The annual report is also available, from most companies, on CD ROM. Some will publish it on their websites and many produce special videos, or hold interactive conferences, to explain to staff what the results and projections actually are.

The involvement of staff is new to the last decade. Companies now spend quite a lot of money retaining well-known TV personalities to introduce a specially commissioned 'programme', which explains the contents of the annual report, and often, interviews the chief executive about particulars contained in it.

Companies recognise and value their staff and so make efforts to include them, even in the most financially fog-bound predictions so that they, in turn, act as ambassadors for the company and believe in the security (or otherwise) of their own jobs.

The Accounting Standards Board (ASB) issued a discussion paper, in 2000, entitled 'Year-End Financial Reports: Improving Communication?' The paper made a number of recommendations regarding annual reports, all of which were intended to simplify financial information and encourage the use of plain language. Among the key recommendations were the suggestion that financial statements should be brief. 'Key information should not be buried within less significant information, and reports should also be balanced and objective' and 'the overall impression created by the summary financial statements should be consistent with that which would be conveyed to knowledgeable users of full financial statements'.[41]

Annual Report and Financial Information on the Web

The ASB paper also recommended that companies should make greater use of the internet. Company sites could contain financial statements. 'Hyperlinks could be used to allow users to jump from an area to another area where the same topic is discussed. They have the potential to make it easier for readers to find the information they need within financial statements, by moving directly from a high-level overview to more detailed information or graphs on topics of interest'.[42]

In 2000, the British Government began planning changes in legislation which would allow internet delivery of annual reports and accounts and even shareholder voting over the net.[43]

Some companies are already providing detailed information on their websites. 'The site (www.nokia.com/investor/) offers the visitor an ability to adjust charts of the company's stock price performance against variable criteria; a sound archive of investor relations conference calls; fast facts for investors and the latest Nokia IR news; as well as the more usual annual and interim financials'.[44]

Of the top 100 of the Fortune 500 companies, 93 include corporate financial information on their websites. In 1997, 92 per cent of top companies in Britain had their own website, and 68 per cent of these included financial details. In the same year, 90 per cent of listed companies in Finland had websites (with 82 per cent including financials); and 87 per cent of Germany's DAX 30 companies had sites (of which 83 per cent included financial details). However, this trend is not worldwide. In 1999, 45 per cent of the top companies listed on the Madrid exchange in Spain had sites, with only 56 per cent of those including financial information.[45]

CONCLUSION

The role of the financial PR specialist is one that will continue to evolve as e-commerce develops and information is transmitted, worldwide, in seconds.

Shareholder profiles have changed. Individual investors command media coverage.

Institutional investors comment publicly. Internal publics (employees) have become shareholders. The media are more aggressive (investigative?) in their coverage of financial matters.

Trust between a company and its publics will always be an important issue. Honesty, openness and quality of information are vital. Rumour can seriously damage a company.

Management is under constant scrutiny from external influencers. Corporate reputation is paramount. Publicly quoted companies would be well advised in the future to pay even more attention to their financial publics.

Telecom Éireann — A Case Study

The flotation of Telecom Éireann is worth looking at, in some detail, because it was the first time the Irish Government sold some of the 'family jewels' and it was the first time that a major national advertising campaign to invest in shares was targeted at Joe and Josephine public.

Government Changed Some of the Board Members in Advance of Flotation

In advance of the flotation, some of the board members of Telecom Éireann were changed. The directors are appointed by Government and the first thing the Government did was review the strength of the directors in the light of the flotation initiative. These directors were eminently suited to serve on the board in previous times, but the Government felt that it needed more financial/stock exchange expertise on the board before going into the flotation in detail.

Government Rejected the Idea of Changing the Name to Eircom before Flotation

Telecom Éireann changed its name to Eircom after the flotation. It was said that the board wanted to change the name before the flotation, but the government blocked it — a wise move. Telecom Éireann was well established in the public mind, and its predecessor (Posts & Telegraphs) was long forgotten. By keeping the name, the board saved itself the huge difficulty of having to explain who the company was at a time when it was trying to sell shares. The established understanding of Telecom, the name recognition and the identity of the logo made it easier to promote the company to the public. (The change of name to Eircom was undoubtedly recommended to reflect the changes happening within the company itself, but the timing, in advance of the flotation, would probably have been wrong.)

Government Deeply Involved in Photo Calls, Speaking Opportunities and Media Interviews in Support of People Buying Shares

The Government was deeply involved in the promotion of the flotation at all times. Mary O'Rourke in particular, as the minister with responsibility, took a high profile at media events like photo calls and interviews. The Government supported the launch (obviously as it had agreed it) and threw its weight behind a campaign in support of people buying shares.

Debates raged in the media about whether or not the share price was a fair one (with many suggesting that more money could have been raised from the sale of the company). Banks and building societies seemed to support the flotation whole-heartedly, with most writing to customers offering to lend them money to invest in Telecom Éireann shares.

Advertising Campaign on TV Tapped into an 'Irishness' about the Company — a Sense of Shared Ownership (although we already owned it).

In my opinion, the advertising campaign was brilliant. It played on the 'Irishness' of the company — greatly enhanced by the visuals and music which were used in the campaign. It generated a feeling of us all being in it together — a sort of national movement to buy the telephone industry. The campaign was a great success, with people, evidently, forgetting that they already owned the company (the Government held it in trust for the people) and rushing, in sizeable numbers, to buy a piece of it.

Many of the elements of the promotion of the flotation were superbly done. The choice of music on the ads reminded us of the uniquely Irish nature of the company. The photographs used on brochures and the prospectus were visually memorable. The photos were mixed — male/female (six men, six women), young/old, people who looked Irish, African and Asian. The mix suggested a multicultural society, an inclusive society, a new world — the future of the country almost — of which Telecom was a part. The cleverness of asking people to register for details, but making it abundantly clear that they were under no obligation to buy, was perfect. It encouraged people who might otherwise have felt somewhat 'out of their league' to send for information. And the cleverest part was the 'without obligation' element which was widely promoted — no fear of someone putting you under pressure to buy just because you had enquired.

Even the envelopes reflected the corporate style of the brochures (smaller versions of the photos on the top of all envelopes). It made them stand out when they arrived through the letterbox.

A range of brochures was also produced. One explained what Telecom Éireann was (Introducing Telecom Éireann and the Share Offer). Another brochure explained the actual share offer (Mini-Prospectus).

The entire country seemed to be caught up in the buzz.

Share Price Performance

There was a downside, however. Although many bought shares, they bought without reading the fine print of the prospectus — they were caught up in the buzz (and complained loudly afterwards that information had not been brought to their attention). Many bought shares out of sheer greed. They expected to be able to sell them in a hurry and make a better profit than they would have achieved by putting money on deposit with a bank or building society. Many borrowed in order to invest — encouraged, no doubt, by the enthusiasm of financial institutions which offered funding for shares.

The shares did not perform as well as expected. Those who understood the market, and had anticipated a drop in share price, sold their shares quickly on the 'grey market' (i.e. before they legally owned them). This practice, known as 'stagging', is perfectly legal. However, the majority of the shareholders, new to the stock exchange, were dismayed and felt 'cheated'. Had they sold faster, they argued, had they even known that they could sell faster, they might not now be holding shares, waiting for them to realise a return on their investment. The low interest rates from financial institutions, coupled with the ease of getting a loan and the anticipated high return on the share price, had encouraged people to believe that they could 'make a killing', on Telecom shares. It was this that caused the greatest amount of dismay, public outcry and shareholder fury.

Shareholder fury surfaced at the first AGM of the newly named Eircom, when media coverage on television and in newspapers showed long queues of shareholders waiting to gain entry. Media coverage also showed shareholders inside the hall arguing that the company theme-song (used on all of their advertising and on their hold music on phones) — 'Your love is my love' — should be turned off because it was insulting and aggravating people. Those same media also carried scenes of shareholders publicly calling for the resignations of the board of directors, and objecting to the bonuses to be paid to directors on the basis that, if no one made money out of buying the shares, why on earth should the directors be paid a bonus for successfully launching them? Shareholders even asked about the level of investment of each of the directors in the company, and Dick Spring TD, a board member, made the news in all of the papers and on radio and TV the following day when he told the meeting that he held no shares in the company because, at the time that they were offered to him, he could not afford to invest.

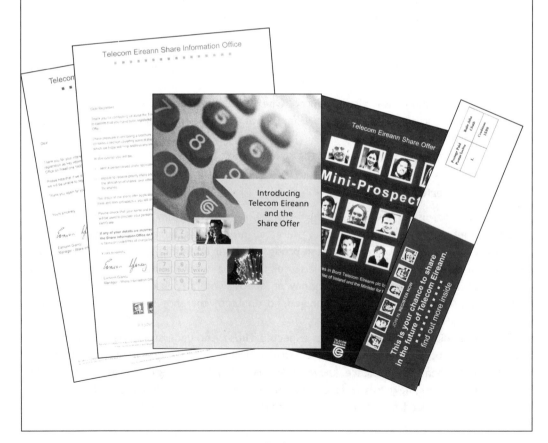

REFERENCES

1. Michael Forde, *Company Law*, Dublin and Cork: Mercier Press, 1992.
2. The Stock Exchange Act, 1995 (SEA), came into force on 29 September 1995.
3. *Strategic Financial Management*, CIMA Study Text, Stage 4, Paper 13, London: BPP Publishing, 1998.
4. Michael Forde, Op cit.
5. 'Methods of Issue of New Shares', in *Investment Planning*, course text, the Institute of Bankers in Ireland, 1998.
6. Michael Forde, Op cit.
7. *Strategic Financial Management*, Op cit.
8. Michael Forde, Op cit.
9. *Strategic Financial Management*, Op cit.
10. Ibid.
11. Michael Forde, Op cit.
12. Company Law, Education Programme, Institute of Public Administration, 1993.
13. Michael Forde, Op cit.
14. Ibid.
15. Amsterdam Exchanges (22 October 99), 'Conclusion AEX: KLM in contravention of Listing Rules', Amsterdam: www.aex.nl/scripts/nieuws in Kevin Traverse-Healy, 'Have you taken your Financial e yet?', *Frontline 21*, IPRA, July/August 2000.
16. Kevin Traverse-Healy, 'Have you taken your Financial e yet?', *Frontline 21*, IPRA, July/August 2000.
17. Brendan McGrath, 'Fyffes sues DCC over timing of major share sale', *The Irish Times*, 25 January 2002, Business this week column.
18. Colm Keena, 'Jury clears executive of insider trading charges', *The Irish Times*, 30 January 2002, Business & Finance section; Colm Keena, 'Former Dunloe chief denies insider trading charges', *The Irish Times*, 15 January 2002, Business & Finance section.
19. Colm Keena, 'Emotions high after verdict of not guilty returned', *The Irish Times*, 15 January 2002, Business & Finance section.
20. Pat Boyle, 'Kingpin deal maker who often bears fruit', *Irish Independent*, 26 January 2002, Business section.
21. Tom Goldin, 'Dot.com dottiness turns the market upside down', *Sunday Business Post*, 9 April 2000.
22. Ibid.
23. National Investor Relations Institute (1988) Definition, Washington DC, in Kevin Traverse-Healy, Op cit.
24. Pat Bowman, *Handbook of Financial Public Relations*, Oxford: Heinemann, 1989, in Kevin Traverse-Healy, Op cit.
25. Kevin Traverse-Healy, Op cit.

26. *Strategic Financial Management*, Op cit.
27. Paul O'Kane, 'Smurfit to retire as CEO in October', *Sunday Tribune*, 3 February 2002, Business section.
28. Siobhán Creaton, 'IAIM welcomes Smurfit resignation', *The Irish Times*, 4 February 2002, Business & Finance section.
29. 'Bombshell as FF deputy is named in tax scam', *Irish Independent*, 20 June 1998.
30. Elaine Lafferty, 'Investors hold nerve despite bear noises', *The Irish Times*, 14 April 2000.
31. Hamish McRae, 'Enron's legacy will be a new breed of accountant' (Independent News Service), *Irish Independent*, 24 January 2002.
32. Shane Coleman, 'Ahern steps in to repair split over Aer Rianta float', *Sunday Tribune*, 23 April 2000.
33. Kevin Traverse-Healy, Op cit.
34. Colm Rapple is a taxation consultant, author and commentator; Dr Dan McLaughlin is chief economist with Bank of Ireland.
35. Jean-Pierre Beaudoin, 'Volatility, opinion and stockmarkets — lessons of the dot.com experience', *Frontline 21*, IPRA, July/August 2000.
36. Dragon International Consultancy, 'Views from the City', research, 1993.
37. Jean-Pierre Beaudoin, Op cit.
38. Frank Mulrennan, 'Dishing the DIRT from the floor at Bankcentre', *Irish Independent*, 20 April 2000.
39. Brian Carey, 'Current still flows against Riverdeep', *Sunday Tribune*, 23 April 2000.
40. Andrew Porter, 'Whitehall wakes up to the internet', London: Sunday Business (4 June 2000) in Kevin Traverse-Healy, Op cit.
41. Cáit Carmody, 'Shareholder communication in the 21st Century', *Sunday Business Post*, 23 April 2000.
42. Ibid.
43. Andrew Porter, Op cit.
44. Kevin Traverse-Healy, Op cit.
45. Ibid.

CHAPTER 19

Political PR

It is difficult to look at political public relations as one topic. The area is so varied and so very interesting. In order to look at political PR, we need to look at four different areas — public relations for political parties, PR for government, departmental PR and political lobbying.

PR FOR POLITICAL PARTIES

The role of the public relations officer in a political party is very varied. The job encompasses a number of different information tasks. We will look at each in turn.

Creating Awareness

Political public relations officers need to create awareness of the party and its policies. The electorate needs a clear 'vision' of what the party stands for.

Since the Progressive Democrats (PDs) first formed in 1985, they have built a profile of a party which stands for law and order, fiscal rectitude and morals/high standards in government. In the period 2000–2002, their membership numbers were believed to be declining. Karl Brophy, political correspondent of the *Irish Independent*, wrote that: 'in marketing terms, the PD brand is so weak that it is incapable of carrying a candidate anywhere near Leinster House'.[1] He was not alone among commentators in holding this view. No one anticipated the electoral rejuvenation of the party which occurred in 2002.

What is the awareness of the Labour Party, now amalgamated with Democratic Left? It has always been associated with the 'working man' and the party secures some of its funding from the trade union movement. It would traditionally have been seen as 'strong' in the poorer rural and urban communities. However, the party's Dáil representation has remained quite static in recent years.

Fianna Fáil's identity is as a republican party and its members are proud of their record of achievement with the peace process in Northern Ireland. But the tribunals of enquiry will cause the party many years of suffering.

Sinn Féin had for years been associated with 'the Armalite in one hand and the ballot box in the other'. However, the party made enormous progress with the peace process in Northern Ireland, which won it much support north and south of the border.

The Green Party is clearly interested in care for the environment and conservation. However, until 2001, when Trevor Sargent was elected as leader, the party lacked a cohesion that other political parties had.

At the time of writing, Fine Gael is struggling to create an awareness of the party and its policies. Karl Brophy has written that: 'Fine Gael are becoming…dead brand increasingly dependent on small numbers of charismatic and hard-working candidates for rare successes'.[2] In 2002, under the leadership of Enda Kenny, the party began a series of meetings, discussions and a recruitment drive for new members in an effort to re-establish itself on the Irish political scene. This party, too, will be haunted by the ghost of Fine Gael's past in the tribunal investigations.

Although it is always dangerous to generalise, the public is not particularly interested in party policies. However, it is necessary for the public to have an image of the party (made up partly of policy issues) which positions it in the mind of the voter.

Personality Profiling

Party PR people also need to generate interest in their leading figures — both their leaders and the people who will be their future ministers (often current spokespersons). This is more the 'personality profiling' part of their job, but a very important part nonetheless.

This is a specialised skill in itself. You have only to look at the film, *The War Room*, to understand the communications passion, drive, determination, effort and sheer brilliance of James Carville and George Stephanopoulos as they drove Bill Clinton's presidential campaign from the first primary in New Hampshire to the victory celebrations in Little Rock almost ten months later.[3]

We are disinclined to vote for people we know nothing about. You need only look to the political past of Mary McAleese to see that. When she first stood for election (for Fianna Fáil in the Dublin South East constituency), very few people knew her. When she stood as the Fianna Fáil candidate for the presidency, however, a lot of time, money, effort and energy were spent informing people of who she was, what she had achieved, and how she could represent the country as president.

The job of the party PR person is to create opportunities to make the party leaders better known. In the case of Fianna Fáil, the party PR people have succeeded — Bertie Ahern is known, jokingly, as the man who turns up everywhere. He has commentated (on RTÉ) on football matches. He has appeared on *The Late Late Show*. He is known as a lover of and frequent attender at GAA matches. And he brings with him a reputation as a negotiator (or fixer, depending on your perspective) — the most cunning and most devious of them all, according to his former leader, Charles Haughey (1992).

Mary Harney, as leader of the PDs, is also very well known and highly regarded as a hard worker. She is not inclined to grant personal interviews. She broke out of the mould when she gave an interview to Marian Finucane just before Christmas 2000 in which she spoke of the loneliness of being a single woman in politics.[4]

Gerry Adams is very well known from his interviews, and, most notably, his auto-biography, *Before the Dawn*,[5] which revealed the 'human' behind the party leader.

Fine Gael's Enda Kenny had just been elected at the time of writing. His national profile will undoubtedly increase in the coming years.

If you move beyond the party leaders themselves, which of their leadership figures (spokespersons and potential ministers) could you name? Who is the opposition spokesperson on health, education or social welfare? The promotion of each of these different figures is indeed a difficult job for the party PR person and often involves promoting issues on which they have spoken, which may not, in fact, relate to the spokesperson's position.

Research

The party PR person also needs to provide information and research for the party. The research is often conducted by volunteers. These people work on committees, usually in the evenings, and are supporters of the party. The advantage of being in government is that you have staff available to you to conduct research. The opposition parties do not have the same facilities and therefore rely much more on voluntary help. It is often from the ranks of these voluntary helpers that government advisers are later appointed.

The research needs to be ongoing and very broad — across a wide range of issues. And the party PRO needs to disseminate the information to all members of the party — the front bench, the executive councils, the constituency bodies, and the ordinary members. It is a huge task in itself.

Support

The party PRO also needs to support local officers in each constituency — organising regular meetings with headquarters, keeping an ear to the ground locally, informing them of developments, training them in the roles and functions of the different officers, from chairing meetings, to taking minutes, setting agendas, balancing the books as the treasurer, or promoting the party as the local PRO.

They also need to provide support to local candidates at constituency level. This is most obviously done in times of election when the candidates are brought together for briefings on key issues. But the party PRO should also be involved in creating or supporting initiatives to get the candidates better known — a difficult task which the incumbents (be they sitting TDs or councillors) will be disinclined to support. PROs must provide the support through headquarters, but more importantly through the local officers, and, at the same time, satisfy their existing representatives that they are not in any way being disadvantaged by the promotion of the newcomer.

Finally, the party PRO's job also involves reaching us — Joe and Josephine public

— through these same grass-roots members (and the media) and ensuring that we have an understanding of the party. We, after all, are the electorate who decide the outcome of the next local or national election.

Internal Communications

Internally, there are various groups with whom the party PRO needs to liaise, keeping a constant free-flow of information from the PR section to the group, and vice versa. The party front bench needs to be kept informed of developments, as does the parliamentary party (made up of TDs and senators). These, at least, are relatively easy to reach as they all congregate in Dublin at regular intervals for scheduled meetings and can therefore be reached as a group.

Councillors and town commissioners are a tougher group to reach as they are spread throughout the country, often with little contact between councillors in different counties (except at the time of a Seanad election). They too need to be kept abreast of party developments and position papers, and their input is needed by the parties.

Without their input, policy would become the product of a Dublin-based think-tank, and the impact of developments on rural and local constituencies would be lost. The final internal group with whom communication is necessary is probably the largest and most disparate group of them all — the constituency officers and the party members — all of whom also need to be kept abreast of developments and each of whom can valuably contribute to party policy. They need to be kept informed of developments, by newsletters, and by occasional access to top party members (usually by arranging constituency visits by spokespersons). These are the people who go out, in all weathers, knocking on doors, seeking support for party candidates. Without them, political parties would not have any 'machine' to speak of.

These are the front line of the communications network with the electorate. Not every member of the electorate will get to meet the candidate, or sitting TD, or party leader on a visit to the constituency but, if the job is well done, every member of the electorate should be canvassed by one of these grass-roots members of the party.

HQ

Within party headquarters, the PR person needs to keep abreast of the research being conducted. Party PR people should be constantly analysing issues to see how they will be received and reported. Their skill, after all, is in deciding what the story should be, how it should be told, and how it will impact on the general public.

The PR person is also responsible for articulating policy, often in one-to-one meetings with journalists. Party PROs need to have a very good understanding of party policy to be able to explain and debate it with journalists whose job is to report on political issues. Their briefings give valuable detailed information to journalists, but also allow them to gather valuable information for the leader/spokesperson on how the policy is being received, reported, or interpreted/misinterpreted.

Internally, the party PRO will also be involved in writing speeches for the leader, and issuing guidelines for speeches for front-bench spokespersons. Often, speeches will be reviewed by the PRO before delivery, to ensure that there is no possibility of misunderstanding, or simply to include a few 'quotable quotes' for media.

Party PR people are also responsible for writing, editing, and distributing the party newsletter to all members of the party — a vital tool in keeping people abreast of the party's position on different issues. The newsletter also lets people know of older members who have passed away, or future dates for commemorative ceremonies, constituency visits, annual dinner dances, or new fundraising initiatives.

The party PR person is a key influencer at national level, interpreting, recommending, and counselling on issues and policies. The party PRO is also, in part, a troubleshooter, liaising with the various bodies, committees, constituency organisations and elected representatives in the party, and 'flagging' issues to the leadership. Party PROs are also constantly trying to involve backbenchers and others in the work of the party — partly because they are always short of bodies and partly because it allows them to gauge the strengths or weaknesses of individuals.

The PR person may also be responsible for promoting new fund-raising initiatives within the party. All political parties claim to be lacking in funds — hence the introduction of the Electoral Act, 1997, to give parties funding based on the numbers of their elected representatives.[6] While parties now declare donations in excess of €5,078 from any one individual, there are many ways in which funds can be legitimately raised from members and well-wishers, and the party PRO is responsible for promoting these ideas to members and ensuring a good up-take on the initiative.

Presentation of Party Policy

This has become more difficult over the years with personalities seeming to dominate debate. It is therefore necessary to put forward lively, capable and media-trained spokespersons to present your policies.

There will always be divisions within parties, however, and these need to be carefully co-ordinated. If the party policy is to close a number of hospitals in rural areas, for example, and open newer, bigger, better-equipped but fewer centralised hospitals, the local TDs in areas where hospitals are closing must be allowed to protest at the closure (they will not be re-elected otherwise). Thus, parties walk a thin line between policy and 'local' rebellion. The rebellion is only serious, however, when someone is expelled from the party or publicly censured. Everything else, usually, merits only a slap on the wrist — distancing the party from the individual, but allowing the individual to show the constituents that their representative 'told them in Dublin' on their behalf.

TDs and Senators

In opposition, parties need to provide platforms for the presentation of policies. The PRO must create good photo opportunities, and write timely speeches (when the leader is in a particular constituency). The opposition parties need constantly to put the government under pressure — that, after all, is the function of an opposition. They constantly generate news items about the government's poor policies, oversights, or lack of caring. The PRO needs to keep finding items in the news media (a great source of constituent thinking) which should be raised in the house as a question to the relevant minister.

Most local TDs and councillors do not need to be told that they should attend factory openings and local regattas — they do this instinctively. But they should have the help of the local PRO (guided by the party PRO) in promoting their attendance at these functions. It is often said that Irish politics is weaker than British politics, for example, because elected representatives spend so much time in their own constituencies attending functions. Yet we, the electorate, demand that they do. It is important to us that they be seen.

Interestingly, in the changing times in which we live, a lot of people will be aware of the attendance of their representative at a function only if it is covered by local media (print or radio). We all live more stressful and time-conscious lives and therefore have less time to participate. We catch the news through the media.

Media Training

In the current era it is not enough to be a good communicator; you must be seen to be one. Party PR people spend a lot of time arranging media training for spokespersons. This is vital.

Look at the way in which professional politicians use the media. Take the Rev. Ian Paisley — a master of the art of getting his message across through the media. He has been known to 'prime' camera people that he will stand up and leave the studio, by the left exit, as soon as Mr X walks in. The cameras, therefore, catch his indignant exit. It is brilliant PR.

Think of Pat Rabbitte or Mary O'Rourke — consummate media performers. They are comfortable with the media and quite unflappable under questioning. In fact, Mary O'Rourke (sometimes referred to derogatorily as 'the school marm') is known for her quick wit and cutting tongue, delivered with a girlish smile. One of her most famous comments was when Albert Reynolds, in 1992, removed many of the ministers who had served in C. J. Haughey's government. Mary O'Rourke was removed with the others. Albert Reynolds had said that he was promoting people on merit. Mary O'Rourke, on being accosted by the media who had learned of her sacking, commented, with a smile, that she had been 'demoted on merit' — a wonderful response!

Media performance or profile or lack of it affects our judgement of ministers probably more than we realise. In an article in *The Irish Times*, Síle de Valera wrote of her record of achievement in the Department of Arts, Heritage, Gaeltacht and the Islands: 'what it amounts to is solid, evidenced progress....What it doesn't amount to, in my view, is an opportunity for personal PR...I prioritise substance rather than publicity'.[7]

In my opinion, however, it is not a matter of prioritising. The public expects its ministers to work hard and have a complete mastery of their brief. But the public also needs to be kept informed of, and included in, decisions. This is, at least in part, achieved by journalists debating and writing about political issues. These debates are a vital part of the two-way flow of information, from electorate to government.

When television cameras were introduced into the Dáil for the first time, TDs were given grooming courses. They were given simple rules — like making sure that their hair was combed before they went into the chamber, and that they wore a freshly pressed suit and a clean shirt and tie. They would be seen on television in the background, and so would create an impression with the viewers.

For those great annual gatherings of party faithful, the party conference or árd fheis, think of how cleverly most of the women TDs use the opportunity of sitting on the podium for the leader's speech. Men are mostly confined to wearing dark colours — black, grey, brown — and since there are so many of them, they are inclined to blend together. The cleverer of the women make sure that they are wearing bright colours — reds, yellows, white, flashy blue — anything that makes them stand out in the group and therefore draws the eye of the viewer and gets them noticed.

Attitudes

Political parties are fighting an uphill battle to gain the genuine interest of the electorate. In years gone by, people knew, by the newspaper you read, which political party you supported. Entire families voted for the same party for generations — it was like a religion.

Now, like religious practice, dedicated voting is in decline. People are either not going to the polls (and young people are staying away in large numbers) or they are changing their vote at each election.

Politicians need to make it easier for people to vote (longer opening hours at polling stations, voting on-line, swipe cards which can be used in booths in shopping malls, and so on).

Additionally, and perhaps more importantly, they need to change the perception of politics. In the coming decade, political parties will need to apply themselves seriously to the task of winning back the interest — and respect — of the electorate.

Spending by Political Parties in Ireland

The spending patterns of the political parties reflect their level of dependence on voluntary help. Of just over €1.26 million paid in party leaders' allowances in 1999, Fianna Fáil, the Labour Party and the Green Party spent nothing on research, education, training or policy formulation. Sinn Féin spent approximately €3,200. Most of the money given to the parties went into general administration.[8]

PR FOR GOVERNMENT

Press Secretary

The most high-profile person in the PR armoury of the government is the Government Press Secretary and the role is a very powerful one. This person is close to government, abreast of the decision-making process and conscious of the internal debates about positive and negative perceptions.

Government press secretaries deal with an exclusive group of journalists — the pol corrs (political correspondents). They brief them regularly about government developments — very often in off-the-record briefings — and they control access, primarily to the Taoiseach.

They are irreverently known as national handlers, national fondlers or spin doctors. The terms are applied by the media. A government press secretary can be drawn from public relations, politics or journalism. There are two over-riding requirements for the job: the person must be able to communicate effectively, and must have the total trust of the government.

Eamon Delaney, in his book, *An Accidental Diplomat*, tells the story of Margaret Thatcher's Press Secretary — Bernard Ingham — and how he completely controlled a briefing with journalists at Dublin Castle. He allowed those media favourable to Thatcher to ask her the first questions so that, by the time the negative media were allowed to ask questions, she could dismiss them by telling them that the question had already been answered.[9]

Seán Duignan, in his book, *One Spin on the Merry-go-Round*,[10] explains how easy it is to underestimate the importance politicians place on the media. Albert Reynolds needed to be updated throughout the day on what the media were writing about, broadcasting, saying and thinking.

The briefings by government press secretaries are understood to be off-the-record — what they say is not attributable to them. Seldom does a comment of the government press secretary escape into print. P. J. Mara, perhaps the most famous press secretary of them all, was the exception. Some of his comments will survive to the next century. A colourful character, he was well liked by the national media who understood his sense of humour. He was also a vital link between his 'leader', C. J. Haughey, and the media. The media, notoriously hostile to Haughey, liked Mara. Through him, Haughey could get his point of view across. Interestingly, according to Eamon Delaney, Mara's style was not appreciated (perhaps not understood?) by European correspondents.[11]

The role of the press secretary is vital. This person tries to inform and persuade people about the government's point of view, the reasons for the introduction of new legislation, the thinking behind changes in the budget, the rationale for cuts in the health service, etc. Press secretaries are skilful and adept at using a wide range of media — TV, radio, print (national and local) — to get their points of view across.

Their job is often one of persuasion and is, therefore, often thought of more as propaganda than public relations. Their primary function is to have the government message understood and they therefore work hard at convincing, persuading, cajoling and influencing people to accept their point of view.

They play a vital role in defending the actions of their political masters. Take, for example, the statement by Albert Reynolds in which he claimed that he had been vindicated by the beef tribunal. The statement was issued by Seán Duignan and contained some dots: 'been…vindicated'. The report was issued on a Friday night, and was nearly 2,000 pages long. The media covered the story as issued by the press secretary.[12]

The relationship between press secretaries and the media is a close one. The Horseshoe Bar in the Shelbourne Hotel is famous as a meeting place for the glitterati, politicians, the government press secretary and pol corrs. Many 'nuggets' of information have been acquired in this hostelry over the years.

Finally, government press secretaries throughout the world have also been accused of using and misleading the media. They are quite capable of dropping a nugget — the government is thinking of X initiative — which is really just 'flying a kite' to see how the public will react. If the reaction is negative — and especially since the original idea came from a 'government source' and not a named individual — the minister or press secretary can go 'on the record' and deny that the government ever had any such intention.

PR FOR GOVERNMENT DEPARTMENTS

Departmental public relations is a contentious area. Many of the in-house departments were originally staffed by people who had no formal training in public relations, and had, instead, been trained on the job. These were the permanent civil servants who were given the responsibility of promoting the department and its minister.

In times past, their role was seen as a lowly one. Ministers brought in their own PR people and relied on the in-house PR staff to issue ministerial speeches. One civil servant described it to me as putting speeches on faxes all day, only to be replaced by the next speech (all 20–30 pages of it), which needed to be faxed to the same media. It was a thankless job and one not particularly valued by ministers either.

Nowadays, the role of the in-house departmental PR is very different. Staff members are usually PR trained, and are involved in writing and issuing the releases, creating the photo opportunities, advising the minister, and writing the speeches.

Although they work closely with the minister, ministers usually have their own PR person. Their function, as civil servants, is primarily to promote the work of the department, and ensure that departmental initiatives are understood by the public.

Eamon Delaney's book highlights how in-house PR people can virtually write their own ticket if they have been successful in the Department of Foreign Affairs.[13]

The departmental PR people have a deep, inside knowledge of their 'industry' be it finance, social welfare, health, etc. They are expert at knowing what has been tried before, and why it has failed, how media are likely to react to initiatives, and what timing is best. They have very close links with the media who report their area, and each gets to know the other very well over time.

As in any industry, there are differences in strengths. While conducting research for my thesis,[14] I had reason to interview journalists about the departmental PR people they worked with. While the journalists pointed to PR people in the past who were 'useless' or 'stonewallers', each of the (then) current departmental PROs they spoke about was regarded as excellent and, consequently, 'overqualified' to work as a PR person.

POLITICAL LOBBYING

One of the biggest growth areas in recent years in public relations has been the area of the political lobbyist. These are the PR professionals who understand the work ings of government and how to influence it. They are retained by corporations who wish to gain access to government, and opposition, to put their point of view and influence parliamentary opinion.

Bribery

The perception — of media and the general public — is that lobbying is inextricably linked with payments/money/bribery. This is unfortunate, and results, at least in part, from the ongoing work of the tribunals.

The Irish Times journalist, Fintan O'Toole, has written: 'The purpose of a bribe is to influence the conduct of public business in a way which will benefit the person handing over the money'.[15] If you need to pay someone to get them to agree with your point of view, you are quite simply bribing them — you are not lobbying. Lobbying, however, has nothing to do with paying people (in money or goods or holidays) in order to influence their decision.

Much has been written by the media about the PR lobbyist Frank Dunlop who appeared before the Flood Tribunal in April 2000. Dunlop was retained to lobby for the lifting of a development cap of 220,000 sq. feet on the Quarryvale development. 'Mr Dunlop...confirmed that it had involved extensive lobbying of members of Dublin County Council'.[16]

However, when the payment of monies to public representatives and others became public knowledge, we were no longer talking about lobbying. The media — once his friends — were ruthless and highly personalised in their condemnation.

Writing about Dunlop's appearance at the tribunal, the *Sunday Independent* journalist, John Drennan, said of the cross-examination: 'it was enough to destroy the dapper bumptiousness we normally associate with Dunlop…The normal supercilious tones had been replaced by a hoarse whisper…the maestro of the spin doctors visibly shrank away from the media posse….Everything he had scrambled to possess — his business, his reputation, his wealth — was being turned to dust by his own mouth. Like Michael Lowry, he is effectively at the jaws of Mountjoy'.[17]

Ethics and Lobbying

The art of lobbying is to put your argument, clearly and concisely, in order to show the inequality of a possible government/local government decision. The nature of the inequality, and how well you demonstrate it, should help the person being lobbied to understand your point of view.

What is Lobbying?

The term originated in the Willard Hotel, Washington DC, when congressmen and senators, including Abraham Lincoln, lived there. People would gather in the lobby to meet them — it was the ideal place to 'influence' or seek 'favours'.

In Ireland, we were slow to adopt the culture of the lobbyist. After all, our politicians are eminently approachable. People felt that it was easy to lobby politicians — all you had to do was go down to see them in their clinic, or meet them in the local pub, or have a word when you ran into them at a function.

Maol Muire Tynan has said that: 'lobbyists are those who are paid, often a lot of money to persuade, pressurise, influence or campaign on behalf of an interested client. Lobbying is a mixed science, using media relations, face-to-face lobbying and organised campaigns to try to shape public policy'.[18] As a definition, it works quite well, with the exception of the word 'pressurise'. If you are pressurising, you are using undue influence to achieve the result that you require. That is not lobbying.

Virtually everyone in the country has lobbied for something at one time or another. You lobbied when you signed a petition to have a bus stop removed or installed; when you joined a protest to stop trucks using a narrow road; when you carried a placard to prevent your local hospital from being closed down; when you voted as a member of the residents' association not to pay local charges; or when you joined a student protest.

Businesses, corporations, companies, charities and organisations lobby too. It is just that they do it in a more structured way.

The journalist Emer O'Kelly believes that 'the notion of lobbying as a trade is in itself dubious. After all, if a project is viable, and to the common good, there should be no need to lobby for it'.[19] However, charities lobbied the government long and hard to allow corporations make charitable donations which would be tax deductible. The charities argued that the corporations would give them more money if there was a tangible benefit — i.e. tax write-offs. It would cost the state very little, but the benefit to the charities would be enormous. Who could object to such a lobby?

Groups lobbied government to give people with disabilities greater accessibility — introduce taxis capable of taking wheelchairs, put ramps/slopes into pathways, buy buses which could drop their floors to allow wheelchairs access, and put sloped entrances to all public buildings so that those with disabilities could gain access. Is this a cause that anyone could disagree with? Yet it is a cause that would have been overlooked had no one made a conscious effort to lobby for it.

One of the most successful lobby groups in the country is the Irish Farmers'Association (IFA), and just look at all of the things that farming groups have achieved over the years! The IFA also has a permanent staff of lobbyists in the EU headquarters in Brussels, to influence European as well as Irish Legislation. They are representing farmers, on a daily basis, and looking after their interests. Anything that arises at local, national or EU level, which might impact either positively or negatively on farmers, is immediately identified and a lobby begins. It is a wonderful example of how one group of people can use the lobbying system to protect its own interests properly.

Professional Lobbyists

In the United States, lobbyists are classified in three main groups: public interest groups, trade associations and professional lobbyists. No such classification exists in Ireland, nor are lobbyists defined by law. The Labour Party published a 'Registration of Lobbyists Bill' in 1999, but no law was subsequently enacted.[20] In 2002, the Public Relations Institute of Ireland was looking at the possible introduction of a voluntary register of lobbyists in Ireland.

It is difficult to define lobbyists; often they are also PR people, although, increasingly, the lobbyist is a specialist in that area alone. Often lobbyists are people who have worked with government in the past (like Jackie Gallagher) or who have been political representatives (like Nuala Fennell) and therefore know their way around the system.

Former Fianna Fáil government press secretary P. J. Mara lobbies on behalf of companies like AerFi (formerly GPA), Esat and the Élan Corporation. Jackie Gallagher quit his job as adviser and strategist to the Fianna Fáil government and, after a short spell with Fleishman Hilliard Saunders, established his own consultancy firm with Declan Kelly. Paddy Duffy, former chef de cabinet in Taoiseach Bertie Ahern's department, and the manager of the 'communications unit', Marty Whelan, have moved to the PR/lobbying profession.

Former Progressive Democrats assistant press secretary Stephen O'Byrnes, assistant press officer Ray Gordon, and general secretary of the PDs Michael Parker have moved to corporate PR and lobbying.

Fine Gael's former press secretary, Peter White has moved to public relations and lobbying. Fergus Finlay, adviser to the former Tánaiste Dick Spring of the Labour Party, moved to public relations but returned to politics as adviser to Pat Rabbite, leader of the labour party.[21]

Public Representatives as Lobbyists

PR consultancies can also retain the services of elected representatives to lobby on behalf of their clients.

The IPR (UK) keeps a public list of all Members of Parliament who are retained by consultancies as lobbyists. There is no such list in Ireland. Members of the Dáil are required, through the register of Oireachtas members' interests, to make a declaration of interests, including any consultancy services they provide.

Personally, I have deep reservations about public representatives working as lobbyists. TDs and councillors are elected to represent the interests of their constituents — and their job certainly includes lobbying on their behalf. However, when public representatives are retained (and separately paid) to lobby, I believe that the perception of those clients for whom they work is that they are buying 'inside' services — politicians have access to other politicians in a way that ordinary constituents do not (in the Dáil bar for example). And the perception of their constituents is that their representatives are working on behalf of 'big business', and not on behalf of the people who elected them.

There are many members of the Oireachtas who offer consultancy services of one kind or another — not all, by any means, in the area of lobbying. The list of interests is wide and varied.

Dick Spring (Labour Party) lists, among his directorships, his role as 'consultant/international counsel' for Boston consultancy ML Strategies — a subsidiary of prestigious law firm Mintz, Levin, Cohn, Ferris, Glovsky and Popeo.

Richard Bruton (Fine Gael) gave advice on development policy in Kazakhstan as part of an EU project, and his party colleague, Gay Mitchell, has an occupational income from Impac Ltd.

Conor Lenihan (Fianna Fáil) has advised Esat Digifone (now O2) and Torc Telecom, and former Taoiseach Albert Reynolds is a director of Smurfit and chairman of Bula Resources.[22]

Single Issue Lobby Groups

In earlier chapters, we looked in some detail at activist groups. However, in terms of politics, lobby groups — organisations of people who lobby on individual environmental issues, for example, or seek legislative or constitutional change — like political parties, are monitored for donations.

The Electoral Amendment Act defines a political donation as any contribution 'to promote or oppose, directly or indirectly, the interests of a third party in connection with the conduct or management of any campaign conducted with a view to promoting or procuring a particular outcome in relation to a policy or policies or functions of the Government or any public authority'.

The legislation requires lobby groups to register formally with the Standards in Public Office Commission (SPOC), outlining their political objectives and goals. As of January 2002, any organisation accepting a donation of more than €127 will have its accounts audited by SPOC.

These lobby groups may not accept donations from the same person, in any one year, which exceed €6,348. With the exception of an Irish citizen, any individual who resides outside Ireland may not make donations. Nor are foreign-based groups or organisations allowed to make donations, unless they have a significant office in Ireland.[23]

While these provisions will not provide any great hardship for most groups, they will undoubtedly affect the conduct of constitutional referenda where, in the past, foreign-based or international groups were believed to have contributed significant amounts of money to influence the outcome of constitutional votes.

Key Rules of Political Lobbying

There are five key rules of political lobbying, according to Myles Tierney.[24] These are:

1　Determine the inequality;
2　Demonstrate the fact of the inequality;
3　Dramatise the issue;
4　Have it brought to decision;
5　Anticipate the recourse to principle of which there are five:
　　❏ A denial of fact
　　❏ A denial of intent
　　❏ A denial of means
　　❏ A denial of capacity
　　❏ A denial of right.

We will look at each in turn.

Determine the inequality. Is there an inequality at present? Who is being treated unfairly? How are others being treated as more equal? It is not enough simply to say that 'it is unfair to us' — life is unfair. You need to show how, and in particular, why this unfairness results in inequality. It may be that your sports organisation does not receive as much government funding, pro rata, as other organisations. Your body, therefore, has to spend much more time and effort raising funds. You are being treated unequally. Other sports organisations are receiving more money. Why? Because they are more worthy? This creates an inequality. All sports persons are not being treated equally. You have established a case which can be put to government.

Determine the fact of the inequality. How does it manifest itself? Exactly how much money is given to each sporting group? How many members does each group have? What has each group achieved over the past 5–10 years? How much grant-aid, per head, does the government actually give to each group? Start to lay out your stall; put the facts together — undeniable facts of inequality. A sports metaphor is used here, but you could equally use any change in legislation which affects corporations or organisations or individuals.

Dramatise the issue. Make it public. Get people on your side. Get them annoyed. Myles Tierney handled the lobbying by the Restaurant Association of Ireland to have the right to sell alcohol in restaurants. As part of the campaign, he introduced little cards which sat on each table in every restaurant. The cards simply said 'no Irish served here'. When people became, naturally, outraged and asked what it was all about, they were told that French wines could be served, but not Irish whiskey or beers. The campaign was ultimately successful.[25]

The farmers' groups are very good at dramatising issues by bringing sheep into the centre of Dublin city, or dumping grain outside Department of Agriculture headquarters. Groups campaigning for people with disabilities have chained themselves to the railings of government buildings in an effort to dramatise and bring attention to their issue. The gardaí had blue flu days and took to the streets in an unprecedented protest against conditions.

The object of the exercise is to highlight the issue, not only to the politicians, but more importantly to the public. Politicians seek public approval of their actions. If you can get the public on your side, get the 'constituents' of the TDs arguing that your case is a good one, then you are well on the road to seeing a resolution of your inequality.

Bring the issue to decision. Identify the person who has responsibility for the area or section in which the inequality appears and, crucially, lobby the person who has the power to change the situation.

Tierney warns about five recourses to principle which are worthy of a more detailed look.

- *A denial of fact*. You got it wrong. Your argument is built on the wrong premise or presumption. You did not do your homework. Your facts are wrong. You have no case to put.
- *A denial of intent*. The legislation was never intended to have the effect that it is having on your group. Fine. But now that we have established that this is the outcome, can we change it, please?
- *A denial of means*. Politicians accept that you have a good case, but deny that they have the means by which to change it. It would cost too much money. Times are tough. It will have to wait until there are more funds in the economy. It is unfortunate that it has happened, but the cost implications of changing it could not be justified (and by implication, would not be supported by the general public).
- *A denial of capacity*. The politicians/decision makers argue that they do not have the capacity to change the situation. Essentially, you have identified the wrong person/body. It would need to be changed at local level (not national) or vice versa.

It is a European decision, not a local one. It is not a legislative matter — it is custom and practice of the organisation which controls this area of sport, the profession, etc.

- *A denial of right.* The politician argues that you do not have the right to what you are lobbying for — usually because the abolition of your inequality will result in the creation of a greater inequality for a larger group of people. For example, legislation dictates that we, in Ireland, drive on the left-hand side of the road. You could lobby politicians that it is your right to decide to drive on the right-hand side, and that you are being deprived of your free will and choice when you are being forced to drive on the left-hand side of the road. Admittedly, this is an extreme example, but it is one that shows how a politician could agree that you are undoubtedly being forced to drive on the left-hand side of the road, and this is an inequality. However, you do not have the right to drive on the right-hand side because you would cause traffic mayhem. Your actions would most likely lead to accidents which might result in injury and death, and the exercise of your right would definitely create a greater inequality for all other road users who would be living on their nerves trying to figure out where traffic was approaching from. Your right to choose which side of the road on which to drive, therefore, would be denied.

Over the years, Myles Tierney, a former county councillor and highly respected PR practitioner and lobbyist, developed his theory on two strong premises. The first was that politicians always try to act in the Common Good, i.e. the best possible interest of each citizen. The second is that politicians always strive for Public Repose, i.e. an absence of political tension. They hate the pressure of being lobbied, or negative public attention being directed towards them. Their natural inclination is to alleviate the tension.

However, politicians also have a natural tendency to bat to base — that is, to send things off to a committee for review or recommendation. In this way, they have taken the problem off their desks, but they can honestly argue that an expert group is looking into the situation and will advise them in due course. They can honestly tell you to stop shouting, lobbying, demonstrating — as they are already doing something.

REFERENCES

1. Karl Brophy, 'PDs hail "new dawn" but life-support system still on', *Irish Independent*, 21 January 2002.
2. Ibid.
3. *The War Room*. A film by Chris Hegedus and Da Pennebaker. Downtown Video Ltd. BALF 002. Produced by R.J. Cutler, Wendy Ettinger, Frazer Pennebaker.
4. Date of Mary Harney's interview confirmed by John Higgins, General Secretary, Progressive Democrats, 10 April 2002.

5. Gerry Adams, *Before the Dawn, An Autobiography*, Dingle, Co. Kerry: Brandon Books, 1996.

6. The Electoral Act of 1997 had a donations figure of €3,809. The act was amended in 2001. It increased funding from the state to the parties, and the donations figure increased to €5,078 (£4,000). There is a link to the Act on the Attorney General website in the Statute Book page, at http://193.120.124.98/ZZA23Y1992.html. Information provided by Ben Dunne, Government Press Office, 8 April 2002.

7. Síle de Valera, Minister for Arts, Heritage, Gaeltacht and the Islands, 'Action in place of PR', *The Irish Times*, 12 March 2002.

8. Chris Glennon, 'Parties share £1m allowance', *Irish Independent*, 17 May 2000.

9. Eamon Delaney, *An Accidental Diplomat, My Years in the Irish Foreign Service 1987–1995*, Dublin: New Island, 2001.

10. Seán Duignan, *One Spin on the Merry-go-Round*, Dublin: Blackwater Press, 1995.

11. Eamon Delaney, Op cit.

12. 'Reynolds cleared by Beef Tribunal', *Irish Independent*, 30 July 1994, headline.

13. Eamon Delaney, Op cit.

14. Ellen Gunning, 'Agenda Setting: A Study of the Blue Flu', Thesis submitted in part fulfilment of the requirements for the awarding of the degree of Masters in Communications and Cultural Studies, Dublin City University, August 1999.

15. Fintan O'Toole, 'Time to ban all forms of political contribution', *The Irish Times*, 25 April 2000.

16. Christine Newman and Colman Cassidy, '£300,000 success fee paid when building cap lifted', *The Irish Times*, 20 April 2000.

17. John Drennan, 'Flattened by a glacier of titanic proportions', *Sunday Independent*, 23 April 2000.

18. Maol Muire Tynan, 'What is a lobbyist, anyway?', *Sunday Business Post*, 23 April 2000.

19. Emer O'Kelly, 'Moral integrity is for the little people', *Sunday Independent*, 23 April 2000.

20. Registration of Lobbyists Bill, 1999. (First schedule — Public Bodies. Second Schedule — Lobbyists' Code of Conduct.)

21. Maol Muire Tynan, Op cit.

22. Shane Coleman, 'How Dick Spring has embraced capitalism', *Sunday Tribune*, May 2000.

23. Karl Brophy, 'Political lobby groups facing new funds curb from today', *Irish Independent*, 24 January 2002.

24. Myles Tierney MPRII, study notes for students, PRII Certificate in Public Relations course, 1985–87.

25. Antoinette Harbourne, 'No Irish Served here — The Lobby to Allow Restaurants Serve Beer and Spirits' in Francis Xavier Carty (ed.), From *John Paul to Saint Jack — Public Relations in Ireland*, Abel Press, 1995.

CHAPTER 20

Internal PR

Internal Public Relations is a specialist area which has grown in importance since the mid-1990s. The introduction of new or amended national and international employment legislation, changes in work practices, a growing openness and transparency in relationships with employees, and the difficulty of recruiting and retaining staff will ensure that this area increases in importance in the coming decade.

A lot of the tools of public relations, used for employee communications, are also used with other publics. Some of these issues have been referred to as staff issues in other chapters — like video presentation of shares for employees (Chapter 18), or newsletters (Chapter 7).

This specialist area of internal PR is sometimes referred to as employee communications. It is found in larger companies, and it has real, tangible, measurable benefits to employers and employees.

ROLE OF INTERNAL PR

We will begin by separating internal communications from the role of in-house public relations. The in-house PR department is charged with many responsibilities — corporate image, media relations, financial PR — and internal communications. Internal communications is employee-focused — it deals with one internal public only, namely staff.

The purpose of internal public relations is to develop, encourage and promote internal communications among employees. Most large companies will already have industrial relations or human resource mechanisms in place. All will have designated structures for management/employee communication. Internal PR is separate from all of these. It does not deal with issues of salary, promotion or industrial relations. Its purpose is to generate a good flow of communications among all levels of employees.

CHANGING EMPLOYEE PROFILE

The profile of employees and their expectations has changed through the years.

Employees are no longer single-skilled. They have become what Prema Sagar, principal and founder of Genesis PR, India, calls 'gold-collar' workers. This new employee is 'a highly skilled multi-disciplinarian who combines the mind of the white-collar worker with the hands of the blue-collar employee'.[1]

The age profile of workers in some industries has also changed. In 2000, when the supermarket chain, Tesco, sought to fill 1,000 new jobs, Maurice Pratt, the managing director, stated that the company was putting 'an increased emphasis on 'grey power' and an openness towards recruiting more students and foreign nationals'.[2]

The need to work is still strong. Employment provides an income, but, more importantly, being employed 'ensures participation in a community…with the main risk associated to the loss of it being social exclusion'. However, employees are no longer satisfied with the concept of a secure job for life. Employee mobility is a key issue for employers. The workers of the present generation 'have been educated to be loyal to themselves rather than to their employer of the day'.[3]

UNSTRUCTURED EMPLOYEE COMMUNICATIONS

Unstructured employee communication, as a general rule, is inclined to be emotive rather than factual. The unofficial grapevine, which operates in every organisation, is speedy, often inaccurate and prone to gossip, scandal and rumour.

When you are dealing with internal communications, you are dealing horizontally — employee to employee communications. The purpose of internal communications is not to act as a mouthpiece for management or, for that matter, unions. The purpose is to generate staff interest in the organisation, to develop a pride in the organisation, and to increase employee morale.

STRUCTURED EMPLOYEE COMMUNICATIONS

For good internal communications, you need a skilled communications manager and a recognition, at board level, of the real value of employee communications.

It should be noted that it is a manager's job to manage. Internal communications is an additional tool in the armoury of communications within the company. It is not in any way intended to take away from a manager's duty to make decisions, to issue instructions and to see that those instructions are implemented.

Internal communication complements existing management structures by offering opportunities for explanation of decisions, by generating an esprit de corps among the workforce, and by encouraging feedback and input from staff. This is primarily — though not exclusively — done by face-to-face communications.

To Contribute to Company Goals

The ideal form of communications, always, is face to face. Employees may already have face-to-face communications through staff meetings, but these can be largely ritualistic and only marginally informative. Staff meetings — generally held to impart management decisions — are nominally consultative. They do not, however, provide an opportunity for true face-to-face communications, or real participation in the decision-making process.

Internal communications tries to encourage this more real form of communication, through, for example, informal staff groups. These groups meet to participate in the management and structure of the organisation. Their purpose is to meet the organisational goals of the company, as well as meeting the needs of each individual member. They work together in collaboration, making suggestions and recommendations for changes in work practices, or product displays, or product presentation, for example. These groups, and their suggestions, should not be confused with unions, whose role is to meet with members, represent their demands, and ensure that workers are given fair remuneration for work that is done in suitable environments.

These informal staff groups harness the knowledge that company employees have, and use that knowledge to benefit the entire organisation, including individual employees.

Induction and Explanation

More and more companies are seeing the wisdom of *explaining* the reasons for the introduction of policy issues, rather than merely communicating the fact of the change. Staff members who understand the rationale behind a decision are much more likely to support it and implement it. It is also a good discipline for companies to evaluate constantly the way in which things are done. Companies that fail to do this end up like the monkeys in 'Company Policy' (next page).

Induction sessions used to be popular up to the 1980s when they declined in significance for major companies. They are now making a serious comeback in the 2000s. The purpose of an induction course, particularly in very large companies, is to give the new employee a 'feeling' for the organisation they have joined, and how it works.

Induction sessions, usually done in small groups, are intended to introduce the employee to the company. By video, PowerPoint and personal presentation, employees are given a history of the company. They are introduced to the founding fathers, the original plant, the first employees and the company's range of products at that time. The history of the company brings them right up to date by giving them an understanding of the development of the company down through the years.

A graph or schematic of the company structure can also be explained. How is the company run? How many divisions does it contain? Are they all based in one city or spread throughout the country? Is the company Irish-owned, foreign-owned, or part of a multinational organisation?

Within each division, what does the division do? How many people work in that section? How does their job interlink with the rest of the company (it is easier to do a job if you know its value to the end product).

Is the company a publicly quoted company? Is there an employee scheme for purchasing shares? When is the annual general meeting held?

New employees learn a little about the board of directors — who they are, what their backgrounds are, how long they have been with the company. They learn about the company's history and vision for the future.

Finally, induction sessions also give new employees an opportunity to develop an understanding of the market: the products the company produces and the customers to which it sells.

Company Policy

Start with a cage containing five monkeys. Inside the cage, hang a banana on a string and place a set of stairs under it. Before long, a monkey will go to the stairs and start to climb towards the banana. As soon as he touches the stairs, spray all of the other monkeys with cold water. After a while, another monkey makes an attempt with the same result — all the other monkeys are sprayed with cold water. Pretty soon, when another monkey tries to climb the stairs, the other monkeys will try to prevent it. Now, put away the cold water. Remove one monkey from the cage and replace it with a new one. The new monkey sees the banana and wants to climb the stairs. To his surprise and horror, all of the other monkeys attack him. After another attempt and attack, he knows that if he tries to climb the stairs, he will be assaulted. Next, remove another of the original five monkeys and replace it with a new one. The newcomer goes to the stairs and is attacked. The previous newcomer takes part in the punishment with enthusiasm! Likewise, replace a third original monkey with a new one, then a fourth, then the fifth. Every time the newest monkey takes to the stairs, he is attacked. Most of the monkeys that are beating him have no idea why they were not permitted to climb the stairs or why they are participating in the beating of the newest monkey. After replacing all the original monkeys, none of the remaining monkeys have ever been sprayed with cold water. Nevertheless, no monkey ever again approaches the stairs to try for the banana.
   Why not?
   Because as far as they know that's the way it's always been done around here.
   And that, my friends, is how company policy begins.

Company Policy

Employees also need to understand company policy. What are the policies of the company; why were they introduced; how are they implemented? Employees (like consumers) are keenly interested in the company for which they work. They want to know that the company treats its staff well, has a good industrial relations/human relations policy, and that the company has a pro-active environmental policy.

They need to understand EU regulations or legislation which impact on their business. They need to know that the company is operating to best-practice standards which are nationally or internationally recognised.

They should be told of any awards the company has won — or has entered for. They should know of initiatives the company is planning to undertake (within commercially sensitive limits, of course).

GENERATING GOOD COMPANY SPIRIT

If employees are more mobile, less 'loyal' by nature, and more inclined to seek to make work part of their life, then companies need to work harder to generate good company spirit. Employees need to make connections with each other through societies, outings, newsletters, family days, open days, children's Christmas parties, social occasions, and awards schemes.

Companies are offering employees internet access also, as a means of keeping in touch. The US energy company, Georgia Power, introduced universal access to the internet for all of its employees after an evaluation of non-inclusive practices within the company. The evaluation found that traditional white-collar workers had internet access, but employees who worked in power plants and as field representatives did not.

The plan, called 'The Outlet', gave every employee their own e-mail address. The company created 175 new kiosk workstations in 115 sites located throughout Georgia and involved more than 1,700 employees.

According to Lisa Frederick, supervisor of internal communication for Georgia Power, the programme 'helped Georgia Power's non-white-collar workers feel valued and connected'.[4]

INTERNAL PR MEDIA AND TECHNIQUES (TOOLS)

There are many techniques and tools available to the internal PR specialist. The staff newsletter is one obvious tool. Many companies — particularly large manufacturing companies — have electronic notice boards in their factories with constantly changing news updates. Some companies use ideas schemes — offering awards or rewards to employees for coming forward with good ideas. Others have speak-up days, where the managing director, head of personnel, etc. are available to take an employee's call and deal with any issue they care to raise (this is mostly used in the United States of America).

Internal PR tools include:

- Clubs and societies
- Functions for staff families
- House journals
- Ideas and awards schemes
- Induction literature and training
- Internet access
- Meetings with company executives
- Notice boards
- PowerPoint presentations
- Staff conferences
- Staff events
- Speak-up schemes
- Staff meetings
- Videotape presentations.

APPLYING THE TOOLS

The following example shows how a breadth of PR tools was used, successfully, in employee communications. (This real-life example won IPRA's Golden World Awards for best overall public relations campaign of 1997, as well as for the best employee communications programme.)

Two of the world's largest aerospace companies, the Boeing Company and its arch-rival, McDonnell Douglas, decided to amalgamate in 1996.

Because the merger negotiations took place unannounced and over a short period of time, no action could be taken on employee communications until after the initial public announcement, which was made on Sunday, 15 December 1996.

Following the announcement, intensive research was undertaken to measure employee reaction. Information packs were on the desks of managers on Monday morning, for sharing with all workers. Twenty-one employee focus groups were held, and all reported that employees of neither company were ready to work together as a team.

In the seven-month period from the announcement in December 1996 to July 1997, an intensive communication programme, directed by eleven transition communications teams, was introduced. Every medium, from company publications to websites, was used.

Following completion of the merger, information packs, containing videotapes and brochures, were delivered to all 220,000 employees' homes. Special events were arranged to give employees an opportunity to hear directly from the merger leaders Phil Condit, chief executive officer, and Harry Stonecipher, chief operations officer.

The two men also toured the United States in a five-day period, visiting thousands of workers in fourteen cities, walking production lines, shaking hands, signing autographs and answering questions.

More than 176,000 employees gathered at special events to hear from Phil Condit and Harry Stonecipher, and 150 employees, each with a guest, were flown to Washington for an employee-only 'Town hall' meeting.

The benefits of implementing this strategy were obvious one year later. Staff numbers had increased by 18,000, morale was high, and the merged company revealed sales of $45.8 billion — almost $10 billion greater than the sum of what the companies had recorded separately in 1996.[5]

BENEFITS TO EMPLOYEES

The benefits to employees are virtually self-evident. The creation of a better working environment leads to more pride in the work, and more pleasure in working. Employees know that they are respected and valued. Their input is welcomed and heeded. They feel closer to the employer and therefore more loyal. Their working life has been recognised as an important part of their entire lives.

BENEFITS TO MANAGEMENT

There are real and tangible benefits to a company in having good internal relations, which possibly outweigh the benefits to employees. The most obvious one is that a happy workforce will have fewer days' uncertified absences. This, in itself, is a commercially viable reason for employee PR.

Staff retention rates are also higher if there is a good atmosphere and communication levels among employees are good. This makes sense from a company's perspective. It costs more money to employ and train new people continually than it does to put communications structures in place which encourage the employees to stay.

Good employee communications also brings less tangible benefits. It spreads the good name of, and goodwill towards, the company, which may help in recruiting future employees. It usually generates positive community support for the company, as a lot of employees will live in the local community.

Good internal communication, generating a better quality of working experience, leads to increased productivity, fewer quality-control problems, lower absenteeism, greater customer satisfaction, and more recommendations and referrals. Conversely, poor internal communications leads to poor motivation, boredom, and an increase in quality-control problems, absenteeism, etc.

Douglas McGregor, in his book, *The Human Side of Enterprise*, 'proved that to truly succeed, companies must cultivate an organisation that is built on enduring relationships with its employees'. He suggested that 'what people are actually looking for is challenge and interest, and that the task of management is to maximise commitment and liberate their ideas and abilities....Knowledgeable employees offer superior service and...are becoming an increasingly important source of business advantage'.[6]

In addition, national parliaments are beginning to focus on the role of the employee, and limit the downsizing capabilities of companies. 'Just weeks after Michelin announced simultaneously higher profits and job cuts in the fall of 1999, the French parliament passed legislation putting new constraints on profitable companies wanting to reduce employment'. The growing focus on social issues across Europe 'is signalled by the fact that the European Commission is thinking of formulating a directive demanding from companies initiating any merger and acquisition project that they develop a "social report" as binding as the "financial report" currently required by the equity markets'.[7]

The power of the consumer must also be taken into account. A study by SWR, Weber Shandwick's research arm, revealed that 'aside from price and quality, how a company treats its employees is the most important factor for consumers when they make a decision to purchase a product'.[8]

Companies have also recognised the power of influence of their employees over customers. Dawn James calls these employees living, breathing brand builders.

At a time of industrial unrest in BA (1997), she took a shuttle from Manchester to London. 'The stewardess spent most of the fifty-minute flight...telling me how unhappy all the employees she knew were; that they all disliked working for the airline and that in her opinion the management were a complete shambles. I don't know how much BA spent with its advertising agency Saatchi's that year...but it was largely wasted in my judgement. The company would have been better off spending the money on a decent employee communications programme which got the staff first to understand and second to involve them in solving the problems' she wrote. According to Martin George, director of marketing and communications with BA, the company has since placed a special emphasis 'on improving communication with both union representatives and the broad range of British Airways employees'.[9]

REFERENCES

1. Prema Sagar, 'The Need to Nurture Talent and Add Value', *IPRA Frontline Magazine*, March 2002.
2. Jamie Smyth, 'Tesco boss tapping into "grey power" to fill job vacancies', *The Irish Times*, 14 April 2000.
3. Jean-Pierre Beaudoin, 'The Vocabulary of Labour', *IPRA Frontline Magazine*, March 2001.
4. Anne Deeley, 'Bringing in the outlet', *IPRA Frontline Magazine*, December 2001.
5. 'The Employee Factor in Success of a Mega-Merger', *International Public Relations Review*, June 1998.
6. Prema Sagar, Op cit.
7. Jean-Pierre Beaudoin, Op cit.
8. Dawn James, 'Living, Breathing Brand Builders', *IPRA Frontline Magazine*, December 2001.
9. Ibid.

CHAPTER 21

Public Consultation

Public consultation is quite new to Ireland.[1] It is the process by which government or local councils seek the input of the people in advance of introducing any new infrastructural arrangements in their area. While the examples used in this chapter are based on macro projects like the Dublin Transportation Initiative (which covered Dublin, Wicklow, Meath and Kildare), it is worth pointing out that public consultation is also used for micro projects like a village development plan by a local council.

Public consultation — government of the people by the people — is not exactly a new concept, but it provides a new role for public relations practitioners, and is a new departure for the state.

The EU could probably take the credit for the introduction of the initiative. Because of the breadth of EU funding available for infrastructure projects, and because of the country's dire need for infrastructural improvement, it was only natural that Ireland, like every other Member State of the Union, would seek its fair share of European funding.

The European Union was not about to throw money at any project, however. It was mandatory that people be consulted in advance, to establish the need for each infrastructural change, to give them an input into the way in which those changes would be implemented, and to seek their consent for the final plans.

Further — and more importantly from a PR practitioner's point of view — the EU insisted that the proof of consultations, inputs and consent, be laid before people for inspection. It would not be good enough merely to state that the people had been consulted; it would be necessary to show how the consultation process was handled.

This is a job for a communications specialist. The EU required that a communications system be put in place and opportunities be offered to people to make an input. Those inputs needed a response; the response was to be brought back to the people; and their consent was to be sought for the implementation of the proposals. This is pure public relations.

The budget for public consultation is 1 per cent (usually) of the total budget for the project. If you think that the national development plan currently has an allocation of €51 billion (£40 billion) for infrastructure projects, that means that the consultation element is valued at €510 million (£400 million). That's a lot of PR spend.

The EU focus was on infrastructure, but it was also on people. There was a consciousness at EU level that any infrastructural change would affect people, farms

342

and communities, and the funding bodies wanted to be certain that the changes were being introduced with the people's consent. However, because the consultation process is so detailed, delays in the implementation of infrastructural changes can amount to decades! This may lead to a change in approach in the future.

There is a school of thought which argues that decisions should be taken nationally, by central government, in the best interests of the majority of citizens. Only after a decision has been taken should an inquiry be held to deal with the concerns and objections of affected communities. In other words, the local democratic participation would be reactive, and would kick in only after the decision has been taken.

However — back to the present!

PUBLIC CONSULTATION COMPARISONS

Britain and Ireland suffer from the same problems when it comes to the development of major infrastructural projects — problems different from those of our continental neighbours.

Geography plays a part, if only because building big infrastructural projects in empty spaces is far easier than building them on a crowded island.

Infrastructure projects take a long time to plan in western countries because of consultancy requirements and environmental issues. But planning regulations are more protective in Ireland and Britain. Property densities and values are much higher than in France. The compulsory-purchase regulation is much more difficult to use than in France.

France

All big projects are driven by the French government and developed through state-controlled companies. This makes fund raising simpler since taxpayers take on the financial risk. Concessions are also often made to allay local misgivings, even if it adds to the cost. With plenty of spare land, France has been able to proceed swiftly with projects.

Spain

All major construction projects are initiated by central government and although local authorities and lobby groups are consulted, it is the public interest that prevails. As a result, Spain is being equipped with a road and rail network that is the envy of Europe.

Germany

As a federal country, key planning decisions do not have to be referred to central government for approval. Each case is treated as a regional issue. A process of political and public discussion is usually adhered to, and construction is monitored closely.

The Netherlands

The Dutch government periodically produces its own guidelines on planning policy to help those taking decisions at regional level. Large-scale national planning decisions take far longer to agree upon; so although it took twelve years for work to begin on a fifth runway for Amsterdam's Schipol Airport, an extension of the terminal building took less than a year.

WHY SHOULD PROPOSERS CONSULT?

Not only are proposers required by legislation to consult, but it is in their interest to consult with the broader community, primarily for four key reasons:

- To make more information available to the public;
- To listen to a wider range of interests;
- To obtain more and better information from the affected parties;
- To be more responsive to what is heard.

Public consultation is important because it allows the proposers to make information available to the affected public. The provision of information, in advance of a project planning application or commencement, should also significantly reduce the number of objections at the planning application stage.

Consultation enables the proposer to listen to a wide range of interests. No matter how much research is done in advance, no one body can expect to understand fully the perspectives of all of the local communities or interest groups that might be affected by the proposals. Genuine consultation allows the proposers to find out what the concerns are and, where possible, to address them.

The proposers also get more detailed and better information from the affected parties. The more they know, the better they can address the issues.

Finally, it allows the proposers to be genuinely responsive to what they have heard and to make a real effort to address the grievances or concerns of their publics.

WHAT CAN CONSULTATION ACHIEVE?

A well-designed and well-implemented programme of consultation can achieve a number of goals which benefit the regulating body, the proposer, and the business and residential communities. It can:

- Contribute to higher-quality regulations
- Identify more effective alternatives
- Lower costs to business and administration
- Ensure better compliance
- Help speed regulatory responses
- Improve credibility and legitimacy of government action
- Win support of groups involved in the decision process
- Increase acceptance by those affected.

A well-designed and well-implemented programme can contribute to higher-quality regulations. Issues may be raised which could be dealt with by 'local agreement' but which the proposer might feel should be incorporated into binding regulations which will serve to help future proposers to address these particular concerns.

The proposers will also be able to identify more effective alternatives. Every proposal must, by its nature, begin with an outline. But an outline merely provides the foundation for a discussion. Issues raised at meetings or by submission give the proposer an opportunity to look at alternative approaches — sometimes more effective, sometimes more cost-effective, sometimes more costly (but better for the community) — which they can implement.

A good consultation process can also reveal ways in which changes can be implemented which will make compliance by business and administration relatively easy. The consultation can prevent needless additional costs being incurred by businesses and administration. By dealing with the interest groups, it is possible to look at, for example, the impact of road widening on hauliers. This, in turn, may lead to adopting an approach which would minimise disruption and additional cost to those hauliers. There will be disruption in order to introduce anything new, but if the disruption can be kept to a minimum, and specifically structured to suit affected bodies, the cost and inconvenience to business can be minimised.

Everyone likes to be consulted about changes in their local community or business behaviour. If the consultation process has been true, and has taken your concerns on board, you are more likely as a business or private citizen to support the initiative and comply with it. It does not really matter that your problems have been solved. What matters is that someone tried to solve them, explained to you why they could not be solved in the way that you had wished, and secured your consent for the solution adopted.

Early identification of a problem, particularly a problem that will affect a broad sweep of the community, can happen and the problem be addressed without waiting for the consultation process to be complete. If it is obvious that the introduction of new regulations would make the implementation of the proposal better for the entire community, the proposer can begin to work on that almost immediately.

One of the greatest benefits of the public consultation process is that it improves the credibility and legitimacy of government action. By being involved in the decision-making process, members of the public feel that they are a part of it (as they are). This in turn gives greater credibility to the plans introduced by the government or local authority. It also gives legitimacy to their actions. People have been consulted, and their views and opinions have been listened to and then responded to. In theory at least, everyone now agrees that this is the fairest approach to the project, which all agree is necessary. This legitimacy, in turn, reduces the level of negativity towards the disruption which will inevitably happen when the project begins.

Public consultation also wins the support of groups involved. Their support means that they have, in effect, become a voice in favour of the project. They are more likely to explain why disruption is happening than they are to take to the streets and protest against it.

Finally, it goes without saying that there is an increased acceptance of the project by the communities involved.

CONSULTATIVE APPROACHES

We will look, in the first instance, at the broad sweep of consultative approaches which are relevant to public consultation initiatives. Later we will look at the implementation of these approaches, as adopted by the Dublin Transportation Initiative.

Among the key approaches are:

- Publication of future plans
- Informal consultation
- Circulation for comments
- Public notice and comment hearings
- Advisory bodies
- Complaint/ombudsman procedures
- Use of information technologies.

Publication of future plans allows people to see all of the phases of a development, not only the current one under discussion, but, arising from that, what phase two or three will involve. Informal consultations with key opinion leaders will be ongoing, and will help to guide and influence the final decision. Circulation of information for comments is important. Circulation of reports of local community meetings should encourage feedback and further comment. Allowing people a forum, usually through public meetings, in which they can discuss the proposal, is also important. These meetings or discussion sessions should be widely and publicly advertised.

Advisory bodies also need to be consulted as these represent groups of people with common interests. Advisory bodies would range from the Chambers of Commerce to the Institute of Engineers of Ireland to residents' associations. Those involved in the consultation process should also be aware of any other forum in which they can make their point of view known, from whom they can request further information, or to whom they can complain. If there is a role for the office of the Ombudsman, then participants should know under what circumstances the Ombudsman should become involved. Finally, it is almost self-evident to say that all forms of information technology should be incorporated into any plan which seeks to make information as widely available as possible to the affected communities.

ELEMENTS OF PUBLIC PARTICIPATION

The consultation process itself must have clear goals and rules. One of the goals must be to encourage as much open participation as possible. Another goal would have to be a recognition of the obligation on government or local authority to account for its use of the citizens' input (i.e. how were the recommendations or objections of the citizens dealt with?) The rules might well involve details of the numbers of meetings to be held in each area, and the length of time between the meeting and publication of a report. All of the goals and rules also need to be made known to the public.

Eamon Brady[2] of Luas lists five key elements of public participation, namely:

- *Publicity*: building public understanding/support
- *Public education*: disseminating information
- *Public input*: collecting information
- *Public interaction*: two-way communication
- *Public partnership*: securing advice and consent

Publicity is used to build public understanding and support. Public education allows the organisation to disseminate information. Public input is the collection of information from the publics involved. Interaction is the basic tool of PR — a two-way flow of communication — and public partnership involves securing the consent of the public for the proposals.

Publicity

Publicity, used to build public understanding and support, includes advertising, public relations, direct marketing, research, exhibitions and public meetings.

Public Education

Public education involves the dissemination of information. At all times, information must be:

1 *Complete*. Information that is unfavourable to the proposal cannot be excluded, nor can elements which the proposers do not favour be 'overlooked'. All of the available information must be put before the people.
2 *Objective*. The information must contain third-party analysis of the options available, or the cost implications. The information cannot seek to lead people in a particular direction — it must objectively put the case for and against, and allow the public to decide.
3 *Reliable*. The information must be from reputable sources. These sources should be named and the dates of their research given. Every statistic given or costing outlined must be referenced back to a source.
4 *Easy to find*. If, for example, information were made available only on the internet, thousands of members of the relevant publics might be excluded — hence the very wide range of media used to disseminate information, reaction, proposals and decisions to the publics.

Public Input

Public input involves the collection of information from the publics involved, and the compilation of this information, area by area, meeting by meeting, to build a complete picture of public response and reaction to the initiative.

Public Interaction

Sufficient time must be allowed for the citizen to participate in the process. This means allowing enough time to give adequate notice of meetings and exhibitions; allowing sufficient time during meetings for all views to be aired; and allowing time after the meetings for people to return with further feedback.

Public Partnership

The time must also be flexible enough to permit new ideas and mechanisms to be integrated into the policy-making process. There must be sufficient time for engineers and technical people to review, evaluate, cost and integrate new processes and approaches into the project. If members of the public have put forward good ideas, there must be sufficient time, within the system, for the technicians to make those ideas become a reality.

It might also be necessary to allow time for legislative changes or amendments to policy regulations to allow the ideas to be implemented.

PUBLIC CONSULTATION — APPROACHES

Seán O'Connor,[3] a PR consultant who worked on the DTI public consultation programme, outlined the key approaches which were used. These included:

- Advertising
- Seeking Submissions from Interest Groups
- Newsletters
- Public Meetings
- Direct Mail
- House-to-House Visits
- Websites
- TV/Video
- Schools Visits/Promotions
- Database of Community Groups/Opinion Formers
- Public Representatives
- Freephones
- Local/National Print Media
- Local/National Radio — debate
- Exhibitions
- Freepost

- Public Office
- No Agenda — must show all options.

Advertising

Advertising is widely used at all stages throughout the process, in local and national press, radio and, in some cases, television.

Advertising is used to promote and encourage attendance at local residents' meetings, to tell people where plans may be viewed, and to encourage people to make submissions for consideration. It is also used to tell people the outcome of the consultation process.

Seeking Submissions from Interest Groups

Each public consultation process must seek submissions from interest groups. These groups vary from residents' associations, representatives of people with disabilities, commercial institutes and Chambers of Commerce — anyone, in fact, with an interest in the proposed development.

Each must be contacted and encouraged to make a submission about, for example, the changes they see as necessary or unnecessary; the routes they feel that a proposed rail or road development should follow; or the likely impact on residents or shopkeepers.

Newsletters

Newsletters are a widely used and, in my opinion, widely read tool in the public relations armoury of public consultation. Newsletters may be produced on a regular basis to update people on developments in advance of the decisions and, possibly more importantly, after the beginning of the implementation phase.

The Dublin Docklands Development Authority is a particularly good example of an organisation which produces newsletters on a regular basis and distributes them, door to door, within its catchment areas.

The newsletters contain information about future developments within the area and local initiatives like sponsorships, a local art competition around the theme of the docklands, or the uptake on third-level education offers within the area.

The newsletters are A3 in size and produced in full colour. They are well laid out, and, as a consequence, well read.

Public Meetings

It is important that people living in local areas are given an opportunity to voice their concerns and this is best done at public meetings. At these meetings, neighbours have an opportunity to come together and discuss the development. They can highlight their fears and have them either allayed or taken on board for the future. They all share a common interest, as they work or live in the area. In most cases, people will know each other, so an informal, neighbourly, community atmosphere prevails.

The organisation of public meetings is difficult. There is no database, for example, of all of the local groups in any area. Some of the Dublin Corporation community officers have names and addresses of chairpersons and secretaries of residents' associations, but it is a huge task for the PR person to put together a list of every voluntary and representative group in one, small community area. Each of these groups must be contacted, and they, in turn, must be given sufficient time to contact each of their members.

Advertising in the local media will help to promote the meeting, but pro-actively approaching people, explaining the reasons for the meeting and encouraging their attendance, is vital.

At these public meetings, members of the local community are joined by the initiative's representatives who put their case for the project and listen to contributions from the floor. Local and national public representatives for the area will also be invited to attend. And, of course, a chairperson must be found to conduct the meeting.

It is best if the chairperson can be appointed from within the local community. You need to choose wisely — the meeting will be a disaster if the chairperson is poor at the job — but a local chairperson also adds a community feel to the meeting. It is far nicer to have someone say, 'Mrs Murphy has a point she wants to make,' than to hear the chairperson say, 'The woman at the back, in the black coat, wants to make a point.' It is a small detail but an important one.

Public representatives will provide a lot of help and assistance in putting together the database of names and addresses of the officers of local organisations whom you should contact. They, as a separate group, may need the courtesy of a private showing of the presentation which you will use at public meetings in their areas. However, because the public meeting provides public representatives with a platform within their constituency, they can tend to speak for far too long, or make too many contributions.

Because you also require information to be presented in the same way at each meeting, and because these meetings will be held throughout the area (necessitating more than one presenter), it might be best to produce a video which can be shown. This ensures that the information is imparted in exactly the same way to each of the groups. Printed material — a brochure, for example — could also be distributed at the meeting. This brochure could give the key statistics and facts (costs, number of houses involved, length of time for the developments, etc.) as well as serving as a reminder of the key points of the video.

Direct Mail

Direct mail, addressed to each homeowner or occupant (information available from the electoral register), can also be used within the area. However, door-to-door drops may prove equally as effective and more cost-efficient.

Direct mail can certainly be used very effectively to keep the key influencers abreast of developments. Members of the Dáil, Seanad, local corporations and councils, interest groups like IBEC or ICTU and professional bodies will all appreciate a regular mailing with details of the developments as they occur.

House-to-House Visits

House-to-house visits by trained interviewers, working from pre-designed question-naires, can also be a very useful way of getting feedback. This feedback may differ in some ways from the feedback received at the public meetings.

Public meetings, by their nature, are inclined to attract the 'activists' within the area. They are perfectly entitled to attend and put their point of view but they are often so well versed in the business of meetings that they can tend to discourage other members of the public from participating. House-to-house meetings allow you to get a 'personal' impression of the proposals and their impact. In their own homes, people may (and very often do) tell you things that they would not voice at a public meeting. Moreover, researchers will tell you that if you ask people what they think their neighbours think (rather than what they themselves think) you may get a much more accurate response.

House-to-house meetings can be very time-consuming. It is necessary, in the first instance, to get an answer at the door — not always the easiest thing to do in an era where people work long hours, and may have deliberately installed spy holes and intercom systems to shield them from unwanted visitors. Having got an answer at the door, it is often necessary to make an appointment. People are much more inclined to co-operate with you if you ask them to nominate a time that suits them. Few people will make themselves instantly available for questioning. An appointment also allows people time to think about the project, and you therefore get a more reflective, thoughtful input.

Websites

It would be difficult to imagine any campaign, in the western world, in the twenty-first century, which does not have a website. The number of people with access to the web is large and growing, and it is another means of communication with an audience. The website must be advertised so that people know where to find it, which means that it must be promoted at the end of the video, and on all advertising and printed leaflets which are distributed throughout the campaign.

The website allows you to show clips from the video, putting the key points of the presentation. It allows you to outline the rationale behind the drive and identify the key people involved. It can list the forthcoming public meetings, or exhibitions, and encourage attendance. And, of course, the website must contain an e-mail facility, which allows people the opportunity to contribute their thoughts and feelings about the project.

There are two things to note here: (1) the website must be kept fully up to date, and (2) all e-mails should be responded to — even if it is just an acknowledgement of receipt. People like to know that their voice, input, or opinion has in some way been recorded.

TV/Video

Perhaps the greatest benefit of video is that it allows the public to visualise new concepts like modern trams on the streets of Dublin. Although a lot can be done in print, video and DVD give the consultant an opportunity to animate the concepts, and thus bring them to life for the viewing public.

We have already touched on the usefulness of video for the public meetings. The video can also be sent to interested parties to view at private meetings, or at council or committee level. And, of course, video can be distributed to the schools.

The role of television, particularly in a national campaign, is also vital. This involves not only advertising on television, but, more importantly, using PR tools on TV. It involves training spokespersons, finding opportunities for them to be interviewed, encouraging documentary programmes to be made, or making them yourself for broadcast.

Schools Visits/Promotions

Every good marketer knows the value of the influence of children. In his book, Bill Cullen tells the story of his grandmother selling fish on the street.[4] When families bought from her, she always gave the children a lollipop. This gesture ensured that the next time the children were out shopping with the parents, they brought the parents to buy fish (so that they could receive the lollipop). Also, one of the greatest complaints from parents is that TV advertising, especially in the pre-Christmas season, puts them under pressure from their children.

However, from the perspective of a public consultation programme, the involvement of children is crucial. They will, of course, involve their parents — although, in this instance, they are highly unlikely to influence them. Visits to local schools can provide opportunities to give leaflets and information. Competitions for children — art competitions, essay competitions — encourage them to think about the impact of a tunnel under the water, to visualise what a tram might look like, to study the history of bicycles, or simply to tell you about their vision for the future of their area.

Database of Community Groups/Opinion Formers

Putting together a database of community groups and opinion formers is time-consuming and fraught with difficulties. Even if you manage to get hold of a list, the chances are that the list will be out of date. Clubs and associations hold annual meetings at which the officer positions (chair, secretary, treasurer, etc.) are filled. Although the roles often seem to revolve among three or four key people, in many cases they are filled by new people each year. And there are always new organisations emerging.

Think about any local community or village and try to count the number of sports clubs, old folk's clubs, parent and toddler groups, voluntary bodies, residents' associations, and environmental bodies. Then try to add to these all of the opinion formers in this small area — the parish priest, local minister, rabbi, members of the Garda Síochána, teachers in the local schools, publicans, the post master/mistress, the local chemist, and others. The list would be very long indeed! Try multiplying that by the number of such communities spread throughout, say, the greater Dublin area, and you have some idea of the size of the task that needs to be undertaken.

Remember, also — the person you forget will cause you the greatest grief!

Public Representatives

Public representatives need to be involved. Local representatives (city or county councillors, town commissioners), non-elected local representatives (self-styled, selected by a political party to run in the next election), and national representatives (TDs, ministers or senators) from within the area must all be invited to attend each of the local meetings.

Freephones

It was always thought that freephone services were a great way of giving citizens an opportunity to participate in the public consultation process. Certainly it meant that anyone, irrespective of their economic status, could phone with their input or enquiry, or could check details of a meeting or the progress of developments.

However, controversy about the freephone facility in late 2001, with horror stories of people ringing freephone lines and leaving them jammed for hours, may well cause a change, over time, to lo-call (or low-cost) numbers instead.

Either way, the idea of being able to put your query to someone at the end of a phone line is a good one and should be incorporated into every public consultation programme.

Local/National Print Media

Local and national media will be widely used throughout the consultation process. Both will provide opportunities for interviews, feature articles outlining the plans, and graphics showing proposed routes.

Local/National Radio

There are people who gain most of their 'news' information from radio. Debate on radio (whether local or national) allows people to hear both sides of an argument and to listen to the pros and cons on each side. The value of participating in discussions with Joe Duffy, or Gerry Ryan, or any of the broadcasters on local radio, cannot be overstated.

Again, from a PR perspective, it requires that you set up the interview or debate opportunities, and train your people to participate.

The media, of course, can also be used to highlight a series of public meetings, to give live or edited footage from the meetings, or to promote the winners of school competitions.

Exhibitions

Exhibitions bring the proposals to life. An exhibition allows the public to view the changes in context. Mock-ups can be used to show where roads will run in relation to current housing, to allow people to gain a perspective on the size of a development, or just to get a really good idea of the finished project and how it will impact on the quality of their living environment.

Freepost

Freepost addresses (the snail-mail equivalent of the web address) can encourage people to write to you with submissions or comments or queries. Freepost cards can be included in door-to-door drops and newsletters, encouraging people to send away for more information about the project.

Public Office

You might also consider the possibility of opening a public office, manned by trained and qualified people who will be available to deal with enquiries over a public counter.

No Agenda

The most important thing to remember about public consultation is that you are consulting — openly, honestly, and with no agenda. You are not trying to win people over to your opinion — you do not actually have one. You should, of course, lay out all of the options before the people. For example, the Dublin Transportation Initiative would have shown people a number of options including widening roads to create dual carriageways, pedestrianising areas, introducing trams, cycle lanes, a rail system under Dublin, tunnels, flyovers, bus lanes, etc. It is your duty to bring these possibilities alive to people so that they clearly understand their options. But you must not, under any circumstances, seek to influence the outcome.

City planners will have certain preferences. Engineers will have valid objections to certain suggestions because they are not technically feasible. But no one may decide, in advance, what the outcome will be.

The EU monitors carefully to ensure that people are given an almost blank canvas on which to paint, and they will withdraw funding if there is any suggestion that the consultation process was in any way directed towards a particular outcome.

DUBLIN TRANSPORTATION INITIATIVE

The Dublin Transportation Initiative (1988–95) was the first major exercise in Ireland in public consultation.[5] It broke all of the rules of PR pitches as well! Unlike most pitches, where a few consultancies are invited to tender proposals, the DTI contacted just about every consultancy in Dublin, possibly in the country. And again, unlike the usual response from consultancies, just about every consultancy attended the briefing session. Everyone knew that this was going to be one of the biggest contracts ever awarded. Every consultant probably also suspected that there would be others like it in the future, and developing an expertise in this area could be a wise, long-term business strategy.

The DTI was followed by major public consultation projects for the Dublin Port Tunnel and Luas. It is now commonplace for major projects to have a public consultation element to them, although the size of the project usually determines the level of public consultation.

The Luas Tram

Lessons Learnt

The DTI was the first public consultation project undertaken in Ireland. A number of lessons were learned from it, which helped, in turn, to shape future consultation programmes.

Special Interest Groups Can Dominate

One of the things that people had not anticipated was the dominance of special interest groups at public meetings. The special interest groups, who had their own agenda, participated in each of the public meetings held to discuss the DTI options. This was their right. They were perfectly entitled to do so. But their presence at every meeting, in every community in the city, probably skewed the reports of these meetings in some ways.

In particular, the groups representing people with disabilities used these public meetings very effectively. They attended every public meeting and their wheelchair-bound representatives always took the front row at the meeting. They were passionate about their cause, and articulate in expounding their needs. And they, undoubtedly, influenced the DTI. Their agenda was access for the disabled — buses and taxis which could be used by people in wheelchairs (which also, of course, benefits the infirm and the old). Theirs was a cause with which few could disagree. And they succeeded in putting their issue on the DTI agenda. However, from a DTI perspective, the weight of their influence at each meeting probably greatly outweighed their influence within each community.

Their approach was a clever and legitimate one. In fact, if you were the PR consultant advising people with disabilities, this is a strategy you would advise them to adopt, and you would celebrate their success on completion of the meetings.

However, because it was not anticipated, it posed reporting and statistical problems.

Community/Interest Group Databases

The development of databases which covered community and interest groups in Dublin was also greatly underestimated. No one really anticipated the amount of time, effort and energy involved in assembling, inputting and cross-checking community databases. There is still no central, publicly available database of community groups in the country.

Local Content/Message Vital

The importance of your message having a local context could not be overestimated. It is one of the primary rules of PR that you should make your communication relevant to the group you are addressing, but it is an added pressure if you are organising on behalf of a group like the DTI. Consider for a moment the time and presentation implications of adopting this strategy.

You are trying to put the options, for the greater Dublin area, to a public meeting in Ringsend. The people there are conscious of certain issues — the East Link Bridge; Pearse Street as one of the main arteries into and out of the city (through Ringsend); the narrowness of Ringsend Bridge; the impact of additional traffic on old housing stock.

Now visualise a meeting the following evening in Ballyfermot. None of the Ringsend issues are relevant to the people of Ballyfermot!

Yet, in both cases, the overall job of the meeting is to secure input on the plan for the greater Dublin area. It gives you some idea of the amount of research, and the targeting of presentations, necessary to do the job well.

Getting agreement and accurately recording all opinions expressed at public meetings can be extremely difficult. The nature of a public meeting is that all sorts of issues will be highlighted. Many differences of opinion will emerge. There may be consensus on one particular element of a plan — that no one wants a road to be widened which causes a row of cottages to be lost — but, across the broader span of issues, it is difficult to reach any form of agreement.

The report of the meeting must reflect the divergence of views, and possibly try to quantify the level of support for each view as expressed at the meeting.

Time-wasters

It is a sad fact of life that time-wasters are also attracted to public meetings. We have all seen them in action — people who have nothing better to do with their time than attend meetings and listen to the sound of their own voices. They may be against a proposal at 7 p.m., in favour of it at 7.15 p.m. and against it again at 7.30 p.m. They thoroughly enjoy being on their feet, making points, whether relevant or not. Every community has them and, if you watch a meeting carefully, you can actually see people's eyes glaze over when the time-waster rises to speak. However, time-wasters are entitled to be there.

The only good counter measure to time-wasters is a good chairperson. In fact, the only way to achieve anything from a meeting is to appoint the right chairperson — someone who is capable of allowing everyone the space and time to put their point of view, but who also has the ability to shorten someone's contribution, encapsulate the key points made and move the meeting along to ensure that a full agenda is covered.

Access Issues

It is important that public meetings are arranged at a time which best suits the community — usually evening time when businesses are (mostly) closed and residents are home from work. There is another issue of transport, however, which needs to be addressed. It is important that an evening meeting does not exclude any members of the community. Arranging transport to and from a meeting ensures that less mobile people have an opportunity to attend, and have a safe (and reliable) mode of transport.

Minority Groups

We briefly touched on this issue already when we were looking at the compilation of databases. It is important that minority groups be included in invitations to attend meetings and make submissions. These groups are often harder to find, categorise, and detail on a database than others. While most will know who the chairperson or secretary of the residents' association or senior citizens' club is, fewer will know who the chairperson of the local autistic children's group is, for example.

Engineers/Officials May Need Training in Advance

Engineers and technical people are specialists in their own fields, but they are not trained communicators. In order for them to be enabled to put across their point of view, in a way that is easily understood by those attending meetings, it will probably be necessary to give them media training.

We all use the language of the business we are in. Technical jargon slides easily into our normal speech and we do not even notice it — usually because those with whom we are speaking share the same knowledge.

When you attend a public meeting, however, it is very important to recognise that while some of those in attendance may be familiar with engineering or technical terms, most will not. So, in addition to preparing a presentation for each of these specialists to make at the meetings, you may also need to ensure that they are trained in the language to use and the actual skills of making a presentation. They might even need to undergo question-and-answer sessions in preparation for dealing with contributions from the floor.

The purpose of having specialists attend the meeting, after all, is to give the attendees an opportunity to get the benefit of their input. You have gone to a lot of effort organising a meeting. It will all be wasted if the technical information imparted serves as a barrier rather than an aid to communication.

Technical Matters Need to be Made Simple

One of the greatest benefits of using video, PowerPoint or printed material is that it gives you an opportunity to put the proposal before the people visually. In the same way as exhibitions bring the concept alive, good and clever use of graphics, cartoon sequences or mock film footage will bring technical details (like tunnelling under ground, removing telephone or electricity cables, etc.) alive for those with an interest in the issue.

Dedicated Staff and Lots of Filing Space

Public consultation contracts require the involvement of many staff-members on the PR side. The professionalism and dedication required are enormous. People are needed to handle the media aspects, to look after the video and print-material productions, to organise the exhibitions, to plan the specialist interest groups and public meetings, to book the halls and buses, to record what happens at the meetings, to write up the reports, and to file and categorise all of the comments received through the public offices, freephone services and e-mails. People are needed to set up the media interviews, arrange media or presentation-skills training, monitor media coverage, and rectify inaccuracies. It will also, probably, be necessary to have a member of the team who understands the technical details of the project — possibly a specialist employed, on contract, by the consultancy.

Demanding on Staff

There are particular time demands on staff, especially when it comes to the organisation of, attendance at, and reporting from public meetings. The nature of any public consultation contract is that the consultation must be completed within a given time-frame. Public meetings, especially because so many need to be organised, are often arranged on nights following each other, or with a gap of one night between meetings — after all, you can hold meetings only on evenings from Monday to Thursday (people would not attend on a weekend evening).

This puts enormous pressure on staff-members who have, in most cases, worked a full day in the office, before leaving to attend a public meeting. The following day, they need to filter back the information and get the report written before attending another public meeting that evening or the next. The reality is that there are only so many people who will be available to handle public meetings, and this element of the work is particularly exhausting and time-consuming.

Venues for Meetings/Exhibitions

Because of the very local nature of the meetings to be held, it is often difficult to find suitable venues. There is no problem if your meetings are being held city centre — there are numerous hotels available. However, when you move to smaller local areas, where you are looking for the use of the local community centre, rugby club or CYMS hall, the organisation of the hire of the venues and the provision of refreshments can be a problem.

Writing Reports

Writing up reports of each of the meetings is a major undertaking. Each meeting should probably be recorded for accuracy. But the nature of a report is that it encapsu-lates the key presentations, points raised from the floor, issues of hot debate and areas of agreement. It cannot be a verbatim transcript of the meeting because it would be too long, and far too difficult to discern the key points, and not even the European bureaucrats have that amount of time available to them!

So, the report needs to represent, fairly and accurately, the points raised, the counter-arguments put forward, the mood of the meeting, the level of representation of local groups, the numbers attending, the rough proportions of those in favour of and against certain proposals. This report is a well-crafted, professionally written doc-ument, which will be studied, acted upon, and reacted to, and will form the basis of the next communication with that individual community. There is no point in asking people for their opinions if you do not revert to them with responses to the issues they have raised. Remember too that these reports will also form part of the overall report issued to Europe, and will become, in themselves, historical documents. They cannot be written quickly.

Environmental Impact Study

It is often a requirement when introducing a proposal for a project that an environmental impact assessment/study be undertaken. The results of this study must also be presented to the public by all of the communications means available to the PR consultancy.

Public Representatives, Interest Groups and the Media

Public representatives and interest groups can unbalance the process via media, very easily, very unexpectedly and with devastating consequences. The nature of public representatives is that they seek to reflect the views of their constituents (not to lead them). If feelings in a local area are against a particular proposal, the local representatives may use their right to exercise their own concerns, through the media, to that community. The difficulty with this (and they are perfectly entitled to do it) is that it might serve to get people thinking negatively (or positively) about a proposal before a presentation has ever been made to them. This skews the content and outcome of the public meetings and makes genuine public consultation more difficult. Similarly interest groups may also use the media to unbalance the agenda.

Few Case Studies — Growing Business

One of the difficulties arising from the newness of the public consultation process is that, until now, there have been no case studies available, or books written on the subject, or training courses for PR people in how to tackle this growing, and profitable, area of public relations. Public consultation processes are undertaken through the EU and will be even bigger business in the future.

PR Person Needs to Understand the Key Technical Matters

Not only the 'outside expert' but also the key public relations executive must take the time to immerse themselves in the technical issues and develop a full understanding of them. It would be virtually impossible to participate in public meetings, or brief journalists, if the PR person did not fully understand all details of the project to be introduced.

Project Managers Often Do Not Understand the Role of PR

Project managers often do not understand the public relations approach, and, of course, the PR person also needs to educate the client. Government and local authority bodies often do not understand fully the need for PR, the need for the consultation to be so detailed, or the nature and value of the PR tools used. These things need to be explained to the client — often after the contract has been signed — in order to secure everyone's full co-operation with the implementation of proposals, and to make sure that they fully understand their role in the process.

Getting it wrong means a loss of millions of euro. It is in everyone's interest to get it right.

REFERENCES

1. Public Consultation is covered in the Local Government Act of 2001.
2. Eamon Brady has been involved with the Luas project since its inception. He developed the public consultation process for the project while with Bill O'Herlihy Communications. He is now publicity manager with the Railway Procurement Agency, which has the responsibility for the Luas system and the development of Dublin Metro.
3. Seán O'Connor was the lead consultant on the DTI and Luas Public Consultation process. A former senator, he has worked as a public relations professional in the Middle East, Europe and Ireland since 1980. He is currently researching a post-graduate thesis at DIT, on Sport Marketing.
4. Bill Cullen, *It's a Long Way from Penny Apples*, Dublin and Cork: Mercier Press, 2001.
5. Dublin Transport Initiative, final report, see: http://www.epe.be/workbooks/tcui/example10.html

CHAPTER 22

International PR

One of the biggest growth opportunities for western corporations, and in turn for PR people, is in the developing countries and the emerging markets of Eastern Europe. Major corporations are looking to the developing world to generate growth in product sales which they could not hope to generate in the first world. They are looking to the former communist countries (and many are already there) to provide them with a lower-cost labour base, a hub from which to supply the European market, and a new product base. The western market is well tapped — although corporations continue to refine and redefine their products in order to get us to trade up and change constantly.

The real growth area, however, is in the as-yet-untapped developing countries. Some of the major American companies — Coca-Cola and Pepsi, in particular — have already made substantial inroads into these areas.

The key public relations opportunities are in the food, tobacco, motoring, energy, banking, pharmaceutical and agricultural industries.

ROLE OF PR

The main job of the PR person in developing countries is to inform, educate, create understanding and spread knowledge — usually to prime the market in advance of or during a sales period. We will deal with each in turn.

Inform

In developing countries, information campaigns play a huge role in health care — everything from healthy-eating campaigns to contraception.

In Cuba, on arrival, you are struck by the number of posters showing healthy happy people at work. The message, presumably, is that as a Cuban you are lucky to live here and are doing well — a message which, in some respects at least, is at odds with reality.

In Jamaica, some years ago, the most popular rap song played on every radio station, had the words: 'Respect the man who comes home at night, respect the man who has only one wife'. If it was not part of a public campaign to prevent the spread of AIDS, it should have been.

Educate

PR people play a huge role in education in the developing world — actually explaining to people what a product does, how it can help them, how it should be used, and what benefits it brings to them or their children. There is no point in introducing a range of multi-vitamins into a country which does not have a tradition of taking tablets and where a PR campaign has not been initiated to inform the locals of the benefits of these tablets.

Similarly, the introduction of western cars into Cuba will necessitate a huge information campaign about the range of cars available, and the changes in engine structure (it will be sad to see the decline of the old American saloon cars in Cuba, but it will happen when the market eventually opens). There will be a need to re-educate mechanics who, for in excess of twenty years or more, have needed to repair only two types of car — the American saloon and the LADA (known fondly by the Jamaicans as the Life And Death Association).

An environmental awareness campaign in Mongolia would be difficult to undertake. Food scraps, empty bottles and the like are automatically thrown onto the wide-open spaces of the Steppes and left there. It is not that the Mongolians are dirty — just that there is so much space, litter doesn't cause a problem. The campaign would need to begin by creating an understanding of the issues before you ever progressed to implementing preventative measures.

In China, you could spend a fortune on a 'be safe' campaign, but to no avail. Beijing is a city in which handbags are not snatched, people are not mugged, and it is safe to walk the streets at night. In a safe climate such as that, try selling house insurance!

There are other issues of which PR people should be conscious. The lack of good drinking water in sub-Saharan Africa is now legendary. But these countries also need to attract tourists and their money. The tourism industry needs to be particularly conscious of the use of water (in every hotel in South Africa, you will find notices about the re-use of towels or not using running water when brushing your teeth). While this practice has spread somewhat in Western Europe, it has particular relevance in Africa.

Create Understanding

Information campaigns are not confined to developing countries, but they are a huge part of the role of the PR person there. Think of the amount of communications undertaken by the British government for the original introduction of pensions, and imagine, in any of the developing countries, how much time, effort and money it would take to introduce a similar campaign nowadays.

Spread Knowledge

Look at the vast sums of money being spent to prevent the spread of AIDS in developing countries, and the very low level of success these campaigns are achieving. Local knowledge, and respect for local customs, are vital if you are to introduce a campaign.

In Zimbabwe, for example, very few people marry before they have had a child. It is widely and implicitly accepted that the fertility of both partners should be established before a marriage is entered into. And the number of wives a man has reflects his social standing — he is a seriously respected member of the community if he has three wives. Three women, and their children, all living in the same compound, depend on him for financial support. How do you introduce into that culture the notion of no sex before marriage or protected sex?

PRACTISING PR

To practise public relations successfully in developing countries, you need to have a respect for cultural difference, a local knowledge, and, as in everything else you do, you need to behave ethically.

Cultural Differences

There is a need for a deep, locally based, source of information about culture — otherwise you are introducing a western solution, based on western values, into a country that does not necessarily share those values, will not understand your message and, as a result, will not give you the desired outcome.

The situation in Afghanistan in 2000 highlighted to the world the role of tribal leaders, the respect in which they are held, and the sheer numbers of them throughout the country. After the collapse of government in January 1991, the war in Somalia was between rival clans and sub-clans. Trying to introduce any campaign, no matter how well meaning, without first paying the tribal leaders the respect of informing them, and, more importantly, getting their imprimatur on the venture, means that you are doomed to failure.

In many developing countries the communications infrastructure is simply not in place. There is no widespread access to e-mail, for example, which most of the western world takes for granted. There are poor telephone lines, which are used for business or personal calls of a very urgent nature. The telephone does not sit in every room in the house. There might be one in the local village. Similarly fax machines are in very short supply, so the speed at which you can communicate is often phenomenally slower than in western countries.

There is also the issue of who is the messenger. If you need to send people to speak with communities, the people you choose, how you choose them and where they go to makes a huge difference. You often cannot send a member of one tribe to speak with members of another. So the sheer number of people you need to train becomes enormous. The return is much more worthwhile, but the initial investment is costly and time-consuming. Arab, Asian and Latin American countries are high-context cultures (i.e. the meaning of the message is, to a large extent, conveyed by the situation and the sender–receiver relationship). Northern Europe and North

America, by comparison, are low-context cultures (i.e. the face value of the message gives it its meaning).[1]

There is also a difference in language, and in the interpretation of meaning. Something that is clearly understood by members of one culture may cause great confusion when relayed to a member of another. And, of course, even when you are all using the same language, there is the way in which that language is used. The US style of communication has been described as boring, uptight and conservative — some call it 'prissy'. The perception of communications issuing from the Pacific Rim countries is that it tends to be conservative and respectful in style.[2]

There is also the issue of how you portray your message. Do you use western faces on billboards; or local faces? It is not as simple a question as it seems. Again it is based on cultural perceptions. Do the people of that country/region look to America and the west? Would it enhance your campaign that westerners are seen to endorse your product? On the other hand, would it be seen as insulting to the local population — and somewhat arrogant — if all of the faces had blond hair and white skin? There are deep-rooted cultural issues which need to be resolved.

The assertiveness and equality of women is another example of cultural difference. In Thailand, women's demeanour is submissive (this is not to say that the women are, but their demeanour is). It is difficult for a man to do business with an assertive western woman — the whole notion is alien to him.

In Hungary, some years ago, I spoke of the BMW as a car of 'status' that people wanted to be seen driving. It said something about the fact that you had 'arrived' that you could afford to drive this car. I was surprised by the reaction I received from the assembled group as I had seen BMWs since my arrival. It was only later that I was informed that it was a very different type of businessperson who used a BMW in Hungary.

In some countries, it is important that you work with the church or churches. Some countries have a tradition of faith and look to spiritual leaders for guidance about a campaign. In others, religious practice is not an issue and you would be creating additional and unnecessary layers in your campaign if you included the clergy.

There are also cultural sensitivities of which you should be aware. The Saami People of Northern Finland object to their traditional clothing being used by the Tourist Board in tourism promotions. Their permission was not sought, and they believe that the practice is exploitative. They have likened it to cultural imperialism by the tourist board.[3]

The journalist, Hafizur Rahman, queried the value of foreign expertise in Pakistan, in a witty and thought-provoking article in which he contrasted American and Pakistani cultural differences. He contrasted the fortunes of US presidential candidate Gary Hart who 'had to drop out of the race for the US presidency when his intimate connection with a show biz girl became known', with Sardarji, a Sikh candidate in East Punjab, who was 'caught in the act with a woman of easy virtue'. His political opponents tried to make capital out of it, but Sardarji was having none of it.

Undaunted, he announced that he would address a public meeting on the matter. 'All the world turned up to hear what excuse he would make. Sardarji made no excuses. Instead he boasted brazen-facedly about his exploit as an act of male macho, saying that if he got the opportunity he would do it again. Thunderous applause greeted this ultra-masculine confession'. As the author rightly points out, it is difficult to imagine any western consultancy giving the candidate this advice![4]

Literacy and Oramedia

Language is also an obstacle. In many of the developing countries there are multitudes of different languages, and different dialects. The problem of translation, and of being clearly understood, multiplies by a factor of hundreds.

There is also the problem of literacy. In developing countries, literacy levels are low. If messages are written, how many people will be capable of reading them? And, even if they are, how widespread is the distribution of media? Do newspapers reach people on a daily basis? In how many newspapers would you need to secure coverage in order to achieve even 50 per cent coverage of the country? And that 50 per cent coverage reaches only a small percentage of people who actually read newspapers.

In Ireland, years ago, the power of the storyteller was well known, and the art of

---

Oramedia

Making a Drama out of a Crisis
by Marie O'Halloran

The message is blunt, direct and in dramatic form. Free shows in schools, market places and wherever people meet, tell a story with the anti-AIDS warning, 'change your behaviour'.

The tale is of a father and son, living in the same home. Unbeknownst to each other, both of them are sleeping with the maid.

The son is a 'man about town', with three or four girlfriends. One of his girlfriends hasn't yet slept with him. He proposes marriage and then pleads, according to a translation of the drama: 'We have been in love for the last two weeks, why don't we have sex?'

She responds: 'We are in the modern society, we don't have sex before marriage and we have to be screened for HIV before marriage'. So the son gets screened and turns out to be HIV-positive. He confesses to the father: 'I have committed sex with many girls, including the servant. So please excuse me, I have done wrong'.

'You have AIDS and you slept with my servant,' asks the father, who collapses. He has realised he probably is HIV-positive as well. The maid, in the background, hears the revelations and realises that she, too, is most likely positive. It is a disaster. They are all HIV-positive.

But the message at the end of the drama is 'having HIV doesn't mean the end of life. You can live if you take care of yourself. We have to tell others and teach them to change their ways'.

Dramatic presentation is one of the most effective ways of getting a message across in an area where 70 per cent of the population is illiterate. The message reflects 'the Dawn of Hope', the name of an organisation of people in the Ethiopian city of Bahir Dar, who are living with HIV/AIDS.

Source: *The Irish Times*, 28 January 2002.

---

storytelling was highly regarded. In the developing countries, it still is. They do not have television sets in their homes, so people relate stories to each other: of olden days, of things they saw on a visit to town, of people they met. This is oramedia. An opportunity to attend a meeting or a function in the locality will get much greater attendances in rural areas of the developing countries than it will in cities. It is an opportunity for the community to meet together, hear something new (irrespective of what it is) and debate it for some time to come. For a good example of oramedia, have a look at 'Making a Drama out of a Crisis'.

Films, shown by mobile cinemas (often a screen mounted on the top of a van) are another popular means of communication in countries with poor literacy. Showing a film creates an 'occasion' for people to meet and socialise, and gives a visual and aural message to those attending. (Mobile cinemas are not confined to developing countries either — Leitrim County Council also operates one![5])

Local Knowledge

Public relations in developing countries will be successful only if undertaken in conjunction with a local agency or, at a minimum, with local expertise. No matter how many books you read about a culture, they will never fully prepare you. You need someone, locally based, who can bring you up to speed — at a distance and in situ — about the simple things you might do which would cause lasting offence or be completely misinterpreted.

In Zimbabwe, my host brought me into local communities to meet the people. Everyone who met him smiled at him and clapped their hands. By contrast, I shook hands with everyone to whom I was introduced. After the second meeting, I asked my host if I should be clapping hands instead, and he explained that I should not. People clapped their hands at him as a mark of respect — he was highly regarded within the community. If I clapped at everyone I met, I would be giving them a status they had not earned, and, at the very least, would cause confusion.

In Mongolia, it is customary to offer a guest some snuff. The snuff bottle is always passed with the left hand — it causes great offence if it is passed with the right hand.

Local Public Relations Practice

In Greece, PR has either a confused, blurred image or an unreliable and unrespectable one! Major companies are interested in PR and in acquiring the services of PR people, but their understanding of the value of public relations is confined to publicity (mostly for brands) and networking.

Advertising agencies in Greece now call themselves 'Communications Consultants' and it is they who handle the weightier (and more profitable) areas of public relations, like Corporate Communication Strategy, Corporate Identity, Corporate Image, Corporate (Institutional) Communication, Political Communication, and Social-Cultural Sponsorship.[6]

The Irish Academy of Public Relations has been involved in training in Hungary where public relations is still relatively new, but growing quickly. Hungarian PR people believe that the future of public relations in their country lies with the newer PR tools: WEB PR, NET PR and on-line PR. Hungarian practitioners use an e-group (called MPR list) to exchange ideas, questions and offers of business.[7]

In Nigeria, like Greece, the advertising industry was the first established and is still the more favoured method of spending by major corporations. Public relations is growing, however, but will need to establish itself, and its measurability (in terms of results achieved) before it can really be widely accepted.[8]

Local Media

The practice of public relations in Russia made international news in 2001 when the local Moscow custom of paying cash for editorial — *Zakazukha* in Russian — became an item of debate in the PR community. *Zakazukha* is the 'accepted' policy of media requesting payment to print news releases. The practice became news when Pomaco, a Russian PR consultancy, held a press conference to announce the result of having sent out a fictitious news release to the Moscow media, concerning the opening of a new store. The press release attracted *Zakazukha* offers from sixteen media, thirteen of whom were eventually paid to run a story about the opening of a non-existent company at a non-existent address.

While it was the Russian media which attracted this attention, it should be noted that this practice is not unusual in many of the countries emerging from communist regimes. Media, used to covering government propaganda, regard any commercial information as a form of advertising, and believe that they are entitled to charge for publication. Dr Alexei Sitnikov, President of Image-Contact public relations in Moscow, points out that: 'it is important for Westerners to understand that many people here do not yet grasp the concept of a free press, and believe that everything has still got to be paid for'.[9] The practice, frowned upon by professional PR practitioners throughout the world, is, however, widespread. In March 2001, Alison Tipping of Comm Direct PR wrote of issuing a press release to the British media 'and no fewer than 10 trade publications said they'd love to publish providing we paid between £60 and £120'.[10]

There are two other points which should be made in relation to *Zakazukha*. The first is that a number of colleagues have questioned the difference between paying for editorial (unacceptable) and paying for colour separations in trade press (acceptable). 'Why single out Russia — what is the difference of the trade and technical media practices, common in the UK, USA, continental Europe and many other places, of providing "free editorial" with advertising or advertorials, or photocaption stories in exchange for colour transparency costs?'[11]

The second is that clients sometimes assume that payment is needed. In Denmark, editors have been approached by CEOs of major companies seeking corporate profiles and offering leading daily papers money for getting the lead story in a human resource column. The cases were turned down, but it reveals a need for greater client education as well![12]

Different media restrictions also operate in different countries.

In Zimbabwe, the introduction, in 2002, of a law limiting the freedom of the press makes it virtually impossible for an independent (national or foreign) press to report on events in that country.[13]

In China, the authorities have blocked access to many websites, including a number of key foreign news organisations such as CNN, BBC, the *Washington Post* and *Time* magazine.[14]

The difficulty of communicating effectively through media (or other means) is increased when you look at the cultural diversity evident in one country alone. In South Africa, there are 28 distinctly different ethnic groups and eleven official languages. Each of these groupings and languages represents a very different value system.[15]

Ethics

The developing countries have disproportionately large numbers of young people. Theirs is not an old culture — and you can be quite 'old' at 50. The youth provide a huge market for products — everything from football jerseys to soft drinks to the music industry. Developing countries also provide new and expanding markets for just about every type of product you could imagine.

Unfortunately they also provide opportunities for less ethical companies to dispose of products which are past their sell-by date, to sell paints which are now banned in EU countries, to test products, or to dispose of product which would not be of a high enough standard to sell in the west. Not only do PR people have to behave ethically, but companies do too. And every PR person needs to decide for themselves if they believe that the company for which they are working is an ethical company or, rather, is ethical in the developing world.

Mary Robinson, then UN High Commissioner for Human Rights, was interviewed on RTÉ's *Late Late Show* in January 2002. She spoke of her desire, in the future, to promote ethical globalisation: 'One of the issues that we have to look at in a more deep and thoughtful way, a reflective way, is that part of the threat of what we call "globalisation" is a cultural threat....So part of what I am interested in is looking at ethical globalisation...to value cultural diversity, to respect, to not want globalisation with an American, Coca-Cola, McDonald's flag on it, which is what is greatly feared.'[16] She said that society, and business in particular, had a vested interest 'in working together to shape the ethical foundation of a new globalisation that ensured respect for the human rights of all'.[17] 'Our task is to ensure that the promises globalisation holds for fostering higher standards of living and more open and inclusive societies are realised for all people,' she added.[18]

And there are wider issues for consultancies to handle. Hill & Knowlton was retained by Kuwait to generate American interest in the Iraqi invasion of that country.[19]

INTERNATIONAL PR

If you are handling an international public relations campaign, you will find it easier if you divide by segments: Ireland and Britain; pan-European; pan-language e.g. Spanish; pan-regional — e.g. Arab; and by media — e.g. trade press only.

Seán O'Connor,[20] who delivered a guest lecture to my Dublin students in November 2001, identified the key issues as follows:

- Time zones *v.* target markets *v.* target media
- Cultural issues — do not offend
- Translation — takes time and much is often lost by direct translations
- Media structure and culture
- Means of expression — avoid using Irish/local expressions
- Currency — Euro will help in explaining costs
- Technology level of different markets (many do not use internet yet)
- Work culture — can be different from ours — watch deadlines
- Embargoes — often do not work on a pan or global campaign
- Budgets — can be affected by currency changes
- Monitoring — can be difficult
- Local PR operative — build relationship with this person
- Media queries — if possible, let a local handle these — language and relationship reasons
- Key publications — even if you can't read the language, ask for copies of these to view style, photo content, etc.
- Stories — look for a local angle — photos always work best
- Formats required by media — check — TV and photos.

For international events, he recommends paying particular attention to the following:

- Accreditation system
- Quality of suppliers — avoid being let down on the day
- Advance visit — recce
- Local language systems
- Awareness of local customs
- Advance knowledge of media needs
- Care in mixing nationalities
- Flights — avoid jet lag and tight schedules — arrive early
- Event management — visas, etc.
- Local language press kits if required
- Filter system for interviews if required because of numbers

- Good local advice — vital
- Photos/video for your own reporting/files.

PUBLIC RELATIONS MEDIA

The public relations media in emerging nations differ slightly from the media available in the western world. Obviously, you will use press, radio and television. Bear in mind that the press may be read by only a small, educated, cultural élite within the country; radio may be widely listened to, but only if batteries are freely available; and television may be the preserve of the wealthy or hotel population.

Cinema is a useful medium — both fixed and travelling cinema — particularly for documentary films. It also overcomes literacy problems and benefits the practitioner who knows that people remember more quickly what they have seen and heard, rather than heard or seen only.

House journals are an extremely useful tool, particularly if paper is in short supply. Journals may be kept for many years and used as a teaching aid. Journals also provide a long-term source of reference, particularly if clear and easily understood graphics are used in them. The same rule applies to boxes of product — clear graphics will prove to be of much greater assistance than paragraphs of text.

Exhibitions are another useful tool in the PR armoury, once again overcoming the literacy problem. Finally, do not forget oramedia — the power of the spoken word can be the greatest asset of all.

REFERENCES

1. CERP Conference, Copenhagen, October 1996.
2. Tracy Shilobrit, in IPRA Digest, no. 162, 2001.
3. IPRA World Congress, Helsinki, 1997.
4. Hafizur Rahman, 'Image Building', in 'Zia Islam Zuberi', *IPRA Digest*, no. 88, 2001.
5. 'Mobile cinema is popular', *Sunday Business Post*, 20 January 2002.
6. Thalis P. Coutoupis (Greece), in *IPRA Digest*, August 2000.
7. Tamás Barát (Hungary), in *IPRA Digest*, August 2000.
8. Andy Odeh (Nigeria), in *IPRA Digest*, August 2000.
9. Jacques Dinan, in *IPRA Digest*, no. 76, 2001.
10. Alison Tipping, in *IPRA Digest*, no. 76, 2001.
11. Peter L. Walker, in *IPRA Digest*, no. 76, 2001.
12. Katrine Steen, in *IPRA Digest*, no. 76, 2001.
13. Reuters, 'Harare curbs on press', *The Irish Times*, 1 February 2002.
14. Miriam Donohoe, 'China adopts new laws curbing access to web', *The Irish Times*, 19 January 2002.
15. Michael de Kock, in *IPRA Digest*, no. 163, 2001.
16. Mary Robinson, UN High Commissioner for Human Rights, speaking on

The Late Late Show in an interview with Pat Kenny, 18 January 2002 (RTÉ 1).

17. Frank Kahn, 'Teach good business rules, academics told', *Irish Independent*, 19 January 2002.

18. Christine Newman, 'Robinson advocates "a new globalisation"', *The Irish Times*, 19 January 2002.

19. 'PR-ISM — Bad Ideas of the 20th century', *Without Walls* programme, Channel Four.

20. Seán O'Connor was the lead consultant on the DTI and Luas Public Consultation process. A former senator, he has worked as a public relations professional in the Middle East, Europe and Ireland since 1980. He is currently researching a postgraduate thesis at DIT, on Sport Marketing.

Section 6
PR in the
Twenty-First Century

CHAPTER 23

The Future of Public Relations

No book on public relations would be complete without an attempt to address trends and issues in society, business and communications, which will impact on the world of public relations. As I don't have access to a crystal ball, it may transpire, in years to come, that my predictions were very wrong. I might also discover that I was an oracle! However, if only to stimulate debate, here are the changes I foresee.

PRODUCT PR/BRANDING

Teenagers and young people will continue to have high disposable income. This is the age group (15–25 years) that has least respect for money, and is most influenced by brands. Designer products, in particular, are 'must have' items for young people.

Products geared to this group will continue to attract high PR spends. Public relations people are extraordinarily good at creating lifestyles, and these lifestyles get wrapped up in the products. Third-party endorsement, from the worlds of music, film and television, will continue to play a huge role. Being hip will still be all-important in 2020.

The decline in product PR spend will be seen in the mid-20 to mid-40 age groups. These are the people who are already investing more time in their careers, who have less free time and often have young families to support. They have lower disposable income.

An increase in product PR budgets will be seen at the upper (age) end of the market — the people in and beyond middle age. Carolyn Fazio, former president of IPRA, says that, 'Boomers have already succeeded in renaming their middle age "middle youth", and are using every tool at their disposal to stave off the inevitable. Smart marketers will play along with the mass delusion.'[1]

Those beyond middle age are what Linda Grant, journalist with the *Independent on Sunday*, refers to as the 'crumblies and wrinklies' — people like Gloria Hunniford (of UTV fame), and actors like Joan Collins, Clint Eastwood or Paul Newman (all in the 60–80 age group). Older generations have more disposable income and they are living longer — with women still outnumbering men.[2] These are the high-spend product PR targets of the future.

Finally, consumer power will continue to influence products and their manufacturers. The power of the consumer varies around the world — but companies overlook it at their peril. Consumers are very active in the United States (particularly with the growth of 'class action' suits where similar cases are all taken together), and they are becoming more active throughout Europe (helped greatly by cross-border enforceable consumer legislation). Consumerism is in its infancy in Mexico, Italy and Japan, and Canadians are passive consumers.[3]

MISSION STATEMENTS

Mission statements will become more important to companies, employees, customers, shareholders and stakeholders.

The Dean of Katz Business School, Fredrick Winter, believes that mission statements should:

1. Be durable enough to stand the test of time
2. Point you in certain directions
3. Suggest new opportunities
4. Differentiate your company from your competitors.

However, he cautions companies that the information contained in the statement will be sensitive, and companies may not want to share it. He offers the following (worrying) advice to companies: 'If you do it right, you may not want to hang the results up in your lobby where customers and competitors can actually see them....if you'd like, you can create a grand but innocuous statement for public consumption'.[4]

Stephen Robbins and Mary Coulter list the seven key components of a mission statement as:

- Customers
- Products or services
- Markets
- Technology
- Concern for survival/growth/profitability
- Philosophy
- Self-concept
- Concern for public image and concern for employees.[5]

Gary Dessler believes that a mission statement should reflect management vision. According to him, a mission statement 'broadly outlines the organization's future course and serves to communicate "who we are, what we do, and where we're headed"'.[6]

Serious companies are making efforts to design meaningful mission statements. The Tesco mission statement reads: 'Our core purpose is to create value for customers to earn their lifetime loyalty'. While this statement is short and specific, and indicates that the company is customer-focused, it makes no mention of stakeholders or employees, and it assumes an exclusive customer focus on value for money.[7]

In the future, mission statements will go much further. They will reflect the company culture, the values the organisation holds and the behavioural standards the company adopts. Mission statements will reflect the company's goals, and its attitude towards its employees, the environment and the community. A mission statement will be a symbol of the common cause shared by all of the stakeholders in a company, and it will influence the purchasing power of consumers and investors. That is why companies will spend more time designing, implementing and promoting mission statements that go beyond a statement of product and profit.

CORPORATE SOCIAL RESPONSIBILITY

The onus on companies and organisations to behave responsibly will increase and magnify with the coming years. They will be required (by legislation, consumers and stakeholders) to behave responsibly towards their employees, the environment and their shareholders. Corporate social responsibility (or the higher common good) will become more important for companies in the future.

Since 2001, the European Commission has been encouraging dialogue on corporate social responsibility, notably by trying to find methods for implementing voluntary commitments.[8]

PUBLIC CONSULTATION

Public consultation will provide challenges and opportunities for PR people in the future. The emphasis on working with communities, representing their needs, taking their concerns on board, and finding solutions to national and local issues, will continue to grow. The public will demand to be consulted and the EU will continue to demand that serious and meaningful consultations take place with local communities. This area of public relations will undoubtedly become a specialist area of the future.

MULTICULTURAL COMMUNICATIONS

One of the greatest changes since about the 1980s has been the growth of multi-cultural societies worldwide. No longer is it possible to think of an Irish person, or a German, or a Dutch citizen, and think of only one culture, one race, or one attitude. The death of colonisation, freedom of movement within the EU, and the growth in numbers of refugees and asylum seekers fleeing oppression have all changed national 'societies'. In the future, communications programmes will need to take account of the variety of cultures within a nation. The very nature of communications pro-grammes will become multicultural, and this will be a continuing and more noticeable trend in the future.

PR ACCOUNTABILITY

Public relations people will have to be more accountable to clients — they will need to evaluate more thoroughly in the future. PR people, who have always known the value of public relations, will need to spend more time educating the client about its value, and proving its worth.

Consultancies will spend more time analysing and quantifying the impact of campaigns. For media relations, they will invest more time in proving the effectiveness of coverage in achieving impact, generating interest and enhancing corporate image and reputation.

For the implementation of all other proposals, PR professionals will provide clients with an evaluation of the change in attitude achieved, or the improvement in morale, etc. More money will be invested, by the consultancies themselves, in proving their worth to their clients.

The specialist areas of public relations will continue to develop. There are already financial, IT, agricultural, lobbying and publicist consultancies. Perhaps the trend of the future will be to see a further specialisation — in public consultation and corporate reputation, for example.

EUROPEAN UNION

The EU will have a greater impact on industry — our clients. With the introduction of each new measure, the PR industry will face two challenges. In the first instance, there will be a continuing need to educate EU publics about the directives and legislation. Individual companies will also need to communicate their compliance with EU measures, and, in many cases, show how they have gone beyond what is required of them, in law, in order to protect the consumer or the environment.

The EU will continue to have an impact on the media of communication, through the introduction of controls on direct mail, the use of databases and information held on computers, and cross-ownership of media themselves. The EU will compel PR people to re-think the ways in which they communicate, on behalf of their clients, with the public.

NATIONAL INITIATIVES

Public Relations is becoming much more pro-active in the twenty-first century. There are various national initiatives which the PR industry is undertaking, and some which it might look at in the future.

In 2002, the Public Relations Institute of Ireland was reviewing proposals for the introduction of a voluntary register of lobbyists. Lobbying belongs in the PR 'family' — it is, after all, a form of communication which, ultimately, works in the public interest. A clear definition of the role and function of lobbyists (professional and voluntary) is needed. Perhaps a separate code of ethics for lobbyists should be introduced? This would benefit clients, media, politicians and the public, and make them aware of the standards adopted by professional practitioners.

A hobby-horse of mine, which the industry might look at in the future, is the retention of serving politicians, by consultancies, to act as lobbyists. At a minimum, I believe that a list of serving politicians, the consultancies retaining them, and the nature of the work they are retained to do, should be made available through the

PRII. (Such a system currently exists in Britain.) The list would be available through the PRII for inspection by interested parties — other lobbyists, media, activist groups or representative bodies.

Also in 2002, the Public Relations Institute of Ireland was looking at new codes of professional conduct for practitioners in Ireland. Again, this move is to be welcomed. The Codes of Athens and Lisbon are excellent, but somewhat dated. An additional code, which would clarify professional conduct in the twenty-first century, would be of benefit to practitioners and clients alike.

PACIFIC RIM/ASIAN COUNTRIES

Under new trade agreements, the Pacific Rim/Asian countries are now becoming part of a two-way economic flow. These were previously tightly controlled markets and are now becoming much more open economies.

As these markets open more to western products, so too will the opportunities for PR people. This will mean western consultancies forming local alliances in places like Indonesia, Korea, Malaysia, Taiwan, Thailand, Japan and China.

Western PR consultancies will need to develop an understanding of how these economic markets operate; deal with cultural differences; and learn to overcome language barriers.

If there are economic opportunities there, major corporations will find and exploit them (as they should). PR people will be working with them priming the market in advance of the introduction of new products, creating speaking opportunities for key corporations, enhancing the understanding of 'other' cultures, designing and explaining employment policies, and promoting the company, its corporate ethos and its products.

EMERGING NATIONS

The potential offered by emerging nations — the Czech Republic, Hungary, Slovenia, Slovakia, Poland or Estonia — is enormous. All of the former Eastern European nations are signing or seeking to sign accession treaties with the EU. They will provide new markets for our clients and new challenges for PR people.

The free flow of people within the EU will increase and enhance the multicultural nature of Irish society. This will also provide communications challenges in the future.

CHANGES IN BROADCASTING

Ireland has seen major changes in broadcasting in the 1990s, with much more to come in the 2000s. Regional and local radio stations will continue to grow in number, and they will increasingly target 'niche' audiences.

TG4, in particular, will grow in importance in the future. A market must exist for practitioners to train people in the spoken Irish language (most people profess to have some Irish, but most are equally reluctant to use it in public). There will also be opportunities for consultancies specialising in Irish-language businesses and media.

Digital television will enhance the opportunities for public relations practitioners — and our clients — but will also make it more difficult to target specific publics.

Of course, there is also the whole issue of whether or not people will continue to watch television. Research in the 1990s in the United States showed a declining interest among viewers in watching foreign news or investigative journalism. Audiences for network news stations in the US are declining; young people are not reading newspapers; less investigative journalism is appearing — or being read; and journalists are better educated but less dedicated, according to research.[9]

International sports marketing/PR, in particular, will continue to grow in the future. The audience for televised sport is increasing every year. These large audiences provide companies with a cost-effective opportunity to raise awareness and build loyalty. In addition, sportspeople of the future will continue to be players, product endorsers and celebrity speakers.

And what of the internet? It was said that newspapers would be the death of the book; television would cause the death of the newspaper; and the internet would kill them all off. Instead of one medium replacing another, we continually add to the range of media available to us. There is a very real question mark over the future of the net. Viruses and hackers continue to cause major disruption and cost to businesses. If unchecked, these trends could lead to the abandonment of the net as a business and communications tool. However, I believe that that this medium will survive.

E-MAIL

E-mail itself will provide challenges for PR people. As companies make e-mail available on each employee's desk, they grant the right to the employee to 'represent' the company when they reply to an enquiry. PR people have a role to play in training people in the language of e-mail, and the way to project the right image using a medium which requires brevity and informality.

INTRANET AND XTRANET

The intranet and xtranet also provide additional communication opportunities for PR people. They will create efficiencies of scale, increase the level and value of communication with employees and clients, and, undoubtedly, develop beyond their current uses.

CONSULTANCY CHANGES

In the late 1990s and early 2000s, there was a trend for the smaller and generally more specialised consultancies to be bought for large sums of money. (These, it should be stressed, are the consultancies working in specialist areas.) Eileen Gleeson sold FCC (Financial and Corporate Communications) for a reputed €3.8 million while Gallagher and Kelly (a lobbying consultancy) was reportedly sold for €15.25

million. Larger consultancies are buying the specialisations rather than building them in-house, and this trend looks set to continue.

The smaller, non-specialist consultancies will continue to form cross-national alliances with other small consultancies. Pan-European, pan-Asian, and pan-African alliances will become the order of the day. There will always be a role in each country for non-linked consultancies, but they will be increasingly confined to local communications.

There will also be a growth in freelance PR in the future. In the past, sub-areas of PR have developed into specialisations (like event management or conference organisation), and these separate entities have been subcontracted out by consultancies. In the future, consultancies will keep more areas in-house and recruit freelance assistance for specific projects.

The freelancers will be multi-skilled professionals, at a senior level, who have possibly reduced their annual working hours (because they live abroad in winter) or had left PR to raise a family (and do not want to re-enter the industry on a full-time basis). These people will be taken on for fixed contracts of work, possibly for specific projects, on an annual basis.

AMERICAN PREDICTIONS

In a guest lecture to my Cork students in April 2000, Eileen Perrigo, made ten predictions for the future of PR.[10] Although presented from an American perspective, they seem to encapsulate some of the key challenges facing the industry worldwide:

1. Growth — the PR boom will continue and broaden;
2. Globalism — as the world shrinks, the importance of PR will loom larger;
3. Research — research will improve or PR will suffer the consequences;
4. Education — the importance of education will finally be acknowledged;
5. Recruitment — PR pros will increasingly come from other professions;
6. Technology — PR will embrace technology to transform itself;
7. Tactics — tactics will be used to target narrower audiences;
8. Strategic counsel — strategic counsel will become more important to the corporation;
9. Ethics — there will be more stringent codes;
10. The reputation of PR — top corporate CEOs will continue to recognise the value of public relations.

PR EDUCATION AND RECRUITMENT

What of the entrants into the field? What level of education will be required of them as they start a career in PR?

One of the great debates, which has raged for years in PR circles, concerns whether or not PR education should be academic or vocational in nature. A mix of both, probably, will continue to provide the best of all possible worlds. However, with the speed of change, it will probably be necessary for practitioners to upgrade their skills after a number of years' practice. Already, the industry has a Continuing Professional Development (CPD) programme which provides half-and full-day programmes of training.

In the future, it might be necessary to look at other structures — such as a Higher Diploma, for example — which would deal with broader management and reputation issues. These issues would really be relevant only at a higher level, to people with a number of years' practical experience behind them.

Or perhaps the future lies in specialisation. Having acquired the Diploma in Public Relations, and perhaps after a few years' working in the business, practitioners might return to specialise in public consultation, or financial PR, or any of the other specialist areas.

Finally, languages are becoming more important as the global village shrinks. Fluency in any of the major languages is currently a bonus to anyone entering public relations practice, but it will become a necessity in the future. Most of our European colleagues are fluent in several languages. The enlargement of the European Union and the continuing development of international linkages (for consultancies and professional bodies) will ensure that the Irish practitioner of the future is multi-lingual.

One thing that's certain is that the number of people entering courses of study in public relations will increase each year. In the United States, the focus is on degree programmes. In 2000, there were 16,679 undergraduate students studying for PR degrees, and a further 5,004 studying for combined advertising and PR degrees.[11] In Ireland, where the population is smaller, the figures show that approximately 500–600 people were studying for recognised diplomas in Public Relations in 2002.

International and European recognition of qualifications will become even more important in the future. The Irish Diploma in Public Relations currently has European recognition (through CERP), and heads of agreement have been signed with other countries. The ultimate aim — and the size of the challenge should not be underestimated — must be to establish an internationally recognised standard of education.

EDUCATION v. CONSULTANCY

An IPRA colleague, Alison Tipping, points to a growing problem for market research companies, posed by educational establishments. She says that in Britain, universities 'are obtaining European funding for providing market research free of charge to companies — it threatens the market research companies because they can't provide free services, but boosts the universities' profits'.[12] It is an interesting point. Might PR consultancies be similarly threatened? Might the EU, in the future, commission PR students to design pan-European information programmes?

PR FOR THE PUBLIC RELATIONS INDUSTRY

The industry has never, by tradition, promoted itself. Corporate clients who have not previously retained the services of PR people are still, in the twenty-first century, unsure of what PR entails. The industry needs to become pro-active. There is a huge benefit in running targeted campaigns — to graduates, journalists, corporate bodies — explaining to them what public relations is all about, how it is used, and what benefits it would bring to their industry.

It is in the profession's interest to spend some money on the promotion of the business on which we depend for our livelihoods.

EUROPEAN AND INTERNATIONAL ASSOCIATIONS

Groups like the European Public Relations Confederation (CERP) and the International Public Relations Association (IPRA) will continue to grow. The world is becoming a smaller place — a global village — and each nation's professionals need to share information with and learn from the professionals of other nations. It is only by association with fellow professionals that we all grow as businesspeople and communicators.

Whether by legislative, regulatory or professional agreement, it is ultimately in the interests of the industry to establish international standards of practice to which all will subscribe. There are already international codes of ethics. It is a huge challenge — the practice of public relations varies greatly from country to country — but it is something which, I believe, the industry must tackle in the future.

THE TWENTY-FIRST CENTURY

Leaving aside all of the particular or specific predictions, the public relations industry will continue to grow and prosper. Companies, charities, organisations, political parties, lobby groups and governments, among others, will all need to communicate in the future. The diversity of publics, and the breadth of media, will ensure that communications experts will be needed well into the twenty-second century.

The industry will continue to be professional — more hard-working than people suspect, and certainly more diversified. It will continue to attract multi-talented, multi-skilled practitioners who will enhance its reputation. It will, I hope, remain an industry in which practitioners respect each other, and each other's work, and treat each other with fairness and courtesy. The industry will continue to offer great earning potential — and high stress levels! But above all, I believe that it will remain the best industry in the world in which to work.

So, whatever area of public relations you go into — enjoy it!

REFERENCES

1. Carolyn Fazio, e-mail, 10 January 2001.
2. Department of Health website, www.doh.ie/statistics/stats/sectiona_files/sheet001.htm
3. IPRA World Congress, Helsinki, 1997.
4. Fredrick Winter, in 'The Secret of Powerful Mission Statements — Not All of Them Hang in the Lobby', <http://www.imakenews.com>™.
5. Stephen P. Robbins and Mary Coulter, *Management*, New Jersey: Prentice Hall, 2002 (seventh edition) (based on F. David, *Strategic Management*, New Jersey: Prentice Hall, 2001 (eighth edition)).
6. Gary Dessler, *A Framework for Management*, New Jersey: Prentice Hall, 2002.
7. www.ncl.ac.uk/aefm/student_resources/aefi14.117/MissionStat&Tesco.pdf
8. Richard Linning, discussion of European Commission document, 'Best business practices for corporate social responsibility: Management tools for implementing the Organisation for Economic Cooperation and Development (OECD) Guide lines for Multinational Enterprises', *IPRA Digest*, no. 96, 2001.
9. IPRA World Congress, Helsinki, 1997.
10. Eileen M. Perrigo, M. Ed, APR, 'The Future of Public Relations', presentation to the students of the Irish Academy of Public Relations, 29 April 2000.
11. Steve Mackey, in *IPRA Digest*, no. 71, 2001.
12. Alison Tipping, in *IPRA Digest*, no. 67, 2001.

Section 7
Examinations

CHAPTER 24

Analysis of Past Examination Papers
(Introduction to PR)

The Introduction to Public Relations course is taught by the Irish Academy of Public Relations. It is taught in three locations — Dublin, Cork and Galway. Lectures are held over an eight-week period, with one two-hour lecture session per week. Lecturers write their own examination papers, which means that the papers not only reflect the syllabus content, but, more importantly, they reflect the emphasis of the individual lecturers and the particular issues which arose in discussion with each group of students. Individual papers for each location can reflect local interest and offer students an opportunity to showcase local knowledge.

Each paper is approved, in advance, by the Academy's external examiner who ensures that the questions are a fair reflection of the syllabus and offer students a fair opportunity to show the knowledge they have gained. The external examiner also approves all final grades awarded to students.

Each paper is corrected by the local lecturer, and then sent to the external examiner for ratification or change in grade. It is the job of the external examiner to ensure that the standard awarded is consistent across all locations so that the grade awarded is, truly, a national standard.

Each of the papers contains six questions of which Question 1 is compulsory, and the student has a choice of three of the remaining five questions (i.e. four questions in total must be answered). All questions carry equal marks.

QUESTION 1 (COMPULSORY)

Question 1, as you would expect, reflects the core topic of the course. It is, by tradition, a 'what is PR?' question. We will look at three examples from November/December 2001.

Q In 1906 Ivy Ledbetter Lee promised unequivocally that he would '...supply prompt and accurate information concerning subjects which it is of interest and value to the public to know about...' and so began modern-day Public Relations. In your opinion, what is Public Relations and where did it come from?

(Dublin)

Q Your friend laughed when you told him that you were studying public relations. 'You mean to tell me that people actually give lessons in how to be nice to people?' he asked. Write him a letter explaining what public relations is all about.

(Galway)

Q Public Relations is a cheap form of advertising.
From what you know about Public Relations is this statement correct? *(Cork)*

The questions, while similar in style, encourage different types of response. The Dublin question asks you to define public relations, and discuss the history of the industry. In your response to this question, you would be expected to give a recognised definition (and explain it) and outline the history of public relations from cave drawings to modern PR. The question gives ample scope to the studious student to list key dates and key events in the history of the development of the industry.

The Galway question, by comparison, seeks no history of public relations at all. Instead, it asks the student to defend the industry, by letter. It encourages the student not only to define public relations, but also to give examples of its modern-day use and value to companies, organisations, charitable bodies and governments.

In Cork, the question relates public relations to advertising. Again, it encourages you to define and explain public relations. But this question is really encouraging you to compare public relations with the other communications industries, like advertising, sales promotion, and marketing. You could compare the uses, benefits and costs of each.

QUESTIONS PER TOPIC

The series of lectures covers, in addition, six other topics, any of which might arise in the examination papers. We will look at them topic by topic — again using November/December 2001 as an example. As you will see, the Cork papers contained an either/or option in each topic, while the Dublin and Galway papers did not.

In general, the questions are a mix of what might be called 'study' and 'application' questions. The 'study' questions allow the student who has studied the notes and learned the key points to do well. They offer an opportunity to list key dates, checklists or important points. The 'application' questions are broader and offer scope to the student not only to list the key points but then to apply them to the scenario that they have been given. These questions offer more scope to show how you would apply the techniques of PR, rather that detailing what the techniques are.

As with every exam, it is important to read the questions fully and be sure that you are answering the question you were asked. As you will see from the following examples, the questions are quite similar in nature. The answers required, however, differ with each question. You need to understand what the examiner is looking for first, and then start to answer the question.

Newsletters

Q Write a paragraph on each of the key questions that must be answered before deciding to establish an internal company newsletter. *(Cork)*

This is a 'study' question. It asks the student to list all of the key issues involved in reaching a decision to introduce a staff newsletter. The question also clearly tells you that you are expected to write a paragraph on each of the issues you list.

Q What considerations should be taken into account before deciding to publish a brochure on a new product line for your company? *(Cork)*

This is a much broader question. It asks you again to list key decisions, but the print item, in this case, is a product brochure. Therefore, as part of a public relations challenge, your answer should include not only the publication of the brochure, but the other PR tools that you would use in promoting it — like photo calls, news releases, exhibitions, etc.

Photography

Q Your client, a small convenience-store owner, has finished building new premises (double the size of the original building). You have been asked to organise a photo call on the opening day. You have secured a local TD to cut the ribbon How do you go about organising the photo call and how do you brief the photographer? Describe the coverage you anticipate, as a result of your assignment, and, apart from the media, indicate other relevant outlets for the pictures. *(Dublin)*

This is really a multi-part question. You are given the scenario, and the guest of honour. You are then asked about (a) the preparatory steps involved in organising the photo call, (b) the brief you would give to the photographer, (c) the media you would expect coverage in, and (d) other outlets for your pictures. It is a very detailed question.

The (a) section asks you to detail the selection of the photographer, the venue, the recce, etc. The (b) section requires a detailed brief about timing, venue, lighting, etc. The (c) section means that you must decide where the function will be held, and target media on that basis (e.g. if the function is in Cork, the local TD might get coverage in a national newspaper — the *Irish Examiner* — and local papers like the *Carrigdhoun Weekly*). Finally the (d) section requires you to note that magazines like *Shelflife* might be interested in covering the event. Local freesheet newspapers and parish bulletins might also provide an outlet for coverage, and possibly a publication like *Marketing* magazine or the journal of the local Chamber of Commerce (if your store owner is a member) could also provide coverage opportunities.

It is a detailed question which might, under the time constraints of the exam, be difficult to score well on. There is no indication about a division of marks per section so it must be assumed that each section carries equal marks. Therefore, if you answer two sections well and in some detail, but then run out of time, you can, at best, score only half-marks on this question.

Q The photo call is often an under-utilised weapon in the armoury of the public relations professional. Discuss with examples. *(Galway)*

The question offers you the opportunity to explain the uses of a photo call; it encourages you to offer an opinion about a paragraph of text versus a photograph; and it asks you to discuss with examples. Examples of photo calls would have been discussed in class and, in addition, photo calls are covered in the papers daily. It is a question that offers great scope to students who apply the theory to their everyday lives (as opposed to the student who studies once a week in isolation from current media).

Q As part of a Public Relations programme for a client, you decide to organise a photo call. Describe (a) what essential requirements you should take into consideration when hiring a photographer, (b) how you would organise the photo call, (c) how you would distribute the resultant photographs to obtain maximum publicity for your client. *(Cork)*

This question is very similar in style to the Dublin question. There are two key differences though: the Cork question divides the items you are asked to deal with (the Dublin question does not) and, crucially, the Cork question does not give you any information about the client. This means, in effect, that you must begin by deciding who the client is, and why you are holding a photo call — you cannot adequately answer the question otherwise. So, you would need to begin your answer by stating, for example, that your client is a national chain of cosmetics stores, called The Beauty Business, and the company has arranged for Cindy Crawford to open its newest outlet on Patrick Street (or anything else that comes into your head). Basically, begin by sketching a scenario which will allow you to get good photo coverage (the examiner has given you the space to do so — use it wisely). The other elements of the question would be dealt with as per the Dublin question.

News Release

Q One of the basic qualities that a PR Practitioner needs is the ability to communicate verbally and in writing, and one of the most basic tools of PR is the news release.
What other qualities does a PR Practitioner need to have? (5)
What is the purpose of a news release? (10)
How should a news release be written? (10) *(Dublin)*

This is a very nice question. It divides the marks for each section, so there is no fear that you will spend too much time on the first section and too little on the third. It is also one of those great questions if you are running out of time, or having difficulty with the paper. It allows you to play to your strengths. If, for example, you know that you could write well about the qualities a practitioner needs, and you could really do justice to 'how a release should be written', then — because of lack of either time or knowledge — you might decide to answer two sections only, giving yourself a maximum mark of 15 out of 25.

As to each of the sections, the first section (for 5 marks) asks you to list all of the qualities that are useful to a PR practitioner — things like verbal communication skills, knowledge of advertising and marketing, understanding of media, etc. The third section about writing a press release is easy if you know the rules. The second section requires the most work. Your answer here needs to incorporate what news actually is, why you would issue a release (as opposed to holding a press conference, for example), who releases are sent to, etc. It requires a broader answer by far than the other two sections.

Q What are the vital elements in ensuring your news release gets noticed by a news editor? Discuss. *(Galway)*

This is also quite a broad question. It requires you to explain what a news release is, in the first instance, and you should then explain how it is structured. The element of the question which will gain you most marks, however, is the 'getting it noticed' part. This means that you will need to deal with targeting the right journalists, issuing information of interest to their readers, selecting the right 'angle', etc.

Q Itemise what you would consider to be the 'essentials' of good news release writing. *(Cork)*

This is one of those beautiful questions where 25 marks are just sitting on the table waiting to be picked up! The answer required is very straightforward: the essentials encompassing the style of writing, angles and targeted submissions.

Press Officer

Q What are the functions of a Press Officer? What skills are necessary to be a good Press Officer? *(Dublin)*

This is a 'study'-type question — very straightforward. List all of the functions of a press officer and write a paragraph on each. Then outline the skills which make a good practitioner. This question allows no room for padding but, if you know the answer, the marks are easy.

Q Outline the key functions of a press officer, distinguishing his or her role from that of a PR consultant. *(Galway)*

This question is slightly different. While it also asks you to list the key functions of the press officer, it then goes on to award half of the marks for a discussion of the different roles of press officer and PR consultant. What the examiner is looking to establish is that you have a clear idea in your head regarding the division of roles, and can adequately discuss the difference between each.

Event Organisation

Q Your client has asked you to organise a function to preview the company's new product for all staff members and their families, two months before its commercial launch. Identify the product, and explain how you will organise such an event. *(Dublin)*

The examiner is looking for two things in this question. The first is that you would clearly show that you know how to organise a function — everything from the initial selection of the venue through to the 'goody bag' on departure. The second element of the question is the lateral thinking element — you need to select the company and the product.

The really nice thing about this question is that you can use your own organisation as an example if you work in a product-based industry (obviously you cannot if you are, for example, a teacher). However, your selection can reflect your personal interests. So, you could choose to launch a new software package for computers, or a learning aid for children, or a drug to cure AIDS, or a new range of designer towels. Your choice is endless.

Be aware that you must first decide the product, and then tackle the answer. All of the elements will interlink, after all. The choice of venue will reflect the product you are launching — you would not launch the children's learning aid in a senior citizens' home. And it is unlikely, two months in advance of the commercial launch, that you would give people a sample on departure. Once you have a picture of the product in your head, the launch event will crystallise itself.

However, there is one thing to be very careful about with this question. The product is being previewed to staff, two months in advance of the launch. You will not, obviously, be inviting media or the trade to the event, nor will you be seeking publicity for it, with the possible exception of coverage in the staff newsletter.

Q Your company is hosting a reception at which the 'Galway Business Person of the Year' will be announced. Representatives of businesses in the city and county, politicians, and lecturers/professors of business studies will attend.
You have been retained to organise the function. How will you go about it?
(Galway)

This is a more difficult question to answer. The function, presumably, will be an up-market one, to judge from the list of invitees. You will need to determine how many people will attend the function, and where you will find the 'representatives' (e.g. database lists). The timing of the function will probably be evening, as all of these people work during the day. Furthermore, if I were the sponsoring company, I would expect your organisation to include media coverage on the west coast of Ireland. This is a broader question than it would seem.

Q You are the Public Relations Officer for your organisation.
The Chief Executive informs you that the company is about to launch an important new product, and asks you to arrange an appropriate PR function. Describe what you would do.
(Cork)

This question is similar to the one on the Dublin paper, except that the function is a public one. You will need to outline the guests who will be invited to attend the launch — staff, customers, suppliers, media, etc. — but again you have the scope to choose the product, which allows you to organise a fabulous function, and use a special guest. You have not been confined to a budget — so, spend! You could take a very ordinary product — like a new eye-liner — and have it launched by Catherine Zeta Jones, whom you would specially fly in from Hollywood — mega publicity and guaranteed attendance by all who are invited!

Sponsorship

Q What is sponsorship? Why do companies choose to sponsor an event? Who are the parties involved in a sponsorship? Name a sponsorship with which you are familiar and explain why in your view it has proved to be a successful sponsorship.
(Dublin)

This is a detailed question. Begin by splitting it into those sections which you are required to answer. There are five: (1) a definition of sponsorship, (2) an explanation of why companies choose sponsorship (instead of, say, advertising), (3) an analysis of who is involved (presumably the sports body or charity and the corporate body), (4) an example of a sponsorship with which you are familiar (which means naming it and explaining what the sponsorship involves), and (5) saying why you believe that your sample sponsorship was successful.

The first section requires a definition, possibly use sponsorship *v.* charitable donation. The second section encourages you to talk about the key benefits of sponsorship, like name recognition. The third section needs your explanation of the benefits of sponsorship to both parties. The fourth and fifth sections require you to give details of a sponsorship, and show how it was successful by reference to your answer in the second section — i.e. what were the key benefits that the sponsoring company achieved?

Q Sponsorship should always deliver a return on your investment. Outline the key steps involved when deciding to enter a sponsorship. *(Galway)*

This is a nice, straightforward, non-fluffy question (i.e. there's no room for fluffiness in your answer). You should refer to the opening section — 'the return on invest-ment' — and list some of the returns (like name awareness). But that is for extra points. What the answer really needs is a list of the key steps involved, and a para-graph on each, explaining the steps in more detail.

Q As a Public Relations consultant you have been commissioned to organise a sponsorship for a multinational company. Write a submission to the Chief Execu-tive outlining the key elements of the sponsorship. *(Cork)*

This question is not as simple as it looks. Before you begin to answer it, you need to sketch the scenario in your head. The multinational company is looking for a spon-sorship — is it in Ireland only? Does the company have other sponsorships? (If so, does the company want to keep its sponsorships in the same area — like sport?) What does the multinational want to achieve from the sponsorship (you would pre-sumably have been told this when you were given the brief). You should answer the question by first stating your assumptions, and then writing the submission to the chief executive, outlining all of the key points.

CHAPTER 25

Analysis of Past Examination Papers (Diploma in PR)

In each year of the diploma, public relations is examined by project and examination. The project carries 40 per cent of the subject marks for that year, and the examination carries the balance of 60 per cent. In each year, each of the two elements must be independently passed before a grade for that subject can be awarded.

The examination papers are set by a national examiner (for the Public Relations Institute of Ireland) and approved, in advance, by a national external examiner. Students who study the Diploma course in Dublin, Cork and Galway all sit the same examination, at the same time, on the same day.

The scripts are sent to the examiner for correction, and then go to an external examiner and an examination board for ratification or change.

The first-and second-year papers differ substantially, one from the other. The syllabus for each year is different, but, more importantly, the level of reply required from the student differs between first and second year.

For this reason, we will look at each paper separately.

For full-time students, the paper is a combination of first- and second-year questions. The advice regarding examination approaches to Year One and Year Two should be separately applied to each of the two sections of the full-time paper.

YEAR ONE

The Year One paper contains six questions. Question 1 is compulsory, and students are required to answer four of the remaining five questions. The purpose of the syllabus and examination in Year One is to establish that students have learned the tools of the trade — the building blocks which will be used in the construction of PR proposals. This is not to say that the examination is easy — it is not. The basic standard required to pass any question (i.e. secure a D grade) is a thorough knowledge of the subject. If you are going to practise as a competent PR professional, and be awarded an internationally recognised diploma, no lower standard could be set.

This chapter deals with questions on a topic-by-topic basis. The examples below are all taken from the May 2000 and May 2001 first-year examination papers.

Irrespective of which question you are answering, you should always try to define the 'issue' to be debated. You should try to quote at least two authors on the subject and you should always try to incorporate a current example.

QUESTION 1 (COMPULSORY)

The first thing to note about the compulsory question on the diploma paper is that it is always a 'what is PR?' question. It is assumed that students who have studied past papers could reasonably anticipate this type of question as the compulsory one, and should, therefore, be well prepared to answer it. There are no easy marks on this question.

We will look at two examples:

Q 'What comes to mind when you think about a PR consultant? The stereotype is that they are loud-mouthed poseurs with Southern accents, continually on their mobile phones, swigging G&Ts or champagne between calls, and speeding from one superficial and gimmicky event to another in their GTi cabriolets, the hood down in all weathers'. (*The DIY Guide to Public Relations*, UK) Discuss.

You have just completed a gruelling year of study and you are faced with a quote which tells you, in effect, that PR people are useless wasters — marvellous. While the quote is wonderful, and needs to be addressed in your answer, the question is a simple 'what is PR?' and that is the issue you should be addressing in your answer.

The question requires you to give at least one definition of public relations, explain something of its history and origins, possibly contrast PR with other communication forms, give some examples of companies which successfully (or unsuccessfully) use PR techniques, and possibly name some of the key PR practitioners nationally or internationally. You are being asked, quite simply, what you have learned in the last year — tell the examiner all!

The opening quote needs to be addressed, however. Students who respond to this question with 'Public relations is about...' have missed the point. You are specifically asked to discuss the issues raised in the quote.

There is no right or wrong way to address the quote. Some students might write that the author obviously hasn't a clue about public relations. Others might adopt the approach that the comment was obviously made a long time ago as the perception of public relations has changed radically in the last decade. Others again might address each individual item in the quote, pointing out, for example, that everyone nowadays uses mobile phones, etc. Others again will adopt a humorous approach and offer guidance to the author — G&Ts ceased to be trendy after the Second World War! The approach does not matter — and the more confident, the better — but the quote must be referred to. You should also refer to the quote again at the conclusion of your answer, linking back to your original point.

What you are saying, for this question, is that you hope you have proved that PR is a lot more than the quote suggests — but do it in your own style.

Q 'A squirrel is just a rat with good public relations!' (Claire Austin)

With the benefit of your current studies, write Ms Austin a letter explaining what Public Relations is all about.

This question requires you to write a letter. It sounds obvious, but you should begin with an address in the top right-hand corner and a 'Dear Ms Austin,' etc. The style of your reply should also be letter style.

Again, the question is asking you what public relations is all about, but it is giving you a chance to do it in a different format.

In-house *v.* Consultancy

Q Having worked as an in-house PR person within a large organisation for a number of years, you have recently changed jobs to work with one of the larger PR consultancies in the city. The director of your consultancy is interested in your views on the similarities and differences between the functions of in-house PR and consultant. Write him a memo.

Clearly, a memo needs to be written as a memo — not as an exam answer. Memo style means that you write 'To:....From:....Re:....' at the top of the page. Dispense with an opening (do not use 'Dear...'), and dispense with a closing (a memo never ends with 'yours...'). Other than that, the style of writing is exactly as you would answer an exam question.

This is a nice question because it allows you to show off. It is essentially asking you to list the advantages and disadvantages of in-house *v.* consultancy. Beyond that, though, it gives you opportunities to talk about the nature of the work, the actual hours worked, the breadth of PR responsibilities, the specialisations — even the differences in salary structures. You can give as much information as your memory will allow.

Ethics

Q '[Mary] Finan will talk at length about why PR is a worthwhile and necessary profession. She says lying, spinning and misleading don't happen when you deal with reputable clients.... "No client, no matter how much they would spend, would be worth me telling a lie for."' (*Sunday Independent* — 20.2.2000) Are PR practitioners really so ethical? Discuss.

This question goes to the heart of the ethics of the PR industry. It is asking you to explain the Codes of Athens and Lisbon. Do not, by the way, learn the codes off by heart. You are not training to become a parrot. Instead, learn the key obligations and responsibilities which the codes impose on PR professionals, and discuss them from that perspective.

The question also gives you an opportunity to discuss the fact that the codes are voluntary, and you might compare them with the voluntary codes of the NUJ for example.

You might also give examples (always worth extra points) of how the codes are observed or have been breached.

Event Organisation

Q Your company, a large firm of solicitors, has decided to introduce an annual conference. Each year the conference will deal with legal issues which are relevant to company directors and chairpersons. They have asked you to organise the conference, and need your recommendations on every aspect of its organisation.
Write a memo.

There is great scope in this question — and there are also hidden pitfalls. The company is a firm of solicitors. These are serious 'suits' who will not appreciate too much lateral thinking. A colourful, funny photo call, for example, might not only ruin the image of the firm but could destroy the cachet of the conference. So, think serious, corporate, important guests.

The question asks for your recommendations 'on every aspect' — be sure that you cover them all. You will need to invent a name for the firm of solicitors, and put them in a location (e.g. Galway or Cork). You will need to decide whether the conference is being held for clients throughout the entire country — the company might have branch offices, or might handle clients in every county — or whether it is for local companies only.

The fact that you are dealing with company directors and chairpersons means that you are targeting a very specific (and hard-to-reach) audience. The conference venue will need to be excellent in order to attract them. Your list of speakers should be exemplary — can you bring in foreign speakers, the Attorney General, or a well-known business person to talk about the impact of the legislation? You will need to choose your timing carefully so that you do not clash with anything like the IMI conference, for example.

Should your conference consist of speakers only or should directors have an opportunity to ask questions in a workshop session? What kind of printed material will you produce and will it be issued in advance, as a follow-up or on the day? How will you determine which directors should be invited? How many people will attend? This question does not ask you for a list of 'things you should consider'. It asks you, the student, to consider all of the elements and make recommendations. Your answer, therefore, should leave the examiner with the very clear impression that you have thought about all of the elements involved in the organisation of this conference, and your recommendations are logical, thorough and workable.

Don't forget the roles of direct mail, advertising and PR. You might use the first two to promote the conference, and you should presume that your client would also be seeking that, in addition to using your PR skills as a conference organiser, you would also be organising some sort of media coverage for the event.

It is a detailed question to answer, but one on which you could score very good marks. However, a straight list of things to consider would not even get you a D grade.

Definitions

Q Define each of the following terms: Press Conference, Publics, Pubic Relations, Photo Call, Objectives.

Q Define each of the following in 150 words (approx.): Photo Call, Press Conference, Newsletter, OTS, Propaganda.

The definitions question appears on the paper regularly and is generally poorly answered. This question is one which could be answered quickly, and one on which easy marks should be picked up. For most students, however, this question is used to lose marks!

If there are 4–5 marks going for each definition, you must give the examiner four or five different points on which you can be scored. Each definition should be given two–three paragraphs in response.

The crucial word in the question is 'define'. Most of the terms used are not defined in any textbook — therefore, there are no definitions you can learn. The purpose of a definition is to make something clear to someone who has never heard of it. So, to say that a photo call is 'organised for the media by a PR person' tells the uninitiated absolutely nothing! It could be a fashion show, an agricultural fair or a conference telephone call.

After you have defined each, you should expand your answer to give examples of how a photo call, for example, is used. Compare a photo call to other PR tools and show how it differs. And, if possible, give an example of a photo call which recently achieved coverage.

The same rules apply to any term you are asked to define — define it; give examples of how it is used as part of a PR strategy; compare it with other PR techniques; and use a current example, if possible.

PR Tools

Q The managing director has called you into his office this morning, and told you that former EU Commissioner Ray MacSharry has agreed to become a director of the company. He knows that you are familiar with all of the tools of PR, and has asked for your recommendations on how best to inform the media of this development.

This question needs 'thinking' time. It is asking you to look at all of the tools available to a PR person, and select the most appropriate for this particular situation. Begin by listing all of the tools available — you will pick up a few points, but it will also help to clarify your own thinking. List everything from press releases to exhibitions. Then, go through them and construct the best-possible PR proposal.

You will probably organise a function (or functions) to introduce Mr MacSharry to media, customers, staff and shareholders. You will also use your media skills — releases, conferences, photo calls. You might arrange a media lunch briefing, or you might need to conduct media training with existing directors. You will look at the different publics and possibly select different media for each. You may look for coverage in newsletters — perhaps an existing staff or customer newsletter. You could mount a photographic and text exhibition in the reception area, highlighting the new appointment. There must be trade press, relevant to your business, who would be interested in possible feature coverage of the appointment. If the company has a website, the announcement should be published on it. The list is endless.

What the examiner is looking for is a clear answer from you, showing your understanding of all the tools at your disposal and that you have made a logical selection from them.

It is important to note that in an examination such as this — where different lecturers will place different emphasis on PR tools — you are not necessarily required to produce the 'right' answer. Two consultancies given the same brief might adopt two entirely different approaches. What you are required to do is to show that you understand the tools, know how to use them, and have made a logical selection of those that you feel would best meet the challenge the company has set for you.

Q   Your company manufactures baby-food products. One of your products has been found to be mildly contaminated. The contamination would cause illness, but is not life threatening. The company need to inform shopkeepers, supermarkets, and parents that the product should not be used and should be returned to them. They know that, as a PR professional, you are aware of a wide range of tools which could be used to help them to disseminate this information. They have asked for your advice.

(a) Outline the tools available to you (*5 marks*)
    and
(b) Recommend the tools which should be used, and why. (*15 marks*)

Once again, you are being asked to list and then select from the tools of PR which are available to you. In this case, however, the question is more specific and confining — which, in some ways, makes it easier to answer.

You have been given each of the publics in the question and you know that the contamination is confined to one product only. However, as the product is a baby food, you could reasonably anticipate a high level of tension and anxiety from parents.

Part (a) of the question requires a long list of every possible tool which you might use — easy marks.

Part (b) is about the application of those tools. To answer this question fully, you probably need to think outside the 'PR' box a little. You will certainly use PR tools — statements, press conferences, photo calls, newsletters, media, individual contact by phone, etc. — but you will also, probably, need to place advertising in national and local media, brief the salespeople and get them out there on the road to the customers, etc.

The key to answering this section is to be thorough (use as many tools as possible) and be quick (your recommendations should concentrate on the first, crucial 24–48 hours, and then outline the follow-up).

Press Officer

Q You are a newly appointed Press Officer in a large, semi-state organisation, and you are the first person ever to hold this position. Your manager has asked you to prepare a presentation to the board of directors outlining your role and function within the organisation. Draft your presentation.

Your presentation, presumably, will be given on slide or PowerPoint. Your answer, therefore, should contain bullet points, fleshed out with text (your speaking notes) below.

This question gives you plenty of scope. The company has never had a press officer before, so you need to organise an office and everything that goes with it. Presumably no media training has been done; there are no crisis files in existence; no close links have been formed with relevant media; and staff-members have never worked with a PRO before. The directors also need to be briefed on what your role is and how you will fulfil it (e.g. when to refer media queries to you).

Photography

Q Your company has moved to new premises, and senior management want a 'grand opening'. They have booked d'Unbelievables to perform the ceremony, which will be attended by staff, customers, members of the local community and several politicians. You are responsible for photography at the event.

Explain:

how you will brief the photographer in advance of the function. (*13 marks*)

where the photographs will be used afterwards. (*7 marks*)

This question paints the scenario for you, and clearly tells you where most of the marks are to be picked up. Briefing the photographer will include all of the usual things like time, venue, etc., but, in addition, d'Unbelievables will play a key role in determining the type of photographs to be used — great scope for off-the-wall shots. Using d'Unbelievables cleverly in your brief to the photographer will gain you many extra points. The publics, who have all been invited to attend, should all be included, in some way, in the brief.

The key to photographs being used afterwards is that (a) d'Unbelievables should give you a good opportunity to pick up national, local and trade press coverage and (b) you need to find an outlet for the photographs which link up with each of the publics.

Evaluation

Q The purpose of evaluating proposals is to establish their worth, their effectiveness and their benefit to a company. Explain four methods of PR evaluation. (*20 marks*)

This is a 'study' question. You can easily identify four methods of evaluation, but you need to have a lot of information about each to gain the full five marks awarded to each one. To gain good points on this question, you would need to quote the authors/inventors of different systems of evaluation, look at the costs of the different methods and give comparative examples of when each would be used.

YEAR TWO

If the Year One paper deals with the building-blocks of PR, then Year Two is the architectural design. The examination paper in Year Two tests students' ability to apply the tools and theory that they have learned.

Only four questions (out of seven) must be answered on the second-year paper. The depth of your response, consequently, should be much greater.

There is no compulsory question in Year Two, and there are no 'how to' questions. Rather, each question deals with a specialised area of public relations.

The examples below are from the May 2000 and May 2001 papers.

Financial PR

Q 'The financial public relations man is basically a communicator of information. Through his expertness in communications, he helps many people reach the decision to buy or hold his company's stock.' (Eugene Miller, *Lesly's Public Relations Handbook*) Explain the role of the financial public relations practitioner.

The quotation here appears to lead you in one direction, while the actual question leads you in another. The quotation suggests that the role of financial PR revolves around the shareholder — this assumption needs to be tackled at the start of your answer. You need to point out that the role is much broader than that.

The question essentially encourages you to look at the role of financial PR and the breadth of influences upon it. So, you would explain, for example, the background necessary to work in financial PR, the different publics and how they subdivide, the information that each needs, the rules under which financial PR operates, and the consequences of getting it wrong. You would also look at all of the other influences which impact upon financial PR — such as corporate identity, rumour, profit margins, environmental record, etc.

You should be able, for extra points, to name some of the key financial PR people in the country and mention their clients.

This is the closest a second-year paper ever gets to a 'how to' question.

Q At the AGM 'rebel AIB shareholder and former employee, Niall Murphy positively poured forth invective, some of it cringe-inducing, against the nine man team of directors on the podium'. (Frank Mulrennan, *Irish Independent*, 20.4.2000) Explain the role and function of financial PR, concentrating on the variety of tools used to reach each of its audiences.

This question differs somewhat from the first. It certainly asks you to outline the role of the financial PRO, but it then guides you, deliberately, into the tools used to reach each of the audiences.

In tackling this question, you would need first to explain the role, then to detail the publics, and then specify — public by public — which tools are used to communicate. You would also need to use current examples of the different forms of communication in use.

For extra points, discuss the growing media focus on 'ordinary shareholders' and changes in shareholder profile.

PR for Charity

Q The role of PR in a non-profit organisation differs greatly from the role of PR for a corporation. Explain the role of PR for a charitable/non-profit organisation and highlight the differences

This is a nice question if you have a clear understanding of the differences between profit and charity organisations. To tackle this question, you would need first to explain the role of public relations for charity, and the PR role for commercial enterprises. You then need to detail the differences between each (e.g. staff *v.* volunteers). You should look at the actual role of the PR person in each organisation and again highlight the differences in their roles (job descriptions, working hours, etc.) Finally, you would need to use examples, from both areas, to highlight the points you are making.

Q Charities rely on the donor's 'disposition to relieve the wants of others'. In the past, this meant simply asking for a donation. Compassion fatigue, however, has led to the development of new and innovative strategies by charitable organisations. Discuss the role and function of PR for charities.

This is a difficult question to tackle if you have not been aware of 'new and innovative' strategies which charities have adopted. This question does not ask you to compare charity with commercial organisations; rather, it asks you to discuss the unique and highly specialised role of charity PR.

You would need, in the first instance, to refer to the purpose of charities, and to discuss 'compassion fatigue'. This will naturally lead you into the innovative strategies which charities have been adopting, and the societal reasons which have compelled charities to adopt these approaches. These strategies should guide you to the publics at which they are aimed. For extra points (if you had time) you might discuss the other challenges facing charities (in addition to compassion fatigue), and the future challenges you would anticipate, from a PR perspective.

Crisis Management

Q 'The best form of crisis management is thorough preparation. Plan for a crisis before it occurs.' (Claire Austin, *Successful Public Relations in a Week*) Explain the key steps involved in crisis PR and discuss one case study, with which you are familiar.

Although a breakdown of marks is not given for this question, it is obvious that the first part carries considerably fewer marks than the second. You should easily be able to explain the key steps involved; the case study is a little more difficult.

Students are notoriously bad when it comes to writing case studies. They make two mistakes. Firstly, they assume that the examiner already knows all of the details. You will not gain marks for what you presumed others knew and, anyway, you are not addressing the question. In order to discuss the study, you need first to outline the situation.

Secondly, instead of writing a case study, students write a story — a rambling, chatty, often interesting account of what happened. The story, of itself, is of no interest. It is the story, from a PR perspective, which the examiner wants to see discussed.

A case study is a brief, concise outline of what happened, and the key points which had an impact on the way in which the PR people dealt with the crisis. Your answer should then go on to look at an overview of the crisis, and deal specifically with the issues that were either well or badly handled from a communications point of view. You should complete your analysis with an update on how the company or organisation has fared in the meantime and what steps it has taken to ensure that a crisis of this nature could not happen again. If the case study is an old one, you should point out the differences in communication techniques which would be available to the modern-day practitioner.

Q A senior director of your company has been suspended, pending investigation into allegations of sexual harassment. Your board has asked you to write a crisis plan to deal with media, staff and clients. Outline the plan that you will put before them.

This is a crisis question with a difference. Here, you have been given an outline of the situation and you are asked to outline your plan. A list of 'key steps' in crisis management will get you zero points — the board could read a book! This question requires 'thinking' time. What the examiner is looking for is a logical thought process; an understanding of all of the publics involved and the impact of this information on them; the consequences, for the company, of each decision; and sound application of PR tools.

You should outline the assumptions you have made, before tackling this question. For example, you need to state that, as shareholders are not mentioned among the publics, the company must not be publicly quoted. Look for the gaps and pick up the extra points by highlighting the fact that you have noticed them.

There are other issues which you need to clarify to the examiner before tackling this question. 'Sexual harassment' needs to be defined — as the company understands it. You need to let the examiner know exactly what the company is dealing with — are we talking about someone being groped, or publicly humiliated by lewd jokes, or what? It doesn't matter what form of harassment you choose, but you should make it clear to the examiner, and it may, of course, impact on the strategy you adopt. Also, the question uses the term 'allegations' — plural. Were there several allegations from one person, or one allegation from each of several people?

You also need to determine the sex of the people involved. Is the senior director a man or a woman? Is the person who made the complaint a man or woman? So, are we dealing with a senior woman harassing a male junior, a senior male harassing a female junior, a senior male harassing a male junior? Clearly outline the assumptions so that you can design a plan that will suit the situation in which you find yourself.

The director has been suspended. Why? Have there been complaints before? Is this the result of implementing the company policy on sexual harassment? Think the scenario through before you tackle the question.

Now we come to the question itself. You have been given different publics with whom there should be communication. Your answer should outline the speed at which you plan to communicate with all (you are trying to achieve virtually simultaneous flows of information), whether or not a statement will be issued, and what information that statement should contain. You should also look at any additional steps which the company might offer to implement immediately.

Your plan should deal with the crucial first 24–48 hours in detail, and the follow-on in more outline form. But you should outline the plan to its conclusion (reinstatement or dismissal of the director).

Finally, your answer should take into account the impact (internally and externally) of the situation's being made public. You should deal separately with the person/s making the allegations of harassment, and the director. You should comment on the good or bad internal communications among employees, and you will need to take into account the level of media skills which the board already has.

For extra points, use an example of a sexual harassment case recently covered in the media, or a company you are familiar with, which has an excellent harassment policy.

Community PR

Q Many organisations now realise the true value of community relations. Discuss the key elements of community PR, citing examples of companies or organisations with good community relations.

You need to begin by defining community PR and clearly outlining precisely what you believe it to mean. You should also define community. You then need to explain all of the ways in which companies can become involved in their communities, i.e. the range of tools available to them. You will need to cite several examples — you have not been asked for a case study (although you could include one); rather, the examiner is expecting you to give an example of each tool. So, what is expected is real-world examples of companies that e.g. sponsor community events or educational opportunities.

For extra points, you could give examples of where companies have benefited from good community relations, or learned — too late? — that community relations would have been worthy of investment.

Sponsorship

Q Sponsorship is really a function of marketing. Discuss.

As a general rule, I hate short questions because it is more difficult to figure out what the examiner is looking for. In this case, however, it is quite specific — defend sponsorship as part of the PR function. To tackle this question, you need either to feel passionately about the issue, or to steer a clever course through your answer.

You will need to define sponsorship — obviously. You should outline the key benefits of entering a sponsorship arrangement (i.e. what sponsorship can deliver for the company), the costs involved and the evaluation methods used in determining its success or otherwise.

You will definitely comment on the fact that many large companies still do not have PR departments, and therefore everything, including sponsorship, is under the umbrella of the marketing department, and you must cite examples of PR consultancies which specialise in sponsorship.

Above and beyond that — and without getting drawn into the argument which, I feel, could lead you astray in your 'power to pull marks' — you should cite at least one sponsorship with which you are familiar, and outline the public relations and marketing benefits of the sponsorship. If possible, compare it with a second sponsorship.

When in doubt, finish somewhere in the middle. The examiner is not going to mark you on the basis of whether or not they agree with the conclusion you reached — your marks are gained on the way in which you argued your case. Play safe. Conclude with something along the lines of: 'On the one hand...but on the other...the jury is still out' — you will not lose any marks for it and you will have saved yourself the hassle of trying to construct an argument, under exam pressure, which probably will not do you justice.

Product PR

Q 'Product PR is just free advertising.' So said the Marketing Manager when he retained you to handle the launch of a new exclusive perfume for women. Write him a memo — you may either agree or disagree.

This question does not allow you the same freedom of movement as the sponsorship question. The examiner has told you that you must take a position — you may agree or disagree, but there is to be no sitting on the fence here. Pick a side and argue your case. Remember to answer in memo style.

In tackling this question, you should aim to reach your conclusion at the end of your answer. That sounds obvious, but it needs some explanation — the approach is explained below.

You should begin by outlining the role and function of product PR — a highly specialised area of the business. You could outline the 4 Ps of marketing and explain how public relations is taught to marketing people. You could outline the role of product PR in pre-priming the market, generating interest, etc. You could also look at the similarities between product PR and advertising.

You will need to use case studies, or numerous examples, of the power of product PR, and the way in which it 'fits' into the overall scheme of the introduction of a new product. Deal with the role of product PR in national, local and trade press. Look at statistics on brand awareness and customer purchasing trends. Throw in examples of lifestyle changes and the role of PR in promoting lifestyle choices.

In essence, this question asks you to argue the pros and cons of product PR, and draw a conclusion at the end. As you write, you will be formulating more arguments — one idea naturally sparks another. Therefore, when you have written your answer, you should re-read it and evaluate the strength of the points you put — then, reach your conclusion based on what you have written.

PR as a Management Function

Q The management function is often underestimated in Public Relations. Explain the key managerial tasks involved in the management of a PR department.

This is a 'study' question. You would need to begin your answer to this question by explaining what the functions of management are (in all organisations). You should then outline the role and function of a PR department. Explain that management of a PR department means applying the same rules. Select the management tasks that you feel are common to all, and those that you feel are specific to public relations.

Q Discuss the benefits (specific to PR) of good management techniques.

In order to do really well in this question, you (probably) need to quote European or American studies on the management of the public relations function. You could possibly compare and contrast management of a PR department (seldom a separate profit centre) with management of a consultancy, and the different demands which are placed on both.

Environmental PR

Q Activist groups, concerned citizens and environmentalists have achieved tremendous publicity in recent years, with mixed outcomes (successful and unsuccessful). Discuss one environmental campaign with which you are familiar, explaining, in particular, the use of public relations.

What the examiner is looking for in this question is a detailed environmental case study — a study in which you outline each of the parties involved and how the particular environmental issue arose. To do well in this question, you need to be able to explain, in detail, the public relations approaches taken by the activists and the corporation. Your case study will need to be a good one. It will need to take the examiner through each of the steps: the community involvement, the media coverage, the legal battles, the political support or lack of support, the corporate lobbying, etc. This case study should be written almost in a timescale fashion, leading to a conclusion of who, in your opinion, won the PR battle and why.

For extra points, you could draw on other examples of environmental campaigns where additional PR tools were used to good or bad effect. You might also draw on previous environmental campaigns which had an obvious impact on the way in which your chosen case study was handled by either the activists or the corporations.

Internal PR

Q In a Celtic tiger economy, with virtually full employment, there is no need for internal public relations. Investment in this area cannot be justified. Discuss.

Chapter 20 dealt with internal public relations, and I deliberately began it by explaining that it is PR for an internal audience (i.e. employees). Numerous students over the years have misread questions on internal PR as being about in-house PR, and have proceeded to answer a question which they were not asked, and on which they could not, therefore, score any marks.

The question suggests strongly that companies need to invest in their employees only when jobs are hard to find. It is an issue that you need to tackle at the start of your answer.

Once again, you need to define what internal public relations actually is. You need to look at changing corporate attitudes, and societal and work-practice changes which reflect the role of employees as valuable company assets. You need to compare and contrast internal PR with the role of trade unions and human resource departments.

You should list the tools of internal PR, and write a paragraph or two about the benefits of each. Your answer would also benefit from current examples of companies that use these tools.

You could, in addition, discuss the role of employees as brand ambassadors and customer and community influencers. You should use examples of companies with good and bad internal relations, and show how those relations impact on the public perception of the company.

Finally, you should deal with the very real and tangible benefits to the company, of good internal public relations.

Political Lobbying

Q 'The notion of lobbying as a trade is in itself dubious. After all, if a project is viable, and to the common good, there should be no need to lobby for it'. (Emer O'Kelly, *Sunday Independent*, 23.4.2000) Write a letter to Ms O'Kelly putting the case in favour of lobbying.

To begin this question, you need to look at what lobbying actually is. Sketch a brief outline of the history of lobbying, how it all began, through to the present day when it is big PR business.

You will need to explain the rules of lobbying — how a good and ethical lobby is actually conducted. You should mention the public interest, and access to politicians, and the public repose.

You will obviously use examples of lobby organisations, and PR lobbyists, and the roles that they fulfil. You should balance your answer by using examples of lobbyists or lobbying for corporations, charities and local organisations. You should also draw on at least one case study of a lobby which was successful and which counters the argument in the quote above.

However, if I were tackling this question, I would not shy away from the fact that not all lobbyists are ethical. I would mention legislation, voluntary codes of conduct, the PR codes of ethics, public perception, and I might suggest a way forward.

Finally, remember the rule — you have been asked to write a letter — your response should be in letter format.

The Future of PR

Q The one certainty about public relations is that it is constantly changing. Explain the challenges, opportunities, threats and potential developments facing the industry in the 21st century.

This question seeks your analysis of the future trends in public relations. It gives you four clear categories in which to analyse these trends — challenges, opportunities, threats and potential development. Your answer should deal with each of these four areas.

There is no right or wrong answer to this question. No one knows what the future holds for public relations as an industry. What the examiner is looking for is a breadth of vision. What do you see as the future of in-house PR; consultancy; education; specialised areas of PR?

How will societal changes impact on PR? What is the future impact of technology? Will legislation change the way in which we practise? What do you see happening to media? Will client spend increase or decrease in the future? Will there ever be a 'global' PR standard? Will marketing and advertising people take over the PR role?

It matters little what areas you choose. What matters is that you choose a broad mix of areas, and analyse them in depth. After all, this is an industry that you are just about to enter. You are hardly likely to do so if you are predicting its imminent collapse, and you are 'innocent', at best, if you have not thought about the future of the industry, and your future within it.

Use examples, research, statistics and trends to substantiate your points.

Appendices

APPENDIX I

Code of Athens
International Code of Ethics
for Public Relations

CONSIDERING that all Member countries of the United Nations Organisation have agreed to abide by its Charter which reaffirms its faith in fundamental human rights, in the dignity and worth of the human person and that having regard to the very nature of their profession Public Relations practitioners in these countries should undertake to ascertain and observe the principles set out in this charter.

CONSIDERING that, apart from 'rights', human beings have not only physical or material needs but also intellectual, moral and social needs, and that their rights are of real benefit to them only insofar as these needs are essentially met.

CONSIDERING that, in the course of their professional duties and depending on how these duties are performed Public Relations practitioners can substantially help to meet these intellectual, moral and social needs.

And lastly, CONSIDERING that the use of techniques enabling them to come simultaneously into contact with millions of people gives Public Relations practitioners a power that has to be restrained by the observance of a strict moral code.

On all these grounds, the undersigned Public Relations Associations hereby declare that they accept as their moral charter the principle of the following Code of Ethics, and that if, in the light of evidence submitted to the Council, a member of these associations should be found to have infringed this Code in the course of his professional duties, he will be deemed to be guilty of serious misconduct calling for an appropriate penalty.

Accordingly, each Member of this Association:
SHALL ENDEAVOUR:

1. To contribute to the achievement of the moral and cultural conditions enabling human beings to reach their full stature and enjoy the indefeasible rights to which they are entitled under the 'Universal Declaration of Human Rights'.

2. To establish communication patterns and channels which, by fostering the free flow of essential information, will make each member of the group feel that he is being kept informed, and also give him an awareness of his own personal involvement and responsibility, and of his solidarity with other members.

3. To conduct himself always and in all circumstances in such a manner as to deserve and secure the confidence of those with whom he comes into contact

4. To bear in mind that because of the relationship between his profession and the public, his conduct — even in private — will have an impact on the way in which the profession as a whole is appraised.

SHALL UNDERTAKE:

5. To observe, in the course of his professional duties, the moral principles and rules of the Universal Declaration of Human Rights.

6. To pay due regard to and uphold human dignity and to recognise the right of each individual to judge for himself.

7. To establish the moral, psychological and intellectual conditions for dialogue in its true sense and to recognise the right of the parties involved to state their case and express their views.

8. To act, in all circumstances, in such a manner as to take account of the respective interests of the parties involved, both the interests of the organisation which he serves and the interests of the publics concerned.

9. To carry out his undertaking and commitments, which shall always be so worded as to avoid any misunderstanding, and to show loyalty and integrity in all circumstances so as to keep the confidence of his clients or employers, past or present, and of all the publics that are affected by his actions.

SHALL REFRAIN FROM:

10. Subordinating the truth to other requirements

11. Circulating information which is not based on established and ascertainable facts

12. Taking part in any venture or undertaking which is unethical or dishonest or capable of impairing human dignity and integrity

13. Using any manipulative methods or techniques designed to create subconscious motivations which the individual cannot control of his own free will and so cannot be held accountable for the action taken on them.

APPENDIX 2

Code of Lisbon

SECTION I

Criteria and standards of professional qualification of practitioners bound by this code.

Clause 1

Every professional member of (national association) duly admitted as such in accordance with the rules of (national association) is deemed for the purpose of this Code to be a public relations practitioner, and to be bound by the Code.

SECTION II

GENERAL PROFESSIONAL OBLIGATIONS

Clause 2

In the practice of his profession, the public relations practitioner undertakes to respect the principles set forth in the Universal Declaration of Human Rights, and in particular the freedom of expression and the freedom of the press which give effect to the right of the individual to receive information. He likewise undertakes to act in accordance with the public interest and not to harm the dignity or integrity of the individual.

Clause 3

In his professional conduct, the public relations practitioner must show honesty, intellectual integrity and loyalty. In particular he undertakes not to make use of comment or information which, to his knowledge or belief, are false or misleading. In the same spirit he must be careful to avoid the use, even by accident, of practices or methods incompatible with this code.

Clause 4

Public relations activities must be carried out openly: they must be readily identifiable, bear a clear indication of their origin, and must not tend to mislead third parties.

Clause 5

In his relations with other professions and with other branches of social communications, the public relations practitioner must respect the rules and practices appropriate to those professions or occupations, so far as these are compatible with the ethics of his own profession.

A public relations practitioner must respect the national Code of professional conduct and the laws in force in any country in which he practises his profession and exercise restraint in reaching personal publicity.

SECTION III
SPECIFIC PROFESSIONAL OBLIGATIONS
Towards Clients or Employees

Clause 6

A public relations practitioner shall not represent conflicting or competing interests without the express consent of the clients or employers concerned.

Clause 7

In the practice of his profession, a public relations practitioner must observe complete discretion. He must scrupulously respect professional confidence, and in particular must not reveal any confidential information received from his clients or employers, past, present or potential, or make use of such information, without express authorisation.

Clause 8

A public relations practitioner who has an interest which may conflict with that of his client or employer must disclose it as soon as possible.

Clause 9

A public relations practitioner must not recommend to his client or employer the services of any business or organisation in which he has a financial, commercial or other interest without first disclosing that interest.

Clause 10

A public relations practitioner shall not enter a contract with his client or employer under which the practitioner guarantees quantified results.

Clause 11

A public relations practitioner may accept remuneration for his services only in the form of salary or fees, and on no account may he accept payment or other material rewards contingent upon quantifiable professional results.

Clause 12

A public relations practitioner shall not accept for his services to a client or an employer any remuneration from a third party, such as discounts, commissions or payments in kind, except with the agreement of the client or employer.

Clause 13

When the execution of a public relations assignment would be likely to entail serious professional misconduct and imply behaviour contrary to the principles of this Code, the public relations practitioner must take steps to notify his client or employer immediately, and do everything possible to see that the latter respects the requirements of the Code. If the client or employer persists in his intentions, the practitioner must nevertheless observe the Code irrespective of the consequences to him.

Towards Public Opinion and the Information Media

Clause 14

The spirit of this Code and the rules contained in preceding clauses, notably clauses 2, 3, 4 and 5 imply a constant concern on the part of the public relations practitioner with the right to information, and moreover the duty to provide information, within the limits of professional confidence. They imply also a respect for the rights and independence of the information media.

Clause 15

Any attempt to deceive public opinion or its representatives is forbidden. News must be provided without charge or hidden reward for its use or publication.

Clause 16

If it should seem necessary to maintain the initiative in and the control of the distribution of information, within the principles of this Code, the public relations practitioner may buy space or broadcasting time in conformity with the rules, practices and usages in that field.

Towards Fellow-Practioners

Clause 17

The public relations practitioner must refrain from unfair competition with fellow-practitioners. He must neither act nor speak in a way which would tend to deprecate the reputation or business of a fellow-practitioner, subject always to his duty under Clause 19b of this code.

Towards the Profession

Clause 18

The public relations practitioner must refrain from any conduct which may prejudice the reputation of his profession. In particular he must not cause harm to his national association (name), its efficient working or its good name by malicious attacks or by any breach of its constitution or rules.

Clause 19

The reputation of the profession is the responsibility of each of its members. The public relations practitioner has a duty not only to respect this Code himself but also:

a. To assist in making the Code more widely and better known and understood.
b. To report to the competent disciplinary authorities any breach or suspected breach of the Code which comes to his notice.
c. To take any action in his power to ensure that rulings on its application by such authorities are observed and sanctions made effective.

APPENDIX 3

Institute of Public Relations (UK) Code of Professional Conduct

Both the Code of Athens and the Code of Lisbon are incorporated in the Institute of Public Relations (UK) Code of Professional Conduct. It reads as follows:

1. **CONDUCT TOWARDS THE PRACTICE OF PUBLIC RELATIONS**
   A member shall:

1.1 Have a positive duty to observe the highest standards in the practice of public relations and to deal fairly and honestly with employers and clients (past and present), fellow members and professionals, the public relations profession, other professions, suppliers, intermediaries, the media of communications, employees and, above all, the public.

1.2 Be aware of, understand and observe this code, any amendment to it, and any other codes which shall be incorporated into it; remain up to date with the content and recommendations of any guidance or practice papers issued by IPR; and have a duty to conform to good practice as expressed in such guidance or practice papers.

1.3 Uphold this Code and co-operate with fellow members to enforce decisions on any matter arising from its application. A Member who knowingly causes his or her staff to act in a manner inconsistent with this Code should be disciplined by the Member.

1.4 Neither engage in any practice nor be seen to conduct him or her self in any manner detrimental to the reputation of the Institute or the reputation and interests of the public relations profession.

2. **CONDUCT TOWARDS THE PUBLIC, THE MEDIA AND OTHER PROFESSIONS**
   A member shall:

2.1 Conduct his or her professional activities with proper regard to the public interest.

2.2 Have a positive duty at all times to respect the truth and shall not disseminate false or misleading information knowingly or recklessly, and take proper care to check all information prior to its dissemination.

2.3 Have a duty to ensure that the actual interest of any organisation with which he or she may be professionally concerned is adequately declared.

2.4 When working in association with other professionals, identify and respect the codes of those professions.

2.5 Respect any statutory or regulatory codes laid down by any other authorities which are relevant to the actions of his or her employer or client, or taken on behalf of an employer or client.

2.6 Ensure that the names of all directors, executives, and retained advisers of his or her employers or company who hold public office, are members of either House of Parliament, Local Authorities or any statutory organisation or body, are recorded in the IPR register.

2.7 Honour confidences received or given in the course of professional activity.

2.8 Neither propose nor undertake any action which would be an improper influence on government, legislation, or the media of communication.

2.9 Neither offer nor give, or cause an employer or client to give, any inducement to holders of public office or members of any statutory body or organisation who are not directors, executives or retained consultants, with intent to further the interests of the employer or client if such action is inconsistent with the public interest.

3.   CONDUCT TOWARDS EMPLOYERS AND CLIENTS
A member shall:

3.1 Safeguard the confidences of both present and former employers or clients; shall not disclose or use these confidences to the disadvantage or prejudice of such employers or clients, or to the financial advantage of the Member (unless the employer or client has released such information for public use, or has given specific permission for disclosure), except upon the order of a court of law.

3.2 Inform an employer or client of any shareholding or financial interest held by that member or any staff employed by that member in any company or person whose services he or she recommends.

3.3 Be free to accept fees, commissions or other valuable considerations from persons other than an employer or client, if such considerations are disclosed to the employer or client.

3.4 Be free to negotiate, or renegotiate, with an employer or client terms that are a fair reflection of demands of the work involved and take into account factors other than hours worked and the experience involved. These special factors, which are also applied by other professional advisers, shall have regard to all the circumstances of the specific situation and in particular to:

3.4.1 The complexity of the issue, case, problem or assignment, and the difficulties associated with its completion.

3.4.2 The professional or specialised skills required and the degree of responsibility involved.

3.4.3 The amount of documentation necessary to be perused or prepared, and its importance.

3.4.4 The place and circumstances where the work is carried out, in whole or in part.

3.4.5 The scope, scale and value of the task and its importance as an activity, issue or project to the employer or client.

A member shall not:

3.5 Misuse information regarding his or her employer's or client's business for financial or other gain.

3.6 Use inside information for gain. Nor may a member of staff managed or employed by a member directly trade in his or her employer's or client's securities without the prior written permission of the employer or client and of the member's chief executive or chief financial officer or compliance officer.

3.7 Serve an employer or client under terms and conditions which might impair his or her independence, objectivity or integrity.

3.8 Represent conflicting interests but may represent competing interests with the express consent of the parties concerned.

3.9 Guarantee the achievement of results which are beyond the member's direct capacity to achieve or prevent.

4. **CONDUCT TOWARDS COLLEAGUES**
A member shall:

4.1 Adhere to the highest standards of accuracy and truth, avoiding extravagant claims or unfair comparisons and giving credit for ideas and words borrowed from others.

4.2 Be free to represent his or her capabilities and service to any potential employer or client, either on his or her own initiative or at the behest of any client, provided in so doing he or she does not seek to break any existing contract or detract from the reputation or capabilities of any member already serving that employer or client.

A member shall not:

4.3 Injure the professional reputation or practice of another member.

5. **INTERPRETING THE CODE**

5.1 In the interpretation of this code, the Laws of the Land shall apply.

APPENDIX 4

National Union of Journalists
Code of Conduct

1. A journalist has a duty to maintain the highest professional and ethical standards.

2. A journalist shall at all times defend the principle of the freedom of the Press and other media in relation to the collection of information and the expression of comment and criticism. He/she shall strive to eliminate distortion, news suppression and censorship.

3. A journalist shall strive to ensure that the information he/she disseminates is fair and accurate, avoid the expression of comment and conjecture as established fact and falsification by distortion, selection or misrepresentation.

4. A journalist shall rectify promptly any harmful inaccuracies, ensure that correction and apologies receive due prominence and afford the right of reply to persons criticised when the issue is of sufficient importance.

5. A journalist shall obtain information, photographs and illustrations only by straightforward means. The use of other means can be justified only by over-riding considerations of the public interest. The journalist is entitled to exercise a personal conscientious objection to the use of such means.

6. Subject to the justification by over-riding considerations of the public interest, a journalist shall do nothing which entails intrusion into private grief and distress.

7. A journalist shall protect confidential sources of information.

8. A journalist shall not accept bribes nor shall he/she allow other inducements to influence the performance of his/her professional duties.

9. A journalist shall not lend himself/herself to the distortion or suppression of the truth because of advertising or other considerations.

10. A journalist shall only mention a person's age, race, colour, creed, illegitimacy, disability, marital status (or lack of it), gender or sexual orientation if this information is strictly relevant. A journalist shall neither originate nor process material which encourages discrimination, ridicule, prejudice or hatred on any of the above mentioned grounds.

11. A journalist shall not take private advantage of information gained in the course of his/her duties, before the information is public knowledge.

12. A journalist shall not by way of statement, voice or appearance endorse by advertisement any commercial product or service save for the promotion of his/her own work or of the medium by which he/she is employed.

APPENDIX 5

Past Papers (Introduction to PR) November/December 2001 — Dublin, Cork and Galway

IRISH ACADEMY OF
Public Relations

EXAMINATION: INTRODUCTION TO PUBLIC RELATIONS

Venue:	University College Dublin
Date:	Wednesday 5th December 2001
Time:	7.00pm–9.00pm
Examiners:	Ros Murphy BA, MIAPR
	Aidan O'Hanlon MA, FPRII

**Answer Question 1 and three questions of your choice.
All questions carry equal marks.**

QUESTION 1

In 1906 Ivy Ledbetter Lee promised unequivocally that he would '...supply prompt and accurate information concerning subjects which it is of interest and value to the public to know about...' and so began modern-day Public Relations. In your opinion what is Public Relations and where did it come from?   (*25 marks*)

QUESTION 2

Your client, a small convenience store owner, has finished building new premises (double the size of the original building). You have been asked to organise a photo call on the opening day. You have secured a local TD to cut the ribbon. How do you go about organising the photo call and how do you brief the photographer? Describe the coverage you anticipate, as a result of your assignment, and, apart from the media, indicate other relevant outlets for the pictures.   (*25 marks*)

QUESTION 3

One of the basic qualities that a PR Practitioner needs is the ability to communicate verbally and in writing, and one of the most basic tools of PR is the news release.
What other qualities does a PR Practitioner need to have? (*5*)
What is the purpose of a news release? (*10*)
How should a news release be written? (*10*)

QUESTION 4

What are the functions of a Press Officer? What skills are necessary to be a good Press Officer?   (*25 marks*)

QUESTION 5

Your client has asked you to organise a function to preview the company's new product for all staff members and their families, two months before its commercial launch. Identify the product, and explain how you will organise such an event.
(*25 marks*)

QUESTION 6

What is sponsorship? Why do companies choose to sponsor an event? Who are the parties involved in a sponsorship? Name a sponsorship with which you are familiar and explain why in your view it has proved to be a successful sponsorship.
(*25 marks*)

IRISH ACADEMY OF
Public Relations

EXAMINATION: INTRODUCTION TO PUBLIC RELATIONS

Venue: National University of Ireland, Galway
Date: Wednesday 28th November 2001
Time: 7.00pm–9.00pm
Examiners: Ian McKeever MPRII
                  Ellen Gunning MA, MIAPR, MPRII, NUJ
                  Aidan O'Hanlon MA, FPRII

Answer Question 1 and three questions of your choice.
All questions carry equal marks.

QUESTION 1

Your friend laughed when you told him that you were studying public relations.
'You mean to tell me that people actually give lessons in how to be nice to people?'
he asked. Write him a letter explaining what public relations is all about.   (*25 marks*)

QUESTION 2

Sponsorship should always deliver a return on your investment. Outline the key
steps involved when deciding to enter a sponsorship.   (*25 marks*)

QUESTION 3

Your company is hosting a reception at which the 'Galway Business Person of the
Year' will be announced. Representatives of businesses in the city and county, politi-
cians, and lecturers/professors of business studies will attend.
You have been retained to organise the function. How will you go about it?

(*25 marks*)

QUESTION 4

The photo call is often an under-utilised weapon in the armoury of the public relations professional. Discuss with examples. *(25 marks)*

QUESTION 5

What are the vital elements in ensuring your news release gets noticed by a news editor? Discuss. *(25 marks)*

QUESTION 6

Outline the key functions of a press officer, distinguishing his or her role from that of a PR consultant. *(25 marks)*

IRISH ACADEMY OF
Public Relations

EXAMINATION: INTRODUCTION TO PUBLIC RELATIONS

Venue: University College Cork
Date: Saturday 8th December 2001
Time: 10.30am–12.30pm
Examiners: Eamonn Dorney MIAPR
               Finbarr O'Sullivan MIAPR
               Aidan O'Hanlon MA, FPRII

Answer Question 1 and three questions of your choice.
All questions carry equal marks.

QUESTION 1

Public Relations is a cheap form of advertising.
From what you know about Public Relations is this statement correct?   *(25 marks)*

QUESTION 2

As part of a Public Relations programme for a client, you decide to organise a photo call.
Describe (a) what essential requirements you should take into consideration when hiring a photographer, (b) how you would organise the photo call, (c) how you would distribute the resultant photographs to obtain maximum publicity for your client.

(25 marks)

QUESTION 3

As a Public Relations consultant you have been commissioned to organise a sponsorship for a multinational company. Write a submission to the Chief Executive outlining the key elements of the sponsorship. *(25 marks)*

QUESTION 4

You are the Public Relations Officer for your organisation.
The Chief Executive informs you that the company is about to launch an important new product, and asks you to arrange an appropriate PR function. Describe what you would do. *(25 marks)*

QUESTION 5

'The PR practitioner must have a thorough understanding of the workings of the print media.'
Describe what you understand this to mean.
or
Write a paragraph on each of the 5 principles of good media relations. *(25 marks)*

QUESTION 6

Using the information in handout 1, write a news release for either the *Daily Star* (tabloid) or the *Irish Independent* (broadsheet) newspaper.
or
Itemise what you would consider to be the 'essentials' of good news release writing.

(25 marks)

QUESTION 7

Write a paragraph on each of the key questions that must be answered before deciding to establish an internal company newsletter.
or
What considerations should be taken into account before deciding to publish a brochure on a new product line for your company? *(25 marks)*

HANDOUT 1 — PRESS RELEASE INFORMATION

Details of a new package of incentives were announced in the Royal Hospital Kilmainham today at a seminar on 'Boiler Efficiency in the Commercial and Public Sectors'. The new grant aid was introduced today by Peter O'Brien TD, Minister of State at the Department of Transport, Energy & Communications.

'Boilers account for an estimated 40% of national energy use. In the Jo Bloggs Corporation we believe that Irish business currently loses somewhere in the region of £5 million per year because of boiler inefficiency,' said Nuala Murphy, the corporation's manager.

The conference, organised by the Jo Bloggs Corporation, looked at the full range of boilers, maintenance issues and systems controls. Delegates were also given presentations on three specific projects — Esat Digifone, Parkways Ltd and Abbey Hotels — which highlighted the financial and energy-saving benefits of good practice in boilerhouses.

The package will assist companies by making a maximum grant of £100,000 or 40% of project costs available to them. The grant assistance is not confined to any particular type of boiler system and is available for both new-build projects and upgrading schemes.

'This new initiative will help companies to achieve monetary savings. In addition, other benefits include improved reliability of plant, improved maintenance levels and more importantly improved comfort,' said Minister O'Brien.

The Jo Bloggs Corporation introduced a new grant initiative, worth £450,000, to encourage businesses in the industrial, commercial and public sectors to use their boilerhouses more efficiently.

APPENDIX 6

Past Papers (Diploma in PR)
May 2000 and 2001. Year 1 and Year 2

PUBLIC RELATIONS INSTITUTE OF IRELAND

DIPLOMA IN PUBLIC RELATIONS

Subject: Public Relations Techniques – Year I Students
Date: *Thursday 18th May 2000*
Time: *10.00–13.00 hrs*

Question 1 is compulsory.
You should also answer 4 (four) of the remaining 5 (five) questions.
All questions carry equal marks.

Compulsory

Question 1
'What comes to mind when you think about a PR consultant? The stereotype is that they are loud-mouthed poseurs with Southern accents, continually on their mobile phones, swigging G&Ts or champagne between calls, and speeding from one superficial and gimmicky event to another in their GTi cabriolets, the hood down in all weathers'.

The DIY Guide to Public Relations (UK).

Discuss.

(20 marks)

Question 2
Having worked as an in-house PR person within a large organisation for a number of years, you have recently changed jobs to work with one of the larger PR consultancies in the city.

The director of your consultancy is interested in your views on the similarities and differences between the functions of in-house PR and consultant.
Write him a memo.

(20 marks)

Question 3
Mary Finan will talk at length about why PR is a worthwhile and necessary profession. She says lying, spinning and misleading don't happen when you deal with reputable clients . . . 'No client, no matter how much they would spend, would be worth me telling a lie for'. Sunday Independent — 20/2/2000

Are PR practitioners really so ethical? Discuss.

(20 marks)

Question 4

Your company, a large firm of solicitors, has decided to introduce an annual conference. Each year the conference will deal with legal issues which are relevant to company directors and chairpersons. They have asked you to organise the conference, and need your recommendations on every aspect of its organisation. Write a memo.

(20 marks)

Question 5

Define each of the following terms:

1. Press conference
2. Publics
3. Public relations
4. Photo-call
5. Objectives

(20 marks)

Question 6

The managing director has called you into his office this morning, and told you that former EU Commissioner Ray MacSharry has agreed to become a director of the company.

He knows that you are familiar with all the tools of PR, and has asked for your recommendations on how best to inform the media of this development.

(20 marks)

PUBLIC RELATIONS INSTITUTE OF IRELAND

DIPLOMA IN PUBLIC RELATIONS

Subject: Public Relations Techniques – Year I Students
Date: *Monday 21st May 2001*
Time: *10.00–13.00 hrs*

Question 1 is compulsory.
You should also answer 4 (four) of the remaining 5 (five) questions.
All questions carry equal marks.

<u>Compulsory</u>

Question 1

'*A squirrel is just a rat with good public relations!*' (Claire Austin).

With the benefit of your current studies, write Ms Austin a letter explaining what Public Relations is all about.

(20 marks)

Question 2

You are a newly appointed Press Officer in a large, semi-state organisation, and you are the first person ever to hold this position. Your manager has asked you to prepare a presentation to the board of directors outlining your role and function within the organisation.
Draft your presentation.

(20 marks)

Question 3

Your company manufactures baby-food products. One of your products has been found to be mildly contaminated. The contamination would cause illness, but is not life threatening. The company needs to inform shopkeepers, supermarkets, and parents that the product should not be used and should be returned to them.

They know that, as a PR professional, you are aware of a wide range of tools which could be used to help them to disseminate this information. They have asked for your advice.

(a)   Outline the tools available to you. *(5 marks)*
(b)   Recommend the tools which should be used and why. *(15 marks)*

Question 4

Define each of the following in 150 words (approx.):
   1.   Photo-Call
   2.   Press Conference
   3.   Newsletter
   4.   OTS
   5.   Propaganda

(20 marks)

Question 5

Your company has moved to new premises, and senior management want a 'grand opening'. They have booked D'Unbelievables to perform the ceremony, which will be attended by staff, customers, members of the local community and several politicians. You are responsible for photography at the event.

Explain:
(a) How you will brief the photographer in advance of the function. *(13 marks)*
(b) Where the photographs will be used afterwards. *(7 marks)*

Question 6

The purpose of evaluating proposals is to establish their worth, their effectiveness and their benefit to a company. Explain four methods of PR evaluation.

(20 marks)

PUBLIC RELATIONS INSTITUTE OF IRELAND

DIPLOMA IN PUBLIC RELATIONS

Subject: Public Relations Techniques – Year 2 Students
Date: *Thursday 18th May 2000*
Time: *10.00–13.00 hrs*

Answer 4 (four) questions of your choice.
All questions carry equal marks.

Question 1

'The financial public relations man is basically a communicator of information. Through his expertness in communications, he helps many people reach the decision to buy or hold his company's stock.'

Eugene Miller, *Lesly's Public Relations Handbook.*

Explain the role of the financial public relations practitioner.

(25 marks)

Question 2

Explain the role of PR for a charitable/non-profit organisation and highlight the differences.

(25 marks)

Question 3

'The best form of crisis management is thorough preparation. Plan for a crisis before it occurs.'

Claire Austin, *Successful Public Relations in a Week.*

Explain the key steps involved in Crisis PR and discuss one case study with which you are familiar.

(25 marks)

Question 4

Many organisations now realise the true value of community relations. Discuss the key elements of Community PR, citing examples of companies or organisations with good community relations.

(25 marks)

Question 5

Sponsorship is really a function of marketing. Discuss.

(25 marks)

Question 6

'Product PR is just free advertising'. So said the Marketing Manager when he retained you to handle the launch of a new exclusive perfume for women. Write him a memo – you may either agree or disagree.

(25 marks)

Question 7

The management function is often underestimated in Public Relations. Explain the key managerial tasks involved in the management of a PR department.

(25 marks)

PUBLIC RELATIONS INSTITUTE OF IRELAND

DIPLOMA IN PUBLIC RELATIONS

Subject: Public Relations Techniques – Year 2 Students
Date: *Monday 21st May 2001*
Time: *10.00–13.00 hrs*

Answer 4 (four) questions of your choice.
All questions carry equal marks.

Question 1

At the AGM 'rebel AIB shareholder and former employee, Niall Murphy positively poured forth invective, some of it cringe-inducing, against the nine man team of directors on the podium'.
Frank Mulrennan, *Irish Independent*, 20/4/2000

Explain the role and function of Financial PR, concentrating on the variety of tools used to reach each of its audiences.

(25 marks)

Question 2

Activist groups, concerned citizens and environmentalists have achieved tremendous publicity in recent years, with mixed outcomes (successful and unsuccessful).

Discuss one environmental campaign with which you are familiar, explaining, in particular, their use of public relations.

(25 marks)

Question 3

In a Celtic tiger economy, with virtually full employment, there is no need for internal public relations. Investment in this area cannot be justified.
Discuss.

(25 marks)

Question 4

'The notion of lobbying as a trade is in itself dubious. After all, if a project is viable, and to the common good, there should be no need to lobby for it'. Emer O'Kelly, *Sunday Independent*, 23/4/2000

Write a letter to Ms O'Kelly putting the case in favour of lobbying.

(25 marks)

Question 5

The one certainty about public relations is that it is constantly changing. Explain the challenges, opportunities, threats and potential development facing the industry in the 21st century.

(25 marks)

Question 6

Charities rely on the donor's 'disposition to relieve the wants of others'. In the past, this meant simply asking for a donation. Compassion fatigue, however, has led to the development of new and innovative strategies by charitable organisations.
Discuss the role and function of PR for charities.

(25 marks)

Question 7

A senior director of your company has been suspended, pending investigation into allegations of sexual harassment. Your board has asked you to write a crisis plan to deal with media, staff and clients. Outline the plan that you will put before them.

(25 marks)

APPENDIX 7

PRII National Syllabus
Diploma in Public Relations
PR Project 1 May 2000

TOPIC

St Jude's is a new hospital in your area. It opened its doors on 1 January 2001 and has been built to replace the old city centre Children's Hospital, the Regional Maternity Hospital and the County General and Surgical Hospital which was located on the west side of the city. The new hospital has 450 beds and is located just off the newly constructed orbital route around the city. Opening night was difficult and most of the admissions were through the Casualty Unit and were principally made up of New Year's Eve revellers. Unfortunately, this was recorded by a photographer and one national tabloid reported opening night in an unflattering manner.

At a recent meeting of the Board of Governors, the Development (fundraising) Division has just announced that the first initiative to raise funds will be a sponsored walk in the Andes Mountain Range in Peru. Participants will have to raise a minimum of £50,000 for the hospital and the numbers are restricted to 250 plus 5 hospital representatives. They will fly from Ireland on the August Bank Holiday and return the following Friday week.

You have just been appointed to the post of PRO and have been set the task of developing a Public Relations Programme to launch and support this new initiative. The overall PR budget is £40,000 and separate funds have been allocated to Marketing and Advertising for this initiative. The proposed timescale for the programme that you have to develop is 16 weeks beginning just after Easter and finishing the week before departure.

St Jude's Hospital, Cork

Marie Crimmins MIAPR

Sample PR Project (Grade A)

Year 1, Diploma in Public Relations

Irish Academy of Public Relations

St Jude's Hospital Cork

PR Proposal

May 2001

Contents

Appendices

1.0 INTRODUCTION

This is a Public Relations proposal for St Jude's Hospital, Cork. The proposal outlines the main objectives and events which will be undertaken within the project period. There are a number of important areas which are outlined in the various sections of the proposal, with ancillary diagrams and explanatory reference material in the Appendices to the rear of the proposal.

Firstly in order to get a description for the job at hand let us turn to the Brief for the project.

2.0 THE BRIEF

2.1 St Jude's is a hospital in the Cork area. Unfortunately its opening night was difficult, made worse by the fact that a photographer took damaging photographs and one national tabloid reported the night in an unflattering manner.

At a recent meeting of the board of governors, the Development (fundraising) Division announced that the first initiative to raise funds will be a sponsored walk in the Andes Mountain Range in Peru. Participants will have to raise a minimum of £5,000 for the hospital and numbers are restricted to 250 plus 5 hospital representatives. They will fly from Ireland on the August bank holiday and return the following Friday week.

The overall PR budget is £40,000 and separate funds have been allocated to marketing and advertising for this initiative.

3.0 ASSUMPTIONS

3.1 The New Hospital

St Jude's is a new hospital in the Cork Area. It was built to replace the old city centre Children's Hospital, the Regional Maternity Hospital and the County General and Surgical Hospital which was located on the west side of the city. The new hospital, which opened its doors on the 1st of January last (2001) has 450 beds and is located just off the newly constructed orbital route around the city.

3.2 The Three Hospitals, pre 1st January 2001

In order to get a profile of the new hospital it is important to understand the ethos of the individual hospitals, pre amalgamation.

3.2.1 The Children's Hospital was a 150-bed hospital located in the city centre. While every effort was being made to establish a 'child-friendly' environment, it became difficult to accommodate the increasing needs both in terms of medical technological advances and because the building itself was in need of some modernisation. Among the requests put forward by the staff and management of the Children's Hospital was the provision of a large indoor and outdoor play facility for the children and purpose-built rooms for parents who wish to stay with their children, as parents are seen as a vital part of the care team.

3.2.2 The Maternity Hospital had approximately 100 beds and had a long history in Cork. Again, due to its size and inadequate facilities it became apparent that the only solution was to relocate the hospital. The main requests put forward here were to provide a bright and cheerful design and also a large crèche facility for children of the hospital staff.

3.2.3 The County General and Surgical Hospital had approximately 200 beds, well under capacity for a hospital with an expanding catchment area. It was felt that accessibility, including public transport and adequate car-parking facilities both for staff and visitors, and a heli-pad were facilities which would need to be improved.

St Jude's, the new hospital, is equipped with state-of-the-art facilities and the requests of the individual hospitals have been met.

3.3   The Area

St Jude's is located just off the newly constructed orbital route around the city. It falls under the jurisdiction of the Southern Health Board, and will cater for patients mainly from the 'North Lee' and 'South Lee' areas, which have a total population of 303,645.[1] There are many well-established companies and business parks in the Greater Cork area;[2] these will form part of the 'publics' – section 6.0. Also Cork City and Suburbs has a long list of primary and secondary schools and two third-level institutions. There are a number of walking clubs — within these second/third-level institutions. The larger employers (for example Cork County Council has a walking club) and within the Cork area itself, the 'Cork Walkers Group'.

3.4   The Walk

A separate committee will be set up by the Board of Governors to deal with the actual walk itself. The health and safety of the walkers is paramount and this committee will deal with the fundraising elements. The chairperson of this committee will liaise with the PR Consultancy and attend regular meetings to exchange views and ideas.

4.0   THE PROBLEMS

4.1   The bad publicity regarding the opening night at the hospital has generated a bad initial perception of the hospital.

4.2   As St Jude's is a new hospital it does not have a previous 'track record' to dismiss such claims by tabloid newspapers, especially regarding photographs. Thus the attempts to dismiss the opening night problems did not, or could not have totally dismissed the photographs.

4.3   Staff at the hospital seem to be divided — since the opening night there is a tension between different sections. This, coupled with the fact that each of the hospitals is searching to find its new 'place' or identity, is proving difficult.

4.4   The larger 'Greater Cork Area' community including the City Centre has no allegiance to the new hospital. There is a need to build up the community's perception of the new hospital and also create an awareness of the new hospital and the range of facilities it has to offer.

4.5   The Southern Health Board is aware that cardiovascular diseases are a major killer in Ireland, and the Southern Health Board region is no different. 45% of all deaths in the Southern Health Board area are due to such diseases.[3]

5.0 AIMS AND OBJECTIVES

5.1 Increase awareness of St Jude's as a hospital in its own right.

5.2 Increase people's awareness of the walk and inform them about the facilities that are on offer there.

5.3 Create a better image of the hospital as a place to work for existing and potential employees.

5.4 Create an awareness of the dangers of heart disease and motivate people to join walking groups (for example).

6.0 PUBLICS

As noted previously there are a wide number of publics which must be contacted or reached. Firstly, let us examine the complete list. See Appendix A for Event – Publics Matrix.

6.1 Hospital Publics which include: Management and Staff (all levels, both current and potential), Patients (both current and potential). Also with the assistance of after care – the families and those close to the patients.

6.2 The Greater Cork area communities, Community Groups – those living in the area, who are potential visitors, patients in the hospital.

6.3 Sports Clubs, Mountaineering Clubs, Walking Clubs, Community Centres, those with an interest in sport and travel.

6.4 Local Schools both Primary and Secondary and also Third Level Institutions, University College Cork and Cork Institute of Technology.

6.5 The Business and Enterprise Community, including the Pharmaceutical Industry which is so strong in the Cork area and the Shopping Centres in the Greater Cork area.

6.6 Local and National Media – The Southern Star, the Imokilly People, The Corkman, Local Community radio, 96FM and National media – newspapers, TV and radio presenters.

6.7 Opinion Leaders – The Department of Health and Children, Minister Micheál Martin TD, Cork Corporation and Cork County Council, Southern Health Boards, Doctors and Public Representatives.

6.8 National Organisations – The Happy Heart Foundation.

7.0 SOME GENERAL RECOMMENDATIONS

7.1 Following research and consultation with the main committees and public bodies, it has been decided that the 4-month public relations campaign shall commence on 9 April, one week earlier than specified.[4]

7.2 The title of the campaign or the campaign slogan is 'St Jude's Healthy Heart Walkers', as this encompasses the main aims of the project.

7.3 St Jude's is not the first hospital to amalgamate three different hospitals and the different approaches employed in similar hospitals around the country shall be used in order to monitor the success of the project.

7.4 The project shall consist of three main phases:
1. Pre-launch (6 April–11 May)
2. Launch (12 May)
3. Post launch (13 May–30 August)

8.0 THE PRE-LAUNCH PHASE

8.1 Create awareness about the campaign – Community
Drop leaflets into households in the vicinity of the hospital. This should aim to do the following:
- Highlight St Jude's – phone numbers, departments, visitor facilities, etc.
- Raise awareness about the campaign 'St Jude's Healthy Heart Walkers' – and the phone numbers to contact to receive information pack.
- Should also mention the Launch date (12 May)

8.2 Design and print posters A0 and A3 size to be distributed in the local bus stops and shopping centres, and any other public places, also in work places, medical centres – health facilities, community care centres and in the hospital itself.

8.3 Set up an information stand in the large reception area of the hospital – this will be manned on specific information days. This stand will show the construction of the hospital (to include photos taken by the locals), and also official photos, and information about Peru and the 'St Jude's Healthy Heart Walkers'.

8.4 The TV/Radio Personality
The TV/Radio Personality to be used in this campaign is John Creedon, who is a well-known 'local' – Cork personality. He has also agreed to highlight the campaign on his morning show on RTE Radio One. Because of the nature of the campaign – combating heart disease – a number of other personalities will agree to support the campaign.

8.5 Walking Groups and Mountaineering Groups
It is imperative that all of Cork's walking/mountaineering groups are informed about the walk. They will be written to and contacted by phone to assess the level of interest.

8.6 Primary and Secondary Schools
A separate competition has been set up for the different age groups in the schools. John Creedon and a Hospital Representative together with some native

Peruvians will visit the larger Primary schools and announce details of the 'St Jude's Healthy Heart Competition'.

9.0 THE LAUNCH

9.1 The Launch is to take place on Saturday 12 May in the Conference area of the Hospital. John Creedon will introduce Minister for Health and Children, Mícheál Martin, who has agreed to launch the campaign. In his address he will cover the most salient aspects of the campaign;
- St Jude's, joining of three hospitals who have given exemplary service to the people of Munster for decades, and this new hospital has continued in this proud tradition.
- The frightening statistics produced each year regarding cardiovascular diseases – state-of-the-art facilities and expert care available in St Jude's.
- In light of this, St Jude's Hospital promotes the Summer 2001 Walk in Peru. Raising money for a new cardiac ambulance for the Cork area.
  Light Refreshments will be available in the Hospital Gardens, following the official photographs taken by a PR photographer. 100 heart-shaped balloons will be set off to launch the project.

10.0 POST-LAUNCH STAGE[5]

10.1 Healthy Heart Promotion Week
This will be a seven-day event – for anyone who wishes to have blood pressure and cholesterol measured by the hospital staff. A special unit will be set up for this from Monday to Friday, and on Saturday and Sunday, they will set up a road show and visit two local shopping centres. This will be free of charge and will generate good publicity for the hospital. Also an aerobics session will take place in the shopping centre at lunchtime. Aerobics instructors from the local gym have volunteered their time.

10.2 Staff Sports Day
A sports day will be organised for St Jude's hospital staff, group sports as well as individual sporting activities will be held. Part of the competition will be held in the nearby gym, which has recently opened.

10.3 Membership Discount for Hospital Staff and Walkers
10.3.1   This Gym has offered a reduction in joining fees for St Jude's hospital staff. Also in an effort to raise the profile of the walkers and exercise, the gym has provided the St Jude's Healthy Heart Walkers with half-price joining fees.
10.3.2   Also, an activity shop in Cork City has agreed to help finance the provision of walking equipment including walking boots and knap sacks.

10.4 Evening Talks

The staff of the hospital will arrange a series of three evening talks. They will deal with the following topics:

- Talk for community on Lifestyle Changes, the importance of exercise
- Talk for community, 'You are what you eat' – given by hospital dieticians
- Talk aimed specifically at the walkers/out-door activity clubs in the Cork area about first aid in sport, given by Casualty staff

10.5 Garden Fête

One of the Development Committee members has volunteered the use of her garden for a garden fête, which will include a 'bring and buy' section. This event will provide another opportunity for staff to mix and locals (especially the elderly in the community) to come along.

10.6 Cork Youth Orchestra

The Orchestra has helped with fundraisers in the past, and has proved very success-ful. They will play an outdoor concert (weather permitting) and will play a variety of South American music to fit in with the 'Peruvian' theme of the walk. As patron of the Orchestra, the Lord Mayor will attend this concert.

10.7 'A Midsummer Night's Dream'

The Maryborough House Hotel will be the venue for this fancy dress ball. The aim of this evening is to get the business community to 'dig deep'. Hospital staff will also be invited to attend this gala evening. The evening will begin with a reception in the garden, where a PR photographer will be present and distribute pictures to the key media groups.

10.8 Children's Sports Day

A sports day will be held for the local children including those children who entered the project competitions. Secondary schools students will help with the organisation of this event, which will be similar to that of the staff sports day. A prize-giving ceremony will be held for all the children that evening and a party will be organised for the children after that.

10.9 Documentary

A local film company, Econ Ltd, has expressed an interest in making a documentary about the hospital, including the campaign and the walking trip to Peru. This docu-mentary will be part funded by the hospital and will be made available for sale to the major networks for viewing.

11.0 BUDGET

Items/Events	Quantity	Cost
11.1 Promotion of Campaign		
Celebrity Fee		£3,000
Leaflets & balloons	20,000	£2,000
Posters		
A0		
A3		£2,000
Information Pack Folders		£1,800
Information Stand at Hospital		£400
(Hire stands etc.)		
11.2 Official Launch		
PR Photographer/Press Release		£600
Invitations	2,000	£700
Food Catering – cost covered by Hospital		£0
Reception/Conference Area of Hospital —		£0
Free of charge		
11.3 Healthy Heart Promotion Week		
2 Nurses (for 7 days)		£1,000
Aerobics Instructor (5 hours total)		£250
PR Photographer/Press Release		£500
Medical Supplies and Analysis[6]		£1,000
11.4 Staff Sports Day		
Total Prize Money		£1,000[7]
Cost of Hiring Gym		£600
Refreshments		£600
PR Photographer/Press Release		£400
11.5 Evening Talks		
Costs included in 11.1		
11.6 Garden Fête		
Refreshments		£1,000
Musical Entertainment		£500
11.7 Cork Youth Orchestra		
Programmes		£100
Refreshments		£1,000
Raffle prizes and donations		£1,000[8]
PR Photographs and Press Release		£500
11.8 'A Midsummer Night's Dream'		
Maryborough House Hotel		£1,000

Meals	300 @ £25 per head	£7,500
Music		£500
Decorations		£500
PR Photographs/Press Release		£500

11.9 Children's Sports Day

Prizes (Sports) – medals	1,000	£600
Prizes (projects) – computers sponsored by EMC		£0
Refreshments		£600
PR Photographs/Press Release		£500

11.10 Evaluation	
Facilitators (three-day interview process)	£600
11.11 Documentary	
Finances from the PR budget[9]	£7,000
11.12 Expenses	
Miscellaneous	£500
Total Cost	**£39,750**

NOTE
All prices include VAT.

12.0 EVALUATION

12.1 Media General

Together with the Hospital Spokesperson and Hospital Board of Governor (Fundraising Division), the media reaction to the different events will be monitored.

12.2 In-depth analysis of Media Coverage

The level, quality and quantity of media coverage of the 'St Jude's Healthy Heart Walk' will be assessed both during and after the campaign. There will also be a level of publicity when the walkers return and the measure of success of the project will, to a certain extent, be underlined by this coverage. The frequency and tone of the media content both written and spoken will be analysed.

12.3 Measure of interest in the Walk

The level of interest in the Peru walk will be determined by the number of information packs requested and also by the hospital stand.

12.4 Hospital Staff

Specialised facilitators will interview a random sample of hospital staff. They will be asked how they find working in the hospital and whether the gym deal was seen to be an added bonus to those interested in joining St Jude's staff. The results of these structured interviews will be presented to the hospital Board of Governors.

12.5 Level of Participation at the events

Another measure of the success of the campaign is the level of participation at the fund-raising events, and children's sports day, and the Healthy Heart Week — blood pressure and cholesterol testing sessions, and aerobics.

12.6 Feedback from the Walking Groups and the Hospital Walkers

It is important that the walkers themselves are satisfied with the campaign and the level of support and fundraising that is generated by the publicity.

12.7 The SHB Statistics regarding heart disease should also provide an indicator as to whether the campaign helped to influence life-style changes for the people of the Greater Cork area.

Appendix A
Matrix demonstrating projects/events aimed at particular publics

Date/Month	Project/Event	Specific Publics and Action
Commences 9 April	Campaign Awareness Drop leaflet to 10 local housing estates	Residents in the locality Again, all publics, hospital, staff and patients
18 April	Set up information stand at St Jude's Hospital	Youth 4- to 12-year-olds
18 April	Visit to local primary schools	
Week of 23-27 April	Visit to local secondary schools	Youth 12- to 18-year-olds
12 May	Official launch	Invitations to walking groups, staff, local and national media, representatives from local heart foundation – medical/health centres local representatives
21-27 May	Healthy Heart Promotion Week	Community
7 June	Staff Sports Day	Staff of St Jude's Hospital
From 14 May (announce at the Launch)	Discounts for local gym and sports shop	Walkers and St Jude's Hospital staff
28 May 30 May 6 June	Evening talks	Local community, especially those with an interest in health issues. Also aimed at the walking groups.
7 July	Garden Fête	Hospital staff and local community
11 July	Cork Youth Orchestra	Community (local interest in Cork Youth Orchestra)
21 July	'Midsummer Night's Dream'	Commercial groups and business people
23 June	Children's Sports Day	Youth of the Community
All during campaign and while in Peru and after walkers come home	Documentary about the 'Walk to Peru' – fundraising activities, the actual walk, etc.	All Publics mentioned here including publics, communities at a wider level.
Mid August	Assess 'post' walk media interest	For purposes of Evaluation
End August	Prepare report for hospital Board of Governors	To assess project and learn for future campaigns.

APPENDIX B

Southern Health Board – Healthy Heart Campaign

The main findings of the report include:

- Cardiovascular disease is a major cause of death in Irish men and women.
- We in Ireland have higher death rates than our EU colleagues.
- There is a downward trend regionally and nationally in these diseases.
- Also there is a fall in mortality which is greatest in the 65 years of age cohort.
- Highest mortality rates from heart attack
- Cardiac interventions on the increase.

These graphs represent some of the Southern Health Board's data.

[Pie chart — Principal Causes of Deaths, 1994–1998]

[Bar chart — Number of Cardiac Procedures Carried out in the SHB in 1998]

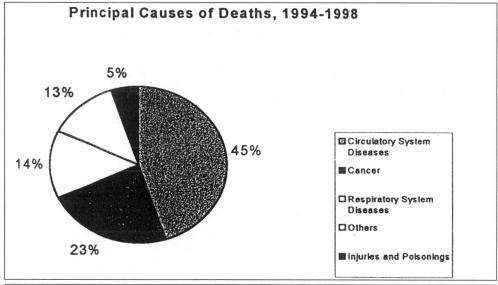

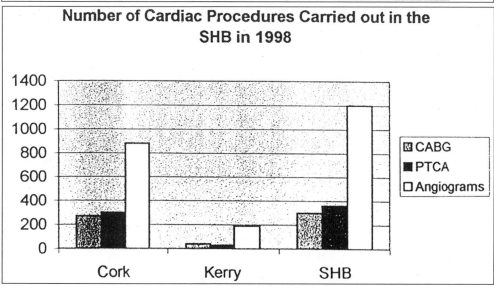

APPENDIX C
John Creedon's Duties[10]

- To promote the campaign on his radio show, interview some of the walkers before and after the walk.
- Visit the schools and introduce the Peruvians, act as a 'facilitator'.
- Attend the launch and introduce the theme of the campaign and Health Minister Micheál Martin.
- Attend the Healthy Heart Promotion week – at the shopping centre where he will formally announce its commencement, and perhaps get his own blood pressure and cholesterol measured!
- Attend and compere the Cork Youth Orchestra Concert.
- Attend the 'Midsummer Night's Dream' dinner, raise awareness and importance of funding for the walkers.
- Attend the Children's sports day – present the prizes at the prize-giving ceremony.
- To be available for any additional interviews necessary for the documentary.

APPENDIX D

References

Public Relations

Jefkins, F., *Public Relations Techniques*, Butterworth Heinemann, England (1994)
Public Relations Hand Book (2000-2001)

Southern Health Board

Report of the Director of Public Health, November 2000, Stationery Office, Dublin
The National Health Promotion Strategy 2000-2005, July 2000, Stationery Office, Dublin
Corporate Development Plan 2000-2003, Stationery Office, Dublin
Building Healthier Hearts – Southern Health Board – 5 Year Action Plan 2000-2004, Stationery Office, Dublin
An Information Guide to Southern Health Board Services, July 2000, Stationery Office, Dublin

Websites:
www.maryborough.com
www.irlgov.ie
www.doh.ie
www.irlgov.ie/educ

APPENDIX E

Other Hospitals in the Cork Area

University College Hospital
Wilton, Cork, Co. Cork
Telephone: 021-546400
Fax: 021-342690

Erinville Hospital
Western Road, Cork, Co. Cork
Telephone: 021-275211
Fax: 021-275502

General Hospital Bantry
Bantry, Co. Cork
Telephone: 027-50133
Fax: 027-51209

General Hospital Mallow
Mallow, Co. Cork
Telephone: 022-21251
Fax: 022-43110

Mental Health Centre
Midleton, Co. Cork
Telephone: 021-631751

Mercy Hospital
Grenville Place, Cork, Co. Cork
Telephone: 021-271971
Fax: 021-276341

Our Lady's Psychiatric Hospital
Lee Road, Cork, Co. Cork
Telephone: 021-541901
Fax: 021-303017

St Finbarr's Hospital
2 Douglas Road, Cork, Co. Cork
Telephone: 021-966555
Fax: 021-966563

St Mary's Orthopaedic Hospital
Gurranebraher, Cork, Co. Cork
Telephone: 021-303264
Fax: 021-303527

St Stephen's Psychiatric Hospital
Sarsfieldcourt, Glanmire, Cork, Co. Cork
Telephone: 021-821411
Fax: 024-866872

South Infirmary/Victoria Hospital
Old Blackrock Road, Cork, Co. Cork
Telephone: 021-964333
Fax: 021-310153

District Hospital Bandon
Bandon, Co. Cork
Telephone: 023-41403
Fax: 023-41403

District Hospital Castletownbere
Castletownbere, Co. Cork
Telephone: 027-70004
Fax: 027-70881

District Hospital Clonakilty
Clonakilty, Co. Cork
Telephone: 023-33205
Fax: 023-35643

District Hospital Dunmanway
Dunmanway, Co. Cork
Telephone: 023-45102
Fax: 023-45344

District Hospital Fermoy
Fermoy, Co. Cork
Telephone: 025-31300
Fax: 025-33686

District Hospital Kanturk
Kanturk, Co. Cork
Telephone: 029-50024
Fax: 029-51292

District Hospital Kinsale
Kinsale, Co. Cork
Telephone: 021-772202
Fax: 021-773386

District Hospital Macroom
Macroom, Co. Cork
Telephone: 026-41002
Fax: 026-42878

District Hospital Midleton
Midleton, Co. Cork
Telephone: 021-631516
Fax: 021-633463

District Hospital Millstreet
Millstreet, Co. Cork
Telephone: 029-70003
Fax: 029-71148

District Hospital Schull
Schull, Co. Cork
Telephone: 028-28120
Fax: 028-28398

District Hospital Skibbereen
Skibbereen, Co. Cork
Telephone: 028-21677
Fax: 028-22583

District Hospital Youghal
Youghal, Co. Cork
Telephone: 024-92106
Fax: 024-92651

(Note: Since submission of the project the telephone numbers in the 021 district have had an extra digit added before the number.)

REFERENCES

1. Southern Health Board, Annual Report, 1999. It should be noted that there are other hospitals within the Cork area to help deal with this population.
2. For the purposes of this promotion, the Greater Cork Area is defined as Cork City, and its surrounding suburbs, and its catchment areas (North Lee and South Lee) as outlined by the Southern Health Board.
3. Such diseases include coronary heart disease, stroke, angina, heart failure, and diseases of the arteries, hypertensive disease and rheumatic heart disease. (Southern Health Board, 2000, p. 30)
4. The brief outlined the starting date as 'after Easter'. However this would not fit in with the commencement date – 'the week before departure'. Thus it was decided to begin one week earlier.
5. All of these events will be advertised on local newspapers and radio.
6. Hospital has agreed to fund any expenses over this amount.
7. Prizes were also donated by local businesses and also Cork Swansea Car Ferries and Cork Airport/Aer Rianta.
8. Again, spot prizes were donated by local businesses.
9. Some of the additional costs will be funded by the Marketing and Advertisement budget.
10. John Creedon has expressed an interest in taking part in the walk in Peru (which will give the documentary an added interest). This, however, is not formally considered to be one of his duties.

APPENDIX 8

PRII National Syllabus
Diploma in Public Relations
PR Project 2 May 2000

TOPIC

You work in-house as a Public Relations Manager for a state owned service provider. Due to changes in your industry, particularly deregulation, your organisation has decided to undergo a complete corporate name and identification change.

You have been given the responsibility to manage this undertaking and have been requested to ensure that the change-over is as smooth as possible.

Company employees and customers are a priority. However, this change impacts on all of your stakeholders and your task is to maximise the positive aspects of this new development and your company's evolving role in society.

A budget of €6 million has been allocated to the actual design and implementation of the new name and identification and €63,500 for public relations activities. You must detail a budget for all of the public relations strategies and techniques which you are advocating. The time frame is a six month lead-up to the launch of the name and identification and a six week period after the official launch for continuing techniques and evaluation.

The project should be no more than 16 typed pages, excluding appendices. Only relevant appendices need be attached.

Developing Our Future Identity
Ita Glavin MIAPR
Sample PR Project (Grade A)
Year 2, Diploma in Public Relations

Developing our Future Identity

Food Technology Services

An In-house Public Relations Proposal

Submitted: Saturday, 12 May 2001

ASSUMPTIONS

Recognising the constraints of the Brief, with regard to time and budget, the following assumptions have been made:

In line with an EU Directive and recommendations from the OECD, Ireland is preparing its food research and services industry for deregulation in January 2002. This has given Teagasc subsidiary, Food Technology Services, an opportunity to draw up a strategic plan to face rigorous competition in the Irish food research market. It plans to sharpen its image and focus on establishing itself as the leading food research and advisory body in Ireland. The National Food Safety Authority will be the industry regulator.

The Minister for Agriculture and Food and the Board of Directors of Food Technology Services are responding to this challenge by launching the Company under a new corporate name and identity.

The existing Board of Directors will remain unchanged.

A discussion framework has been set with Trade Unions and talks are well under way.

The Teagasc Group derives its annual funding from the Oireachtas, the EU, grants, donations, voluntary levies and operational income. Internal financial and accounting systems are operating in Irish Pounds at present and provisions have been made for a smooth changeover to the Euro on 1 January 2002. The Company may face privatisation or seek an industry partnership in a few years but no firm decision has been made at this time.

A corporate identity steering group has been formed to oversee the development of this project. It includes the in-house Communications Department of Food Technology Services which has qualified professionals in the fields of advertising, marketing and public relations. It works closely with the Board of Directors, Human Resources, Finance, Research and Advisory Strategy Committees, Training and Education Committee and the Department of Agriculture and Food.

Behaviour & Attitudes Ltd has been engaged to train the management team of Food Technology Services in the delivery phase of name change and conduct of media relations. This will be paid from the Public Relations Budget.

Interbrand Newell & Sorrell has been engaged to oversee the selection of a new corporate name. If a suitable one isn't recommended from employees they have their own brand name in reserve.

Carton Le Vert will create a new visual image/logo.

The above two items will be paid from the €6 million campaign budget.

Design and Print have also been contracted out.

Other members of the project steering committee are taking charge of areas that require alteration in the changeover to new corporate name and identity. Their activities are listed in Appendix 1. Expenses for all of these activities including the advertising and marketing campaigns will be taken from the €6 million budget.

The budget of €6 million is probably realistic given that the sales market from food and agri-business companies in Ireland was over £9,000 million in 1997. However, it represents approximately 7.5% of Food Technology Service's annual budget, which is quite high.

This proposal will be submitted to the Board of Directors for examination, and subject to approval, the campaign will be rolled out from 4 June 2001.

The public relations proposal is only one element of the overall plan.

Contents

Section 1

INTRODUCTION

The Brief

Food Technology Services is a constituent part of Teagasc, the state-owned Agriculture and Food Development Authority. It is to undergo a complete corporate name and identification change due to proposed deregulation of the food research and services industry in Ireland.

As in-house Public Relations Manager for the project, the author of the proposal will design a planned and sustained programme of activity ensuring a smooth transition for Company employees and customers. It will impact favourably on all stakeholders and ultimately allow the Company to focus more closely on society's evolving needs.

A budget of €6 million has been allocated for the design and implementation of the new corporate name and identification programme, and €63,500 for public relations activities.

The proposal covers a six month-period, June–November 2001, at the end of which the official launch takes place. There will be a six-week period post-launch for ongoing activities and evaluation.

Section 2

SITUATION ANALYSIS

Market Background

The international agri-food industries are undergoing revolutionary change. Markets are changing in response to consumer demands for greater product quality and safety, improved animal management systems and environmentally sustainable farming and land-use systems. Emerging technologies are allowing modification of plants, food ingredients, packaging and food which in turn lead to new products.

Survival of the agri-food industries will in part depend on their ability to grasp the potential of these advances and innovate as a way to gain commercial advantage. Deregulation of the food research and advisory industry in Ireland will provide more competition in the market place, with wider choice and lower prices for industry and consumers. Agri-food industries in Ireland will have to cope with international markets and competition if they wish to expand and share in the new opportunities.

Teagasc Group

The Teagasc Group provides integrated research, advisory and training services for the agriculture and food industry and for rural communities in Ireland. It employs 1,500 people at 120 locations (see Appendix 2). It has played a vital role in the development of the Irish economy.

Research services are delivered by 200 scientists at eight dedicated centres covering food processing, dairying, beef, sheep, arable crops, horticulture, environmental protection, economics and rural development.

Independent advice to farmers and rural dwellers is provided by 550 local advisers and regional specialists located at 100 centres. Through its advisory and training services Teagasc has contact with over 80,000 farmers, almost half of whom are contracted clients.

Training for young entrants, adult farmers, rural dwellers and the food industry is provided by 200 teachers and technologists at 14 colleges, 45 local training centres and research centres.

The corporate identity of the Company is bound up with a sense of nationality and is highly visible across the country via tradeshows, sponsorships, seminars and training courses. Its corporate image is very positive in the academic, scientific and rural communities.

In order to prepare itself for deregulation Teagasc has decided to split its organisation into two segments:

(a) Food Technology Services, representing their food research and advisory services, will be launched under a new corporate name, a new logo and corporate identity. Existing identity guidelines were last updated in 1983.
(b) Teagasc, whose name is synonymous with agriculture, will continue using that name to provide top-class advice, research and expertise to the agricultural industry.

Food Technology Services

Structure
This body comprises eight Research Centres, serving over 600 clients, located at Grange, Co. Meath, Oak Park, Co. Carlow, Johnstown Castle, Co. Wexford, Clonroche, Co. Wexford, Athenry, Co. Galway, Raheen, Co. Limerick, Dunsinea, Co. Dublin, and Moorepark, Co. Cork.

Activities
The food centres at Moorepark, Fermoy and Dunsinea, Dublin, undertake technology transfer to the food industry through technical consultancy, contract research and training programmes.

In 1999, sixty-nine projects were undertaken at Dublin and Moorepark. These led to significant advances in research and innovation across the entire food spectrum. A measure of the scientific excellence of the food research programme is that food researchers published 71 reports in international scientific journals. A further 300 reports were published by research staff in non-scientific publications. (Teagasc Annual Report 2000)

Food Technology Services has economists attached to the FAPRI-Ireland Partnership, the policy analysis unit formed by Teagasc and Irish universities in conjunction with the University of Missouri. They published their first analysis on the impact of the Agenda 2000 agreement on the reform of the Common Agricultural Policy in May 1999.

Many advisory activities, including food safety training programmes, are provided at the research centres and through the Teagasc network of some 55 training centres and 45 local offices strategically located throughout Ireland.

Mission Statement
'To provide innovation and technology transfer services for the sustainable development of the agri-food sector and rural communities through integrated research, advisory and training programmes.'

Deregulation – the Climate for Change

The clear focus of government policy in deregulating the food industry is to equip the agriculture and food industry as an innovative, high-productivity, high-quality and high-skilled sector which can successfully compete in a more liberalised world food market.

Meeting the future demands of competitiveness will involve moving away from the old 'agriculture oriented' image to a more international, dynamic, innovative and futuristic one.

The new image will encapsulate modern trends, techniques and research, a highly educated and skilled workforce, an impressive portfolio of corporate clients, a knowledgeable audience and informed consumers.

Through promotion of its new name, logo and personality the Company will reach new plateaus.

To assess the impact of deregulation a SWOT Analysis has been completed (see Appendix 3).

465

Section 3

<u>OBJECTIVES</u>

This planned and sustained Public Relations campaign will strive to:
1. Maximise awareness and successfully launch the new corporate name and identification of the Company.
2. Mobilise a positive and participative communications programme for all employees, focusing on the positive aspects of competition and the exciting challenges ahead.
3. Protect and develop the reputation of the Company through effective communication with customers, stakeholders and prime key audiences.

A continuous programme of activities will also cover the following objectives:
(i)   Promote the Company as the national flagship for research and development, innovation and technical services.
(ii) Serve customers better than anyone else and be the envy of competitors and peers.
(iii) Extend the vision of the rebranded Company into colleges, universities, institutes of technology, the scientific and rural communities.
(iv) Develop an interactive website under the new Company name with established links to the Teagasc website.
(v)   Maintain the synergy between Teagasc and the renamed Company.

Section 4

STRATEGY

This six-month Public Relations campaign will provide the framework for comprehensive cultural change within the renamed Technical Food Services Company as the food industry in Ireland prepares itself for deregulation. The new brand name will be the Company anchor and all communication must reflect this, both in terms of positioning and core values.

Relaunch
The relaunch of Technical Food Services will consist of:
- An effective integrated communications strategy involving an informed workforce
- A new logo
- A new mission statement
- New advertising
- A revised portfolio of products and services

There will be a 360-degree programme of events designed to work at every level within the Company's internal and external audiences.

Employees
It will be crucial for Management to get close to its staff as they will be anxious about their positions within the Company and their future prospects. The challenge of successfully managing change will lie in helping people overcome their resistance to it. The vital ingredient of change will be sustained action ensuring progress which ensures change.

SWOT Analysis
Deregulation is about competition, accountability, transparency and change. Now the Company must dramatically improve its efficiency to survive. Change will mean experiencing a significant difference. The Company will no longer operate as a closed system. The SWOT Analysis will define the Company's future as positive with great opportunities ahead but it must also factor in contingency plans for the unexpected.

Communication
Contact with customers, stakeholders and opinion leaders will be through the regular channels of newsletters, mailshots and briefings, with information evenings and presentations being made at the eight Research Centres nationwide.

The general and specialist media will be invited to certain functions.

The wider public audiences will be reached via the general media.

Section 5

PUBLICS

A targeted and sustained Public Relations campaign aimed at key audiences, with particular emphasis on the first three, will be crucial in achieving smooth transition to the new corporate name and identification.

As competition develops in the market place, so too will new audiences develop. It will be important to monitor this trend and to meet the challenges as they arise.

- *Employees*
  Executives, Management, Regional Managers, Directors of Colleges, Specialist Researchers, Technical, Secretarial, Sales and Field Staff

- *Customers*
  Co-Ops, Brewers, Food Producers, Food Processors, Farmhouse Industries, Supermarket Industry

- *Stakeholders*
  The Government, Trade Unions, Dept. Agriculture, Food & Rural Development, ESRI, Forfás, Bórd Glas, UCD – Faculty of Agriculture, UCC – Dept of Food Science, Bórd Bia, The Food Development Authority.

- *Opinion Leaders*
  Minister for Agriculture & Food, All TDs and Senators, IBEC, ISME, IDA, IFA, ICMSA.

- *Interest Groups*
  OECD, EU Office Dublin. Groups against Genetically Modified Foods.

- *Media*
  Print, TV, Radio, Video, Audio; addressing Employees, Trade, Science and National audiences.

- *Rural Communities*
  Dissemination of information via Teagasc Rural Network.

- *Future audiences*
  Economists – maybe privatisation, European Food Fairs (e.g. Frankfurt), European Food Producers and Processors, Potential Employees, Potential Customers.

Section 6

PROPOSALS

Corporate change within the organisation needs to be organic and it needs to occur under the conditions of strict project management for it to succeed. Given the short lead-up time to the launch, the campaign will be intense.

The strategy will be to work from the inside out – starting with employees and their representatives, and through them communicating with customers, stakeholders and key audiences. A strong corporate name and identification is important so as to reap the benefits of competition and market deregulation.

6.1 MANAGEMENT PARTICIPATION

Building Skills
Building trusting relationships will be crucial to the success of the changeover to new corporate name and identification.

Behaviour & Attitudes Ltd will train selected members of the management team and project steering group in conducting delivery sessions of name change, problem solving, image building and media skills. These team members will be selected for being thoughtful, enlightened and farsighted individuals.

Management will need to achieve the following objectives:
- Establish clear communication, via a special campaign newsletter, with employees so that they understand and support the need for change.
- Articulate the Company aspiration, describing what the Company intends to become.
- Show how this aspiration will guide decision-making and action at all levels and help employees to connect their jobs to the larger Company purpose.
- Communicate with customers at the highest level, cementing existing relationships and showing appreciation for their custom.
- Keep stakeholders and opinion leaders informed. Invite them to important events.
- Participate in the production of a corporate video for the launch.

Media: Issue Press Release to national press and industry journals advising how deregulation will affect Food Technology Services and how they are embarking on an internal communications programme to adapt to market and society's needs   (Month 1)

6.2 STAFF PARTICIPATION

Reaching Employees

The Public Relations team will:

- Send a letter to all employees, signed by Chairman, informing them of
  (i) what deregulation of the industry means,
  (ii) how it will affect them, the Company and customers,
  (iii) emphasising that change is important to meet the demands of an evolving society.
- Include 'talking points' that employees can use to inform themselves and to answer questions from customers, family, fellow employees and others.
- Include a series of questions and answers.
- Include a chronology of key events leading up to the launch.
- Advise on the date of the Information Evening at their nearest Research Centre. Encourage staff to attend.

It will be important to engage line management and mobilise key players who have leadership roles in crucial domains.

It is envisaged that an interactive and sustained programme of events will help allay any fears that some staff may have with regard to moving from a stable market environment to a competitive one.

Change will happen at an individual level, at a group level, and at an organisational level. It will be both top-down and bottom-up and will ultimately focus on improved results. Any issue that will imperil change will be addressed in a timely fashion. Staff will be encouraged to be responsible for change – make it – and live with it.

Employee Information Evenings

The Public Relations team will initially assist the Chairman in addressing the Head Office staff at the start of the campaign. They will then embark on a nationwide information tour, with members of Management and the Communications team, visiting staff at the eight Research Centres.

Information evenings will provide an excellent opportunity for interaction and active listening between the team and employees of each particular region. (see Appendix 4)

Various techniques, including the skills of social psychology, will be used to move the process forward. (See Appendix 5)   (Months 2–3)

Ongoing Staff Support

Area Co-Ordinators

Programme Corporate Changeover Area Co-Ordinators will be appointed from the in-house Management Team at each of the eight Research Centres and will be trained and supported by the Public Relations team. The appointees will have the responsibility of briefing staff with campaign updates, disseminating information to the Advisory Offices, Field Staff, and Agricultural Colleges. A list of names of clients to contact in their areas will be provided and the Co-Ordinators will arrange an information evening for such clients. They will also arrange the Launch Day at their centres, with regard to staff viewing launch link, food, entertainment, merchandising, promotion etc.

(Months 2-6)

Staff Newsletter

Progress reports will be issued monthly via the staff newsletter. During the campaign important historical features on the Company will also be printed in the newsletter. It will give employees a sense of being an integral part of change within the Company. This will positively and progressively build the momentum for change.

(Months 1-6)

Designated Phone Line

A Staff Hot Line will be set up for the course of the six-month public relations programme. This expenditure will be covered centrally. It will operate Monday to Friday 12-4 p.m. daily.

(Months 1-6)

Company Intranet

Campaign information pages will be set up on the Company Intranet where staff can read the progress of the campaign and can e-mail in suggestions or comments. It will be updated weekly. Paid by central budget.

(Months 1-6)

Staff Incentives

A sense of excitement and appreciation of staff must be in-built to the campaign and in this regard it is proposed to:

- Hold a Staff Competition – Best suggestion of a new corporate name for the Company – the Company will reserve the right to present its own name if a suitable one isn't found. Prize – 1 week holiday in the sun for two (value €1,300) and €650 spending money. Distribute competition forms at the information evenings and to offices nationwide.
- Present a range of Staff Awards over a 12-month period – Best suggestions on improving service and support systems both internally and externally. Prizes will include shopping vouchers and weekends away.
- Staff Bonus: All staff will receive a once-off extra day's annual leave in 2002.
- Staff Gift: All female staff will receive a silver brooch and male staff a tie pin, in the design of the new corporate logo.

Media

A contracted photographer will travel with the Public Relations roadshow team, compiling photos for a souvenir brochure which each staff member will receive on the day of the launch.

(Months 2–3)

Press Releases will be issued to national and trade newspapers with a supply of some photos with an interesting angle on the information evenings, e.g. Food Technology Services – planning early for deregulation, etc.

(Month 3)

6.3 EXTERNAL PUBLICS

Company Clients

- The Company's customers are its most important publics. A strength of the organisation is that some individuals have established an excellent reputation and one-to-one relation-ship with some valuable corporate clients. This medium must be exploited to its fullest potential.
- In-house Marketing Dept conducted a 'Company Services Survey' through its top 100customers in January 2001. The Survey results will shape future customer product development and delivery. It will be vital to keep this segment informed on any structural or product enhancements as they occur within the industry.

  Retention of existing client base will be essential.

(Months 4–5)

Information Evenings

Area Co-Ordinators will hold Information Evenings at the Research Centres for all clients in their area, discussing the results of the survey, discussing the way forward and thanking them for their business. It will be an opportunity to cement relationships. (see Appendix 4 again)

- Local Public Representatives, Opinion Leaders and selected representatives from Industry Bodies in the local areas will also be invited to attend these evenings.
- Information leaflets will be distributed.
- Tea, coffee and light snacks will be provided.

(Month 4)

Other Stakeholders & Audiences

- Trade Union Representatives will play an integral and important part in formulating plans for job enhancement reward in the new forward-looking organisation. They will be included at all round-table discussions concerning staff issues and will be invited to attend meetings at the Regional Centres.
- Government Departments and other stakeholders will be briefed through information packs and general literature (paid out of central budget).

Media

'Moorepark News', distributed three times annually to all dairy farmers, and 'Teagasc Today', the corporate newsletter also distributed three times annually to all politicians, co-operatives, food processors, employees, academic institutions, etc. will cover some of the unfolding events in the organisation. This will coincide with in-house publishing of the results of the customer survey and customer information evenings.

Trade-journal, 'Irish Food', will contain a feature on exciting changes in the pipeline at Food Technology Services.

(Month 4)

6.4 PRE-LAUNCH STRATEGY

1 Month Prior to Launch:

- All members of the Board, the Project Steering Group, the Communications Department, including Public Relations, will meet to discuss strategy, cross-check and co-ordinate their duties for Launch Day.
- Invitations will be prepared for the VIP list, guest speakers and other guests.
- Executives from each Research Centre will telephone their blue-chip clients and personally invite them to attend the Launch Day function at their centre. A special invitation card will also issue.
- Media will be contacted and invited to attend (see Appendix 6).
- Public Relations photographer booked.
- Chairman to confirm that the Corporate Video has been completed.
- In-house Marketing and Advertising will arrange to have stationery, merchandising and promotional materials distributed to the Regional Centres in time for the launch. These items will be kept under the strict control of the Co-Ordinator until launch day.
- Confirm Launch Day date, name of reserved room, numbers and menus with Hotel.
- Confirm Launch Day details with Area Co-Ordinators.

6.5 LAUNCH DAY – NEW CORPORATE NAME AND IDENTIFICATION

Launch Time: 11.00 a.m.
Launch Date: Monday 25 November 2001
Launch Venue: The Burlington Hotel, Dublin.

A celebratory Launch lunch has been organised for Dublin and other activities arranged for the eight Research Centres (see Appendix 7).

Launch Activities – Dublin

- There will be a photo call at 10.00 a.m. with An Taoiseach, Minister for Agriculture & Food, and Chairman of Food Technology Services.
- A photo opportunity with the Minister for Agriculture and Food cutting a cake in the shape of the new Company Logo.
- Key journalists from the trade press, national press and media will be invited to a special briefing in advance of the photo call.
- A video-taped interview with the Chairman will provide the historical context and rationale for the decision to change corporate name and identification and will be given to these key journalists.
- An embargo on release of this information will be in place until after the launch has taken place.
- Press Packs will be given to all the media, including a history of the Company, and an explanation of the Corporate logo, name and identification.
- There will be a video link from Head Office to all Research Centres where all staff will hear the Chairman's launch speech.

6.6 POST LAUNCH

- Video and audio tapes of the Launch speeches will be distributed to ensure that every employee has the opportunity to review the message.
- All customers will receive a letter from the Chairman of the Board outlining the new corporate name and identity, and emphasising the Company's commitment to serving them better even in a more competitive environment.

(Month 6+)

Section 7

EVALUATION

The six-week post-launch period is very tight to give an accurate assessment of evaluation.

Media: Research and coverage of launch on TV and radio, and column inches generated in national, scientific and trade press will assess how visually successful the campaign has been externally.

Staff: Ongoing evaluation of the Staff Information Campaign will identify its strengths and weaknesses. It will give an opportunity to address any loopholes in the campaign. The launch should provide benefits for staff in morale and prestige. There will be a challenge for everyone to show how training and commitment will position them to compete with other organisations.

Staff Newsletter: Ask staff how effective it was as an information medium for them.
Hotline: Important source of feedback – one-to-one basis – gets close to staff issues.
Intranet: Important medium of contact – 24-hour facility. Monitor number of hits.
Staff Competition re Corporate Name: The volume of returns will be one measure the level of interest in the campaign.
Staff Awards Scheme will keep the impetus of change going for some months.
Staff Bonus will be seen as a gesture of goodwill and an influencing factor in change.
Staff Gift: Symbol of pride for staff. Object of promotion for the Company.

Photographers assigned to all the Regional Centres for Launch Day will capture the spirit and memories of the day. The photos will be circulated in 'Teagasc Today' and a special souvenir booklet for staff a few weeks after the launch.
New Corporate Name and Identification will add to the stability of the Company and make it a very exciting place to work.

Customers: Turnout of customers at the Information Evenings and the Launch will be a measure of support for the organisation. True evaluation of success will be measured by retention and further development of their business in the future.

ONGOING FUTURE TECHNIQUES

Plans are underway to:
- Launch a new Corporate Magazine
- Develop a new website.

These will build and maintain image and contact.

A senior-level Steering Group will continue to monitor how the Organisation is publicly perceived and will suggest ways to perform up to those perceptions.

Sponsorship would enhance and build the Company's image, and getting involved in some of the following areas could be considered:

(i) Best Farmhouse Cheese of the Year
(ii) Young Scientist of the Year
(iii) Two Scholarships to UCC – Degree in Food Science
   Selection from top students to progress to degree level, having completed their Certificates in Agriculture/Horticulture at the Teagasc Colleges.

Once competition between various organisations commences, it will take comprehensive communications efforts, driven by overall business strategies, to retain, cement and strengthen the critical bond between the Company and the customer.

A further ongoing task will be to balance the interest of employees, customers and stakeholders.

The Organisation will have succeeded when:

- customers and competitors regard it as the industry leader
- the professionalism of Management and the quality of the Company's services is envied and emulated.

Section 8

BUDGET

Breakdown	Euro
Administration (Press/Media Releases, telephones, letters, postage etc)	6,000
Behaviour & Attitudes Ltd (Management & Project Group Sessions)	6,000
Co-Ordinators (8) Training Expenses	5,080
Communication Team to Research Centres re Staff Delivery	2,400
(Marketing/PR/HR/Photographer – incl accommodation & mileage)	
Staff Information Evenings (Refreshments & Snacks / 1500 Staff)	8,000
Corporate Name Staff Competition	1,950
Competition Entry Forms: A5 b/w one side recycled 90 gsm* - 5,000	215
Staff Award/Suggestion Scheme	6,000
Entry Forms: A4 b/w one side recycled 90 gsm* - 5,000	300
Staff Campaign Special Newsletter,	2,000
Size A4/Double Sided/Full Colour* 6 months x 1500	
Staff Gifts – Brooches/Tie Pins	9,000

Customers:

Information evenings @ 8 Research Centres – Food/Refreshments	3,500
Letters & Leaflet re new Company logo, mission statement, identification etc.	2,500

Launch:

VIP Invitations – Dignitaries & Guest Speakers	500
6" x 4" Gilt Edge Invitation Cards & Envs Qty 100	
Video – Launch – Copies for Research Centres and Regional Outlets (x 100)	1,000
Pre-recorded interview with Chairman for key Journalists (TV Quality x 10)	1,000
Audio Cassettes for Research Centres/Field Staff etc. (x 200)	1,250

Subtotal:	Euro	56,695
Contingency 10%		5,669
Total	**Euro**	**62,364**

*Printing non inclusive of VAT

Section 9

<u>APPENDICES</u>

1.   ITEMS REQUIRING ALTERATION TO NEW CORPORATE NAME

2.   TEAGASC AGRI-FOOD LOCATIONS

3.   SWOT ANALYSIS

4.   STAFF AND CUSTOMER INFORMATION EVENING AGENDAS

5.   SOCIAL PSYCHOLOGY – THE CONCEPT OF CHANGE TECHNIQUE

6.   MEDIA CONTACTS

7.   CORPORATE LAUNCH – INVITATION LIST

8.   CAMPAIGN SCHEDULE

APPENDIX 1

Sample of some items requiring alteration to new Corporate Name and Identification.

Funds for these activities will be taken from the €6 million budget.

1. The livery of vans.
2. Stationery including letterheads, news release heads, invoices, order forms.
3. Name displays on premises, e.g. head office, research centres, plaques at Teagasc regional and advisory offices.
4. Exhibition stands, showrooms, mobile exhibitions, road signage to premises, sponsorship banners, flags, etc.
5. Sales literature, price lists, catalogues, sales promotion material, merchandising, etc.
6. Labels, packaging and containers.
7. External and internal newsletters.
8. Instruction leaflets, service manuals.
9. Work wear, laboratory clothing, field staff jackets, umbrellas, etc.
10. Advertisements in all visible media.
11. Credits on documentary research films, video tapes, slide presentations.
12. Diaries and calendars.
13. Annual reports, project reports, etc.
14. Website and e-mail references.

Other major expenditure includes:

Carton Le Vert – New Logo/Image
Interbrand Newell & Sorrell – Selection of Corporate Name
Design & Print
Advertising
Marketing – Corporate Video
Staff Hotline
Launch Day Celebrations

APPENDIX 2

Teagasc

AGRICULTURE AND FOOD DEVELOPMENT AUTHORITY

Headquarters
19 Sandymount Ave, Dublin 4	(01) 6688023
Economics Unit	(01) 6688443
Director's Office	(01) 6603673
Finance Depot	(01) 6603776
Personnel Dept	(01) 6376191

Regional Offices
NORTH
Grange, Dunsany, Co. Meath	(046) 25187

SOUTH
Kildalton College, Piltown, Co. Kilkenny	(051) 643446

Rural Development
Rural Development Centre, Athenry, Co. Galway	(091) 844296

Research Centres/Stations/Sites
CARLOW
Oak Park Research Centre, Carlow	(0503) 42423

CLARE
Kilmaley Farm, Inch, Ennis, Co. Clare	(065) 6839430

CORK
Moorepark Production Research Directorate, Fermoy	(025) 42384
Moorepark Production Research Centre, Fermoy	(025) 42340
Dairy Products Research Centre, Fermoy	(025) 42340

DUBLIN
Kinsealy, Malahide Road, Dublin 17	(01) 8460524
National Food Centre, Dunsinea, Castleknock, Dublin 15	(01) 8059550

GALWAY
Research Centre, Athenry	(091) 845847
Belclare Research Station, Belclare, Tuam	(093) 55430

KILDARE
Lullymore Research Station, Rathangan	(045) 860481

LIMERICK
National Food Centre, Food Dev Facility, Raheen	(061) 301172

MAYO
Hill Sheep Farm, Leenane	(095) 42297

MEATH
Grange Research Centre, Dunsany	(046) 26154

TIPPERARY
Solohead Farm, Limerick Junction	(062) 47118

WEXFORD
Johnstown Castle Research Centre	(053) 42004
Johnstown Castle Lab/Research	(053) 42213
Clonroche Research Station, Clonroche	(054) 44544

Advisory Offices
CARLOW
Headquarters, The Green, Tullow	(0503) 51931
Barret Street, Bagenalstown	(0503) 21537

CAVAN
Headquarters, Adv Office, Ballyhaise College, Ballyhaise	(049) 4338304
Kells Road, Bailieboro	(042) 9666492

CLARE
Headquarters, Station Road, Ennis	(065) 6828301
Fossabeg, Scariff	(061) 921525
Ardnaculla, Ennistymon	(065) 7071261
Ballyurra, Kilrush	(065) 9051459

CORK EAST
Headquarters, Farranlea Road, Cork	(021) 4343598
Knockgriffin, Midleton	(021) 4631745
Moorepark, Fermoy	(025) 42384
Sandfield, Mallow	(022) 42657
James O'Keeffe Institute, Newmarket	(029) 60675
Carnegie Hall, Millstreet	(029) 70886
Bluepool, Kanturk	(029) 51181

CORK WEST
Headquarters, Kilbarry Road, Dunmanway	(023) 45161
Codrum, Macroom	(026) 42317
Aras Beanntrai, The Square, Bantry	(027) 51869
Connolly Street, Bandon	(023) 44038
Coronea, Skibbereen	(028) 22398

Advisory Office, Darrara College, Clonakilty	(023) 34449

DONEGAL
Headquarters, Cavan Lower, Ballybofey	(074) 32062
Carnamuggagh, Letterkenny	(074) 26659
Doonan, Donegal	(073) 21918
Main Street, Buncrana	(077) 61265
Pound Street, Carndonagh	(077) 74233

DUBLIN
Headquarters, Kinsealy Research Centre, Malahide Road, Dublin 17	(01) 8461218
Corduff, Lusk, Co. Dublin	(01) 8439013

GALWAY
Headquarters, County Advisory Office, Athenry	(091) 845830
Terryland Retail Park, Headford Road	(091) 561353
C/O M. Keady, The Square, Headford	(093) 35210
Deerpark, Ballinasloe	(0905) 42973
Barrack Street, Loughrea	(091) 841114
Upper Dublin Road, Tuam	(093) 28895

KERRY
Headquarters, The Pavilion, Austin Stack Park, Tralee	(066) 7125558
Clieveragh, Listowel	(068) 22700
Cleeney, Killarney	(064) 32366

KILDARE
Headquarters, Friary Road, Naas	(045) 879093
Rathstewart, Athy	(0507) 38261

KILKENNY
Headquarters, Kells Road	(0506) 21852
Mullinavat	(051) 898204

LAOIS
Headquarters, 1 Park Villas, Portlaoise	(0502) 22974
Knockiel, Rathdowney	(0505) 46601

LEITRIM
Headquarters, Bridge Street, Carrick-On-Shannon	(078) 21363
	(078) 21363
Hill Street, Mohill	(078) 31989
Sligo Road, Manorhamilton	(072) 56151

LIMERICK
Headquarters, Parnell Street, Limerick	(061) 310835
Killmallock	(063) 98580
Gortboy, Newcastlewest	(069) 61094

LONGFORD
Headquarters, Town Centre	(043) 41025

LOUTH
Headquarters, Dublin Road, Dundalk	(042) 9332316

MAYO
Headquarters, Michael Davitt House, Castlebar	(094) 24572
Bunree Road, Ardnaree, Ballina	(096) 71188
Newport Road, Westport	(098) 27295
Abbey Road, Ballinrobe	(092) 41869
Lower James Street, Claremorris	(094) 71913
Abbey Street, Ballyhaunis	(0907) 31032
Bridge Street, Swinford	(094) 52305
Shore Road, Belmullet	(097) 82302
Mullinmore Street, Crossmolina	(096) 31979

MEATH
Headquarters, Kells Road, Navan	(046) 22811
Willowfield, Navan Road, Kells	(046) 40312
Advisory Office, Grange, Dunsany	(046) 26154

MONAGHAN
Headquarters, Coolshannagh	(047) 81408
Lakeview, Castleblaney	(042) 9746659

OFFALY
Headquarters, 'Sheena', Charleville Road, Tullamore	(0506) 21659
St Brendan's House, Oxmanstown Mall, Birr	(0509) 21630

ROSCOMMON
Headquarters, Abbey Street	(0903) 25494
St Patrick's Street, Castlerea	(0907) 20917
Magazine Road, Athlone	(0902) 94636
The Crescent, Boyle	(079) 62586

SLIGO
Headquarters, Riverside	(071) 42677
Carrownanty, Ballymote, Co. Sligo	(071) 83246

TIPPERARY NR
Headquarters, Dromin Road, Nenagh	(067) 31130
Castlemeadows, Thurles	(0504) 21405

TIPPERARY SR
Headquarters, Carrigeen, Clonmel	(052) 21199
Davis Road, Tipperary	(062) 51180

Courthouse, Hogan Square, Cashel	(062) 61160

WATERFORD
Headquarters, Shandon, Dungarvan	(058) 43551
Main Street West, Lismore	(058) 54126
C/O Waterford/Ross Marts, Old Kilmeaden Road	(051) 352239

WESTMEATH
Headquarters, Dublin Road, Mullingar	(044) 40327
Dublin Road, Moate	(0902) 82085

WEXFORD
Headquarters, Adv & Tr Ctr, Johnstown Castle	(053) 45880
Barrett's Park, New Ross	(051) 425490
Dublin Road, Enniscorthy	(054) 33830
Showgrounds, Gorey	(055) 21548

WICKLOW
Headquarters, Wentworth Place, Wicklow	(0404) 69898
Coolruss, Tinahely	(0402) 38640
Kiltegan Road, Baltinglass	(0508) 81432

Colleges
CAVAN
Ballyhaise Agricultural College, Ballyhaise	(049) 4338540

CORK
Darrara Agricultural College, Clonakilty	(023) 34449

DUBLIN
College of Amenity Horticulture, Botanic Gardens, Glasnevin, Dublin 9	(01) 8040212

GALWAY
Mellows Agricultural College, Athenry	(091) 845146

KILKENNY
Kildalton Agricultural & Horticulture College, Piltown	(051) 643797

APPENDIX 3

SWOT ANALYSIS

Strengths
1. Food Technology Services is the national provider of food research consultancy and training to the food industry.
2. It is committed to serving industry through consultancy and technology transfer.
3. It retains a high profile both at home and abroad.
4. It has earned the respect of the international scientific community.
5. Its staff are highly educated and skilfully trained.
6. It disseminates research results and follow-up to 600 food companies through the Non Commissioned Food Research Programme (NCFRP).

Weaknesses
1. Company is unsure how the market will react to new competitors
2. Supply of work no longer guaranteed.
3. Internal systems and standards open to more scrutiny.

Opportunities
1. Opportunity for company to launch itself onto international platforms.
2. New logo and name will express its mission statement, enhance staff morale, build on existing relationships and challenge competitors.
3. Opportunity to develop new business both at home and abroad.
4. Opportunity for staff to develop their careers as company becomes more 'internationally oriented'.
5. Shifting patterns of consumerism will allow the company to adapt more quickly to market demands.
6. Sales of the company's expertise through Research & Advisory Services and Technology will be an important source of income.

Threats
1. Company could lose some of its customer base.
2. Competition could make Company look gauche and outdated.
3. Staff could feel threatened and may resist change.
4. Food manufacturers and consumers may become price-sensitive.

APPENDIX 4

Staff Information Evening
AGENDA

1. Situation Analysis
2. Strategic Plan for Food Technology Services over next three years
3. Deregulation of the Food Research and Advisory Industry in Ireland
4. Legal and Financial implications of compliance
5. Comparative slide-show on similar industry that deregulated in another country
6. Changing our Corporate Name and Identification
7. Schedule of Events and Timetable
8. Human Resources
   — New roles emerging; new training and development opportunities
9. Introduce Area Co-Ordinator for relevant Research Centre
10. Questions and Answers Session
11. Thank everyone for attending – close meeting.

Customer Information Evening
AGENDA

1. Situation Analysis
2. Deregulation of the Food Research and Advisory Industry in Ireland
3. Results of Company Survey – due to time constraints it wasn't possible to survey all customers.
4. The Future of Food Technology Services in serving its customers better.
5. Introduce Area Co-Ordinator for relevant Research Centre
6. Information leaflets on deregulation available
7. Questions and Answers Session
8. Thank everyone for attending, and their custom – close meeting.

APPENDIX 5

Social Psychology – The Concept of Change Technique

    (i)   The psychological contract of change
    (ii) Communication
    (iii) Conceptualisation
    (iv) Commitment

By progressing through these four elements staff will be helped to understand the power of attitude and culture, the lead time of change and the necessity of change both in broad terms and in specific terms. They will be further encouraged to make specific behavioural change that will be permanent.

Summary of how the Concepts of Change will work:

(i)   *Psychological contract*
Without this people will not fully commit themselves. Building a change programme will require a solid foundation. While agreement is passive, commitment is an act of integrity and that will be necessary. Management will need to be successful in 'capturing' both the heads and hearts of their staff. Strive to achieve internalisation.

(ii)   *Communication*
Establishing how staff perceive the management plan will dictate the pace of change. Affirm how important their talents, commitment and vision are in building the company of tomorrow. Hold a question and answer session. Encourage staff to discuss what they like best about the company and what annoys them. Asking staff for their opinion on what things they would like to retain, and images or colours they might like to see in the new logo, will help in determining how the staff feel they are effective and inclusive participants in the process of change.

(iii)   *Conceptualisation*
To understand the reason for change will require concepts. The Public Relations team will generate the right concepts at exactly the right time so that all staff members will fully understand how they themselves form part of the transition process.

(iv)   *Commitment*
This embodies three separate but closely related attitudes:
(a) A sense of identification with the organisational mission
(b) A feeling of involvement in the organisational duties
(c) A feeling of loyalty to the company as a place to live and work.

APPENDIX 6

MEDIA CONTACTS

NATIONAL DAILY PAPERS

Irish Examiner	Business: Kevin Mills	News: Brian Carroll*
Irish Times	Business: Bill Murdoch	News: Willy Clingan*
Irish Independent	Business: Frank Mulrennan	News: Philip Molloy*

SUNDAY PAPERS

Sunday Business Post	Business: Ted Harding	News: Aileen O'Toole
Sunday Independent	Business: Shane Ross	
Sunday Tribune	Business: Brian Carey	News: Martin Wall
Sunday Times		News: Charles Hymas

REGIONAL PAPERS

(Relevant to Research Centre catchment areas)

Co. Meath	The Meath Chronicle
Co. Carlow	The Nationalist
Co. Wexford	The Wexford People
Co. Galway	The Tuam Herald/Connaught Tribune
Co. Limerick	The Limerick Leader
Co. Dublin	The Evening Herald
Co. Cork	The Avondhu/Evening Echo

RADIO

RTÉ Radio 1	George Lee
Cork 96 & 103 FM	
Today FM	

TELEVISION

RTÉ 1	George Lee/Charlie Bird*
TV3	
TG4	
UTV	

SPECIALIST MEDIA/TRADE PRESS

In-house Magazines: Teagasc Today, Moorepark News
Irish Food
Irish Farmer's Journal
Irish Farmer's Monthly

FEATURES

RTÉ – Ear to the Ground – Mairéad McGuinness*

* Key Journalists

APPENDIX 7

CORPORATE LAUNCH
INVITATION LIST

Dublin Launch:

VIP

An Taoiseach – Mr Bertie Ahern
An Tánaiste – Ms Mary Harney
Minister at Department Agriculture, Food & Rural Development
Minister at Department of Enterprise, Trade & Enterprise

Launch Address

Chairman of the Board, Dan Browne
Minister Joe Walsh

Guest Speakers

Mr Denis Brosnan (Kerry Foods plc)
Darina Allen (Ballymaloe Cookery School)

Other Guests to include

TDs, Senators, Lord Mayor of Dublin, Senior Civil Servants
Corporate Customers
Representatives from OECD, IBEC, ISME, IFA, ICMSA, ICTUP, SIPTU, Food Processors and Distributors

Co-Ordinated Launch at Research Centres

Invitations to

Customers in catchment areas
Local Government Representatives
Rural Community Groups
Farmhouse Food-Industry Groups

Telephone invitations will issue to local and national media to attend Corporate launch in Dublin and Research Centres nationwide.

APPENDIX 8

CAMPAIGN SCHEDULE

Commencing 4 June 2001   Launch Date 30 November 2001

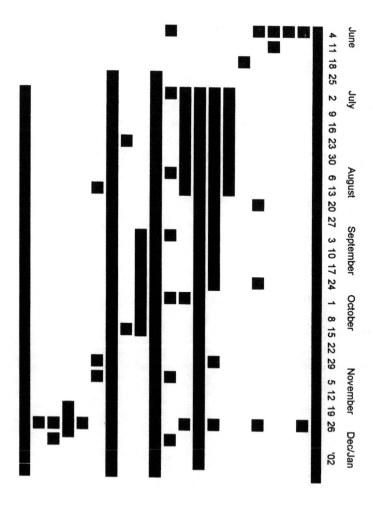

EVENT	June				July					August				September				October				November				Dec/Jan
	4	11	18	25	2	9	16	23	30	6	13	20	27	3	10	17	24	1	8	15	22	29	5	12	19	26	'02

Staff Awareness Programme
Management Training
Steering Group Training
Co-Ordinators Training
Press Release / Features
Employee Info. Pack
Staff Information Evenings
Name Competition/Judge/Prize
Staff Suggestion Scheme
Photogapher
Staff Newsletter
Staff Hotline
Customer Stakeholder Info Evng
Teagasc Today Publication
Intranet Web Page Updates
Customer Mailshots/Invitations re Launch
Entertainment
Merchandising/Promotion Deliveries
Distribute Video & Audio Cassettes
Staff Gift
Campaign Evaluation

Index

Page numbers in italics indicate illustrations